WITHDRAWN

Politics As If Women Mattered
A Political Analysis of the National Action Committee on the Status of Women

The National Action Committee on the Status of Women marked the twentieth anniversary of its founding in 1992. Today, it is the umbrella organization for roughly six hundred women's groups in Canada. The authors of this study argue that, if women's movements are to achieve their equality goals, they must develop enduring institutions that allow women's efforts to be organized over the course of several generations. The authors examine the process of institutionalization through an in-depth study of the National Action Committee.

In the belief that women's movements in Canada have become more or less permanent features of the political system, operating parallel to its official structures, the authors argue the need for a feminist political science that can accommodate the study of both women's politics in their autonomous movements and women's conventional activities in official politics. Indeed, this book undertakes political analysis 'as if women mattered': it focuses on women's interests and draws on feminist theory while remaining connected to the broad framework of political science.

The book documents NAC's evolution as a 'parliament of women.' It shows how the organization moved from a fairly narrow status-of-women focus in its policies to a broadly conceived policy framework that linked such apparently sex-neutral issues as free trade, federalism, and taxation to feminism. Although the more comprehensive feminist approach to public policy proved dangerous for NAC in a conservative era, it also solidified its role and reputation as a major player in equality-seeking politics in Canada.

Jill Vickers is Professor in the School of Canadian Studies, Carleton University. **Pauline Rankin** is an instructor in the School of Canadian Studies, Carleton University. **Christine Appelle** is a psychotherapist in private practice in Ottawa.

Politics As If Women Mattered:
A Political Analysis of the
National Action Committee
on the Status of Women

Jill Vickers, Pauline Rankin,
and Christine Appelle

UNIVERSITY OF TORONTO PRESS
Toronto Buffalo London

© University of Toronto Press Incorporated 1993
Toronto Buffalo London
Printed in Canada

Paperback reprinted 1993

ISBN 0-8020-5850-7 (cloth)
ISBN 0-8020-6757-3 (paper)

Printed on acid-free paper

Canadian Cataloguing in Publication Data

Vickers, Jill, 1942–
  Politics as if women mattered

  Includes bibliographical references and index.
  ISBN 0-8020-5850-7 (bound). – ISBN 0-8020-6757-3 (pbk.)

  1. National Action Committee on the Status of Women.
  2. Women's rights – Canada.   3. Women – Canada –
  Social conditions.   I. Rankin, Pauline.   II. Appelle,
  Christine.   III. Title.

  HQ1453.V52 1993   305.42'06'071   C93-093172-6

This book has been published with the help of a grant from the Social
Science Federation of Canada, using funds provided by the Social Science
and Humanities Research Council of Canada.

To the women of NAC, who have made
women matter in Canadian politics

Contents

Preface

In this book, we offer a fundamental challenge to conventional, male-centred ways of understanding politics. At the heart of this challenge is our belief that the current crisis in public confidence in the 'official' politics of parties, elections, and legislatures is attributable, in part, to the narrow focus by the media, politicians, and academics on those political events that most resemble gladiatorial combat. We argue that understanding politics 'as if women mattered' requires a new framework, one that comprehends the many diverse strategies people employ to gain more control over their lives and to influence public policy.

Politics as reconceptualized in woman-centred terms means far more than participation in public governance. In our examination of the political life of the National Action Committee on the Status of Women (NAC), the major institution of the contemporary women's movement in English Canada, we identify the many ways in which women have attempted to achieve change in the course of the past century.

Conventional political institutions and ideologies were created by men in an era of strict demarcation between the political and domestic spheres. Political parties, courts, bureaucracies, and legislatures all developed in a context in which women were legally excluded as political actors, being largely restricted to domestic roles. Thus, throughout the past century, women have had to search for ways to participate in institutions created by and for men and structured in ways consistent with the life circumstances of a small strata of dominant men. Even traditional views of politics admit that politics functions through élite accommodation and the exclusion of non-élites, including most women.

As women's first century of struggle drew to a close, women in English Canada focused their efforts to achieve change in their lives increasingly on groups that they themselves created, as women, and that operated in ways that accommodated and reflected women's life circumstances. They also began to emphasize the development of stable, woman-centred institutions such as NAC. Formed for the pragmatic purpose of lobbying governments to implement the recommendations of the Royal Commission on the Status of Women, NAC quickly evolved into a modern-day 'parliament of women,' following in the footsteps of the National Council of Women of Canada, which celebrates its hundredth birthday in 1993.

We conclude that women will need stable, woman-centred institutions in the future, because their campaigns for equality and justice will take several more generations to complete. In fact, we argue that there will be a need for woman-centred institutions operating parallel to the structures of official politics throughout the liberal democracies. The success of women's movements in Canada in creating such institutions bodes well for the future development of a 'politics as if women mattered.'

Acknowledgments

Many people contributed to this text at various stages of its development. Our partners and our children provided interest and support. Carleton University gave support at various stages; in particular, Dean Marilyn Marshall provided financial support for production of the index. Vi Augustine cheerfully word-processed the text more times than any of us thought possible. Marcella Munro checked references and notes with skill and energy. Thanks go to Gaby Lévesque for compiling the index.

We must also thank the seven anonymous readers whose suggestions and insights enriched the final text. Doris Anderson, Nancy Adamson, and Anne Molgat each read the text at different stages, offering encouragement, insight, and inspiration. Our thanks go to Virgil Duff for his faith in the project and to Darlene Zeleney for her careful and insightful copy-editing of the manuscript. Thanks are also due to the Social Sciences Federation for a grant in aid of publication.

Our largest debt of thanks is owed to the many women of NAC who gave generously of their time and insight. They let us observe them, read their records, and poke and prod at their motivations. We value their trust. We are very aware that this text represents only one of many possible accounts of NAC's political life. We hope it will provoke many more accounts to correct any misinterpretations we may have made and to flesh out the bare spots that we know remain. We also hope this account will provoke further research and analysis of women's politics in general: It does matter!

All errors, of course, remain our responsibility, and we look forward to the process of scholarship and exploration that will enable us to correct them.

Abbreviations

AFWUF	Alberta Federation of Women United for Families
AGM	Annual General Meeting
AFC	Association des femmes collaboratrices
AFÉAS	Association féminine d'éducation et d'action sociale
ASK	Association for Social Knowledge
CARAL	Canadian Abortion Rights Action League
CACSW	Canadian Advisory Council on the Status of Women
CCF	Cooperative Commonwealth Federation
CCLOW	Canadian Congress of Learning Opportunities for Women
CFUW	Canadian Federation of University Women
CFBPWC	Canadian Federation of Business and Professional Women's Clubs
CLC	Canadian Labour Congress
CORP	Canadian Organization for the Rights of Prostitutes
CNA	Canadian Nurses' Association
CRIAW/ICREF	Canadian Research Institute for the Advancement of Women/Institut canadien de recherches sur les femmes
CUPTE	Canadian Union of Professional and Technical Employees
CUPW	Canadian Union of Postal Workers
CUPE	Canadian Union of Public Employees
CWL	Catholic Women's League
CEW	Committee for Equality for Women
CSN	Confédération des syndicats nationaux
DAWN	Disabled Women's Network

EPC	Equal Pay Coalition
ERA (U.S.)	Equal Rights Amendment
FFQ	Fédération des femmes du Québec
FWIC	Federated Women's Institutes of Canada
FTA	Free Trade Agreement
IODE	Imperial Order of Daughters of the Empire
LEAF	(Women's) Legal Education and Action Fund
MAWS	Mothers Are Women
NAC	National Action Committee on the Status of Women
NAWL	National Association of Women and the Law
NCJW	National Council of Jewish Women
NCWC	National Council of Women of Canada
NDP	New Democratic Party
NOW (U.S.)	National Organization of Women
NUPGE	National Union of Provincial Government Employees
NWAC	Native Women's Association of Canada
OCSW	Ontario Committee on the Status of Women
OWW	Organized Working Women
PLQ	Parti Libéral du Québec
PQ	Parti Québécois
REAL Women	Realistic, Equal and Active for Life
RAIF	Réseau d'action et d'information pour les femmes
ROC	(the) rest of Canada (outside Québec and the First Nations)
SNCC (U.S.)	Student Non-Violent Coordinating Committee
SDS (U.S.)	Students for a Democratic Society
TAC	Therapeutic Abortion Committees
UNESCO	United Nations Economic, Social and Cultural Organization
VOW	Voice of Women
WFH	Wages for Housework
WCTU	Woman's Christian Temperance Union
WAVAW	Women Against Violence Against Women
WPA	Women for Political Action
WAC	Women's Action Committee
WAM	Women's Action Movement
WJC	Women's Joint Committee (of the CCF)
WLM	Women's Liberation Movement
YWCA	Young Women's Christian Association

Politics As If Women Mattered:

A Political Analysis of the
National Action Committee
on the Status of Women

Introduction

For more than a hundred years, women have been trying to make their concerns matter in Canadian politics. And yet, the status of women has never constituted a major issue in any party platform, election campaign, or Speech from the Throne, and no government has ever been defeated because of its views on the subject. Nor have the media or academic communities ever seriously challenged these omissions and silences. Based on this evidence, we begin by assuming that women's movements in Canada represent demands and needs that cannot be met during the course of one or even several generations and, therefore, that their ideas and personnel cannot be expected to be integrated quickly or easily into official politics. In fact, it is the basic premise of this book that, in order to be successful in Canada, women's movements can and must develop enduring institutions through which their efforts to gain equality can be organized over the course of several generations. We will examine this process of institutionalization through an in-depth study of the development of the National Action Committee on the Status of Women (NAC).

To argue that the long-term success of women's movements depends on their ability to develop enduring institutions seems, at first blush, to go against women's experience and wisdom. Too many women have suffered the effects of the institutionalization of male power not to be suspicious of the phenomenon in general. Some observers have identified the concept of institutionalization with the co-optation of women's organizations and their agendas by state institutions (Adamson et al. 1988). Mary O'Brien, in *The Politics of Reproduction* (1981), has even suggested that men create institutions to carry their projects forward in time because, unlike women, they lack a direct connection to the genetic time of reproduction (with the implication that women do not need such structures). In this text, we dispute such views, arguing that women need structures to sustain their projects over time just as men do. As long as we could believe that the goals of women's movements could be achieved within a single generation, this point had no great urgency. Now that it is apparent – at least to us – that we must persuade women in the future to complete our projects, it is necessary to appropriate the concept of 'institution' and reconceptualize it to interpret women's political practice. In discussing NAC as an institution of a women's movement, we embark on this task.

NAC was formed during 1971–2 by a coalition of thirty-odd member groups, to monitor the implementation of the recommendations of the Royal Commission on the Status of Women, tabled in 1970. But the new organization quickly became a magnet for various other forces operating in women's politics, especially in English Canada. Leaders of the more traditional groups – those with roots in the suffrage campaigns of the late-nineteenth and early-twentieth centuries – found themselves rubbing elbows in the NAC arena with women influenced by the feminist ideas of the 1960s. NAC thus became an umbrella structure with a grafted-on, radical grass roots. By 1988, it had roughly six hundred member groups, representing one-third of the organized women's movement (Burt 1986a), and was being viewed increasingly by its activists as an embryonic 'parliament of women,' in which the representation of women's diversity was as important as the representation of their common interests.[1] This greatly enhanced NAC's legitimacy, but at the same time put many stresses on its emerging structure.

As we explained above, we start from the premise that women's movements, at least in Canada, must establish institutions to be successful, because the achievement of their goal of equality requires the organization of activity over a number of generations. With this extended vision, we recognize that such institutions may become near-permanent features of politics in Canada, existing alongside its more traditional institutions. Indeed, we see that women's movements are not similar to many other movements for change, which tend to either realize their goals and become integrated into official politics or fade away. Our extended vision therefore compels us to ask new questions and focus on new aspects of women's politics. First, we must explore how the pattern of women's politics differs from country to country, even within the liberal democracies.[2] Second, we must look beyond an analysis that makes too sharp a distinction between what is commonly known as first- and second-wave women's politics, since the history of women's movements in Canada also suggests the importance of continuities between early and later periods of mobilization. Indeed, it was the important continuities of political culture in English Canada in particular that created the basis for NAC's institutional role in recent decades. Third, we must develop new measures of success for these multigenerational movements. As we have argued thus far, one such measure is a movement's ability to create stable institutions; we will suggest other measures in the chapters that follow.

Throughout this book, we advance a second, counterpoint theme. Because of our belief that women's movements in Canada have become more or less permanent, parallel features of our political system, we also believe it is important to develop a feminist political science that includes both the study of women's politics in autonomous movements and local groups and the study of women's conventional activities in official politics. We have conceptualized this task as undertaking political analysis 'as if women mattered.' In this book, then, we focus on women's interests and concerns while remaining connected to the broad framework of political science. We attempt to provide an introduction to the general categories of political science that is enriched by the use of feminist theory – an approach that should make our analysis accessible both to those who are involved in women's movements but have little background in political science and to those who work within the discipline of political science but have little background in women's politics.[3] We are determined, however, to treat women's politics within the groups that women control as the main focus of this study, rather than as a residual category; that is, we do not conceptualize women's politics as 'just another interest.'[4] We hope that our development of the concept of a parliament of women will convey the fact that our approach goes well beyond an interest-group treatment of women's politics.

It is important to state that this study is not intended as a history of NAC. It is intended as a piece of political analysis based primarily on our reading of the documentary evidence – records, briefs, minutes, and publications. Moreover, our choice of the period of the study, 1972 to 1988, is purely pragmatic. Our entry point is the work of NAC in bringing together (aggregating) and expressing to the federal state (articulating) the views of the women represented by its member organizations. The period of study ends in 1988 because the organizational crises of that year resulted in a rapid contraction of NAC's

Toronto office, making the basic documents largely unavailable for further study. Our analysis also relies on a number of interviews, but these were limited in purpose to filling in the basic narrative in places where the documentary evidence failed us. We were not attempting to produce a comprehensive oral history. Our particular interest was to understand how an organization that had begun with the limited mandate of lobbying to get the recommendations of the Royal Commission on the Status of Women implemented quickly developed into a major new source of policy initiatives on a range of issues that went well beyond the traditional status-of-women portfolio.

We must also note, however, that this study is by no means complete even as a piece of political analysis. While it is possible to understand some aspects of women's politics in Canada by examining the politics of NAC, there are important elements that cannot be understood in this way because they relate to interests and groups that have been marginalized or are not involved in NAC at all. Moreover, by focusing on NAC in the federal arena, we cannot identify the trends and currents that have characterized provincial, territorial, and local women's movements. Nor have we been able to look inside NAC's member groups to understand their internal political dynamics. Although not all of these omissions are serious in terms of our central theme, in several instances our inability to go beyond the NAC arena has been significant.

We have included an afterword in this book to provide readers with a necessary, if somewhat sketchy, updating. While some things have remained the same in NAC since 1988, others have changed significantly. Readers must not assume, therefore, that NAC's politics are currently the same as they were during the seventeen years covered in our study.

In this book, we show that NAC achieved legitimization, in part, by claiming that it represented women better than did any other existing political structure. The scope and diversity of NAC's membership base were therefore an important part of both its claim to legitimacy and its capacity to be viewed as part of the institutional fabric of Canadian politics. In some ways, for the period studied, NAC made good on this claim. In particular, the ideological diversity of its membership was remarkable, as was its ability to act as a bridge between generations of feminists. And, although the NAC executive was dominated by a Toronto-based, central Canadian group for much of its history, the organization also developed a regional structure that afforded significant geographic representation. Furthermore, NAC met with some measure of success in recruiting member groups from recently mobilized segments of the female population, including immigrants, women of colour, and women with disabilities. Finally, NAC managed to retain the involvement of many traditional women's groups as members and to sustain sufficiently good relations with other such groups to continue to work in coalitions with them. By contrast, the organization was largely unsuccessful in maintaining more than symbolic links with francophone feminists in Québec and with the women's movements of Canada's First Nations.

NAC and Women's Politics in Québec

One barrier, other than language, between NAC and most parts of the francophone women's movement in Québec was the difference between their conceptions of women's equality: NAC was committed primarily to an individualist notion of women's equality, while the francophone movement was rooted in the belief that liberation must be based on collective rights. A second, related, barrier was the commitment of most francophone feminists, whether federalist or sovereigntist, to decentralization, which would make it possible for them to relate as feminists primarily to the Québec state. Furthermore, the francophone movement was structured differently from the women's movement in English Canada.

NAC was formed with the participation of francophone women from Québec in the optimistic climate that prevailed in the aftermath of the Royal Commission on the Status of Women. NAC's main link to francophone feminists in Québec was through the Fédération des femmes du Québec (FFQ), which some anglophones viewed as a counterpart of NAC. But the women's movement in Québec was ideologically more polarized than that of English Canada, and the FFQ was consequently less representative of the Québec movement than NAC was of the English-Canadian movement. During the 1960s and 1970s, Québec politics in general was polarized between two distinct forces: the liberal modernization bloc (which included the progressive clergy), headed by the Québec Liberal Party (PLQ) and dominant from 1960 to 1976, and the progressive nationalist bloc, headed by the democratic Parti Québécois (PQ), which was formed in 1968. The FFQ was initially oriented to the liberal modernization bloc. Consequently, it was unlikely that women's groups allied with the progressive nationalist bloc or with the more radical nationalist forces could be connected to NAC (Maroney 1988:106ff.).

Although the liberal feminism of the FFQ became more radical in the late 1970s, the organization still viewed women as 'an interest group operating in a pluralistic political milieu' (Maroney 1988:180). Thus, in terms of willingness to interact with the state, NAC and the FFQ had much in common, although the growing presence in NAC of radical grass-roots groups often led to conflict over the appropriateness of the organization's dedication to lobbying. The FFQ, however, lobbied for – and in 1973 achieved – the establishment of the Conseil du statut de la femme (CSF), which tied it firmly to the Québec state, regardless of the party in power.

Women's movements are profoundly affected by the political culture in which they develop and by the nature of the state regime during key periods of their development. In the case of Québec, the result has been a situation that requires clear distinctions to be made among groups (and caution to be exercised in our use of language in reference to them). Francophone feminists in Québec have considered the Québec state, since the beginning of the Quiet Revolution in the 1960s, to be more progressive on women's issues than the federal state. Anglophone, allophone, and First Nations women in Québec, by contrast, have often been more favourably disposed to the federal state. We have therefore deemed it necessary to use the rather cumbersome term *francophone feminists in Québec* to convey this distinction. Similarly, for the sake of convenience, we use the term *English-Canadian movement* in reference to the collective entity coordinated by NAC in its relationship to the federal state. This term, regrettably, fails to reflect the fact that some allophone and First Nations groups involved with NAC do not speak English among themselves and that, while francophone women's groups outside Québec share many of the values we have attributed to the 'English-Canadian movement,' they also share many of the perspectives of francophone feminists within Québec.

The Québec movement has displayed the sort of ideological polarization characteristic of women's politics in Western Europe, where there is little contact among the different elements involved. Francophone feminists of the left were effectively mobilized by the new unions that resulted from the Quiet Revolution, and the militants of both the revolutionary fragment and the radical-feminist fragment were cut off from liberal feminism 'by historical amnesia and ... political choice' (Maroney 1988:262). Most English-Canadian activists within NAC had little sense of the forces at work in francophone Québec. Moreover, as women's politics in both contexts became less élitist, the percentage of bilingual women involved in the movements declined, and communication between potential allies became less possible, even apart from the animosities inherent in the nationalist debates.

In this analysis, we are rarely able to illuminate the women's politics of francophone Québec. Certainly, our examination of the involvement of the FFQ in NAC did not afford insight into the view of some francophone feminists that 'We are to you [anglophone women] what you are to men' (Maroney 1988:264). NAC had reasons to exaggerate the extent of francophone involvement in its activities (a fact that led us to question the documentary record in this regard): its claim to being a parliament of women depended on at least the illusion of francophone involvement from Québec, as did its claim to government funding at least under Liberal governments. In fact, however, many NAC activists failed to comprehend the views of their francophone counterparts on certain key issues, such as support for the Charter of Rights and Freedoms (which would elevate a federal court above a Québec court and legislature). Similarly, with regard to the Meech Lake Accord, the positions of Québec francophones involved in NAC were not generally understood. It was only after the withdrawal of the FFQ in the wake of the conflict over the accord that feminists outside Québec began to understand why Québec feminists supported decentralization. Eventually, NAC developed a 'Three Nations' constitutional position that recognized the legitimacy of decentralized power for Québec and the First Nations.

NAC and Women's Politics in the First Nations

Just as NAC's commitment to a largely individualist conception of women's rights proved to be a barrier to understanding the aspirations of francophone women in Québec, it also stood in the way of an effective, ongoing relationship between NAC and women activists of the First Nations. Although NAC had an impressive record in support of 'Indian Rights for Indian Women' and the elimination of discrimination against women in the Indian Act, it did not make effective common cause with those who believed that the rights of individual native women could not be secured unless the collective rights of the First Nations were secured. During the 1981 ad hoc constitutional conference held by the women's movement in Ottawa, when it appeared that male politicians would ignore both native rights and women's rights in constitutional patriation, the lack of understanding of this issue among many white activists was made painfully apparent in the feminist press. One source reported, for example, that 'native women constituted a strong presence, although their presentation requesting a supportive resolution was set aside because it asked for support of their plea for independent nationhood rather than anything to do with issues of specific concern to native women themselves' (Hastings and Lawrence 1981:4).

Ironically, the free-trade debate, which saw many white, English-Canadian feminists make the connection between independent nationhood and issues of concern to women specifically, may have begun the process of NAC's developing a better analysis of the link between individual and collective rights. The events at Oka in the summer of 1990 also appear to have occasioned a shift of opinion among NAC activists, as NAC publicly supported the Mohawk nation's claim for political autonomy. None the less, as Susan Phillips shows in her analysis of links among movement groups (1990), native women's groups are largely isolated from white women's movements, with the exception of common linkages through the YWCA.

There are other issues that create barriers between native and non-native groups. For example, First Nations women who base their claim to power sharing within their nations on their power of reproduction – that is, on their ability, as women, to perpetuate their nations – may reject what are commonly regarded as fundamental feminist positions, such as the 'right' of individual women to choose abortion. Such differences have made the building of bridges difficult. Our analysis, which focuses on the internal politics of NAC and its interaction with the federal state until 1988, therefore, provides scant basis for understanding women's politics in the First Nations.

NAC and the Politics of the 'New Force'

Until the 1980s, women of the two majority cultures dominated the movements' agendas and debates. Since then, however, that dominance has been challenged by successive waves of women who have been marginalized and made especially vulnerable because of their race, ethnic background or immigrant status, disability, or sexual orientation. Often united only in their shared vulnerability to oppression, these women constitute the 'new force' in Canadian women's politics.

They have formed many groups, organizations and networks through which they have worked for change on their own behalf. Although we do not explore the politics of this new force, we do examine the demands it has placed on the majority women's movements. Indeed, because immigrant women and women of racial minorities, in particular, have typically chosen to operate in English, these demands have been targeted most vigorously at NAC.

In this text, then, we explore the struggle to make NAC 'a voice for all women,' which could articulate 'the many issues of women, not only those of white, middle-class women' (Day 1991:96). Throughout the 1980s, the new force struggled to make 'the politics of inclusion' more than a rhetorical slogan. By 1992, at the time of the national referendum on the Charlottetown Accord, women of the new force made up nearly half of the NAC executive and held major leadership roles. As a result, NAC came to develop policies more supportive of the concerns of new-force women and to back their demands for inclusion in other organizations and processes. Indeed, NAC's opposition to the Charlottetown Accord reflects a new alliance among women who feel especially dependent on the individual-rights guarantees of the Charter and on the federal government's power to provide social programs for women across the country.

Our account of the politics of the 'new force,' like our account of the women's movements of Québec and the First Nations, reflects the positions that the new force brought into NAC, not the politics internal to each of the disparate elements it comprises nor the nature of the political interactions among the women in each of those elements and within their 'home' communities. We do, however, explore the relationship that developed within NAC between mainstream women and the new-force women who challenged their dominance.

NAC as the Coordinating Institution of the English-Canadian Women's Movement

In our view, NAC's existence as an institutionalized parliament of women has contributed to the effectiveness of women's politics in Canada, despite its inability, during the period studied, to maintain effective links with the francophone movement in Québec or to build effective links with the women's movements within the First Nations. NAC provided an arena in which many types of feminisms could interact. It provided the structures within which women with very diverse interests learned to engage in politics collectively. It tried to provide representation for Canadian women within its structures and it articulated the views of the women it represented to the federal government and its agencies. NAC also served as an important arena for the development of feminist approaches to public policy. Certainly, few decision makers in state institutions knew how to craft policy and programs 'as if women mattered.' And although some women and men within political parties, unions, professional associations, and universities were trying to generate policy that took women's interests into account, it was only in institutions such as NAC that women were in charge of setting the policy agenda and of shaping the process through which policy was made. Only in movement organizations such as NAC was women's equality the main order of business.

In the following analysis, we will demonstrate the importance of institutionalizing NAC as a parliament of women to the development of women's politics in English Canada. We will show how NAC's policy making evolved from a fairly narrow status-of-women approach to a broadly conceived policy framework that linked such apparently sex-neutral issues as free trade, federalism, and taxation to feminism. This evolution was also reflected in the shift from an approach of scrutinizing only the *intended* effects of legislation and government programs to one of considering their *unintended* effects as well. Since the fundamental structures of most men's and women's lives remain quite different, the unintended effects of apparently sex-neutral measures often have far-reaching consequences. While traditional decision makers may have listened to women's groups and feminist experts on status-of-women issues, they were often enraged by what they perceived as NAC's 'interference' in 'real politics.' And although its development of a more holistic feminist approach to public policy has proved dangerous for NAC in a conservative era, it has also solidified NAC's role and reputation as a major player in equality-seeking politics in Canada.

Highlights of NAC's Development

We provide the following chronology as a guide to NAC's development as an institution.

1971 • Ontario Committee on the Status of Women formed as the first provincial organization to lobby a provincial government to implement the recommendations of Royal Commission on the Status of Women

- Committee for the Equality of Women reconstitutes itself as the National Ad Hoc Committee on the Status of Women

1972
- 'Strategy for Change' conference, Toronto; NAC formed, with Laura Sabia as chair; 31 member organizations, representing traditional (social) and liberal feminists; $15,000 budget

1974-5
- CUPE Secretary-Treasurer Grace Hartman chairs NAC (in 1975-6, she is also CUPE president)

1976
- 46 women's centres, 35 feminist periodicals, and 26 local and provincial status-of-women action committees are affiliated with NAC

1975-7
- Lorna Marsden, Chair

1977
- First public lobby of MPs
- 120 member groups; $65,000 budget

1977-9
- Kay Macpherson, Chair

1978
- New format for fully bilingual *Status of Women News*, with in-depth articles
- Macpherson supports Fleck strikers

1978-9
- A coalition of the new generation of feminists gains majority on executive

1979
- 2 policy committees; 140 member groups; $131,560 budget

1979-81
- Lynn McDonald, President

1980
- Constitutional changes establish 'Friends' category of membership and add 3 vice-presidents and 5 regional representatives

1981
- FFQ withdraws from NAC
- AGM crisis over Canadian Constitution

1981-2
- Jean Wood, President

1982
- 200 member groups; $296,000 budget
- AGM crisis over NAC Pension Committee

1982-4
- Doris Anderson, President

1983
- New constitution passed with a fully regionalized structure of representation and new accountability procedures
- Efforts to move the NAC office to Ottawa fail (a small, bilingual lobbying office is opened)

1984-6
- Chaviva Hošek, President

1984
- NAC organizes televised leaders' debate for the federal election

- FFQ rejoins NAC, partly in response to its recognition of two official languages and the introduction of simultaneous translation at the AGM

1984–5 • Nine policy committees formed: justice, employment, native women, survival, social services, health, pensions, pornography, the election

1986–8 • Louise Dulude, President (first president from outside Toronto)

1986 • NAC coordinates responses to the review of the Secretary of State's Women's Program

- 458 organizational members; 900 'Friends of NAC'; $679,476 budget

1988 • Organizational Review Report

- 589 organizational members; $813, 475 budget

Notes

1 NAC is not the first umbrella organization to perform the 'parliament of women' role. The National Council of Women of Canada (NCWC), which celebrates its hundredth anniversary in 1993, played that role as well, but it did not bring together as wide a range of ideological perspectives as NAC has.

2 Why, for example, do we find 'state feminism' with no significant autonomous women's movement in Sweden (Gelb 1989)? Why do we find the project of integrating women into the structures of official politics so far advanced in Norway (Haavio-Mannila 1985)?

3 We trust that those with a background in both areas will understand our desire to provide readers from each perspective with an understanding of the conceptual framework of the other.

4 Given that women constitute more than 50 per cent of the population and that NAC affiliates several million women through its approximately six hundred member groups, we consider the 'just another interest group' approach common in political science to be unacceptable as a basis for a feminist political science.

1 The Intellectual and Political Context for the Development of NAC

Because the resurgence of feminism occurred in most Western industrialized countries at approximately the same time, studies of contemporary women's movements have tended to stress the things those movements have in common. By contrast, it is the purpose of this study to demonstrate the unique course that the English-Canadian women's movement took as it interacted with the federal state through its umbrella organization, NAC. This emphasis on differences rather than similarities is especially important for English-Canadian women, who have generally been so overshadowed by the U.S. movement that they lack a full sense of the unique achievements of their activism. Moreover, differences in each country's political opportunity structures, that is, its 'institutions, alignments and ideology, have patterned the development, goals and values of feminist activists in each nation' (Gelb 1989:2). The structure of women's movements and the systemic characteristics of the country in which they operate also shape and constrain opportunities for effective action in each country.

In this chapter, it is our purpose to describe the nature of the environment in which NAC was created and in which it operated. We explore something of the 'institutions, alignments, and ideologies' that have patterned English-Canadian women's goals and values. We also explore ways in which the structure of women's movements in Canada and systemic characteristics, including federalism and the existence of both a French-Canadian nation and aboriginal First Nations within the Canadian federal state, have shaped and constrained women's opportunities for effective action in this country.

This chapter is divided into four sections. In the first section, we present an overview of NAC's place within the context of women's

movements in Canada. In the process, we outline the major characteristics of the English-Canadian movement and locate it in relation to
models developed in the United States and Western Europe. Our
thesis in this section is that NAC's longevity as an umbrella organization uniting (however tenuously) hundreds of diverse groups from
both the reformist and radical 'wings' of the women's movement has
been attributable to three things: (1) the movement's historic experience with coalitions, transmitted by a bridging generation; (2) a political culture of 'radical liberalism,' which directed the English-Canadian movement towards the federal state – an orientation that many
francophone feminists in Québec and women from the First Nations
ultimately rejected; and (3) a long era of activist federal Liberal governments eager to 'integrate' women's concerns and supportive of
organizations that appeared to 'integrate' Québec women into pan-
Canadian structures.

We begin the second section of this chapter by describing the roots
of a women's political culture that grew out of the constraints experienced by English-Canadian women in the decades following their acquisition of the federal franchise in 1918. We will then explore the roots
of *radical liberalism,* which we identify as the political culture of the
English-Canadian women's movement during NAC's formative years.
Radical liberalism has its roots in the general English-Canadian political culture in the postwar period and in the English-Canadian women's
political culture as it was developed during the first five decades of the
century.

In the third section of the chapter, we consider the impact of U.S.
radical feminism on the English-Canadian movement. We will argue
that many elements of U.S. radical feminism, especially its suspicion of
the state, reflected the particular situation of U.S. women facing the
world's most powerful state. In particular, we contrast the ideas of U.S.
women's liberationists of the 'draft-dodger' generation and the ideas
of the liberationist movement that emerged from English Canada's
democratic Left within the Waffle. In concluding this section, we argue
that while the anti-statism that characterized U.S. radical feminism had
little impact on NAC's interaction with the federal state, its ideas about
the proper mode of operation for feminist organizations had considerable impact on debates within NAC.

In the final section of this chapter, we take another look at NAC's
political-opportunity structure, examining, in general terms, the relationship between the English-Canadian movement and the federal

political system. In particular, we argue that the long era of Liberal rule reinforced NAC's state-centred vision of politics, which made it relatively insensitive to more decentralized visions. We argue that this political context left NAC ill-equipped to deal with the changes that have characterized the subsequent period of Conservative rule.

An Overview of Women's Movements and the National Action Committee

In Western Europe and North America, the evidence is that women participate more in movements for change than men do, while men are vastly overrepresented in the offices of formal politics (Lovenduski 1986; McAdam 1988). It would be wrong, however, to assume that women *choose* one arena over the other. As Lovenduski (1986) argues, 'It is because women are marginal to the political system and women's causes are seen as peripheral that it has been necessary for feminists to opt for social movement forms' (62). Traditional analysis stresses the spontaneity of movements, their limited capacity for organization, and their demise as the people, values, and demands they represent are integrated into the official political system. In subsequent chapters we will explore in detail some of the problems inherent in this characterization; here, we simply posit our hypothesis that women's movements represent values and demands that currently cannot be integrated fully into the official political systems of the liberal democracies. For this reason, we argue that, to be successful, women's movements must become institutionalized to ensure a continuity of activity over long periods of time.

Three distinct types of movements for change were evident in Canadian politics during the 1970s and 1980s: (1) equality-seeking movements, which include women's movements; (2) quality-of-life movement, wherein people seek change in such areas as peace and the environment directly, rather than under the auspices of a political party; and (3) reactionary movements, which arose in opposition to the first two types and were motivated by nostalgia for an idealized past. In each case, the movement existed because people shared a vision of change (or restoration) and because existing political parties could not accommodate the ideas, personnel, and energy involved. Women's movements have been at the centre of a new political dynamic in Canada that pertains to the search for equality. Their relative legitimacy and organizational stability has allowed them to play a key role in creating and sustaining coalitions with other equality seekers to achieve concrete ends that would improve the lives of otherwise marginalized people.

The attempt to understand women's movements in Canada is greatly complicated by their complexity. Already a highly decentralized state, Canada has spawned many movements at the provincial and territorial level. In the federal context, at least three distinct women's movements must currently be recognized: the movement we have chosen to term the 'English-Canadian movement' (as defined in the Introduction); the francophone movement in Québec; and the movements of First Nations women. In ideological terms, one common approach has been to categorize feminism as liberal, leftist, or radical, largely ignoring organizational manifestations. Since it is our conviction that women's movements are shaped by the states to which they relate and by the political culture associated with those states, we have chosen to focus on the character of the movement in Canada as manifested in the political behavior of its largest organization.

Understanding current women's movements is further complicated by the survival of feminist values articulated primarily in the language of responsibilities rather than in the language of rights (Vickers 1989). Such values survive in groups that were formed during the so-called first wave of women's mobilization, some of which are now a hundred years old (see Table 1.1). Groups such as the Federated Women's Institutes and the National Council of Women always involved women in Canadian politics even during periods of limited mobilization. These more traditional groups, revitalized by the Royal Commission on the Status of Women's energetic cross-country tour of the late 1960s, played a major role in shaping the current movement, endowing it not only with a capacity for organization, coalition building, and interaction with government, but also with a reformist stance, a preoccupation with service, and a weakness in theoretical development. To the extent that these groups participated in NAC – and many did – their values, rooted in an earlier era, coexisted with contemporary feminist values.

In the course of our research, we isolated some of the basic traits that characterized the English-Canadian women's movement as it related to the federal state between 1965 and 1985. Many of them reflect the mix of traditional and contemporary values and approaches that we have just described. For example, the movement was ideologically diverse, yet capable of maintaining coalitions. Far from rejecting involvement with the state, it relied heavily on government funding;

TABLE 1.1

Some highlights in the history of the Canadian women's movement, 1874–1992

1874 • First Canadian local of Woman's Christian Temperance Union (WCTU) formed in Picton, Ontario
    • Ontario WCTU formed
1876 • Toronto Women's Literary Club founded. It reorganized in 1883 to become the Toronto Women's Suffrage Association.
1885 • Dominion Woman's Christian Temperance Union formed; endorsed suffrage in 1891
1889 • Dominion Women's Enfranchisement Association formed as an umbrella organization incorporating all suffrage groups in Canada. It changed its name to the Canadian Suffrage Association in 1907.
1893 • National Council of Women of Canada (NCWC) founded, with the goal of social reform. It was chapter-based, with affiliates (1,800 affiliates in 1966; 1,500 in 1985).
    • National Council of Jewish Women (NCJW) founded
1894 • National Young Women's Christian Association (YWCA) founded
1902 • Coloured Women's Club of Montreal founded
1908 • Canadian Nurses Association (CNA) formed
1910 • Women's Labor League, dedicated to women's suffrage, formed in Winnipeg
1912 • National Union of Women Suffrage Societies of Canada formed
1917 • Military Voters Act passed
1918 • Women's Franchise Act passed 24 May 1918
1919 • Federated Women's Institutes of Canada (FWIC) founded
    • Canadian Federation of University Women (CFUW) founded
1921 • Agnes Macphail becomes first woman elected to House of Commons
1927–9 • 'Persons Case' – Supreme Court of Canada declares that women are not persons for purposes of appointment to the Senate. The Judicial Committee of the British Privy Council overrules and declares women to be 'persons.'
1930 • Canadian Federation of Business and Professional Women's Clubs (CFBPWC) founded
1934 • New Brunswick women, who gained the provincial franchise in 1919, become eligible to run for office.
1940 • Provincial suffrage and the right to run for office are gained in Québec.
1950 • Congress of Canadian Women (CCW) formed
1951 • Canadian Negro Women's Association founded
1957 • Ellen Fairclough becomes first woman to be appointed to a federal cabinet (Progressive Conservative).
1958 • Canada becomes a member of the U.N. Status of Women Commission. (NCWC, already affiliated through the International Council of Women, becomes an observer for the government.)
1960 • Voice of Women (VOW) formed, with the primary goal of working for peace
    • Status Indians gain the franchise.
1961 • Planned Parenthood of Canada founded

- President's Commission on the Status of Women established in the United States, to report in 1963; state commissions also established

1964
- Association for Social Knowledge (ASK), a group of gay men and lesbians, formed in Vancouver, with the goals of education, community organizing, and reform of criminal laws

1966
- Committee for the Equality of Women established to lobby for the creation of a royal commission on the status of women. It consists of a coalition of thirty-four national and regional associations.
- Association féminine d'éducation et d'action sociale (AFÉAS) founded
- Fédération des femmes du Québec (FFQ) formed. It is an umbrella regroupment, but also has direct members (approximately 40,000 direct and affiliated members by the mid-1980s).

1967
- Royal Commission on the Status of Women in Canada established, with Anne Francis [Florence Bird] as chair. Monique Bégin, research director, says 'it revitalized traditional women's groups and made them all, to some extent, feminist' (Bégin 1988:359).

1969
- Women's liberation groups formed, mostly on campuses in large cities
- National Farmers Union (Women's Division) formed

1970
- National Abortion Caravan
- Royal Commission on the Status of Women tables its report, which contains 167 recommendations.

1971
- National Ad Hoc Committee on the Status of Women formed

1972
- 'Strategy for Change' conference held (with financial support from the federal government), at which the National Action Committee on the Status of Women (NAC) is founded by more than 30 pre-existing groups. Its goal is to press for and monitor the implementation of the royal commission's recommendations. It includes 230 groups by 1982; 575 groups are affiliated by 1988.

1973
- Canadian Advisory Council on the Status of Women (CACSW) formed
- Ontario Advisory Council on the Status of Women (OACSW) formed
- Conseil du statut de la femme (Québec) formed
- First Canadian lesbian conference held in Toronto, at the YWCA
- Canadian Women's Negro Association calls first national conference of black women.
- Canadian Association for the Repeal of the Abortion Laws (CARAL) / Réseau d'action et d'information pour les femmes (RAIF) formed (renamed Canadian Abortion Rights Action League in 1980)
- Centrale de l'enseignement du Québec, comité de la condition feminine, established
- Fédération des travailleurs du Québec, comité de la condition feminine, established

1974
- Native Women's Association of Canada (NWAC) formed
- Canadian Teachers' Federation, Status of Women Program, established
- Confédération des syndicats nationaux, service condition feminine, established

1975
- International Women's Year declared by the U.N.
- Canadian Association of Women Executives formed
- Canadian Research Institute for the Advancement of Women CRIAW/ Institut canadien de recherches sur les femmes (ICREF) formed

- National Association of Women and the Law (NAWL) founded
1976 - Canadian Labour Congress, Women's Bureau, established
1977 - Québec government includes protection from discrimination on the basis of sexual orientation in provincial Charter of Rights.
1978 - Lesbian Mothers' Defence Fund launched in Toronto by a group called Wages Due Lesbians
1979 - Feminist Party of Canada launched
- Association des femmes collaboratrices (AFC)
- *Égalité et indépendance* published by Conseil du statut de la femme
1980 - Canadian Congress of Black Women founded at the seventh annual conference for black women
- Canadian Union of Postal Workers (CUPW) ratifies contract that includes non-discrimination clause protecting 'gay people' – the first such protection for federal government employees
1981 - Canadian Congress for Learning Opportunities for Women founded
- Doris Anderson resigns from CACSW after cancellation of planned National Conference on Women and the Constitution.
- Ad hoc committee rapidly organizes women's constitutional conference (14–15 February), with no government funding. The conference draws 1,300 women.
- Women's lobby succeeds in exempting Section 28 of the Charter of Rights and Freedoms from override.
- Fifth bi-national lesbian conference in Vancouver organizes first lesbian pride march.
1982 - Charter of Rights and Freedoms proclaimed, including Sections 15 and 28.
1984 - During federal campaign, NAC hosts televised leaders' debate focusing on women's issues. All three leaders claim to support equality for women.
- Royal Commission on Equality in Employment, headed by Judge Rosalie Abella, tables its report in the House of Commons.
1985 - Women's Legal Education and Action Fund (LEAF) founded in Toronto
- United Nations World Conference on Women held in Nairobi, Kenya
1986 - Employment Equity Act proclaimed, requiring employers under federal jurisdiction to report on their redress of systemic discrimination against women, the disabled, aboriginal peoples, and visible minorities
1986 - Shirley Carr becomes first woman president of the Canadian Labour Congress.
1988 - Supreme Court rules that Therapeutic Abortion Committees (TACs) are unconstitutional under the 'security of the person' provision in the Charter. Canada's abortion law is struck down.
1989 - Canadian Human Rights Commission defines a homosexual couple as a family.
- NAC's budget is cut from $600,000 to $490,000 by Finance Minister Michael Wilson. Funding is scheduled to drop to $300,000 in 1991.
- Québec judge upholds an injunction by Chantal Daigle's former boyfriend preventing her from having an abortion. The Québec Court of Appeal supports the earlier decision. In August, the Supreme Court of Canada overturns the decision in favour of Daigle, who then reveals that she has already had the abortion, in Boston.

- The Progressive Conservative government introduces a bill to re-criminalize abortion (November 3).
- At the Winnipeg leadership convention of the New Democratic party, Audrey McLaughlin becomes the first woman leader of a federal political party in Canada.
- On December 6, Marc Lepine massacres fourteen women at the École polytechnique in Montreal, while shouting his hatred of feminists. The victims were Anne-Marie Edward, Maryse Leclair, Michèle Richard, Annie St-Arneault, Maryse Laganière, Maud Haviernick, Geneviève Bergeron, Barbara Daigneault, Nathalie Croteau, Annie Turcotte, Anne-Marie Lemay, Barbara Klueznick, Hélène Colgan, and Sonia Pelletier.

1990
- Federal budget cuts funding programs in eighty women's centres across Canada, as well as subsidies for women's magazines, igniting widespread protest by Canadian women. Funding for women's centres is temporarily restored, but many centres are closed permanently when provincial governments decline to assume responsibility for continued funding.
- Dispute concerning unresolved land claims and sovereignty leads to confrontation at Oka, Québec, between the Mohawk Nation and the Québec Provincial Police, later reinforced by Canadian Forces troops.

1991
- Senate defeats Bill C-43, the bill designed to re-criminalize abortion.

1992
- Constitutional negotiations by First Ministers, territorial leaders, and aboriginal leaders produces the Charlottetown Accord, on August 28. Rosemary Kuptana, of the Inuit Tapirisat, and Nellie Cournoyea, NWT government leader, are the first women to participate in official constitutional negotiations.
- NAC opposes the Charlottetown Accord, which is defeated in a national referendum on October 26.

---

nevertheless, it was both autonomous and multipartisan. Largely reformist in its goals, it displayed a high level of solidarity across class lines and generations. It focused on the federal government as best able to provide social support programs for women. Finally, its political culture is best described as radical liberalism. We shall now examine these characteristics in greater detail.

Many European observers distinguish between two 'wings' in current women's movements: an older, *women's rights* wing and a younger, *women's liberation* wing (Lovenduski 1986). Jo Freeman, observing the U.S. movement, argued for a similar model. She saw the liberation groups as emphasizing their radicalism, fearing co-optation, seeing institutional structures as barriers, and rejecting accommodation with the state. The rights groups, by contrast, tended to think in terms of effectiveness and were interested in working within the existing political system (Freeman 1983). While these positions are also evident in the English-Canadian movement, they exist as tendencies present to some degree in most of the autonomous groups and institutions of the movement rather than as organizationally separate wings.

Ideologically, the English-Canadian movement is diverse, but it also displays a significant capacity to undertake collaborative action, maintain coalitions, and hold allegiances to several distinct political positions at the same time. The traditional political spectrum represented in the movement ranges from 'red Tory,' free enterprise, and libertarian feminism through liberal feminism to socialist, working class, and Marxist feminism. A second political spectrum was created initially around women's experiences of sexuality. In addition, there are integrative feminists, described by Angela Miles (1982:23) as women who 'welcome the tremendous variety of participants, activities and thinking in the current movement and take relatively non-sectarian positions ... they tend to welcome diversity and debate as important contributions to growth and development'. What motivates integrative feminists, in Miles's view, is 'their sense of feminism as a potentially complete politics' that 'unites them more closely with each other ... than with other feminists of like self-definition' (12). This strain of integrative feminism is one feature of the English-Canadian movement that enables it to build and maintain diverse coalitions and organizations that can encompass ideological difference. NAC, of course, is an organizational product of this aspect of the movement.

Politically, the movement is both autonomous – that is, independent of the state – and multipartisan, and both features have been a source of controversy. Sylvia Bashevkin (1985:4) identifies a tension between a desire for independence and an acceptance of partisanship in the political history of women in English Canada, and argues that this tension has limited women's political power. For example, many suffragists rejected political parties as corrupt and immoral devices fuelled by booze and male greed; more recently, many women working in small local groups have rejected the traditional structures of politics, including parties, in equally sweeping terms. As a result, fewer women than men seek to hold office in official politics. The desire to maintain an autonomous women's movement, however, has not involved a total rejection of the formal political arena. Even small groups who focus mainly on local projects have found occasion to join together in networks in order to influence government. Anne Collins (1985) has established that the first nationwide feminist network of small groups emerged as a direct result of the abortion issue and in response to the 1970 Abortion Caravan. Significantly, a number of networks comprising small grass-roots groups, along with many individual groups, belonged to NAC during the period of study.

English-Canadian women who are active in official politics and political parties often rely on the autonomous women's movement as a source of ideas, analysis, and political leverage. The fact that there are feminists in all federal political parties and that each party has some sort of internal caucus or group devoted to feminist issues suggests a determination within the movement to reject an either/or choice. Angela Miles (1984) argues that women can and must insist on the right to participate fully in existing political institutions, while at the same time challenging their character and underlying principles. To follow this course, women have to operate on two fronts simultaneously: They must build autonomous, women-centred institutions in which to develop alternative ways of doing politics and they must be present, to whatever extent possible, within existing political institutions, to participate as women and thereby to challenge the logic of those structures. This dual focus need not be maintained by all individuals or groups; rather, the movement as a whole should operate on both fronts. Certainly, in the 1970s and 1980s, the presence in NAC of individuals and groups with experience working in the official political system and from all the political parties reflected this dual focus and enhanced NAC's political skills.

The English-Canadian movement has been largely reformist in character: there have been no elements advocating the use of violence as there were, for example, in Italy (Lovenduski 1986), nor have the transformative goals in the programs of many of the more radical groups involved revolutionary change, whether violent or non-violent in conception (Adamson et al. 1988). During our period of study, these groups aimed at the transformation of society either through the creation of a counter-culture or through changes in individual consciousness. They did not aspire to some mirror-image system that would simply reverse roles, making women the power holders. They were, however, willing to use non-traditional tactics in their projects of transformation.

Although the English-Canadian movement has been largely reformist and transformative in character, it has also been progressive in many important ways. In particular, it displayed stronger solidarity across class lines and across generations than has either the U.S. or the British movement. Moreover, NAC's membership has included a number of unions, union caucuses, and other groups created by working-class feminists. NAC's second president, Grace Hartman, came from, and went on to lead, the Canadian Union of Public Employees (CUPE).

Madeleine Parent, a beloved (or, depending on one's point of view, notorious) union leader from Québec, also played an important role in the organization. (Both these women were jailed for their union activities at one time or another.) The cross-generation continuity that has characterized the movement resulted, in part, from the involvement of first-wave groups in its alliances and coalitions. Perhaps more significant, however, was the presence of a transitional generation of women bridging the early and later periods of mobilization, women who passed their experiences on to the generation that came of age politically in the 1960s and 1970s. This transitional generation founded the Congress of Canadian Women in the 1950s and the Voice of Women in the 1960s. Many of its members remained active in NAC, and one, Kay Macpherson, became NAC's fourth chair.

Nevertheless, some participants of the movement have been very conscious of the limits of its progressive tendencies. For example, Lynn McDonald (1979:39), NAC's fifth president, wrote that '[while the movement] has not been inordinately concerned with the demands of middle class women ... neither has it gone so far as to challenge such basic institutions as private property.' Margrit Eichler (1983), in her survey of NAC policy on the institution of the family and on the stay-at-home mother, argued that NAC followed a far less radical line in relation to the family than did feminists in Britain or the United States. This moderation on some key issues has often been seen as the inevitable dilution of positions that occurs when feminists of different theoretical stripes operate within a single organization. Other observers, however, have pointed to the moderating effects of certain characteristics unique to the English-Canadian movement, such as its ready acceptance of state funding, its service orientation, and its focus on the state as the primary instrument of change.

Historically, women's organizations in English Canada provided an alternative forum in which women could develop and debate public policy (Strong-Boag 1976). Many of the groups formed during the first wave of mobilization met annually with the federal cabinet, and several were designated to represent the government at the United Nations. Given this tradition, along with the strong intergenerational continuity that characterized the movement, it is not surprising that many of the women involved at the start of the wave of mobilization that began in the 1960s looked to the government as their initial policy focus.

The movement's tendency to see government as an instrument of change, combined with its propensity for creating coalitions, formed the basis on which institutions such as NAC could develop. A coalition of thirty-four traditional women's groups from both English and French Canada, formed in 1966, sought and obtained a royal commission on the status of women. With the establishment of the commission, many movement groups adopted a strategy that treated the commission's report as the focal point of their activity. The commission 'received 468 briefs, more than 1,000 letters of opinion, and heard more than 890 witnesses during public hearings held in fourteen cities across the country' (Kome 1985:87).

While some have argued that the report, with its 167 recommendations, 'became the blueprint for mainstream feminist activism during the 1970s' (Kome 1985:87–8), it was criticized by many of the new generation of feminists for failing to identify some of the basic elements of women's oppression. Its analysis of causes satisfied neither radical nor left-wing feminists. Although some representatives of the more radical groups presented briefs, the commission's overall approach was reformist, and it remained silent on certain key issues, such as violence against women and lesbian rights.

Some supporters of the commission's report praised it precisely because it did not offer a radical analysis. None the less, Anthony Westell, writing in the *Toronto Star*, saw it as 'A BOMBSHELL,' 'a political blockbuster,' and 'packed with more explosive potential than any device manufactured by terrorists.' Westell concluded that, 'as a call to revolution, hopefully a quiet one, it is more persuasive than any FLQ manifesto' (cited in Bird 1974:302). In Québec, although few observers found its recommendations radical, the report aroused ferment among women's associations just as it did in English Canada (Dumont et al. 1987). On balance, the judgment on the report was positive: 'If we view the RCSW as an arm, or vehicle, of the women's movement, we must agree with feminist critics that it failed to adequately reflect feminist concerns and commitments. If, on the other hand, we view the RCSW as a step in the Canadian policy-making process, we cannot judge its composition deficient simply because it provided no representation for militant feminists' (Morris 1982:161).

With a focal document in place, both the English-Canadian and the Québec movements created yet another coalition, this time to establish a permanent structure to monitor the implementation of the royal commission's recommendations. The organization, created out of a process of interaction and conflict at the 'Strategy for Change' conference in 1972, was NAC. (The circumstances of NAC's founding will be examined in greater detail in the next chapter.)

By 1972, groups associated with what was then called the women's liberation movement were sufficiently active in the large cities to be represented on the conference planning committee, and many were present at the founding conference itself. The new organization, however, relied heavily on Canadian women's past experiences in developing its political culture. Its umbrella structure was anchored by women from the National Ad Hoc Committee on the Status of Women, which included a coalition of groups experienced in federal politics. (As a result of their experience with 'Cabinet Days,' many of these women were familiar with the conventions governing polite interaction with politicians.) The newest elements in the movement were to be represented in NAC, but they were still a clear minority. We refer to them collectively as 'grass-roots' groups – a myriad of small groups organized for specific purposes, from consciousness raising to undertaking local direct-action projects or initiating education in local workplaces. We distinguish them from the more traditionally organized groups that focused on interaction with governments. In time, these new groups developed an analysis of the oppression of women that was distinctly different from that of the royal commission, and they thereby came to represent a radical and leftist grass roots grafted on to NAC's founding coalition. Initially an organization of convenience, NAC became the arena in which such conflicting understandings of the condition of women could be debated and explored. As a result, it came to take on a unique role as a 'parliament of women.'

During this time, the various women's groups that existed in the United States remained ideologically and structurally separate (Ferguson 1984), despite the fact that they were reacting to many of the same social pressures and were exposed to a similar range of theoretical interpretations of women's subordination or oppression as were women in Canada (Macpherson and Sears 1976; Richardson 1983). What was it, then, about the environment in Canada that permitted enough cooperation across generational, ideological, and, at least initially, language lines to make possible the creation of an autonomous umbrella organization in which many could participate? Certainly, Canada's sparse population in relation to its vast land mass worked against the creation of ideologically distinct groups and services (Kostash 1980; McDonald 1979). But even in a large, densely populated metropolitan centre like Montreal, U.S. anthropologist Joan Richardson (1983:29) was surprised to find that there was no unbridgeable gulf in the 1970s between anglophone women's-rights

organizations and radical-feminist groups. She argues (somewhat dis-
approvingly from her U.S. perspective) that 'there is far too much bor-
rowing from a 'variety of political sources and an absence of the terrific fear and antagonism which characterized U.S. feminist activity in
the 1960's and 70's to allow for the construction of mutually exclusive
categories.' Historically, then, ideology has not been the central structural barrier in English-Canadian feminist organizing (although ideology does hold sway with some force within the francophone movement in Québec [Maroney 1988]). Furthermore, the fact that many of
the movement's groups and activities were funded by some level of
government may have resulted in their depoliticization, making cooperation easier. In 1986, more than seven hundred groups were receiving funding from the federal Secretary of State's Women's Program
(Emergency Consultation of Women's Groups 1986). (At this time,
there were at least two thousand groups that could be considered part
of the women's movement [Burt 1986a].) Although it enabled many
groups and services to develop to the stage of viability, the granting
process reinforced the service components of projects and downplayed
their political aspects. Richardson (1983:37) argued that 'the general
lack of initiative the groups demonstrated in devising stable and independent sources of funding also curtailed their social impact on the
local environment and circumvented a valuable opportunity to incorporate more women in the movement.'

The issue of funding and its effects was particularly critical for NAC
during the period studied. NAC's members were groups, themselves
already strapped for money. Government funding was a logical option
and, in its fundraising efforts, NAC typically emphasized the government's obligation to support its representational costs. The organization's case was supported by the existing generous tax credit to
federal political parties, which faced similar representational costs.
Given the country's vast territory and sparse population, few pan-
Canadian or even provincial/territorial groups could survive without
government support. And government support remained another barrier to cooperation: it diminished competition among groups for
funding from private sources. The federal government, moreover, encouraged cooperation in many ways.

Another characteristic of the English-Canadian women's movement
was its strong service orientation. This was attributable, in part, to the
availability of state funding for service projects, but it also reflected a
strong tradition in Canadian women's political culture of women

organizing locally to construct the services they, their families, and their communities needed (Andrew 1984; Vickers 1988a). In fact, the attitude towards the provision of service within the women's movement is one point of common perspective between feminists of the first and second waves of mobilization. Again, sparse population and vast territory meant that the provision of services had to be shared by people with quite different ideologies. Increasingly, the provision of services in small communities is even coming to require cooperation between feminists and anti-feminists (Angela Miles, personal communication to Jill Vickers, 1987).

The English-Canadian women's movement has also been characterized by its centralized nature and its centrist orientation. Although the francophone movement in Québec considered the Québec state more progressive on equality issues and more open to feminist influence than the federal government, women in English Canada during the period studied considered the latter to be more progressive than most provincial/territorial governments. (The recent election of NDP governments in three provinces may cause this view to change.) In part, this centrist orientation reflected the symbiotic relationship that developed between the long-tenured Liberal government and a pan-Canadian women's movement that Liberals viewed as a positive force for unity with Québec. It also reflected the fact that the movement's focal document was the product of a federal royal commission and that the commission's recommendations applied primarily within the federal jurisdiction. Finally, the movement's centrism was attributable to the nature of Canadian federalism and the division of powers between the levels of government that put criminal justice (encompassing rape, pornography, prostitution, and abortion), constitutional matters, and most economic policies in the federal arena.

Adjusting to the environment of decentralization that has been encouraged by the Progressive Conservative government since its election in 1984 is possibly one of the greatest challenges facing NAC. Indeed, the free-trade debate and the constitutional talks reflected potential shifts in the power structure of Canadian politics that could leave a centrist women's movement targeting the wrong level of government. NAC's umbrella structure has been most effective in managing coalitions in relation to the centre of the federal system. By contrast, a chapter-based organization such as the National Organization of Women (NOW) in the United States, which mobilizes women at the local and state levels in ways an umbrella structure cannot, might be a better model in a decentralized federation. In addition, the English-Canadian movement is struggling to make common cause with many groups of newly mobilized women. These groups, which include women from racial minorities, lesbians, immigrants, prostitutes, battered women, and women with disabilities, see organizations such as NAC as mainstream and privileged, and meet their expressions of 'concern' with demands for full access and equal treatment. The resulting politics of increased diversity within the English-Canadian women's movement has given governments a pretext for attempting to disrupt the cohesion and solidarity that the movement has managed to achieve.

Canadian Political Culture and Canadian Women's Movements

Canadian women's movements have always been somewhat overshadowed by their U.S. counterparts. The media invariably assume that the movements in the two countries are similar, if not identical, when in fact they are very different. As we had already noted, the English-Canadian movement has been skilled at coalition building and management, developing a multipartisan approach, a reliance on government funding, and a service orientation. All of these features are in distinct contrast to the U.S. pattern. Of course, U.S. women did not choose their options any more than Canadian women chose theirs. Rather, the political cultures of their respective societies and the political environments of their respective states have had an enormous influence on the shape of both countries' women's movements.

We understand political culture to encompass (1) norms and values about how to conduct politics; (2) understandings about the nature of politics; and (3) values about the proper limits of political action. Substantial political change, such as that sought by feminists, cannot be sustained without a basis in political culture, and consequently, every aspect of political culture can potentially be a contested zone from a women-centred perspective.

In this section, we argue that the English-Canadian movement's acceptance of radical liberalism as its operational code made possible the strong coalition-building behaviour that would begin to make women matter in federal politics. Radical liberalism, however, involved values that were somewhat familiar in Canada. NAC itself would have been impossible without this basis in Canadian political culture. By contrast, while the values about how to conduct politics that were developed by radical feminism in the United States reflected the character of U.S. politics, they were in conflict with many key aspects of

Canadian political culture. In particular, the capacity of coalitions and umbrella organizations to operate effectively in the politics of the federal state would potentially have been threatened by this U.S. value system. An indigenous feminist political culture, however, was also developing, building on values from the earlier, local feminist traditions in Canada. Even among the women who worked within political parties, feminist values that had developed out of Canadian experience were taking root.

The values of radical liberalism, which we examine in detail below, were the source of the English-Canadian movement's capacity for internal dialogue and cooperation, as well as of its ability to form alliances with other equality seekers. The latter ability contributed to the emergence of a new dynamic of equality seeking in Canadian politics during the 1960s and 1970s. However, the successful mobilization in the 1980s of large numbers of women who did not share the value system of radical liberalism has led to conflict in recent years over both policies and operational norms.

Women's Political Culture

In this section, we examine the values of political culture that were accepted by the member groups and activists of NAC. Given the importance of the revitalized traditional groups in NAC's original coalition, we will first explore the nature of women's political culture during the first seven decades of the movement's history. Once most Canadian women achieved the right to vote, what values did they hold about how to conduct politics? What did they think was political and what things did they think were properly left beyond the scope of politics?

In 1975, Thelma McCormack argued as follows:

Women live in a different political culture from men, a culture based on differences in political socialization ... differences in political opportunity structures, and the way in which the media of communication define each of them. Together, and reinforcing each other, these add up to a female design for political living that is dissimilar from that of the male. Long before a woman reaches voting age or is even told that politics is a 'man's world,' she can see that government is a male preserve. (P. 25)

What McCormack brought home to observers was that, as a consequence of the overwhelmingly male nature of all of the state's institutions and of the dominant political system, women lived, quite literally, in a different political world than men. They conceived of politics essentially as a spectator sport. And, as McCormack also reminds us, men do more than dominate the *conduct* of politics; as journalists, political writers, and political scientists, they also dominate the *interpretation* of it. The inequality of the two political cultures means that men, 'who are the "haves," are in a position to discredit the political behaviour and political insights of women without ever having to reflect on their own' (26).

Male political culture is lodged in formal political institutions, which perpetuate themselves and their values through the law and longevity. Many contemporary women, liberated by the realization that these institutions are neither natural nor inevitable, readily make a distinction between the 'Big *P*' *Politics* of Parliament and elections and the 'small *p*' *politics* of organizing to get things done in their communities (CRIAW 1987; Vickers 1988a). Linda Christiansen-Ruffman (1982) sees women's experience of local, volunteer activities as the source of their broader conception of what is political, and describes women's political culture as 'rooted in the social organization of women's experience, which involves the nurturing of children and the organization of the family' (8). She defines political action as 'all actions aimed at changing or maintaining the established order' (3).

In an empirical test of the existence of two political cultures, Sandra Burt (1986a:57) found that the men and women she interviewed displayed different values of political culture in three areas: (1) the meaning of politics; (2) the reasons for political participation; and (3) conceptions of the ideal citizen in a democracy. (Interestingly, she also found that, in addition to differences between women's and men's values, there were differences between the values of activists involved in traditional women's groups and those of women working at the grass-roots level for feminist goals, in either women's centres or rape crisis centres.)

Many of the value differences reflect women's clear understanding of the limited capacity of the institutions of the dominant political system to provide a context for meaningful participation by women engaged in ordinary women's lives. Many women do not consider the 'right' to vote and hold office a basis for meaningful political participation, an attitude they have inherited from their mothers and grandmothers. Although women of the suffrage era may seem to have been fixated on the vote, we find that they did not, in fact, have a strong tradition of looking to formal politics for the resolution of their own problems. Instead, they had developed a strong tradition of informal ('small *p*') community politics, operating primarily in self-help groups (Vickers 1989; Strong-Boag 1986). The norm of self-help went along with a service-based conception of political life. Values of duty and responsibility motivated these women as much as, if not more than, abstract concepts of rights (Vickers 1989; Rooke and Schnell 1987).

This broad understanding of politics significantly influenced the women's associations of the first wave of mobilization. The values of their political culture influenced women's choice of the political arenas to which they would entrust the issues that concerned them. For example, they undertook intensive grass-roots political activity in what social scientists and government officials alike still call *voluntary groups*. (This term, much like the term *social movement*, has the effect of depoliticizing the efforts of women to achieve change.) Women's voluntary groups usually engaged in a two-pronged strategy: First, they provided a service in response to an immediate, unmet need in their community; second, they solicited government 'for legislation and programs to provide the means for permanent solutions' (Canada, Secretary of State, Women's Program 1974:2). Women thus identified and filled many gaps in local community and social-welfare programs, until some level of government proved ready to provide the needed services. In this way, women were major creators of the Canadian welfare state (Andrew 1984).

Although first-wave women had a strong belief that they should be active in public life, they were also still limited in their ability to be involved in the distant, formal, and increasingly professionalized arenas of the official political system. Instead, they created organizations through which their close-to-home groups could be linked to those in political power. At both the provincial and federal levels, their councils and federations provided an arena in which women could establish priorities, set agendas, and debate policy (Vickers 1989:23). Such organizations, which proved far more accessible and meaningful for many women than political parties, were also conduits for political pressure on governments.

The first local women's church and community groups were formed in English Canada in the early nineteenth century (Armour and Staton 1990); provincial and national councils and federations followed in the latter half of the century. Canada's developing state did little in the areas that concerned many women, such as health and public welfare. Specific issues of concern included high infant and maternal mortality rates, alcoholism, and the lack of clean milk and water. The tactics used by these women's associations were fairly constant: In addition to organizing services locally, they included 'formulating resolutions on policy within their own groups, urging the adoption of their policy at all appropriate levels of government through the presentation of submissions and delegations to the legislatures and to individually elected representatives, while at the same time influencing social attitudes through public education about the issue' (Canada, Secretary of State, Women's Program 1974:4).

The structure of these first-wave associations deserves some comment. At the local level, group activity demanded relatively little of each individual. Offices were rotated, and meetings were often moved from one woman's home to another's. At the local level, therefore, these groups resembled the loosely structured local groups that exist today. Each of the major associations, however, was also organized hierarchically, with local, provincial, and national levels. Policy issues would rise from the local to the provincial level and would eventually be decided at the federal level. The various associations were also loosely federated 'at the top' under the umbrella of the National Council of Women of Canada (NCWC). But local councils, which allowed coordination (and sometimes competition) at the local level, were equally important. The structure of these associations enabled them to engage governments at all levels.

The membership of these associations should be characterized, in general, as white, middle-class, and, for the times, well educated. The rural Federated Women's Institutes of Canada (FWIC), founded in 1919, came to be the model that was adopted by many other countries. Few of the English-Canadian associations took root among franco-phones in Québec, although the Cercles des fermières were similar and, in fact, were among the founders of the FWIC (Dumont et al. 1987; Prentice et al. 1988:269). Finally, all of the activity undertaken by these groups was either self-funded or funded through raffles, bakesales, and the many other devices women had to raise cash. From 1919 through the 1950s, women's associations undertook extensive activity in the attempt to improve the status of their sex:

They consistently presented resolutions and briefs to government on such issues as education and vocational training for women, the right of equal opportunity to work and for equal pay, taxation and pension reform, laws pertaining to marriage, divorce, family planning and citizenship. They made continual requests for proportionate representation of qualified women to governmental boards, commissions, and agencies, to the Senate, the judiciary and the diplomatic corps. They made periodic requests for commissions where women faced discrimination ... [and they] did so in relative isolation from the main currents of national thought. (Canada, Secretary of State, Women's Program 1974:6, 7)

Women's movements underwent dramatic changes after the Second World War. The post-war concern for human rights provided a new intellectual and moral framework within which women's rights would come to be accepted as a credible issue. Canada became a member of the U.N. Status of Women Commission in 1958, and women's groups seized on the implications of such affiliations for the government's obligations to its own female population.

To summarize, women's political culture before the 1960s constituted a practical reflection of the nature of existing opportunities for women (beyond voting) to participate in decision-making roles in the formal political system. Although women did not reject that system, there remained some distaste for political parties. The women who did participate in political parties, however, were generally limited to support roles (Kealey and Sangster 1989; Sangster 1989). Until the 1960s, then, women were both part of and apart from the dominant political culture.

Radical Liberalism

In this section, we examine the values of the political cultures that influenced the contemporary English-Canadian women's movement. In addition to the general historical women's political culture discussed above, the political environment of organizations such as NAC included what we have called 'radical liberalism.' This set of values about politics is heavily influenced by the characteristics of the general political culture. We identify this set of values as the operational code of the English-Canadian women's movement.

Much current scholarship posits a sharp break between the concerns of the so-called first and second waves of women's movements for change. But an approach that discounts continuities between periods of mobilization in Canada makes an analysis of NAC extremely difficult. With its hybrid political culture and its coalitions of old and new forces, NAC's very existence constitutes a repudiation of such a view. The role of U.S. feminism in this account is complex. There is little doubt that U.S. feminist ideas had an impact in Canada. Certain key books by U.S. feminists were influential, and television, dominated by U.S. sources, projected the feminism of the U.S. movement to Canadians. Furthermore, the women of the 'draft-dodger generation' who came to Canada played a part in the formation of certain types of grass-roots groups in the larger cities in which they located. We will argue that their ideas about how to conduct politics within feminist organizations had a considerable influence on the values that were shaped in those groups. By contrast, we observe that the values of U.S. radical feminism pertaining to women's relationship to the politics of the state had far less influence on the English-Canadian movement.

As we have suggested, then, women's movements in English Canada inherited a set of ideas about how to conduct politics to which we refer as 'radical liberalism' (Richardson 1983; Vickers 1992).[1] In brief, this operational code embodied a commitment to the ordinary political process, a belief in the welfare state, a belief in the efficacy of state action in general to remedy injustices, a belief that change is possible, a belief that dialogue is useful and may help promote change, and a belief that service or helping others is a valid contribution to the process of change. The acceptance of this code gave the movement its ability to work and be effective in coalitions. It also limited the influence of ideas from the United States that rejected the ordinary political process and tended towards anti-statism. Certainly, the commitment of Canadian feminists to the welfare state put them strongly in conflict with this U.S. anti-statism, as our examination of NAC policies in Chapter 6 will demonstrate.

Two major forces for the transmission of the values of radical liberalism were the Royal Commission on the Status of Women and the women's peace movement. Both contributed to a revitalization of women's organizations from 1950 to the late 1960s. But while many groups became more or less feminist in their purposes, they remained traditional in their views of politics and organization and adhered to a reformist, rather than radical, analysis of women's situation. Self-defined liberationists claimed the 'grass-roots' label, believing that their movement 'differs greatly from the middle-class women's rights groups which consist mostly of professional and church women' (Canadian Educational Women's Press 1972:9). Generally young, educated, and from

TABLE 1.2
The operational code of 'second-wave' women's movements in English Canada

---

Dominant strand: 'radical liberalism'
- A commitment to the ordinary political process
- Pro-statism; a belief in the efficacy of state actions, especially of welfare-state programs
- Pro-active; a belief that change is possible
- A belief that dialogue with those who differ may be useful
- A belief that helping others, in terms of service, is a valid contribution to change

Counter-strands
- A belief that 'Power is not electoral'; support for community activism
- Concerns for 'the feminization of process' within feminist groups
- A belief that controversial/adversarial tactics are more effective as educative tools than the lobby/influence approach

---

Sources: Richardson 1983; Vickers 1986, 1988b, 1992

white, middle-class backgrounds, these liberationists were ignorant or scornful of the movement's many decades of local activity (which was nothing if not 'grass-roots').[2] None the less, a sense of differentiation was developing, and the new 'grass-roots feminism was already articulating a sense of itself as different from institutionalized feminism' (Adamson et al. 1988:53). (Adamson and colleagues define *grass roots feminism* as 'more community-based, emphasizing collective organizing, consciousness-raising, and reaching out to women "on the street"' [12].)

In English Canada, these attempts at differentiation did not preclude cooperation between older and newer groups. Bonnie Kreps (1972:75) explained to the royal commission that 'Radical feminism is called "radical" because it is struggling to bring about really fundamental changes in our society.' Her description of the indigenous women's liberation movement, however, reveals a position quite different from the determined exclusion of non-radical women in the United States. Describing women's liberation as 'a generic term covering a large spectrum of positions,' she divides it into the three familiar male-derived ideological 'segments' (liberal, Marxist or socialist, and radical), adding that 'all three have their own validity, all three are important. One belongs to one segment rather than another because of personal affinity with the aims being striven for' (74–5). This early example of the Canadian tradition of integrative feminism is no anomaly. In the United States, the very word *feminist* was rigorously reserved for the ideas of young, radical/revolutionary women. But in

English Canada, quite radical women and groups were willing to work with quite traditional women and groups. Moreover, quite radical groups were also willing to accept (and received) state funding for their projects. What, then, are the values of radical liberalism? First, it is characterized by a belief in dialogue and a willingness to engage in debate, not only for the purpose of eliminating differences, but also, in the case of differences that cannot be transcended, to understand them. Hamilton and Barrett (1986:1) put it this way: 'Canadians talk to each other ... across barriers of theory, analysis and politics that in Britain, for example, would long since have created an angry truce of silent pluralism.' They argue that Canadian feminists operate 'from within a political culture built on the recognition rather than the denial of division and differences between people'(2). Finally, they conclude that, in Canada, the task of 'apprehending diversity without becoming totally distracted by it' has been undertaken 'with greater solidarity and less suspicion between activists and intellectuals, academics and reformers than has been the case in Britain or the U.S.' (2).

While a willingness to engage in dialogue was central to the values inherited from first-wave feminists, the development of practices supportive of dialogue was also made necessary by the realities of Canadian political life. Chief among these realities was the need to achieve the involvement of some francophone women in organizations interacting with the federal government. Dialogue was maintained into the 1970s between anglophone and some francophone feminists through a process of élite accommodation, which was a familiar approach in Canadian politics. Laura Sabia revealed the somewhat opportunistic character of this tactic in her description of the delegation she led to Ottawa, on 19 November 1966, in search of a commitment by the government to establish a royal commission: 'We chose women who gave us credibility, women of stature. We asked Thérèse Casgrain to join us, and Rejane Colas, who was not a vocal person but she headed a lot of groups in Québec. The IODE was highly respected and a voice to be contended with in those days and we had Regina Tait, IODE President ... The leading women in Canada were doing our bidding' (interview with Chris Appelle, 10 January 1986).

The next fifteen years saw a rupturing of this tradition of cooperative interaction between anglophone and francophone feminists as feminism in Québec changed its perspective by embracing nationalism (Lamoureaux 1987), and English Canada failed to understand the nature of, and the reasons for, the new position. Nevertheless, a belief in the importance of interaction between English and French persisted in NAC, and other movement organizations, such as the Canadian Research Institute for the Advancement of Women (CRIAW), also adopted it as a goal. Certainly, claims by predominantly anglophone organizations such as NAC and CRIAW to represent Canadian women dictated at least lip-service to bilingualism.

As Hamilton and Barrett (1986:4) note, 'A belief in undivided sisterhood was never very marketable in Canada,' so the value placed on understanding and accommodating some, if not all, differences was considerable. Solidarity has been easier to maintain across class lines and between generations, however, than across the lines of linguistic, racial, and ethnic difference. As we will demonstrate in Chapter 4, NAC has been more successful in accommodating some differences than others, but it has always been open to dialogue with a remarkably diverse collection of groups.

The belief that 'explaining will help' is a feature of radical liberalism that NAC president Lynn McDonald (1979:39) saw as leading to a 'commitment to the ordinary political process [and to] public education and persuasion of politicians and parties within the system, [and] conversely [to an] avoidance of partisan politics [as a movement] and radical political theory.' However, the commitment to dialogue is by no means universal or unconditional. For example, experience with right-wing governments in British Columbia has made Vancouver feminist groups more anti-system than many of their eastern counterparts (Gillian Riddington, personal communication to Jill Vickers, April 1988). Although the commitment to dialogue was epitomized in NAC's multipartisan choices for president, which included women active in the Liberal, New Democratic, and Progressive Conservative parties, such practice was less acceptable in British Columbia, where the notion of a Social Credit feminist would be harder to swallow. In short, a belief in dialogue and in the notion that explaining things will help (along with everything that flows from that belief) is least saleable where the official political system is most fiercely polarized.

Also characteristic of radical liberalism is the belief that change is possible and that state action is an acceptable way of achieving change. The significant role that women played in creating Canada's welfare state may help to explain the greater sense of efficacy *vis-à-vis* the state among women of the English-Canadian movement than among women elsewhere. This belief, however, also reflects the pro-statism that, until recently, went largely unchallenged in Canadian society (Lipset 1990). Although neoliberal debates about welfare-state reform exist in Canada, relatively few feminists seriously question the view that 'the state is turning out to be the main recourse of women' (Piven 1984:14; see also Andrew 1984). Most English-Canadian feminists still see the state as a potentially benign utility engaged in worthy redistributive efforts, provision of services, and necessary regulatory tasks. Only in the area of abortion did the movement seek less government intervention, and even then, it was strictly in the sense of removing abortion from the criminal code, since feminists continued to demand that the state provide significant improvements in abortion services.

It is clear that the position of English-Canadian feminists is in stark contrast to the view that the state is unremittingly patriarchal and oppressive (MacKinnon 1989). Positions on this issue tend to be based on women's concrete experiences with the institutions of particular states in particular eras. In British Columbia, for example, where right-wing governments eliminated services that benefited women, as well as jobs occupied largely by women, the state was seen less as a benign utility and more as an oppressive force. (It is interesting to note that women active in services dealing with male violence against women also have a more critical appraisal of state institutions [Walker 1990]. This may be at least partially attributable to the fact that these women come into contact primarily with the judicial and police institutions of the state.)

Most English-Canadian feminists accept the premise that 'helping others is a valid contribution which has intrinsic value' (Richardson 1983:28). Since most government funding has been tied to a service orientation, many groups have been forced to provide a service in order to gain funding. State funding has also resulted in the professionalization of feminist services, which has meant increased ranks of paid staff and growing bureaucracies – developments that may conflict with the more grass-roots approach that many feminists prefer.

What we have formulated as the operational code of radical liberalism is muted by a counter-force associated with certain local groups and unions. Even these elements, however, realize that 'feminists who act only as critics of the system, and create too much distance from social institutions, run the risk of being unable to reach and activate people' (Adamson et al. 1988:179). Also present as a counter-current is the recurring debate concerning the proper orientation of umbrella groups such as NAC. Women espousing an ideology of egalitarianism, anti-hierarchy, and anti-leadership have repeatedly demanded a re-thinking of the organization's purposes (Morris 1983). The overall picture, then, is of an operational code that generally supports involvement in the ordinary political process, tolerance of ideological diversity, encouragement of dialogue, and a commitment to service. Combined with these elements is a strong strain of dissent by more-radical elements that find themselves uneasily in harness, in NAC, with a coalition of more-conventional forces. Out of this political dynamic has come NAC's unique contribution to feminist politics.

Radical Influences on Feminist Political Culture

Radical feminism is an important, if little understood, influence in Canada. Throughout Québec and the rest of Canada, 'the radical-feminist message injected new energy into the liberal feminism which had existed ... for more than seventy years' (Dumont et al. 1987:364). It was at the level of general theory that radical feminism had its most important impact on women's movements both in Canada and through-out the liberal democracies. As we will demonstrate, however, these theoretical radical-feminist ideas, generated by French, Australian, Canadian, and U.S. writers, were different from the norms of political culture associated with the U.S. Women's Liberation Movement.

The major sources of radical-feminist theory were the writings of Simone de Beauvoir, of France (translated into English in 1952); Kate Millett, of the United States; Shulamith Firestone, of Canada; and Germaine Greer, of Australia. (The writings of the latter three were translated into French in the early 1970s.) These authors popularized ideas that were radical in two respects: They were based on the premise that sex oppression was fundamental and primary and that all other oppression sprang from it, and they held that all of society's institutions were permeated by and perpetuated male dominance. Although not all of these writers used the term, each demonstrated the existence of a political phenomenon called 'patriarchy.' In Canada, the influence of their ideas was threefold: (1) they helped to revitalize the existing traditions of liberal feminism and left feminism; (2) with their emphasis on personal and sexual relationships, they contributed to the widespread mobilization of young women; and (3) they motivated young women to join groups often established by U.S. émigré feminists. In the context of the feminist theory described above, the term *radical* referred to something quite new, because it focused on gender as the source of oppression.

Additionally, in the context of U.S. politics, *radical* was used in reference to socialism, because of the tactics of 'red-baiting' that met the mildest of feminist proposals in the United States during the 1920s. The association of feminism with socialism came to be almost indelibly imprinted on the U.S. consciousness, to the point that arguments condemning childcare outside the home as a Communist plot made sense to many Americans, including Presidents Nixon and Reagan. J. Stanley Lemons (1973:209) describes the process that weakened the progressive impulse in U.S. feminism during the 1920s as distrust and confusion crept into its ranks:

Feminist organizations and leaders were battered by charges of being agents or dupes of a Bolshevist conspiracy to conquer the United States. Anti-feminists, extreme conservatives, open-shop advocates, anti-pacifists, and patriotic groups made such accusations against organizations as diverse as the Women's Trade Union League, League of Women Voters, YWCA, and Woman's Christian Temperance Union. All were denounced as part of a 'Spider Web' to promote communist objectives. These accusations originated among opponents of woman suffrage and were picked up and spread by the National Association of Manufacturers ... and by the American Medical Association ... The efforts of social feminists for peace, infancy and maternity protection, child labor prohibition and industrial reform generated opponents who used the red smear to defeat the reforms and intimidate the women.

The version of U.S. 'radical' feminism that was first introduced into Canada (at a level other than general theory) is best represented by the ideas of Marlene Dixon, who moved to Montreal from the United States in 1969 to teach sociology at McGill University. Dixon felt she had come from a war zone, and her experience taught her that there was no place in an autonomous radical women's movement for liberals, traditional socialists, or women's-rights feminists. She saw no connection at all between her Women's Liberation Movement (WLM) and indigenous Canadian movements. Dixon understood the WLM as emerging out of the struggle against sexism in the organizations of the American New Left – specifically, Students for a Democratic Society (SDS) and the Student Non-Violent Co-ordinating Committee (SNCC) (Dixon 1971). The 'terrific fear' of the police and other social forces mentioned by Joan Richardson (1983) as characteristic of U.S. feminism in the 1960s also contextualizes Dixon's views.

Dixon identifies three orientations in the early WLM in the United States, namely, those represented by the socialist groups, the consciousness-raising (C-R) groups, and the WITCH group, 'with its wild and poetic imagery of Kings, Fairies, Witches and power [that] involved a litany of oppression and rebellion' (1971:53). She notes that 'at the [1965 Chicago] conference ... the basic division is usually referred to as "consciousness-raising" vs "radical" or "bourgeois" vs "revolutionary"' (56).

By 1969, Dixon was in Montreal acting as the prime mover in a group called WAM, the Women's Action Movement (Richardson 1983:14). The group promoted rapid polarization within the emerging WLM in anglophone Montreal. Indeed, the WLM soon splintered, leaving considerable disagreement as to which of the resulting two groups – the Young Socialists or the counter-culture women (as consciousness-raising women were now called) – was the 'splinter group' (14–15).

By 1975, Marlene Dixon saw the conflict within the WLM as one between the 'politicos' and the 'so-called feminists' (1975:57). Announcing that she had become a Marxist-Leninist, she decried the joining of forces in the United States between the liberal feminists of the National Organization of Women (NOW) and 'radical' feminists who espoused an ideology she described as 'reactionary feminism' because of its explicit premise that 'men are the enemy' (58–60). Calling reactionary feminism an 'ideology of vengeance,' she described how, 'with the virtual expulsion of the left leadership,' the 'radical' feminists (previously described as C-R, counter-culture, bourgeois feminists) had assumed leadership over the portion of the U.S. movement that had not yet been co-opted into the reformist camp (NOW) (60). Finally, Dixon repudiated the methodology of consciousness raising, which she had taken in her missionary kitbag to Montreal, arguing that 'the error ... was to substitute understanding psychological oppression for political education' (61). Seeing conciousness raising used as a tool for individualist self-realization (which is what made it attractive to white, middle-class, North American women who could not be 'objectively oppressed,' except by men), she rejected the program that radical feminists had constructed using it, especially the elements of 'man-hating, Lesbian Vanguardism, reactionary separatism [and] virulent anti-communism' ... (61).

Few radical-feminist groups formed by U.S. émigrés in Canada followed the path of the U.S. movement, although the process of frequent splintering does seem to have been characteristic of groups that valued ideological homogeneity (Ricks et al. 1972). U.S. émigré Bonnie Kreps, cited earlier from her 1968 brief to the Royal Commission on the Status of Women, was a founder of the New Feminists (Koedt et al. 1973).

While her brief shows a strong commitment to radical feminism as an ideology, with its focus on patriarchy and sexual oppression, it does not display hostility to other strains of feminism to the degree that Dixon's writings do.

None of these conflicts and divisions were inevitable results of adopting the ideas we attributed to radical feminism as an ideology earlier. Rather, they grew out of conflicts that were born within the U.S. New Left, in the context of U.S. politics. Because the United States was a vibrant imperial power and U.S. feminists shared in that imperialism, the doctrine of a universal sisterhood was especially appealing to U.S. women. Many U.S. feminists, like Dixon, comfortably assumed that women in other countries were against the things they were against and for the things they were for. U.S. women reacted against the sexism of the male leadership of the New Left, who exploited women's sexuality and labour, denied them leadership roles, and denied their grievances status. Even after it emerged as an independent movement, however, the Women's Liberation Movement continued to share ideas about the politics of the state with the New Left, especially with the cultural radicals, who believed that 'the struggle within the state and its institutions [was] hopeless and beside the point' (Aronowitz 1984:22). Radical feminists saw themselves as striking out on a profoundly new course of analysing the condition of women from the perspective of a discourse of oppression and liberation. The sense of being oppressed by all of the large, impersonal institutions of U.S. society, as well as by men, shaped their efforts to define a sisterhood of those who were oppressed *because of their sex*. Ideas about the nature of oppression and liberation were in the air, and WLM women borrowed from them freely.

In the political culture of the U.S. New Left and U.S. radical feminism, change was understood as occurring primarily in the consciousness of individuals. According to Richardson (1983:411), some groups in Montreal did share the view that 'All value accrued to the individual. The transformation sought was that of the individual, not of the community, or of the society.' Because oppression was understood largely as the product of socialization, change required a series of individual struggles to free each individual from false consciousness. It was believed, initially, that such change could occur spontaneously and rapidly. But as people started to realize that this belief was unfounded and that a spontaneous revolution in America was neither inevitable nor imminent, they began to retreat from a politically engaged stance.

As one feminist 'revolutionary' said in 1971, 'Long-term action is required ... Most of us who have been in the movement for more than
two years realized recently that we would have to work for about ten
or twenty years ... It's scaring a lot of people' (Carden 1974:49). In a
movement that had created 'a good deal of consciousness and very
little concerted action' (Freeman 1983:143), there was insufficient organization for even a ten-year struggle.

Women possessing a new world-view with no corresponding new
world on the horizon and no map of how to get there could not easily
go back to living compromised lives. They kept the faith by creating a
fragment of a new world – a feminist community within a patriarchal
society and an imperialist state. Feminist services, clinics, bookstores,
literature, music, and scholarship all emerged as part of the process of
'living our visions' in the here and now (Hawthurst and Morrow 1984).
Simply living in a liberated way came to be seen as contributing to a
feminist 'revolution.' This cultural version of radical feminism not
only celebrated the social fragment that women created, but also involved a political quietism consistent with the ideas of the U.S. New Left.
While it was perhaps an understandable option for women facing the
enormous power of the U.S. imperial state, there was a lack of fit with
the political culture of radical liberalism that prevailed in the English-
Canadian women's movement (see Table 1.3, on page 46).

The Women's Peace Movement and Feminism within the Canadian Left

Why were English-Canadian women influenced less by U.S. radical
feminism's general ideas about politics than by its ideas about the
proper functioning of feminists groups? We have argued that the
intergenerational continuity of the English-Canadian movement allowed for the transmission of the political culture of radical liberalism
to the new generation of feminists. We will now look at several ways in
which that intergenerational communication about politics occurred.
The first important arena of interaction between 'old' and 'new' feminists was the women's peace movement, especially in the context of
the organization called the Voice of Women (VOW), founded in
Toronto in 1960. The second was the caucuses of the democratic left,
especially the Waffle, formed in 1969. We will also identify some of the
features of the Canadian political system that may account for most
feminists' commitment to radical liberalism and pro-statism.

TABLE 1.3
The ideological 'lack of fit' between English-Canadian radical liberalism and
U.S. radical feminism

Radical liberalism	Radical feminism
A commitment to the ordinary political process	A rejection of the ordinary political process; a rejection of politics in favour of change in individual consciousness
Pro-statism; a belief in the efficacy of state actions, especially in the case of the welfare state	Anti-statism; a belief in the absolute sovereignty of the individual versus the state and its institutions
Pro-active; a belief that change is possible	Briefly pro-active; mainly politically quietist, believing that change must occur in the realm of individual consciousness and must be total
A belief that dialogue with those who differ may be useful	A belief that dialogue with those who differ is not useful; advocate splintering or separating
A belief that helping others, in terms of service, is a valid contribution to change	A belief that assisting others in the area of self-help and aiding the victims of male violence is useful

Sources: Aronowitz 1984; Carden 1974; Dixon 1971; Freeman 1983; Richardson 1983

The 1950s and early 1960s were active years for Canadian women, despite the success of societal and governmental pressures on women to return to their homes after the Second World War. In 1950, on International Women's Day, women's organizations, unions, ethnic groups, and peace groups joined together to form a new national women's alliance – the Congress of Canadian Women (CCW) (Macpherson 1975:40). The president was Rae Luckock, one of Ontario's first two women MPP's (the other was Agnes Macphail). The congress passed a Charter of Rights for Canadian Women, in which a commitment to feminism was clear: 'We women of Canada assert that all human rights are women's rights.' The charter's leftism was also evident in its claim to a 'Right to Livelihood, Equal pay ... [and] seniority rights.' Reproductive issues were conceptualized as the 'Right to Motherhood unhampered by lack of economic security, lack of hospital care and shelter, nurseries, hot meals' (Macpherson 1975:40). Finally, the centrepiece of the charter was its claim to the 'Right to Peace.' The CCW was founded in the same week that Canada's first equal-pay legislation was passed in Ontario. In 1954, a coalition of women's groups, including the YWCA, the NCWC, the Canadian Federation of University Women (CFUW), and the Canadian Federation of Business and Professional Women's Clubs (CFBPWC), lobbied successfully for the establishment of a Women's Bureau in the federal Department of Labour (Bannon 1975). As Table 1.4 (on page 48) shows, this was to be the first of a long tradition of coalitions among women's groups to gain legal and structural changes of benefit to women.

As noted above, a major arena for the transmission of ideas about politics between generations was the Voice of Women. It appealed to women directly and was 'dedicated to crusading against the possibility of nuclear war.' VOW had a more respectable image that did earlier 'ban-the-bomb' groups, because its leaders lent themselves to appellations such as 'prominent' or 'wife of the well-known ... '(Macpherson and Sears 1976:72). This aura of respectability won VOW early access to political decision-makers, but most VOW leaders were also genuinely respected for their feminist work. Thérèse Casgrain, who led the fight for suffrage in Québec, for example, founded the Québec VOW and led a four-hundred-member delegation to Ottawa in 1961.

The VOW's activities interacted with those of the U.S. Women's Liberation Movement because of a shared focus on the war in Vietnam. But, as the VOW became increasingly nationalist and eager for 'made-in-Canada' defence and foreign policies, it became critical of U.S. policy in areas that went beyond the conflict in Vietnam. Its members came increasingly to see Canadian economic, social, and political independence as the key to a Canadian role in achieving peace (Duckworth and Hope-Simpson 1981:172). None the less, many 'Voicers' gave shelter and support to draft resisters and their partners, although the relationship was not always easy. Macpherson and Sears (1976:86) describe the 1971 conference in support of Indochinese women as especially difficult. Canadian women, swamped by the avalanche of 'American imperialism of the left ... felt a new awareness of the need to establish their own national identity, while still acknowledging their bond with women everywhere.'

The VOW was an organization within which several generations shared the values of their political culture. Certainly, NAC's deter-

TABLE 1.4
Policy-centred coalitions among women's groups, 1954–92

1954 Coalition to obtain a Women's Bureau in the federal Department of Labour	Included the YWCA, NCWC, and CFBPWC
1966 Committee for the Equality of Women	Formed to seek a royal commission on the status of women
1971 National Ad Hoc Committee on the Status of Women	Formed to seek a mechanism to ensure implementation of the recommendations of the commission
1972 National Action Committee on the Status of Women	Formed as a more permanent coalition structure, with the initial purpose of ensuring implementation of royal commission's recommendations
1981 Ad hoc committee of Canadian women on the constitution	Formed to ensure inclusion in Charter of the equality-rights clause (Section 15) and the sex-equality clause (Section 28) without override; initiated as an equality-rights coalition with other equality seekers
1985 Coalition to lobby for improved affirmative action	Comprising NAC Employment Committee, Urban Alliance on Race Relations, and the Association for the Mentally Handicapped; labour groups join in December 1985
1987 Ad hoc committee of women on the constitution reactivated	Formed to monitor revisions of the Meech Lake Accord and to ensure that the guarantees in the Charter (Section 28) prevail
1992 Ad hoc committee of women on the constitution again reactivated	Reformed to support NAC in its opposition to the Charlottetown Accord

mined multipartisan approach reflects a heedfulness of the warnings of older Voicers, that problems could result if members were allowed to use the VOW for partisan purposes. VOW members also taught the younger generation that 'they could be agents of change in the world,' and not just in the causes of others, but also on their own behalf

(Macpherson and Sears 1976:88). From 1961, the VOW was engaged in the campaign to legalize birth control, and in 1970, many Voicers lent support to the Abortion Caravan, which modelled itself on the old peace trains.

Both the English-Canadian and the Québec movements, then, benefited from the existence of a bridging generation between first- and second-wave feminism. The democratic left also had the advantage of intergenerational continuity, provided through its socialist feminist tradition.[3] Canada had a pattern of parties of the Left that was quite different from that in the United States. The institutionalized Left in Canada offered both a communist and a non-communist option. In the CCF/NDP, moreover, the social gospel, Christian socialism, and rationalist Fabianism were at least as influential as Marxism. (Certainly, in English Canada, God is invoked as often by the Left as by the Right.) Many feminists were mobilized by the social-gospel tradition into left-wing causes, which thereby gained respectability in their communities. In particular, suffragist Nellie McClung's feminist version of the social gospel became a model for other women.

The evolution of socialist feminism within the non-communist Left, however, was hampered by the intense anti-communism of both the CCF and the NDP, which produced a deep suspicion of semi-autonomous groups or caucuses. In the late 1930s, the Toronto CCF Women's Joint Committee (WJC) was expelled from the party for forming common cause with communist women on certain issues (Manley 1980; Sangster 1989). Also in the 1930s, moreover, party traditionalists such as Winnipeg's Beatrice Brigden believed that 'the CCF ... is firmly anchored to the most important social and economic institution, the home and the family' (Manley 1980:103). None the less, even at that time, many women argued that socialism required a feminist analysis to be complete (Sangster 1989). In the 1960s, women in the NDP's Waffle caucus built on experience of that earlier generation of CCF socialist feminists.

On the surface, the Waffle's 'Women's Lib' may have looked like a U.S. import. On closer examination, however, it becomes apparent that the Waffle's version of the New Left and its version of women's liberation are both quite different from their U.S. counterparts. The postwar renewal of the Left in Canada was represented primarily in the formation of the Waffle, but its adherents would reject the 'New Left' label, seeing it as a manifestation of U.S. imperialism of the Left (Laxer 1960). Although the Waffle challenged the NDP's long-held premise that socialism could be attained exclusively through electoral and parliamentary activity, it in no sense rejected the ordinary political process or questioned the importance of state action. It offered community socialism as a supplement to, not a substitute for, the political process focused on the state. Community socialism involved three aspects: labour organizing, local neighbourhood organizing, and research on Canadian society.

Although the Waffle defined itself primarily around the issue of nationalism, it quickly spawned a women's caucus. A panel on the subject of women's liberation appeared on the agenda of the National Waffle Conference in 1970 (Public Archives of Canada [PAC] 1970b). Also, the resolutions booklet *For a Socialist Ontario in an Independent Socialist Canada*, prepared for the 1970 Ontario NDP Convention, included a ten-page section entitled 'The Liberation of Women.'[4] It asserts the right of women to self-organization, arguing that 'the oppression of women can only be overcome through women working together.' And it adds that 'the liberation of women must be a vital part of the struggle for socialism in Canada' (PAC 1970–2).

In an address to the Steelworkers' Political Conference in 1971, Desmond Morton offered a critique of what he called the Waffle's 'Bonnie and Clyde style of socialism' that essentially summarized the party traditionalists' position: 'In the name of Canadian independence, the Waffle has turned out to be the most massive Americanizing force in the history of our movement, working flat out to impose the language and the tactics which have left American socialism a shattered, almost wholly irrelevant force.' Morton concluded that 'there is hardly a Waffle idea, from Women's Lib to the slogans about Yankee imperialism, which has not been imported holus bolus from the United States' (PAC 1970–2).

Perhaps, in retrospect, Morton can be forgiven for failing to look beyond the rhetoric in his assumption that the Waffle's 'Women's Lib' was 'imported holus bolus from the United States' and that it was therefore indistinguishable from the U.S. variant. While the differences between the indigenous liberation movement and the U.S. WLM were not always evident in the rhetoric, Waffle resolutions made pro-statist demands for services for women and, although they called for the reform of trade unions, political parties, and other institutions, they did not demand their elimination (PAC 1970a).

Waffle women went through a process of reaction against the sexism of their male colleagues and, in the process, honed their consciousness as feminists (Pat Smart, personal communication to Jill Vickers, May 1989). The Waffle as a group, however, responded positively to women's demands, providing an arena for the development of an analysis and policy proposals that integrated socialism and feminism in a new way. On the one hand, with their acceptance of the state, the party, and the ordinary political process, the Waffle women shared the operational code of radical liberalism; on the other hand, the values that underlay the community socialism they hoped to build echoed those held by their 1930s predecessors in the CCF, who also believed in extra-parliamentary action and local community decision making.

To summarize, then, Canadian women of the 1960s were the beneficiaries of political cultures developed by women of earlier generations and transmitted through VOW or the CCF/NDP. This intergenerational cohesion would not only serve organizations such as NAC well, but would also prevent the political doctrine of anti-statism characteristic of U.S. radical feminism from making significant inroads in the English-Canadian women's movement.

NAC's Political-Opportunity Structure: The Canadian Political System

The role of women in the formal politics of the Canadian state is equal to that of men only at the level of voting. The literature is replete with analyses identifying the barriers that limit both the 'supply' of and the 'demand' for women activists within political élites (Brodie and Vickers 1982; Brodie 1985b; Bashevkin 1985; CRIAW 1987; Vickers and Brodie 1981; Burt 1986a). Certainly, the nature of the institutions of liberal democracy, such as political parties, is one such barrier. Democracy developed only as a 'top dressing' in liberal states, which served competitive, individualist, market societies 'through a system of freely competing though not democratic political parties' (Macpherson 1966). Indeed, a central feature of mainstream politics during the era of Liberal rule in Canada was élite accommodation. Despite rhetoric about 'participatory democracy,' women were excluded from the central process of political and economic policy making. Only within women's-movement organizations were women 'in charge' and only there were women-centred policies and processes the main order of business.

We have argued that women's movements are profoundly affected by the political culture in which they develop. In this section, we will illustrate that they are also shaped by the level of complexity of the ruling state and the nature of the prevailing regime during key periods of their development. NAC, in its dual role as a 'parliament of women' and an interest group aggregating and representing the views of its member groups to the federal government, was particularly vulnerable to changes in both state institutions and the prevailing regime, especially to significant changes in the federal–provincial division of powers. In this section, we will explore some of the changing elements of Canada's federal political system, thereby providing the context for the actions and development of the English-Canadian movement, in general, and NAC, in particular.

Although the powerful federal state of the Liberal era was centralist and interventionist in both social and economic areas, the political system was initially underdeveloped and vulnerable to U.S. influences, especially prior to the full development of Canadian television.[5] The federal–provincial division of powers gave the federal state control over the money supply and most areas of taxation, which enabled federal Liberal governments to strengthen the welfare state. Most significantly, following the lead of social-democratic Saskatchewan, they introduced medicare, a program of particular importance to women and their children. The expansion of federal services that were needed more by women than men also meant increased employment of women by state institutions.

During this period, political power over policy making rested with two structures, the party system and the bureaucracy, 'both of which achieve[d] an apex in the cabinet' (Pross 1975:18). The impact of women's movements was initially felt through the traditional tactics of lobbying: delegations of women representing coalitions of groups presented briefs to politicians and government officials, and called for commissions. At that time, lobbying was a fairly private activity. As late as the mid-1970s, one lobbyist made this observation: 'When I see members of Parliament being lobbied, it's a sure sign to me that the lobby lost its fight in the civil service and the cabinet' (Van Loon and Whittington 1976:306). Judy LaMarsh (1969:281), who was the sole (if not the token) woman in Liberal cabinets during the 1960s, argued that 'No political party in Canada can claim to be particularly sensitive to the women within its own organization, much less to the women of the electorate at large.'

The expansion of the welfare state by the federal government during the Liberal era (including, thereby, the provision of services important to women) cannot be understood as resulting primarily from the 'ordinary' politics of élite accommodation. LaMarsh (1969:301) states: 'Nothing was so hard to accomplish during all the time I was in cabinet as the appointment of a Royal Commission to inquire into the Status of Women.' She describes the process and, in particular, the negative role of the press:

In early 1965, Pearson seemed at last to be prepared to accept my advice and set up such a commission. I had provided him with a draft of the proposed terms of reference, with a copy of the Kennedy Commission reference and its report, along with a long list of women who might serve on such a commission. When I mentioned a Royal Commission to a national women's meeting, there was an immediate and scathing reaction from some of the responsible press of the country. Pearson backed off as if stung by a nettle. I have no doubt in my mind that I would have been unable to convince the Government to set up the commission without the remarkable organization of Mrs. Laura Sabia ... who, for the first time in history, brought together women's organizations from all over the country to speak with one voice in Ottawa. This was the pressure needed to make Pearson act ... (301–2)

This precedent made it clear to women that the activist Liberal government would respond to massive public pressure from women under certain circumstances. It also taught them, however, that women's groups had to speak with one voice in order to achieve anything and that it helped to have a network of women within state institutions, and especially within the cabinet, working on the movement's projects.

The most important new element in postwar liberal-democratic politics was the rise of new and renewed movements for change. At the beginning of the Liberal era,. they were of two distinct types: equality-seeking movements and quality-of-life movements, especially those concerned with the effects of a possible nuclear war. International human rights movements and the U.S. civil rights movement were the models that launched the equality-seeking dynamic. While women's movements had important links to the past and women enjoyed the basic civil and political rights won by first-wave activists, many felt that those rights had not made them 'matter' in politics. Formal political equality had not resulted in any real political influence for women. Few policies or policy makers paid the slightest attention to women's needs or wants as women. Most women knew that, but they differed in their estimation of whether equality-seeking movements could get the official political system to respond and to change. In the United States, the tragic end of the Kennedy era and the shame of foreign entangle-ments in Vietnam and Cuba persuaded many women that the system was incapable of change. In English Canada, by contrast, most women remained more optimistic about the ability of governments to respond. These new and revitalized movements for change threatened estab-lished political institutions, especially political parties. Federal Liberal governments, however, responded in an activist way. Government funding of the 'voluntary sector' was expanded to include support that would enable citizen participation – even that of radical groups. To some observers this aspect of the Liberal government's activism is seen as an attempt to control and limit the effects of the new move-ments for change. Martin Loney (1977:457), for example, argues that such support served 'to contain the debate within broad, but none the less definable parameters.' During this period, something of a symbi-otic relationship developed between the organized portion of the women's movement, including NAC, and the federal state. The exist-ence of a Liberal government with activist and centralist tendencies, one that was willing to fund movement groups and activities, encour-aged the movement to 'face the state.' Findlay (1987:31) describes the government's approach as follows:

Between 1966 and 1979, the Canadian state was engaged in organizing its for-mal response to women's demands for equality. Although some concrete leg-islative and policy initiatives were introduced in this period, the response of the state focused largely on integrating the representation of women's interests into the policy-making process. This was done both by establishing a network of programs and advisors to represent women's issues in the state bureau-cracy, and by appointing a minister responsible for the status of women to represent women's interests at the executive level of the state.

The infrastructure developed during the era of Liberal rule in-cluded the Canadian Advisory Council on the Status of Women and Status of Women Canada. Such structures may well become permanent additions to the institutional equipment of the federal state, just as Women's Bureaus in Departments of Labour did several decades ear-lier. This Liberal invention of an infrastructure to represent women's interest in the policy-making process, with its 'femocrat' network of women within the state, was not matched by equal efforts on the part of the political parties to increase the number of women nominated to run for them in safe ridings. From 1968 to 1972, NDP member Grace

MacInnis was the sole woman in the House of Commons. In 1972, however, the Liberals did ensure the election of three women in Québec, including Monique Bégin, who had been the research director of the Royal Commission on the Status of Women, and Jeanne Sauvé, who ultimately became a symbol of the female presence of the Liberal era when she became speaker of the House of Commons and, later, Governor General of Canada. After 1972, there was a sudden increase in the number of women joining political parties (Bashevkin 1985:93). In 1974, five more Liberal women took office, including Aideen Nicholson, an activist on the Ontario Committee on the Status of Women.

What, then, were the major effects of the Liberal era with regard to women? Findlay (1987:31) observes that, during this period, 'the state demonstrated a commitment to consult with the women of Canada, and in doing so not only validated the faith of liberal feminists in the strategy of reform by the state, but constructed a relationship with them that established liberal feminism as the "public face" of the women's movement.' Sandra Burt (1986b) has argued that another key feature of this era was the state's deconstruction of feminism's systematic critique into a series of separate issues. The movement was largely accepting of the strategy of reform by the state and, to meet its commitment to provide services to women, found it necessary to develop its own expertise and policy proposals in areas that conformed to government-set agendas. This occurred in policy areas such as battering and child sexual abuse. Some of the early leaders of NAC were comfortable with the Liberal strategy of downplaying direct action (confrontation and demonstrations) in favour of lobbying government for specific policies and programs: it was an approach consistent with their values. Others, such as Lynn McDonald, believed it conflicted with NAC's responsibilities to its regional and community-based member groups and therefore tried to develop a more confrontational approach.

In the United States, the long-time existence of an entrenched Bill of Rights made equality seeking a familiar part of politics. By contrast, equality seeking was not a common feature of Canadian politics before the 1960s (Vickers 1986). During the Liberal era, however, many equality-seeking movements emerged that borrowed from the analysis and tactics of the women's movement, just as women had borrowed from the anti-slavery and civil-rights movements in the past. But this new dynamic in Canadian politics also included movements that adopted the language of collective, rather than individual, rights. The equality aspirations of Québec, for example, were being expressed increasingly in terms of a collective right to self-determination, and campaigns for individual rights in that province became entangled with campaigns for collective rights. The slogan of some members of the Québec feminist movement was 'Pas de libération des femmes sans Québec libre, pas de Québec libre sans libération des femmes' (Lamoureux 1987:53). Third World struggles for national liberation also had influence on movements in Québec during the Liberal era. Two of the central challenges facing the Liberal government, then, were the rise of a radical movement to 'decolonize' Québec and the rise of a democratic movement seeking to acheive Québec's separation from the rest of Canada by peaceful means.

Whether pursued in relation to individual or collective rights, equality seeking in Canadian politics was a contagious process. Racial minorities, gays and lesbians, immigrant groups, and people with disabilities all used civil-rights/equality-rights discourse and adopted tactics pioneered in part by women's movements. In addition, such groups found it possible to build coalitions, in which women were able to play a central role. The relative stability of women's-movement organizations, achieved through the institutionalization of integrative structures such as NAC, allowed them to play a key role in the equality-seeking dynamic.

In the 1970s, an equality-seeking alliance was forged between some native women, including Mary Two Axe Early, and the member groups of the English-Canadian movement to oppose the elements of the Indian Act that discriminated against women. This alliance, whose aim was captured by the slogan 'Indian rights for Indian women,' believed in the primacy of individual rights. Since that time, however, many aboriginal women have become increasingly sympathetic to the claims of First Nations to their collective rights to self-government. Divided from the 'mainstream' white movements on the sorts of issues that also divide Western and Third World women, many aboriginal women are now seeking improved status exclusively within the First Nations. Non-status and Métis women, however, continue to struggle for individual rights and find support from many women's groups.

Although the development of a broadly based equality-seeking dynamic was probably the most significant shift to occur in the *content* of federal politics during the Liberal era, profound changes were also becoming apparent in the *conduct* of politics. Destined to be fully realized only in later years, the following four changes had their roots in the Liberal era: (1) the communications revolution in politics, especially the impact of television; (2) the rise of single-issue groups and the decline of political parties as the primary institutions mediating between the state and the mass of citizens; (3) the increasing role of political staffs and, most recently, of public-affairs firms in the policy-making process and as facilitators of the interplay between single-issue groups and decision makers; and (4) parliamentary reform and, in particular, the increasing role of committees.

The communications revolution profoundly affected all aspects of politics in the liberal democracies. The near-private nature of political interaction became a thing of the past once politics had to be conducted in the full glare of cameras and in hearing distance of the most sensitive microphones. New technology afforded Canadians a closer look at the politics and movements for change of our neighbours to the South. For the English-Canadian women's movement, it meant being swamped with images of the U.S. women's movement. As with politics in general, women's politics had to be 'mediaworthy,' and its leaders preferably young and photogenic. (The media, of course, also insisted that there be leaders to interview.) Canadian politics was transformed from the person-to-person affair that Judy LaMarsh had experienced into a vast, impersonal spectator sport, in which a party leader's cheekbones and fashion sense were more newsworthy than her policy pronouncements.

The rise of single-issue groups is a phenomenon little studied in Canada. It has received more attention in the United States, where single-issue groups have taken the form of Political Action Committees (PACs), which channel the vast sums of money required to conduct politics in an era of mass media to the politicians who are willing to support their causes. The PAC manifestation of single-issue groups has not developed fully in Canada, partly because the parliamentary system makes elected politicians far less attractive targets than their counterparts in a congressional system and partly because Canadian election-expenses legislation limits spending in elections to the 'official agents' of parties and candidates. During the Liberal era, élite lobby groups were the norm; they were willing to avoid conflict with government, focusing instead on quiet accommodations between experts and on consensus-seeking techniques of political communication (Pross 1975:19). Today, non-economic, single-issue groups are like the U.S. PACs; that is, they try to persuade politicians that they will be elected or defeated because of their views on one policy issue. The obvious model is anti-abortion groups, which fund candidates who support their cause and actively try to defeat candidates who do not. The government's response has included fragmenting policy into a series of short-term, discrete single issues, an approach that has affected the women's movement. NAC, which was designed to aggregate the views of diverse groups, for example, contained many single-issue groups within its ranks during the period studied and frequently responded to single issues.

The rise of single-issue groups in the form of PACs, as well as the increased importance of pressure groups generally, reflects, in part, the muddying of the distinctions among state, regime, and party that was an inevitable consequence of the sheer duration of Liberal rule. Although political parties remained the main source of legislative personnel, their importance as sources of policy clearly declined. The shift towards PACs and other pressure groups also reflects the rise in importance of political staffs. At the beginning of the Liberal era, political staffs were virtually non-existent (LaMarsh 1969). Even the prime minister and cabinet ministers were dependent on civil servants (except during elections, when campaign work was undertaken by volunteers in their constituencies – people who *remained* in their constituencies after the election was won). The development of a service role, or ombuds role, for MPs and the near-collapse of the federal wing of the Liberal party as a policy originator during its era as the government party (Whitaker 1977) increased the importance of political staffs both to rank-and-file MPs and to front-benchers.

John Meisel (1985) attributes the decline of the party as a mediating institution in Canadian politics to many causes, including the rise of the bureaucratic state, the acceptance of the norms of pluralism and the rise of interest-group politics, incipient corporatism, direct federal–provincial diplomacy, the rise of the electronic media and investigative reporting, the rise of opinion polling, the primacy of economic interests, and the long period of one-party dominance.[6] Both the rise of single-issue groups and the increased importance of political staff loyal to individual politicians rather than to parties served to disrupt customary relationships of élite accommodation.

The final general change in the way politics was conducted during the Liberal era was the reform of Parliament and, in particular, the increased importance of parliamentary committees in the conduct of public business. Doris Anderson, former president of both NAC and the

CACSW, believes the women's movement, in general, and NAC, in particular, made the most of this change (personal communication to Jill Vickers, May 1987). In subsequent chapters, we will examine in detail NAC's interaction with policy makers, politicians, and the public through the structure of the new parliamentary committees. In general, the ability of the movement to have an impact on parliamentary committees usually depended on the availability of government funding for participation, unless the committee held hearings across the country.

Canadian feminism has always displayed a broader ideological map than has its U.S. counterpart. One reason for this has been the continued presence of economically conservative, libertarian, and, especially, 'red Tory' elements constituting a vigorous strain of feminism within the federal Progressive Conservative party. It is this presence we must keep in mind as we situate the relationship between the English-Canadian women's movement and the Conservative regime in the post-Liberal era.

Until the late 1970s, there was little difference between the federal Liberals and Conservatives with regard to the propriety of state activism, especially in the realm of economics. As Janine Brodie (1985a:73) explains, 'fundamental disagreements between the Liberal and Progressive Conservative parties over the question of state power and economic development have been relatively rare in our political history. The BNA Act provided for a strong federal government and, from the beginning, it was an active participant in Canada's economic development.' In matters of social policy, there was somewhat more differentiation, with the Liberals supporting a more libertarian position on matters such as sex ('The state has no place in the bedrooms of the nation') and the Conservatives supporting a more libertarian position on issues such as gun control. But even in relation to social policy and the changes sought by equality seekers, there was no clear-cut polarization between the two parties.

In the late 1970s, a polarization did develop that has been described as follows: 'The Progressive Conservatives became the party of free enterprise and decentralization while the Liberals became the party of state intervention in the economy and federal power' (Brodie 1985a:74; see also Laxer 1980). (The NDP, meanwhile, continued to support state intervention and federal power.) Although the shift to the right in the political climate of the United States and Europe was having an impact in Canada, Brodie asserts that demands for the decentralization of power in this country initially came from Western provincial governments, which had been in conflict with the federal government throughout the 1970s. (Alberta, in particular, was in rebellion over the federal Liberal government's interventionist energy policies.) Of course, Québec governments profoundly challenged federal power and centralization, but challenges from the Alberta Conservative and the British Columbia Social Credit governments were qualitatively different: they questioned not only *which* government should have more power, but also whether *any* government should be involved in many areas. In short, the pro-statism that had underwritten government activity in Canada at both the federal and provincial levels and by all governing parties was now being challenged.

Some neoliberal forces in this debate believed that the welfare state had become overgrown and was in need of trimming by the new Conservative regime. They also tended to support a libertarian view of state intervention in 'private' matters of social policy (such as abortion).[7] Neoconservative voices were present in this debate as well. Unlike the neoliberals, who favoured a reduction of the welfare state but not its elimination, neoconservatives advocated the virtual elimination of all and any regulation by the state, in order to 'provide a level playing field' in the equal-opportunity 'sweepstakes' (Vickers 1986). Neoconservative groups, such as the National Citizens' Coalition, were explicitly anti-feminist in their attacks on elements within the federal Conservative government that continued to support feminist issues and the funding of feminist organizations.

Neither the federal government nor the English-Canadian women's movement has chosen to pursue gender-gap politics, although polarization in some provinces has led to the emergence of electorally significant gender gaps. In the United States, where it was originated, the gender-gap approach involved an alliance between the Democratic party and major organizations of the women's movement based on the fact that U.S. women were more supportive than U.S. men of the state activism traditionally associated with the Democratic party. To further woo women voters, the Democratic party adopted affirmative action for party and convention offices and favoured policies supported by progressive women. In Canada, an alliance of this sort between women's groups and the second Mulroney administration was impossible, because both the government and the conservative feminists associated with it had come to view the actions of NAC as supportive of the NDP, although those actions reflected opposition to the government more than support for any other party.

Summary

In this section, we have argued that a strong equality-seeking dynamic was introduced into the federal political system in Canada during the 1960s. The ability of the English-Canadian women's movement to create conflict-managing institutions and to sustain coalitions despite differences made it a central player in this dynamic throughout the Liberal era. We have consequently rejected the vision of the Canadian state as a monolithic and unremittingly patriarchal oppressor (MacKinnon 1989), since this view is not sustainable in the light of the Canadian state's actual record of positive changes for women. Our analysis is based instead on a view of the state as a set of institutions that are often not fully consistent in their direction, partly because the government's ability to affect the behaviour of state institutions varies over time and partly because there is a competition within and among state institutions that complicates the implementation of a government's overall plans.

Furthermore, the limited ability of governments to deal with policy in anything other than short time frames can work to the advantage of the women's movement; indeed, it can potentially enhance the degree of influence that a movement with stable institutions engaged in long-term projects can attain. Sue Findlay (1987:48) maintains that 'at times when the state is more vulnerable to women's demands, feminists can play a more active role in the development of state proposals to promote women's equality.' Moreover, 'taking advantage of the state's need for legitimation, they can establish feminist alternatives to the bureaucratic mode of operating that reinforces patterns of inequality, or advocate policies that challenge the ideology of capitalism and patriarchy.' We would agree that, to be effective, strategies for making women matter in Canadian politics in the period under study required an understanding of when openings for the equality-seeking dynamic were imminent and of how they could be best utilized. We will evaluate NAC's ability to develop and pursue such strategies in subsequent chapters.

The development of successful strategies, however, also depended on the presence of networks of feminists within state institutions, as well as within legislatures. Some observers believe that if women are present in the institutions of the political system, they can change the agendas of those institutions (Freda Paltiel, cited in Burt 1986b). Findlay (1987:48) warns, however, that 'the potential for successful challenges depends on the extent to which feminists inside the state have been able to maintain their relations with women's movement and to use their position to advocate reforms that will affect women's lives rather than reforms that have only symbolic value.' Clearly, this could not be just a one-way street. Not only did women within political institutions have to be receptive to the women's movements, movement women also had to be open to women within the state and within political parties.

Finally, we maintain that it was essential for the contemporary movement to become institutionalized and for these channels of interaction to become as permanent as possible. This derives from our conviction that the struggle to gain equality for women is a multi-generational project that cannot succeed if it relies on the interpersonal relationships of a single generation. Reforms gained can never be taken for granted as permanent features. None the less, 'their value should not be underestimated as a response to the immediate needs of women and as a way of weakening the hegemony of the dominant groups that oppose women's equality' (Findlay 1987:48).

In the chapters that follow, we explore a number of structural reforms and policy changes achieved through NAC's interaction with the formal politics of the state over the period studied, arguing that the contribution of NAC to the achievement of the English-Canadian movement's goals reflects its successful institutionalization. In addition, we examine the political dynamic that led to the achievement of significant changes in Canada's Constitution, gained Canadian women their 'ERA,' and, more importantly, resulted in a recognition of the legitimacy of equality seeking by all disadvantaged groups in relation to the Constitution. In our view, the political engagement of the English-Canadian women's movement has contributed significantly to achieving major gains in women's struggle for real equality.

The remainder of our discussion is an assessment of the contribution of NAC to the movement's effectiveness. In particular, we consider the stresses on NAC as it undergoes institutionalization and strives to grapple with the task of providing representation for Canadian women from a wide political spectrum and from many newly mobilized groups. The issue of representation is critical to NAC's legitimacy, as it claims to represent women better than any existing political structure, including political parties. Finally, we discuss the pressures on NAC from various sources for decentralization and address the question of how NAC has adapted to politics since the end of the Liberal era. Our purpose, which is to present an account of politics 'as if women mattered,' will guide us in this project.

Notes

1 Many of these ideas were shared by both anglophones and francophones in the 1960s, when only the revitalized liberal feminism of the FFQ was present in Québec, but fewer are shared today (Micheline Dumont, personal communication to Jill Vickers, May 1989). Aboriginal women accepted the code to the same extent in the 1960s and early 1970s, but it was not shared in the 1980s by many First Nations women.

2 Intergenerational rebellion may well have been an important factor in shaping the attitudes of some young women to their political foremothers. Many considered their biological mothers to be 'wimps' and knew little of their suffrage and post-suffrage grandmothers. One of the authors completed a BA in political science in the 1960s without ever hearing about the suffrage movement.

3 We will use the unhyphenated term *socialist feminism* to refer to this tradition of lived experience in union movements and the politics of the Left. We will reserve the hyphenated designation *socialist-feminism* for the contemporary academic and intellectual tradition that has tried to synthesize Marxist feminism with radical feminism. We will also follow Heather Jon Maroney in identifying a strain of 'working-class feminism' based on women in unions (1987).

4 This section contained twenty-four detailed resolutions calling for state and party action in the areas of reproductive rights; education; child custody; sexist stereotypes in advertising; day care; part-time work; maternity leave; and 'a houseworker's allowance,' to be paid by the state 'to the man or woman who performs household duties while his or her spouse is working outside of the home' (PAC 1970–2).

5 In her *Memoirs of a Bird in a Gilded Cage* (1969), Judy LaMarsh notes that when she was elected as an MP in 1960, there was no Canadian television; her first TV performance was as a panelist on a U.S. program that was beamed into Canada during the October 1960 by-election.

6 Meisel also identifies several short-run causes for the diminished role of

political parties, such as Pierre Trudeau's disdain for Parliament and the decline in ministerial responsibility that characterized the Liberal era.

7 Recent Conservative ministers responsible for the status of women are excellent examples of neoliberal feminists. Highly supportive of free enterprise and of the libertarian position on abortion, they have also been supportive of the federal state's use of its regulative powers to provide equality of opportunity for women. They have been less supportive of material programs (such as a national child-care program) that would in practice equalize opportunity.

2 NAC in the Shadow of the Royal Commission: The Founding Era, 1972–1978

NAC was not initially designed in 1972 to be the central institution of a multigenerational women's movement. Rather, it was created as a coalition to monitor the implementation of the recommendations of the Royal Commission on the Status of Women. Its founding mothers knew, however, that to have a successful impact on the Canadian state, it was necessary to sustain (and enlarge) their coalition and to maintain a common view and an agreement on strategy. This knowledge was the result of their experiences in the 1950s and 1960s of gains made by earlier coalitions. It was also the result of their memory of the era of the 1930s and 1940s, when each women's group made its case to government in isolation from (and often in conflict with) the others.

The NAC founders also knew that they had a radical and dynamic new generation of feminists on their hands. Two generations met at the founding conference and the organization created was to include them both. This brave decision set NAC on the course of becoming an aggregative organization that would try to provide a forum where the different forces of progressive women's politics could interact. The structure envisioned for NAC by its founders, however, primarily reflected their knowledge of how successful lobby coalitions operated. So, NAC was formed with the model of the National Council of Women (NCWC) and the Fédération des Femmes du Québec (FFQ) in mind, and little attention was paid to adapting the structures of representation and policy making to reflect the ideas of the feminist forces. After all, the report of the royal commission, it was thought, existed to provide the policy demands. All that needed to be discussed, the founding mothers believed, were the tactics to be employed. (The old guard believed that the tried-and-true lobby activities that had traditionally been pursued would suffice.) It was only when the report ceased to be sufficient as the sole blueprint for action that the need for processes to determine NAC's policy became apparent. And it was only when the more radical elements that came to be grafted on to the old coalition began to challenge the validity of the traditional tactics that NAC began to experience conflict about the norms of political process.

In the next three chapters, we trace the development of NAC as an embryonic parliament of women in three phases of its development: (1) the *founding* stage (1972–8), during which NAC was a Toronto-based lobby group operating almost entirely in the shadow of the royal commission; (2) a *transitional* period (1979–82), during which the organization was rocked by conflict and crisis until it became clear that no single ideological group could dominate NAC; and (3) a period of *institutionalization* (1983–8), during which the organization became more regionalized, came to terms with government funding and paid staff, and experienced an enormous expansion of its membership. In this chapter, we contextualize the founding of NAC within the framework of a literature on 'social' movements and the political process. We introduce the concept of institutionalization to illuminate our hypothesis about NAC's role in the English-Canadian women's movement. Second, we explore the immediate context of the founding of NAC, especially the founding of the FFQ and NAC's relationship with its francophone minority. Finally, we examine the nature of the political climate within which NAC operated in this founding era.

'Social' Movements and the Political Process

The traditional academic conception of the political associates it with the formal system of elections and appointments to and decisions by the institutions of the state. As Doug McAdam (1988:61) writes, 'the message is unmistakable: politics is something that takes place in the public domains between officially recognized political actors. Moreover, those domains are defined as masculine – they represent authority, rationality, justice and order.' Movements of change are not usually viewed as political in and of themselves, as the terminology 'social' movements suggests. Indeed, an apolitical view of movements for change has characterized most of the paradigms used in social science. 'Social' movements have been viewed as collective therapy for frustration (Kornhauser 1959) and as the precursors of effective responses by official political actors (Smelser 1962). Movements have been seen as part of the same general process as the contagion of fads and fashions within mass publics. These approaches ignore the potential of movements as arenas in which marginalized people can *collectively* develop alternative ways of understanding and conducting politics. From a women-centred perspective, it is essential to maintain a capacity for double vision that views politics within movements for change and within the official politics of the state as equally important. Methodologically, this means we must seek out the insights of equality seekers about the process in which they are engaged (Vickers 1986) in order to comprehend their alternative conceptions and values concerning politics. Too often, scholars have believed that only a movement's 'outputs' – that is, the demands it communicates to the official political system – matter. By contrast, our approach assumes that understanding the politics within movements for change and their organizations, such as NAC, has intrinsic value and is central to comprehending fully the meaning of a movement's expressed demands.

Older models of movements for change were also based on a free-market paradigm of the political process that assumes there is equal opportunity for access to institutions of the state and that political actors are properly individuals rather than collectivities. By contrast, it is clear to women and other marginalized people that there is no free market in access to political power and resources in the liberal democracies. Power is organized by institutions, and gate-keeping structures control access to and upward mobility within these institutions. Feminist political scientists have demonstrated that the political-opportunity structure does not deal even-handedly with women regardless of their class, race, language, ethnicity, or sexual orientation (Bashevkin 1985; Brodie 1985a; Lovenduski and Hills 1981).

The first mobilization of women in the liberal democracies sought to gain women the civil and legal rights necessary to participate in the official political system. Women activists had other objectives, but they wanted the vote because it seemed to be a powerful tool for achieving those other objectives. In the most recent waves of mobilization, women identified the social, economic, and cultural barriers to their participation beyond the citizen level, and, on that basis, produced critiques of formal political equality and issued condemnations of the character of liberal-democratic political systems. This challenge to the legitimacy of liberal democracies should have provoked a crisis of legitimacy of enormous proportions. In fact, the crises thus provoked were usually of more modest proportions, a fact that is probably attributable to the rejection of violence by the women's movements of most countries. (In fact, in countries such as Italy, where violence was not rejected as a tool, the crisis of legitimacy was much greater [Jenson 1982].)

A general theoretical proposition within social science about movements, then, is that they all eventually end by (1) being integrated into the official political system, (2) fading away, or (3) moving towards violence and revolution. By contrast, we have argued that some movements may become institutionalized as more or less permanent features of a political system operating parallel to official institutions. Indeed, this is a simple observation of reality. Despite periods of dormancy, some women's movements have now persisted for more than a century and some movement organizations have survived for many decades. In Canada, certainly, women's movements today are more or less permanent features of the official political system, existing in parallel to its more traditional elements. They will continue as such to the extent that official political institutions cannot respond to the demands they represent and as long as their political culture rejects violence as an option when the official system fails to respond, responds insufficiently or in a hostile way. In this analysis, then, we argue that some movements for change represent values and demands that cannot be integrated fully into the official political system and its institutions at the present time. If this is true, then an important criterion of success lies in the ability of such movements to create and sustain institutions that allow their participants to have an effective impact on government policy over time. We will argue that it has been the ability of the English-Canadian women's movement to achieve such institutionalization through NAC, which has put it at the centre of Canada's equality-seeking dynamic (Vickers 1986, 1983/4).

Our concept of institutionalization comes from Mary Douglas (1986:46): 'Institution will be used in the sense of a legitimized social grouping.' Douglas stresses the importance of legitimizing ideas in the creation of institutions: 'The entrenching of an institution is essentially an intellectual process ... To acquire legitimacy, every kind of institution needs a formula that founds its rightness in reason and nature' (45). The institutions of the official political system gain legitimacy from their longevity, which makes them seem natural, and from the idea that they are sanctioned by democracy. NAC uses as its founding rationale the idea that it is a democratic organization of many women's groups and that it represents women's interests better than any other political organization or institution; in other words, NAC claims to be the legitimate parliament of women.

Since the social science literature does not offer as a category a long-lasting, institutionalized movement that operates parallel to the official institutions of a political system, we will briefly explore the U.S. and European literature for clues to help us conceptualize the English-Canadian experience. Joyce Gelb (1989:4–5), in a recent analysis of the women's movements of the United States, Sweden, and the United Kingdom, proposes a typology of three models of women's activism: (1) *interest-group feminism*, as found in the United States; (2) *ideological*, or *left-wing*, *feminism*, in a decentralized and locally based movement, as found in the United Kingdom; and (3) *state equality*, or *state feminism*, marked by women's involvement in political parties and the absence of an influential, autonomous women's movement, as found in Sweden. In fact, none of these models is appropriate to English Canada, where there is evidence instead of the emergence of an *integrative* model that includes aspects of all three.

European analysis tends to stress the short-run nature of movements and their limited capacity for organization. Recent studies in Canada, by contrast, have established the longevity of women's organizations. As Susan Phillips (1990:70) notes, 'Once created, all of the national women's groups of this century have survived to the present' (see also Gelb 1989; Coote and Campbell 1982; Bouchier 1983; Dahlerup 1986; Jenson 1982; and Rucht 1991). The degree of continuity displayed in Canada is probably unique, although many first-wave organizations have survived in the United States, the United Kingdom, and France as well (Black 1989).

Observers of the U.S. movement find little interaction between organizations of the first and second waves. Contemporary feminism in the United States, as Jo Freeman (1983) points out, emerged in conjunction with other protest movements, and with relatively little assistance from organizations created by the first wave. During the 1970s and 1980s, the feminist movement in the United States did not share networks or access to decision makers with organizations from the first wave, as Phillips found to be the case in Canada. Moreover, Freeman found a sharp distinction between an older and a younger branch of the second-wave U.S. movement, seeing them as essentially separate movements that shared few resources and faced different constraints. The older branch focused on rights and equal opportunity, while the younger branch – the Women's Liberation Movement – sought more radical change. The two, Freeman believes, operated differently in relation to the official political system, with the former accepting institutional structures and the politics of lobbying, while the latter rejected them. In Canada, by contrast, the younger movement was more likely to share resources with first-wave organizations, which had been reinvigorated by the royal commission's cross-country hearings, than with the other new protest movements. This gave Canadian women's movements a leading role in the politics of equality seeking.

European feminist observers see their women's movements as consisting of various organizations, loosely linked to one another and to the movement at large. They point out that movements often consist only of activists, not formal members, and have no real boundaries, but rather shade off into other movements with whom they share resources. Drude Dahlerup and Brita Gulli consider this organizational fluidity to be a strength of women's movements, representing specialization rather than fragmentation (cited in Lovenduski 1986:64–5). Only in English Canada have women from most of the diverse feminist strains and ideologies joined together within one umbrella organization, which has come to represent the material base of Canadian integrative feminism (Miles 1984).

According to Joni Lovenduski (1986), in Europe, formal (centralized and hierarchical) women's-movement organizations are viewed as suitable only for short-run campaigns. Informal, primary groups (decentralized, with only a simple division of labour) are seen as better suited for 'achieving personal changes in orientation and attitude' (66) and, hence, for meeting long-term goals. In other words, long-term campaigns are thought to require involvement in the consensual political processes of non-hierarchical groups.

The Canadian research distinguishes between formal groups, which aggregate interests across time and space, and informal groups, of which it identifies two types: the ad hoc, 'getting things done,' type and the primary feminist groups (consciousness raising, service collectives, crisis centres, and so on). Informal groups have appeared within institutions of the official political system (for example, as caucuses in political parties); within unions; and within universities, as 'free spaces' where women can explore their specificity as women. These groups pay a minimum of attention to such functions as organizational maintenance, recruitment and fund raising. Their emphasis is usually on creating solidarity, and they rely on networking structures to link them to one another and to formal movement organizations, which represent their interests and articulate their views.

European views on the nature of the movement groups reflect the ideological polarization that exists both within the political systems of European countries and within these countries' women's movements. The second wave of British feminism offers a case in point: the fierce polarization of the general political system in Britain provided scant 'middle ground' for moderate liberal and social-democratic views that might foster more interaction between working-class and liberal feminists (Lovenduski 1986; Gelb 1989). Moreover, the polarization within the movement itself between leftist feminists and radical feminists precluded the existence of any coordinating organization after 1978. From 1971 to 1978, the National Women's Committee maintained some cooperation between the two wings, and was able to organize annual national conferences. But in 1978, the fragile alliance was ruptured when the radical and socialist wings of the movement finally split. In organizational terms, then, the British movement is a series of small local groups, including women's centres, linked in loose networks that are able to rally supporters for various national campaigns.[1] According to Lovenduski, the National Women's Committee would be seen as a short-term, disposable structure, while the 'cells,' or primary informal organizations at the base, would be considered the durable entities that are concerned with long-term organizational survival. In fact, the notion that the 'cells' can survive even if the formal organizations to which they are linked are destroyed has long been a feature of European left-wing movement theory and strategy in a fiercely polarized and often violent political environment.

In Canada, women's movements have produced umbrella structures capable of aggregating most strains of feminism and representing their views to governments. Although, as Phillips (1990:94) notes, 'there are no groups ... [with] an explicit ideology of socialist or radical feminism organized at the national level,' NAC does contain many socialist and radical feminist groups as members, and their ideas have an impact on NAC's demands to government. The absence of sharp ideological polarization in the federal political system during the period studied allowed for the development of umbrella groups, such as NAC, that were in many ways similar to Canada's omnibus political parties, except that they did not contest elections. (Umbrella structures also emerged at the provincial level. Indeed, several of them preceded NAC, the most notable being the FFQ.) It was only through these umbrella structures that the many leftist and radical feminist local, or grass-roots, groups were linked to government policy makers.

The FFQ, along with the NCWC, provided the model on which NAC's structure was based. The FFQ was built on an alliance between traditional and liberal feminists. Organized feminism was reborn in Québec in 1965, with Thérèse Casgrain, leader of the struggle for suffrage in that province, acting as the midwife by proposing a conference entitled 'La Femme du Québec hier et aujourd'hui' to celebrate the twenty-fifth anniversary of the acquisition of the Québec franchise for women. The organizing committee included women from the VOW, the Fédération nationale Saint-Jean-Baptiste, the University Women's Club, and the Anciennes des pédagogie familiale. In the closing session of the conference, the women assembled voted unanimously to found the Fédération des femmes du Québec (FFQ).

The convention comprised four hundred women from the thirty-six associations that sent delegates and the thirty-eight that sent observers. It was 'the first time women from all regions, from all social groups and denominations had come together ... Quite obviously a new solidarity had to be forged' (Dumont et al. 1987:338). The federation was to be multi-ethnic, pluralist, non-sectarian, and autonomous from both religious and secular authorities – a mandate that was frightening to some but considered necessary by the majority if an independent women's voice was to be developed. The coalition represented in the FFQ included neither radical-feminist nor leftist-feminist elements. (The Québec women's liberation movement did not emerge until 1969, heavily influenced by the U.S. WLM [359].) Thus, the FFQ initially represented a coalition of traditional and liberal-feminist groups, in the main;[2] by 1980, it also included women's centres, women's services, and some professional and occupational groups.

Participants at the founding conference adopted the umbrella structure of the National Council of Women of Canada, a structure that had also been adopted, in 1907, by the Fédération national Saint-Jean-Baptiste. Like the NCWC, the FFQ was to have regional councils, as well as individual or direct members. The FFQ's umbrella structure achieved cooperation between traditional and liberal-feminist groups – the two predominant strains of the Québec women's movement prior to the emergence of a women's liberation movement and the sovereignty movement. Unlike NAC, the FFQ did not come to integrate the many elements of the new strains of feminism to create a parliament of women. The Québec movement, therefore, does display ideological 'wings' and did not pursue the goal of integrative feminism (Maroney 1988). None the less, the founders of NAC benefited from the experience of the FFQ's 'founding mothers,' which was transmitted to them through the Committee for the Equality of Women, the Royal Commission on the Status of Women, and the National Ad Hoc Committee on the Status of Women.

The Founding of NAC

In politics, as in comedy, timing is everything. Unlike the FFQ, NAC was officially founded, in 1972, only after the tidal wave of the new feminism hit Canada – and the new feminists didn't intend to be excluded. The force of the new feminist ideas was strong enough to have an impact on those shaping the organization but not strong enough to dilute the values of radical liberalism that created the context for NAC's early years. In 1971, many members of the Committee for the Equality of Women (CEW), formed in 1966 to campaign for a royal commission, reconstituted themselves as the National Ad Hoc Committee on the Status of Women. This group included Kay Macpherson, Helen Tucker, and Moira Armour, from the Voice of Women; Elsie Gregory MacGill, who had been a member of the royal commission and was a CEW member; Réjane Laberge-Colas, Regina Tait, and Laura Sabia, of CEW fame; and women such as Grace Hartman of CUPE and Kay Sigurjonsson of the Women Teachers' Federation (Appelle 1987). This group constituted the backbone of the founding coalition.

The question of whether the old and new generations could work together was nowhere more evident than at the 'Strategy for Change' conference, at which NAC was founded. The assembly of more than five hundred women represented groups ranging from the Communist party to the IODE and from the most traditional to the most radical feminists. Laura Sabia, who chaired the conference and was elected NAC's first president, recalls that 'the militants kept grabbing the microphones and shouting down the speakers, and the organizing committee didn't know what to do. We were ladies! ... And yet those radical women taught us a lot' (personal interview with Chris Appelle, 10 January 1986). What became fully apparent later was that, within its umbrella structure, NAC would have to learn to manage the conflict among the many ideological elements in the movement, maintain representation from all of the political parties, and try to include both anglophone and francophone groups. In addition, it would be expected to respond to the range of demands for regional representation typically made on Canadian political organizations.

The founding era of NAC was characterized by agreement on its objectives among its largely Toronto-based executive members. A declaration on the cover of the first issue of *Status of Women News* (Summer 1973) stated that 'NAC does not duplicate nor supersede established organizations. It is non-profit and non-partisan. NAC serves as an educational and communications link for women in Canada who are striving to improve their status and to change the traditional attitudes and habits of prejudice towards women.' In addition to its intended role as a communications centre providing coordination and information for its member groups, NAC was 'to evaluate, update and spearhead implementation of the recommendations of the Report' and increase public awareness about the status of women (Canada, Secretary of State, Women's Program 1974:17).

A comparison of these objectives with those that currently define NAC reveals the limited scope and sharper focus of the original design. For example, a NAC membership brochure published in 1986 formulated the organization's priorities as a movement institution as follows:

1. To unite women and women's groups from across Canada in the struggle for equality;
2. To develop feminist positions on public policy and present these positions through briefs, research papers, and lobbying; and
3. To sensitize the public to women's issues through media contact, public meetings and forums, and publications.

NAC founders had not conceived of uniting women and women's groups in the development of 'feminist positions on public policy.' Consequently, they had not considered the need for a representational structure to legitimize their positions. Because they accepted as a blueprint the recommendations of the royal commission, which were, after all, based on cross-country hearings, they saw no need for structures that would facilitate the development of policy. The purpose of the annual meetings was to help the executive choose among priorities identified by the commission. NAC was to be an *action committee* achieving the implementation of agreed-upon goals. NAC officers were to be seconded from and responsible to their 'home' groups.

The 'Strategy for Change' conference produced a majority report with seventy-eight recommendations that urged all levels of government, labour unions, and big business to improve the status of women (*Strategy for Change Report* 1972:9–22). The recommendations all demanded that action be taken; they did not seek to make policy. A minority emerged at the conference, however, consisting of more than sixty women who 'met in emergency session to discuss basic issues they found missing' and who called themselves the 'radical caucus of women' (*Strategy for Change Report* 1972:23). This caucus issued a statement promoting the use of tactics in pursuit of goals that were more in line with the agenda of the women's liberation movement. It demanded that the conference 'support demonstrations, boycotts, strikes, and other such actions as a means of public education and of effecting change; that it recognize that all levels of action are necessary and in a spirit of sisterhood all women support such actions in the manner they feel to be the most valid' (23). The caucus made its values clear by emphasizing 'the basic issue ... [that had] been ruled out of discussions' – namely, that the problem of the status of women was symptomatic of the more fundamental problem of 'the system itself' (23). Many of the caucus's demands were organizational, focusing on the conduct of NAC activities (no big hotels; natural foods only; table service to be undertaken by participants themselves, not by waitresses; all-female media and film crews; child care; non-sexist entertainment; and so on). However, the four themes it proposed for a future conference reflected its broader goals and more-radical orientation:

a. child care in state-supported child care centres as a right for every child, as education is a right;
b. community control of education at all levels;
c. the including of sexuality in the human rights code;
d. the elimination of poverty which calls for radical change of the whole structure of this society. For we as women understand that the relationship between women and poverty is a necessary and basic part of the present system. (23)

This self-styled radical caucus would not be represented on the NAC executive until 1977. Instead, the original steering committee, which started out as the conference-organizing committee, was made up of women such as Laura Sabia, Helen Tucker, Kay Macpherson, and Moira Armour, of NAC's 'founding generation,' and women such as Kay Sigurjonsson, who would also help establish the umbrella group by committing the resources of their own home organizations. The conference speakers included Québec suffrage hero Thérèse Casgrain;

Florence Bird, who had chaired the royal commission; and Laura Sabia, hero of the movement that had worked for the establishment of the commission. Only union leader Madeleine Parent and artist Maryon Kantaroff sounded more-radical notes (*Strategy for Change Report* 1972:5). Thus, the organization would be run by women who shared the norms of radical liberalism but who held fairly traditional ideas about organization and political process. Their views about the proper shape of NAC would also be affected by the realities of meagre funding and the high cost of consulting widely in a country of such vast distances. (Indeed, during the period studied, NAC had only one president who did not live in Toronto.)

The early NAC's financial resources were limited. Government support during this period never exceeded $60,000 annually (the amount received in 1977–78). Of this amount, the *Status of Women News*, the Annual General Meeting (AGM) and conference, and the small office operation in Toronto each consumed about a third. In the early years, the only women who could serve on the executive from outside Toronto were those who could afford to pay their own way or those whose employers would fund their travel. And because the founding generation saw NAC primarily as a lobby coalition, it chose leaders experienced in the official political process, who would intuitively understand the kind of group that would succeed in the federal system. Unfortunately, the NAC executive was consequently seen by many (who viewed the above-noted factors as excuses) as a traditional Toronto 'club,' reluctant to share power by developing a broader base.

None the less, the impact on the organization of the ideas of a new generation of feminists is clearly reflected on the pages of NAC's first periodical, *Status of Women News*, as is the organization's serious commitment to promoting dialogue between French and English feminists. Women's interests in areas such as contraception, abortion, rape, battering, child care, feminist spirituality, feminist culture, sport, women's health, birthing alternatives, feminist counselling, sexism, equal pay for work of equal value, women and technology, and women's criminality are all explored.[3] The publication was silent, however, on the issues of homosexuality and lesbian rights, with the exception of a single mention in an article on women and sport: the writer wonders whether homosexuality is 'a problem' of female athleticism (Summer 1973:14). Nevertheless, this house organ covered many of the matters of substance, if not of political structure and process, that were important to the new generation of feminists. Leftist-feminist ideas were also reflected in the *News*. The struggles by unionists such as Grace Hartman and Madeleine Parent to win collective-bargaining objectives for working-class women were reported throughout the period studied. Class aspects of issues such as abortion were highlighted. There was also a strong emphasis on honouring the movement's heroes: for example, first-wave women were always honoured on their retirement from active participation. Long-time director of the Women's Bureau of the federal Department of Labour Sylva Gelber, frequently featured in the publication, was so honoured on her retirement.

Issue by issue, an expanding organizational infrastructure was also proudly recorded. From the nineteen 'regional contacts' NAC reported in the summer of 1973, the movement's infrastructure had grown by 1976 to forty-six women's centres, thirty-five women's periodicals, and twenty-six local and provincial status-of-women committees (July 1976: 22–3). This was in addition to both long-time and newly formed national associations, as well as to caucuses existing within parties, unions, union federations, professional associations, and universities. By November 1977, there were fifty-four women's centres, including five organized by and for native women. The number of women's periodicals, however, had begun to decline. There were now thirty-two local and provincial status-of-women committees. In Alberta, the Northwest Territories, the Yukon, Saskatchewan, Manitoba, Ontario, Québec, Nova Scotia, Newfoundland, and Prince Edward Island, there were autonomous status-of-women action committees or councils attached to government, and in British Columbia, there were both city-based status-of-women groups and the B.C. Federation of Women (November 1977:22–3).

The organization emerging under the NAC umbrella was quite different from the chapter-based National Organization of Women (NOW) in the United States. NOW was based on individual memberships organized into local chapters and state conferences. There was also a national headquarters, in Washington, with a lobbying office, legal staff, and so on. NOW members made an active choice as individuals to affiliate with the organization and its objectives. This structure was similar to that of most of Canada's 'national' organizations. In NAC, by contrast, the affiliated members were organizations, not individuals; hence, women who joined an affiliated organization might not even know that they were indirectly affiliated with NAC. Moreover, NAC's member organizations ranged widely in size and type, but, because NAC's founders had paid little attention to the problem of representation, they were all equally represented at the AGM, NAC's only representational structure. (By the same token, they also paid more or less the same affiliation dues, which were low – NAC did not compete seriously with other groups for the movement's scarce resources.)

The political environment for women's politics was rapidly becoming more complex. Within the federal government, structures assigned to status-of-women issues were advisory or dealt with coordination or the delivery of programs. The major elements of the federal political environment in which NAC operated (see Figure 2.1) were established during NAC's formative years. Our discussion will focus on the three structures that were most important to NAC, each of which had been established (if not in its final form) by 1976: the Canadian Advisory Council on the Status of Women (CACSW), the Women's Program of the Secretary of State, and Status of Women Canada.

The federal Advisory Council on the Status of Women (CACSW), a body called for in the recommendations of the royal commission, held its first meeting 10–11 June 1973. With twenty-eight members from across the country, it was chaired by Katie Cook, a respected public public servant and sociologist. NAC was initially represented on the council by its chair, Laura Sabia, and its treasurer, Grace Hartman. The FFQ and NCWC were represented by their presidents, as were several regional status-of-women councils. The Catholic Women's League was represented by a first vice-president and several members. The mandate of CACSW was as follows: 'To advise the Minister [responsible for the status of women] in respect of such matters relating to the Status of Women as the Minister may refer to the Council for its consideration, or the Council considers appropriate' (*Status of Women News* [Summer 1973]:1).

NAC viewed the establishment of the Advisory Council as its first lobbying success, but 'some concern was expressed that only a quarter or a third of the members ... were able to be identified with status of women concerns' (Summer 1973:2). Although appointments to the CACSW have always been geographically and sectorally representative, they have rarely, regardless of the government making the appointments, reflected the range of feminist constituencies as reliably. Furthermore, 'some of NAC's leaders viewed with alarm the few appointments from among industry, business and the professions, and that two of the 28 places were to be taken by men' (2).

On a more positive note, NAC announced it was seeking views from its 'fifty-odd member organizations' about matters to put to the council

FIGURE 2.1
Federal government services and access points for women's movement, 1983

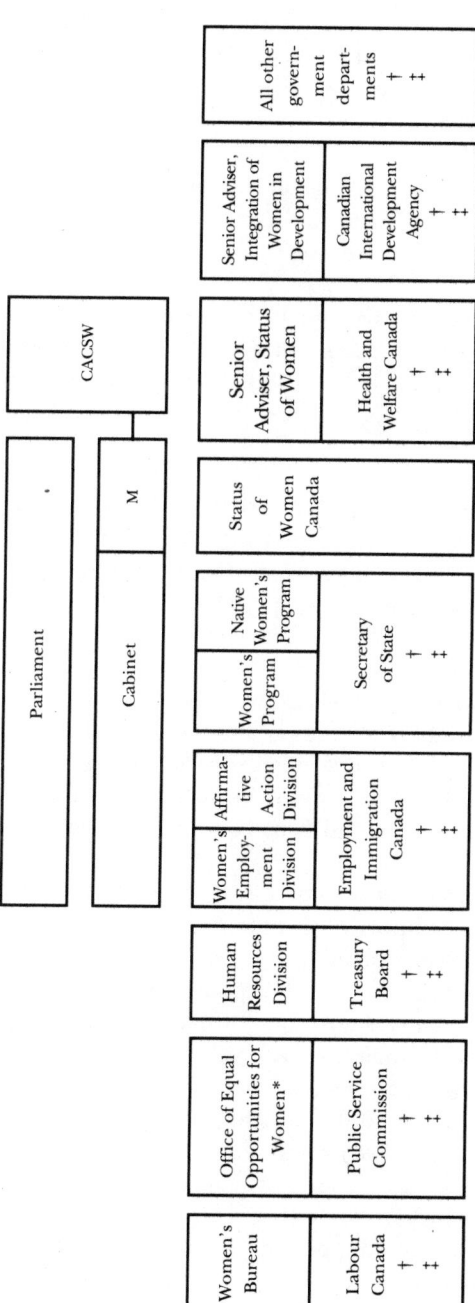

M – Minister responsible for the status of women

CACSW – Canadian Advisory Council on the Status of Women

* Since absorbed into the Public Service Commission

† Integration mechanism in each department (usually a committee to vet policy proposals)

‡ One 'Equal Employment Opportunities Coordinator' and one 'Affirmative Action Officer' in the personnel division of each department

Source: Canadian Advisory Council on the Status of Women, 1983

as priorities. (Questionnaires seeking readers' opinions and priorities were a common feature in the house organ during this founding era.) NAC's priorities for the CACSW, reported in the *Status of Women News* (Summer 1973:2), were as follows:

1. legislation satisfactory to women as non-discriminatory in the Canada Labour Code and the Public Service Employment Act;
2. establishment of a federal Human Rights Commission (preferably with a woman as head);
3. general and accessible child care (with the recommendation that a federal–provincial conference be held as soon as it can be thoroughly prepared);
4. an integrated plan to implement needs for family planning, counselling, convenient clinics and appropriate revision of the Criminal Code to accommodate the plan.

An activist federal government indirectly wooed women's groups in the pages of the *Status of Women News*. In the June 1974 issue (vol. 1, no. 3), a notice compiled by a women's caucus within the Toronto YWCA outlined the objectives of the new Women's Program of the Department of the Secretary of State (Citizenship Branch). It explained the program's funding criteria, which stressed grass-roots, service-oriented, community-based projects, and listed contact names, addresses, and phone numbers for the regional officers of the Secretary of State. Established in 1973, the Women's Program began with an annual fund of $200,000, which, with the exception of International Women's Year, would not exceed $400,000 until the end of the decade.

The royal commission had recommended that all governments increase their financial support to 'women's voluntary associations,' whether 'engaged in projects of public interest' or 'in fields of particular concern to women' (Canada, Royal Commission on the Status of Women, 1970:49). The federal government had already been funding other advocacy groups through the Citizenship Branch, and the funds available for women's groups were very small. The 'Strategy for Change' conference had recommended the pursuit of government funding for NAC 'in order to achieve full representation of the national diversities among Canadian women, i.e., geography, native, ethno-socio-economic groups ...' (*Strategy for Change Report* 1972:22). The government's lack of response during this founding period, however, left NAC dependent largely on donations, subscriptions, voluntarism, and its own fund-raising ventures (such as the sale of medallions, which netted $12,000 one year; a 'two-bits' campaign, which brought in far less; and fund-raising dinners, which were quite successful). NAC started out with office space, time, and staff donated by the Women Teachers' Federation. Volunteers, such as the tireless Helen Tucker, took minutes, kept records, and wrote letters, press releases, and columns (*NAC Memo* [April 1982]:6). Moira Armour donated her creative talents, making films (for example, *Strategies for Change*) and editing the *Status of Women News*.

The function of Status of Women Canada, founded in 1976, would be quite different from either the advisory role of the CACSW or the funding role of the Women's Program. Created as a department of the federal government, it was to play a major coordinating role, acting as a policy secretariat and providing advice internally. It was to ensure liaison both among federal departments and agencies and with provincial governments, advisory councils, national women's organizations, and individual experts. Internationally, it was to coordinate Canada's response to status-of-women concerns and oversee input to the United Nations. The department head was given deputy-minister status and, as was the case with the CACSW, reported to Parliament indirectly, through the minister responsible for the status of women. During its early years, NAC cooperated with Status of Women Canada on numerous national and international issues. Two NAC chairpeople of the 1970s indicated that they had a good working relationship with Status of Women Canada, and at least one NAC executive member moved on to hold a position in that department (Kay Macpherson and Lorna Marsden, personal interviews with Chris Appelle, 10 April 1985 and 19 March 1985, respectively).

These three major structures within, or associated with, the state (the CACSW was semi-autonomous) shaped NAC's political environment during most of the founding era. (The exception was the period during which Marsden was chair, when direct access was available to some cabinet ministers.) But the Women's Bureau of the Department of Labour and the committees and services created in the Departments of Health and Welfare, Employment and Immigration, and Justice, as well as in the Public Service Commission, also became potential entry points for lobbying efforts by NAC. Helen Dawson (1975:46) stressed how important it was to have a wide network of contacts within the bureaucracy to succeed in lobbying in the federal arena. Although women did not constitute an 'élite' group in the normal context of élite accommodation, two of NAC's early chairs, Laura Sabia and Lorna Marsden, had good connections in Ottawa. Marsden, later to become a Liberal senator, had become a player in the governing party through her participation in women's and policy organizations, was consequently able to gain access to groups of cabinet ministers for discussion of NAC's concerns.

It would be misleading to leave readers with the impression of a cozy relationship between a Toronto-based executive comprising women who shared common, traditional values and their Ottawa contacts. Also among NAC's leaders during this founding era was Grace Hartman, a highly respected unionist, who, as head of the Canadian Union of Public Employees, was to lead many strikes of women employees – including one that was declared illegal and for which she was jailed. Kay Macpherson, from the Voice of Women, resists easy categorization. A radical long before the invention of radical feminism, her experience ranged from ban-the-bomb activities to candidacy for the NDP at election time. Together with Thérèse Casgrain, she was detained by police in Paris for participating in a peace demonstration that had offended French authorities. (Within NAC, however, she often acted as a conciliator, able to bridge the gap between different generations and conflicting philosophies.)

Two other features of this era warrant special note. First, the founding generation considered their links with the FFQ and with francophones in Québec to be very important. This was a matter of both conviction and good politics. Federal Liberals considered the women's movement a potential force for unity with Québec, and the Secretary of State began to increase funding to organizations that were willing to become more effectively bilingual. During this period, FFQ presidents attended NAC executive meetings. The *Status of Women News* reported regularly on the Québec movement, and articles and news reports often appeared in French. Starting in December 1978, a fully bilingual version of *Status of Women News* began to appear. Similarly – and this brings us to the second feature noted above – both the executive minutes and *Status of Women News* reflected NAC's concern about, and willingness to expend time and money in the cause of, 'Indian rights for Indian women.' The issue, raised by the royal commission, was a subject for lobbying and education throughout the seventies. NAC also expressed concern for the plight of foreign domestics and of immigrant women in general, but native women's issues constituted a more significant focus.[4]

None the less, the representational structures embodied in NAC remained underdeveloped. An executive was not formed until 1975. Originally, a steering committee was designated, consisting of 'one named person, with an alternate, from each participating organization in NAC' (Index of Policy Recommendations 700.40.1–77). A board of directors (twelve persons from the membership, plus officers, elected by the steering committee, and the immediate past president) was established in April 1974. In 1975, the board of directors became the executive and the steering committee became the Board of NAC, again with one delegate plus alternate for each organization. Individual members were allowed by the 1974 Rules of Association, but no provision was made for them to vote. The now-familiar pattern of ten executive meetings, a mid-year meeting, an AGM, and an annual lobby took some time to establish. There were no internal executive committees during this period and certainly no policy committees. The emphasis was on sharing information, self-education on the issues, and the striking of concrete lobbying priorities for the following year.

The lobby itself, although polite and well prepared, gave women from across Canada the opportunity to make women's concerns matter to politicians, if only for a day. The format of an AGM followed by a day of lobbying was imitated by other women's groups in Canada, such as the Alberta Status of Women Action Committee (ASWAC). Indeed, 'lobby day' was a characteristic feature of the interaction between some first-wave groups and government.

The April 1976 AGM provides a good example of NAC's focus during these early years. The policy resolutions from that meeting cover equal pay, child care, birth-control services, family and property law, pensions, and 'Bills in the Mill on the Hill,' including C-16, which was an 'omnibus bill' on the status of women. On opening the meeting, Chairperson Lorna Marsden welcomed Ministers Lalonde, Basford, and Munro, who then took part in a question-and-answer session. The conference workshops on equal pay, day care, and law reform received the lion's share of the time (the AGM itself took less than a day). Evaluation sheets allowed the women present to indicate their views of the correct priorities for the following year. A lobby on Parliament Hill, prepared for in the Lobby Workshop held the previous evening, ended the event. The presence of Katie Cook as an honored speaker and Lorna Marsden's description of the 'good working relationship' between NAC and the CACSW had set the tone of the meeting. NAC was in harmony with its environment in the realm of the formal politics of the state, even if it was somewhat out of step with the mood of the broader women's movement (*Status of Women News* [May 1976]: 8–9).

The final aspect of NAC's organization and process during this period that we will examine here is the composition and functioning of the executive. We have chosen to focus on executive functioning in 1977 as our example, and we base our description on the minutes for that year. Lorna Marsden was chair for one meeting before the AGM, at which Kay Macpherson was elected to that position. NAC had grown from a membership of 31 groups and a budget of $15,000 in 1972 to a membership of 120 groups and a budget of $65,000 in 1977. The executive in 1977 had about 18 members with 12–14 present at any one meeting, far fewer than would be the case in the 1980s. In proportion to the number of member groups, the executive had represented about one-third of the member groups in 1972, but only one-tenth in 1977. Because NAC did not have the funds to pay travel costs, some organizations were excluded simply because they had no representative living in or near Toronto and could not afford to send a delegate. Several women from outside Toronto, such as Ottawa-based Ruth Bell, paid their own travel costs. The executive also included representatives from the FFQ and from the CACSW. In addition, advisers were co-opted to the executive from time to time, especially when legal advice was needed (lawyers Mary Eberts and Rosalie Abella were two such advisers).

The last meeting of the executive chaired by Lorna Marsden took place on 21 February 1977. The meeting involved a discussion of NAC's presentation (in both English and French) of a brief to cabinet on 17 February 1977. (The cabinet was represented by Ministers Basford, Bégin, Danson, Lalonde, and Sauvé.) Also reported is the meeting between a NAC delegation and Minister Roberts, then secretary of state. The delegation 'discussed the role of NAC within the women's movement in Canada and within the volunteer sector.'[5] Minister Roberts was judged to be 'receptive' to the main message, which was that the Women's Program's funding ought to be increased.

The executive, at this stage, was acting as both an AGM committee and a nominating committee. (The AGM had 108 delegates and 112 observers, as reported by secretary Pearl Blazer in the minutes of the 5 April 1977 meeting.) A decision was taken that guidelines were required to ensure that display materials at the AGM would 'focus on changes for women and not on general matters unrelated to women's issues,' showing the executive's commitment to a fairly constrained status-of-women approach. The elections held at the AGM produced no representation on the new executive from either Québec women or francophone women in other provinces. At the executive meeting of 20 March, the first chaired by Kay Macpherson, 'it was explained ... that no nominations had been received from these groups.' Recruiting an FFQ liaison person to attend NAC executive meetings was proposed, and it was also suggested that NAC pay for the travel costs if such a liaison person could be found. The new executive reflected considerable renewal: Lorenne Clark, whose work on sexual violence was well known, was philosophically linked to the more radical feminist elements, and Marjorie Cohen, Laurel Ritchie, and Lynn Kaye advanced socialist feminist and union views.

Although most of the issues reported in the minutes were educational and the debate apparently placid, one issue provoked conflict. This was the question of whether NAC would lobby against the Anti-Inflation Board (AIB), which was imposing wage controls on Canadians at the time. Although only unionized workers came fully within the AIB's purview, the board's regulations did include a loophole that allowed wages to exceed specified limits in the case of (largely female) groups that had previously suffered wage discrimination. The debate as to whether the AIB in itself, regardless of the existence of the loophole, should be construed as a status-of-women issue runs through the minutes of 1977.

In 1977, it became established practice for groups newly ratified as members to be listed in the minutes. At the 5 April meeting, a number of small action groups were admitted, including Les femmes acadiennes de Clare, Fredericton Women's Action Coalition, Concerned Women of Sault Ste Marie, and the Cape Breton Working Committee on the Status of Women. Two national associations, the Canadian Congress of Black Women and the Canadian Teachers' Federation, were also admitted. At this time, the executive also began to look for ways of making the organization more formal. At the 2 May meeting, Ruth Bell was delegated to investigate the possibility of NAC's becoming incorporated, 'so that members of the Executive would not be liable for debts incurred by NAC.' Procedures for issuing press releases were discussed at the same meeting. It was agreed that texts would require the approval of at least two executive members, including the chair, whenever possible, and the 'specialist' in the issue. Lobbying included activities within Ontario, such as joining the Coalition for Equal Pay for Work of Equal Value in lobbying the premier or protesting the Ontario government's resistance to a provision permitting housewives to be covered in the Canada Pension Plan for periods when they were out of the paid workforce (the 'drop-out' provision). A number of women on NAC's executive at the time had cut their political teeth on the Ontario Committee on the Status of Women, and this was reflected in NAC's agenda throughout the 1970s.

As noted above, the divisive issue of the AIB dogged the executive throughout the year. The minutes reflect that the debate did not concern the content of the AIB policy, but rather the question of NAC's public involvement in an issue that was clearly associated with unions in the public's mind. The minutes from the meeting of July report that ex-chair Grace Hartman had invited Kay Macpherson and other NAC executive members to a meeting that she hoped to set up with the federal finance minister. The reported purpose of the meeting was to press the minister 'for a clearer definition of the sex discrimination clause in the AIB regulations' and to ask for a separate procedure for those claiming the sex-discrimination exemption. The executive decided that NAC should 'not be formally represented at the meeting with the Finance Minister but that another route for dealing with the problem and the AIB be studied.' The issue was considered further at a larger meeting, on 12 July. This is the first instance in our reading of NAC minutes in which a hint of conflict is evident between those representing leftist or working-class feminism and those representing a more traditional, status-of-women orientation. Although reports of such conflicts are rare in this founding era, they were to become common in subsequent years, during what we have termed the 'transitional era.'

There were other signs in the 1977 minutes that foreshadowed later developments and conflicts. First, the practice of having executive members become policy experts responsible for informal committees is anticipated. Lorenne Clark was asked to interact with the Ontario Coalition of Rape Crisis Centres, and she became the specialist who would decide whether NAC would support the coalition's request for funding from the Women's Program. Clark was also made responsible for generating a brief on NAC's behalf in the area of sexual assault. What also emerges is the role individual executive members would play in recruiting new groups to membership – often groups that shared their particular orientation with regard to key issues.

NAC's relationship with the FFQ was stable at this point. The FFQ was represented at almost all of the 1977 meetings by its president, Sheila Finestone (who later became a Liberal MP). The general question of 'stronger regional contacts,' however, was raised by Lynn McDonald at the 3 October meeting, prefiguring the conflict that was to emerge during the transitional period over NAC's lack of effective geographic representation. Although McDonald is often viewed as 'a Toronto person' (having later moved to that city to teach), she first attended a NAC executive meeting as 'a visitor from Nova Scotia' earlier in 1977, and was subsequently nominated to the executive by the Nova Scotia Action Committee as its delegate. Her argument, which was to form part of the substance of her agenda as president, was summarized in the minutes of the 3 October meeting: 'Without altering NAC's goal of communication it may be possible to establish stronger links with the regions of the country and to have more direct regional representation in the Executive with more travel funds to facilitate this representation.' The minutes record that Lorenne Clark proposed a committee be struck 'to examine ways of strengthening NAC's contacts with the regions of the country,' but no committee composition is noted and there is no indication that action was taken on Clark's suggestion.[6]

The minutes of the 26 October meeting record a conflict over control of the *Status of Women News*. At a previous officers' meeting, it had been decided 'to ask the present editor [Moira Armour] ... to relinquish her position so that others might work on the newsletter.' Women of the founding generation objected: Hazel Wigdor, of the Congress of Canadian Women, wrote to the president to express her concern, and Regina Tait informed the officers that 'they had no authority to ask for any officer's (appointed or elected) resignation and had acted out of order.' She also informed them that 'the editor of NAC News should have been invited to the meeting where discussions of the News' developments took place.' How people treated one another on the executive was to become a major issue of controversy during the transitional period, as two generations with quite different values about human interaction came into conflict.

The battle lines over the issue of NAC's house organ were beginning to be drawn. To the founding generation, represented by the views of Moira Armour, the purpose of the paper was to communicate information about lobbying and status-of-women issues, in general, from the executive to the member groups. She stated that 'the newsletter is a collection of material supplied by the executive' to which the editor brought 'her editing, photographic, lay-out and technical skills.' Lorenne Clark and Lynn McDonald 'suggested that a NAC publication might be better and more effective were there more in-depth feature

articles and policy statements.' This anticipates their later goal of producing a commercially viable, high-quality magazine that would have a
direct influence on, and even transform, the ideas of the mass of
women about feminism, as *Ms.* magazine did in the United States.

At this stage, the executive accepted a compromise crafted by Elsie
Gregory MacGill. Costs made it difficult to carry the kind of in-depth
articles that Clark and McDonald wanted to see, but there was nothing standing in the way of creating an editorial committee, which
would report to the editor. Moira Armour was to continue in the
latter role. This was the first permanent committee of the NAC executive to be established. The new format developed for *Status of Women
News* is well illustrated by the theme issue entitled 'In Sickness and in
Health,' which appeared in December 1978 (vol. 5, no. 2). With a
professionally designed cover and a tumbled French/English format,
this issue is the product of an editorial committee of nine, with Armour
as editor. The issue clearly represents a large commitment of volunteer
time, as most of the articles were written by members of the editorial
board or the executive. As Armour had predicted, high-profile journalists were not willing to donate material; women involved in the
women's health movement at the grass-roots level, however, were.
MacGill's compromise was to hold for several years, but the debate
between those who espoused an 'educate to transform' philosophy
and those who held a 'communicate to lobby' view would eventually
resume.

The issue of funding, which would later become the symbolic 'tip
of the iceberg' of the larger conflict over NAC's organizational character, was raised in a new way by Marjorie Cohen, another new executive
member, at the meeting of 7 November. Cohen outlined a proposal
she had prepared for submission to the secretary of state requesting
funding over the long term. The proposal envisioned three phases,
wherein 'each phase would expand NAC's activities and allow for more
travel, more publications and more regional public forums and study
sessions.' Cohen argued that the increased funding 'would also allow
for larger premises and more support staff when needed.' Only Sheila
Finestone of the FFQ is reported to have expressed reservations. She
'advised that ... [NAC] also make inquiries about finance funding, that
is, seeking a large capital grant that would provide enough interest for
operating costs.'[7] There were no other negative reactions to Cohen's
proposal at the time, although the issue of government funding would
eventually drive a deep wedge between those who valued grass-roots

organizing and those who held with more traditional notions of organization. In the next chapter, we will examine how this issue also divided leftist women.

There are certain issues that inevitably arise in Canada – for example, is the status of women a federal or provincial responsibility? – and such issues made their appearance throughout the minutes for 1977. At the 5 December meeting, Jean Woodsworth, of the United Church of Canada, proposed that NAC lobby both provincial and federal governments concerning block funding.[8] Before 1977, transfer payments had been earmarked for particular services, and provinces had been required to match federal amounts from the provincial treasury. Earmarked funds could not be diverted to other uses. In 1977, the federal Liberals, under pressure from some provincial governments (and especially from Québec), proposed a move to block funding, an arrangement whereby transfer payments would not be earmarked for specific purposes. It was feared that provincial governments, given the opportunity, would divert social-service money 'to pay for roads.' (In Canada, the classic economic 'guns or butter' trade-off has always manifested itself as a 'roads or social services' trade-off.)

The minutes of the 5 December meeting report that the executive, guided by Woodsworth, established the following three principles as the basis on which they would lobby both the federal and provincial governments to preserve the underlying philosophy of Canada's complex welfare state: (1) the importance of the concept of matched funding; (2) a commitment to the broader, more progressive social service policy goals (as stated in the Social Services Act) for the achievement of 'personal independence, citizenship participation and enrichment of personal and community life,' as opposed to the limited concept of social services related to economic need; and (3) the value of uniform, public reporting by federal and provincial governments of social service programs and expenditures. A concern with the underlying principles of Canada's welfare state is a thread that runs through the Executive Minutes for most of NAC's existence.

A final note from the 5 December meeting came from Audrey Shepherd, of the Anglican Church Women. NAC's observer at the U.S. Women's Conference in Houston, Texas, she reported that, while 'many of the priorities for women in the U.S. ... [were] the same as for women in Canada,' the style of politics was very different. (She also noted that, in the United States, the two 'languages' to which the term *bilingualism* referred were speech and sign language for the hearing impaired.) Shepherd reported as well that 'Media coverage of the "counter conference" run by Phyllis Schlafly in Houston was fairly extensive, giving a rather warped view of the importance of the counter conference.' In all the minutes for this period, this is the only evidence of discussion about the U.S. women's movement.

Summary

To conclude, let us summarize the major characteristics of NAC's operation as an organization during its founding era. First, there was general agreement on the organization's objectives: NAC was to lobby governments to achieve the implementation of the recommendations of the Royal Commission on the Status of Women. Consequently, policy development was not seen as part of NAC's role. Of course, to the extent that radical feminists were present in NAC, a potential alternative agenda did exist; however, it was adopted only after male violence, especially sexual assault, arose as an issue that, because of the commission's silence about it, demanded a policy position on NAC's part. The original focus on the royal commission's recommendations thus inhibited NAC's initiative as a policy-making entity. *Status of Women News*, however, began to play a major role during this period in communicating to the older feminists of NAC the concerns of the new generation of feminists. It also communicated information about trends arising in the large cities to women living in more-distant and more-sparsely populated areas. Because NAC accepted the royal commission's agenda, the issue of native women's rights received great attention and support, although few native women's groups were members.

Another consequence of NAC's acceptance of the royal commission's report as a blueprint for change was that it largely ignored its own representational structures and used its annual general meeting primarily as an educative assembly to prepare members for the lobby that was always held the following day. The NAC executive, in which initially one-third of NAC's member organizations were represented, soon came to be seen as more representative of the Toronto-based women's movement than of feminism across the country. Not until NAC's minimal funding got beyond the bake-sale level would broad regional representation on the executive become a priority. NAC's emphasis on its lobbying function made it necessary for the executive to meet more frequently than did the executives of other national organizations.

Despite this Toronto dominance, NAC remained focused primarily on federal politics, and effective relationships were maintained between NAC and the FFQ and between NAC and the CACSW.

There were no permanent committees on the NAC executive until 1977, when an editorial board was established. NAC's policy focus in lobbying conformed fairly strictly to a 'status-of-women' approach. In part, this reflected the executive's concern about remaining strictly non-partisan.[9] It also reflected the founding generation's discomfort with broader analyses of women's status that relied on concepts of oppression and liberation – even though this generation agreed emphatically about the importance of all the issues these analyses identified.

By 1978-9, women of the new generation of feminists were in the majority on the executive for the first time. A sufficient contingent of the founding generation remained, however, to make the next few years a period of conflict. But it was also a period during which women from all strains of English-Canadian feminism began to forge a new understanding of women's politics and of acceptable ways of organizing to achieve their goals – partially as a result of having been forced to share an organization in common. Necessity rather than virtue would breed the cooperation that was essential to NAC's survival.

Jo Freeman (1983) argues that an organization's early structure goes a long way in determining the nature of the goals that the organization can achieve in the future and the strategies it can choose for achieving them. Certainly, the decisions made during this founding era were significant in shaping NAC. The choice of an umbrella structure, for example, meant that NAC would always be less able than NOW to mobilize women quickly at the local and provincial/territorial levels, because it lacked the permanent and directable local chapters and provincial councils that make rapid mobilization possible. Similarly, had NAC been created in a less intensely centralist environment than the one that prevailed in Canada during the Liberal era, it might have chosen to align itself more formally with provincial status-of-women committees. From the 'Strategy for Change' conference forward, the majority of NAC leaders and activists assumed that the organization would seek, and eventually receive, federal funding. The *need* for government support was never seriously questioned. The reality was that conducting politics in a territory larger than the United States, but with only one-tenth the population and two official languages, involved all of the same costs of conducting politics but only a fraction of the resources with which to meet them. None the less, as a result of these early circumstances and choices, NAC, unlike NOW, never found itself in direct competition for funds with other women's groups. Neither did it benefit, however, from the vast amounts of time typing, telephoning, writing, and so on, that Canadian women have donated to their primary (member) groups, and that many U.S. women donate to NOW.

In some aspects, Freeman's argument reflects the U.S. context of a political environment crowded with groups and movements all competing for the citizen's loyalty, energy, and money. In Canada, there are far fewer groups and movements. Many groups find themselves serving multiple functions, and people with different points of view are often forced to share the same group. The realities of both geography and economy, then, have led Canadian women to create groups that share resources, contacts, and so on – that is, umbrella or network groups. In the United States, by contrast, the greater population and greater resource base allow most groups and movements to elaborate complete structures within and for themselves. Small group collectives have survived in many parts of Canada only because they created networking groups. These structures became the device through which groups dedicated to radical-feminist ideas about political process could make a contribution to the activities of the more institutionalized elements of the movement. The umbrella structure for which NAC opted allowed for the incorporation of radical, local groups with limited disruption.

The Canadian political environment permitted groups that survived their founding eras to reshape themselves to some degree, as need dictated. As it emerged from the shadow of the royal commission, NAC would require such reshaping and restructuring. Government policy and, especially, government funding would affect NAC's organizational options. Its founding era, however, had equipped NAC for the changes ahead, in that the political experiences of the older generations of feminists had been transmitted to the younger generation. Indeed, this generational bridging has proved to be one of NAC's greatest strengths.

Notes

1 In this, it finds parallels in Canada in the many women's centres linked by Network Nelly in the 1970s and in the rape-crisis, battered women's, and

incest-survivor groups linked by their cooperating networks in the 1980s and 1990s.

2 One of the signatories to the FFQ constitution, dated 1 March 1966, was Monique Bégin, later executive director of the Royal Commission on the Status of Women and long-time minister of health in federal Liberal cabinets. The FFQ, like NAC, has been a political training-ground for women, many of whom have gone on to hold either elected or appointed decision-making positions.

3 This is based on a content analysis of *Status of Women News* for the period 1973–8, conducted by Jill Vickers. Unless otherwise noted, all citations in the following discussion refer to issues of the *Status of Women News*.

4 Initial contact with the Toronto Immigrant Women's Centre was reported at the 12 September meeting, and two native women's organizations from British Columbia were admitted – the Tamitik Women's Organization of Kitimat and the TA'AIKU Women's Centre of Burns Lake.

5 This and all subsequent quotations are from NAC's Executive Minutes of meetings identified by date in the text.

6 However, the minutes of the 26 October meeting do report a successful AGM and lobby organized by the Alberta Status of Women Action Group, which had 36 MLAs in attendance.

7 This 'having your cake and eating it too' solution was pursued by other feminist groups, including CRIAW. It was thought that a substantial single endowment would threaten a group's independence far less than would year-by-year dependency.

8 Historically, many social programs in Canada, including health services and postsecondary education, have been administered by provincial governments, with primary funds coming from the federal government as major tax collector. This arrangement has helped to diminish regional disparities, since 'have-not' provincial governments received more money than they would have been able to collect within their own borders. However, the Conservative government has been withdrawing from this arrangement in recent years.

9 As we will demonstrate in Chapter 3, NAC executives deliberately avoided choosing successive presidents of the same political affiliation. In addition, as the AIB incident demonstrates, they cautiously avoided taking positions that could be construed as partisan.

3 The Struggle for NAC: The Transitional Era, 1979–1982

Until 1979, the alliance of traditional women's groups and liberal feminists that achieved the royal commission and founded NAC also dominated the NAC executive and its AGM. Its values about organization shaped NAC's character and activity, despite an intellectual openness to the ideas of the new generation of feminists. From 1978–9 forward, however, a coalition of groups of the new generation gained a majority, as a radical grass roots was grafted onto the original alliance. In this chapter, we will examine the conflicts that arose during the period 1979–82 in relation to NAC's role, its structure, and its norms of process. In the first section, we will provide an overview of the complex set of issues in dispute between the two coalitions. We will focus on these conflicts in more detail in the second section, discussing in particular the way government funding, regional representation, accountability, and non-partisanship interacted with policy issues such as an entrenched Charter of Rights, wages for housework, and pensions for homemakers.

The Issues in Conflict: Grafting On a Radical Grass Roots

What, then, were the issues that provoked conflict during this stormy transitional period? Our analysis revealed a complex of related issues, which we have formulated as alternatives or questions:

1. Is NAC's basic purpose lobbying within the system or being the focal point of a transformative movement?
2. Is NAC to be independent and self-funding or state funded to a significant degree?

3. Should there be representational structures (regional reps) or continued central control?
4. Who should create policy? Is it to be 'discovered' among the member groups or created by executive-led committees with the help of feminist 'experts'?
5. Are executive members delegates of member groups and free to criticize NAC strategy and policy decisions? Or is the executive an organic body requiring solidarity?
6. Is conflict acceptable within the executive or must the group always achieve consensus?
7. Who speaks for NAC and what should be the roles of leaders and experts?
8. Should NAC have paid staff or depend on volunteers?
9. What should be the role of the membership and must the executive obey resolutions of the AGM?
10. How can people be held accountable? What is conflict of interest in the context of the NAC executive?
11. Should there be a role for individual members in NAC or should groups remain the only voting members?
12. Must the minority be placated or should those who disagree with decisions simply be excluded?

This interrelated set of questions underlay the conflicts that erupted during the transitional period. At times, these issues of process and organization were openly discussed. More often, however, they were expressed only as part of the debate over other issues. The questions concerning NAC's role, for example, had begun to be expressed in discussions about the house organ during the founding era. (During the transitional era, a high-quality magazine called *Status* appeared, along with a mimeographed *NAC Memo*, replacing *Status of Women News* as NAC's communication vehicle. *Status* contained little information about NAC activities, but revealed much about the ideas of the new generation of feminists in Canada.) Disputes about the house organ were part of the larger conflict about NAC's proper role by virtue of the fact that the communications function had existed mainly to strengthen NAC's lobbying at the centre by encouraging member groups, through the publication, to send their letters, speak to their MPs, or address issues in other such ways at the provincial/territorial level. For those who saw NAC primarily as the focal organization for a movement of transformation, the consciousness raising that could be achieved through in-depth articles, book reviews, and other material in *Status* was the main point of communication. Ironically, supporters of a magazine-quality house organ, which would consume a significant portion of the budget in these years, were also often opposed to heavy dependency on state funding. They were, however, willing to accept subventions for the magazine. Other issues onto which the core conflict over NAC's role was displaced during the transitional period were wages for housework; NAC's support for Jean-Claude Parrot, leader of the Canadian Union of Postal Workers (CUPW), who had been jailed for leading a strike in which maternity leave was at issue; the quality of NAC's performance in the constitutional debates that led to patriation; and NAC's policy on pension reform.

The transitional period was marked by charges and counter-charges; motions of censure and motions to repeal; factions and counter-factions; election coups and election defeats. In 1981, Chaviva Hošek, who served as secretary during this era, told Cerise Morris (1983:103) that 'the real split is in terms of the confrontational-adversarial approach versus the lobby-influence approach.' The issues in conflict were, in fact, more complex. Moreover, it was often the case that support for individuals, such as Lynn McDonald and later Jean Wood, determined divisions into separate camps as much as did differences on the issues themselves. (In the Executive Minutes, we noted that there were often as many recorded abstentions during this era as votes pro or con.)

In this discussion of the issues of NAC's structure and organization at the time that a radical grass roots was being grafted onto the founding coalition, we will first explore some of the debates about feminist organization and process. We will also look at some of the changes that were taking place in the broader Canadian movement and in the formal political environment. Finally, we will examine clusters of the questions listed above in an effort to understand how the conflicts that surrounded them, however disruptive, contributed to the process of NAC's institutionalization.

Let us consider initially why questions about the 'how' of politics and organization caused so much conflict within NAC. First, NAC's umbrella structure is a paradox. Although women participated in both the executive and the AGM as delegates from member groups or organizations, feminist egalitarianism demanded that each delegate be treated equally. The founders' purpose in choosing the umbrella structure was to affiliate as many women as possible, through their existing organizations, in order to increase NAC's clout in lobbying and prevent the government from once again disrupting solidarity among women's groups as it had in the interwar period. This original design did not envision a significant role for the many small collectives that were starting to emerge. In addition, the founders had not determined how to incorporate into such a coalition women's groups that were part of a larger organization – for example, union caucuses, party research groups, or feminist programs within organizations such as the YWCA.

The affiliation of many small new groups and caucuses of radical and leftist feminists during this period was matched by a decline in involvement (although not in actual membership) of the large national organizations. This was true in terms of both representation on the executive and involvement in the AGM. The AGM structure was based on a one-delegate–one-vote system. With the same single vote as a collective of ten, groups with large memberships often saw their involvement in NAC as largely symbolic; that is, although they would not go so far as to weaken NAC's legitimacy by withdrawing, they were not very actively engaged. Moreover, by the end of the transitional period, it was acknowledged that executive members would no longer be viewed as delegates of the organization that had nominated them. By 1982, they were described in NAC's literature as representing NAC rather than their original member group; with this shift, it became possible to view the executive as egalitarian.[1]

Women brought to NAC diverse experiences of the political process and often had different views of what feminist politics should be. Women whose only experience had been in small, homogeneous collectives underwent culture shock when they entered a large political arena with women who had extensive experience in partisan or union politics. Many brought with them a view of organizations based on theories of participatory democracy. In particular, we find the view that the basic unit of feminist politics ought to be the small primary group in which consensus can be achieved and conflict avoided. Women who saw movement organizations as the small group or collective 'writ large' found it difficult to operate within the norms of representative democracy.

We have identified five elements of a model of organizational process that would reflect the values of the new generation of feminists, as follows: (1) a valorization of the authenticity of small-group processes, which allowed for a high degree of comfort and a recognition of shared experiences; (2) a belief in the absolute sovereignty of the individual in decision making; (3) a rejection of representative democracy as unfeminist in principle. (Where representative democracy had to be accepted in practice, the principled rejection meant that accountability rules were not developed.); (4) a favouring of the grass roots or the close-to-home over the centre or the far-from-home; (5) a valorization of the goal of transforming individuals, and a lesser emphasis on that of influencing the state.

The role these values played in the conflicts we have identified was not simple. For example, except in their rhetoric, executive members rarely concerned themselves with feminist process in the context of the Annual General Meeting. Their collective view of the AGM was often cynical, and the different factions on the executive tended to try to manipulate the process at that meeting to achieve their desired outcomes. With regard to the executive itself and the shape NAC as a whole was to take, however, these values had a significant impact. They led to conflict among the various elements that were joined together in this common organization, and the resolution of that conflict bore practical fruit. The realities of politics, economics, and geography in Canada had forced women from all factions to come together to conduct politics within a shared structure and, consequently, to deal with, rather than avoid, the conflict that inevitably ensued.[2]

Cerise Morris (1983:102) described the nature of the conflict, which was being played out in public, as follows:

NAC's diversity necessitates discussion, negotiation and compromise in order to arrive at an organizational consensus. Positions adopted through this process cannot please or accurately reflect all of NAC's constituent parts. Since the rhetoric – and to some extent the practice – of NAC is based on participatory democracy, internal dissention can be a draining experience for the organization.

The values of feminist process place a great deal of emphasis on internal solidarity, which, in turn, requires that members put a high premium on non-conflictual internal processes (Richardson 1983; Ricks et al., 1972). Morris (1983:102) reported that NAC 'insiders' feared the organization could 'fall apart over a fundamental issue' and felt they had to 'walk on eggs.' Joyce Rothschild-Witt (1979:513) has observed that social control in small groups influenced by radical-feminist norms is often maintained by 'personalistic' and 'moral appeals,' which makes t necessary for the group to 'select members who share their basic values and world view.' The demand for authenticity meant that attempts to keep conflict impersonal or abstract were viewed negatively. Conflict was both feared and seen in personalistic and moral terms.

Morris (1983:103) interpreted the conflict in NAC in part as a tension between 'centrists' and 'leftists.' She quoted the 'centrists' as saying they feared that a possible 'take-over' by more left-leaning and confrontation-oriented members could destroy NAC. She reported that 'leftists' at the AGM viewed the 'middle of the road approach of NAC' as a serious obstacle to 'real social action on behalf of women's liberation.' The more-radical approaches represented at the 'Strategy for Change' conference now also had a voice on the NAC executive. The central disagreement between the founding coalition and the new coalition over the role NAC was to play was also a disagreement over competing theories of how best to achieve change. Ex-president Lorna Marsden, interviewed by Morris in 1978, argued, 'We're about change, not protest.' She justified the 'brief and lobby' approach as the rational choice because 'if you look at the way social change occurs in Canada most impact comes from influence on institutional authorities challenged in a quiet, straightforward way – not from populist protest' (Morris 1983:100). This classic statement of the liberal-feminist view reflected Marsden's experience as something of a mainstream political insider, with an entrée to the governing party that she was willing to share with NAC. The women who sought 'real social action on behalf of women's liberation' reflected their experience (and that of most women) as outsiders, excluded and alienated from the established structures of official politics. As one NAC insider, who refused to be named, told Morris, 'There [was] no shared analytic understanding of social change; it is more by leadership and luck than by design that NAC has had an impact' (1983:102).

The 'brief-and-lobby' method that NAC had pursued had not required significant policy expertise and, until this period, NAC had concentrated on educating its member groups in the lobby workshops in the ways and means of lobbying. Many of the new feminists were uncomfortable with the use of experts but had sympathy for anything that could empower politically inexperienced women. (Ironically, some of the new feminists themselves became feminist-policy 'experts,' and they often found themselves in conflict with self-help groups, who believed they understood their own needs best.) As NAC began to generate policy, it provided the opportunity within AGM Workshops for the delegates to generate policy. The executive also began to organize policy committees. The minutes of the executive meeting of 26 May 1979 report the formation of the Employment Committee, with a membership almost exclusively from the new-feminist coalition. Other new feminists, however, attacked the élitism that they believed underlay the recruitment of well-educated policy 'experts,' no matter how radical their feminism.[3]

Such conflicts, together with disputes over the more familiar Canadian issue of regional representation and the highly charged issue of government funding, made up a series of confrontations that would end in stalemate. Eventually, it became apparent that no faction could dominate NAC, and that ways of accommodating difference would have to be developed. The 1979 AGM told the story. According to the 26 May 1979 minutes, of the 133 member organizations represented, only 18 were national organizations and 11 were status-of-women committees or councils. The remaining 104 were small groups of caucuses. More telling was the regional breakdown: there were 83 groups from Ontario, 18 from Québec, and only 4 from other provinces or territories. In 1979, NAC planned to hold its mid-year meeting – a mini-AGM – outside Toronto for the first time, and in conjunction with the Alberta Status of Women Action Committee's AGM and lobby. The traditional issue of regional representation was given a new-feminist twist in several ways. First, since one aspect of the organizational values of the new generation of feminists was to privilege the close-to-home, central authorities were seen as potentially oppressive *vis-à-vis* the grass roots. But because the ultimate decision maker was understood to be the 'sovereign individual,' the very concept of representation, not to mention its realities, caused problems for some of the new generation of feminists.

Albertan Pat Preston wrote a text for the executive on the subject of regional representation. In it, she expressed her concern about the possibility of achieving the kind of representation that could measure up to feminist norms: 'When I hear the suggestion that regional representation would include areas such as "the prairie provinces and territories" or "the Atlantic provinces", I shudder.' She explained: 'I cannot conceive of one person providing meaningful representation from areas which are so large. In Alberta, for example, we face the problem of not being able to liaise with women from the far north and even south of the province. Our needs and interests are often quite different and frequently I feel hopelessly inadequate when I attempt to speak for sisters scattered so far apart' (Morris 1983:95). She argued that NAC should establish what the term *regionalism* would mean to it. She believed that, with limited funding, efforts to achieve 'real' representation of regions in NAC 'at the centre' could be achieved only with money and energies diverted from efforts 'at the grassroots.' Finally, she argued against 'tokenism,' which she thought regional representation would be if it involved recruiting to the executive someone 'who has no commitment to working or being actively involved in some specific aspect(s) of NAC' (Morris 1983:95).

In fact, the pressure for an elaborate structure of regional representation came from a group led by Lynn McDonald, who had begun as a representative from Nova Scotia, where regional sentiments have always been especially strong. This was not consistent with the same group's objection to a heavy dependence on governments for funding. The issue of regional representation flowed in part from the regional loyalties held by Canadian feminists; from their belief in the superiority of authentic, local voices; and from the growing understanding that NAC's legitimacy as a policy-making organization required that it represent more than the movement in Toronto or in central Canada. As the shadow of the royal commission receded, the process of generating policy required facing up to the costs of operating a pan-Canadian organization. This meant that the funding issue became key.

Lynn McDonald expressed her opinions on the funding issue clearly: 'In my view, countries much poorer than Canada have independent women's movements ... NAC ought to be the independent group that can fight for all the rest.' (personal interview with Chris Appelle, 18 April 1985). In her President's Report to the AGM in March 1981, she stated, 'My preference is for total independence [from government funding], but many would be satisfied with 3/4 or 1/2 independence.' Her view may well have been influenced by the Liberal government's rejection in 1980 of NAC's request for financial support to organize regional meetings on the Constitution,[4] as well as by her growing belief that the government party had no intention of respecting the political independence of the CACSW.

McDonald also wanted a more theoretically rigorous movement, lamenting the fact that 'there have been a lot of briefs in Canada, but remarkably little theory' (1979:40). Without a doubt, NAC's multiple dependencies – on government funding, on the willingness of member organizations to continue support, on the goodwill of FFQ leaders to confer an aura of biculturalism on it – could be seen as obstacles to its role as the focal point of an independent, theoretically coherent movement for transformative change.

McDonald's support for expensive activities in NAC (a 'magazine-quality' house organ; full regional representation; policy committees), on the one hand, and for independence from government funding, on the other, is understandable in the context of her view of NAC as the focal point of an independent, transformative movement and in the context of her rejection of paid staff (except for a secretary and a typesetter). If virtually all of the activities of the movement were unpaid, the seeming self-contradiction of her position is lessened. It was with McDonald that the legitimizing idea of NAC as a parliament of women (which, of course, required regional representation to make it accept-able in the Canadian political system) took root. Although many other younger feminists rejected volunteerism as one of the self-sacrificing norms of the older generations of feminists, McDonald was motivated by the strain in feminist analysis that viewed paid staff as potential 'bureaucrats' who will dominate the purposes of the organization. (It must be said, however, that this is a position more likely to find support among women with professional qualifications and secure employment than among the majority of women, who face underemployment, un-employment, and inadequate pay for their work.) Radical-feminist practice has been determinedly anti-bureaucratic, beginning with self-conscious efforts to divide tasks and responsibilities in egalitarian and non-hierarchical ways. Even in 'mainstream' women's groups, there had been efforts to develop more participatory structures. Hierarchy, which Ferguson (1984:215) defines as 'horizontally graded authority relations entailing "top-down" supervision and control,'[5] was resisted within the NAC executive during this period. In fact, the executive did not become more structured internally until McDonald's presidency.

Changes in the English-Canadian women's movement during the seventies, together with changes in the mainstream political environ-ment, also contributed to the turbulence of this era within NAC. The coalition between traditional feminists and liberal feminists had pro-duced something of a blueprint for action. But, as Eisenstein (1981) argues, once the women's movement embarked on action related to abortion, child care, and the rights of working mothers, women's private and public domains could no longer be considered separately, and this forced liberal feminism to move beyond its own theory. Liberal feminism's ideological potential for radicalism, therefore, became more apparent just as its organizational centrality in NAC declined. By 1979, the period of growth of large national feminist organizations was drawing to a close, while new local groups creating politics out of women's experiences continued to emerge, and to form their own networks and coalitions, at a rapid rate. Mobilization occurred in waves around issues from the 'private' domain, such as rape, battering, pornography, incest, and prostitution. Women-centred services were created for help and self-help. Network organizations to link service and advocacy groups were also being formed. And the issues of representation and government funding were being debated within these networks at the same time that they were at issue within NAC. In the eighties, as we will outline in the next chapter, networks continued to be elaborated across the country, and new equality-seeking groups mobilized thousands of women around issues of ethnicity, race, disability, immigrant status, and lesbian rights.

Both the English-Canadian and the Québec movements met with success in getting their issues onto the agendas of public authorities. The three-pronged approach of a feminist network within the state, pressure from the 'brief and lobby' feminists, and the radical grassroots groups' energetic and unconventional demonstrations made an impact on government. Findlay (1987:47) reports that, by 1980, infrastructural changes to deal with these new agenda items had been introduced at the federal level. They included a Cabinet Directive to coordinate federal policies on sexual violence, a position entitled Coordinator of the Status of Women in the deputy ministers' committee of the newly created Ministry of State for Social Development, and a Cabinet requirement that all documents include a section on the implications for the status of women of all new federal policies.

It was increasingly apparent to most observers, however, that the state's response brought few substantive changes to women's lives and did little to change the balance of power between men and women in social, economic, or political institutions. Tangible changes, such as a comprehensive child-care system, the decriminalization of abortion, or pensions for home-makers, were simply not being made. Although government regulations paid lip-service to women's goal of equality, in practice – for example, in cases such as the AIB's 'exemption' for female groups – concrete action or extra money in the paycheque was rarely the result. A series of dramatic strikes by women employees (at such companies as Purex, Tandy/Radio Shack, Fleck, Bell Canada, and Blue Cross) revealed that the action for working-class feminists was primarily on the picket line and that leftist feminists expected –

and got – support from their non-union colleagues within NAC. The strikes also showed that employers were unwilling to give up the 'benefit' of underpaid female workers without a major struggle.

A stalemate, or, as Findlay (1987:48) calls it, 'an "unstable equilibrium" of compromise between the state and most of the movement,' led NAC's two internal coalitions to consider different options. The coalition of traditional and liberal feminists adopted the strategy of getting more women elected to the official political system and enhancing the movement's credibility with the public and government. The coalition of radical and left feminists sought to reorient the movement away from the official political system and towards strategies of social transformation. (Evidence during this period of the enormous potential of the pornography issue to mobilize women was certainly a shot in the arm for the transformative elements of the movement.)

The issue of the patriation of Canada's Constitution from Britain after more than a century did not, in itself, galvanize women, although there had been concern about the jurisdictional fate of family law – a concern that divided anglophone and Québec francophone women. The incredible resistance of men within both the federal and provincial governments to women's demands for consultation, participation, and inclusion, however, did galvanize women as 'a stunning display of the limits of state commitment to actively promote women's equality' (Findlay 1987:31). The events surrounding the constitutional debate thus re-energized the movement and, some would argue, led to its finest hour, as Canadian women won the equality guarantees that their U.S. sisters had so bitterly lost. For others, however, the emphasis on legal equality represented a hijacking of the movement's activities away from its original goals. Certainly, although the constitutional debate tipped the balance once again in favour of action in the realm of official politics, it also strengthened each coalition in its opposite view of the usefulness of working to gain change through state action.

In NAC, the constitutional debates of 1981–2 caused conflict and some loss of legitimacy, because the organization had been unable to play an effective role. We will not explore in detail the substance of the issues involved in the constitutional debates here. Although the constitutional equality guarantees were not something the movement had sought, NAC and the CACSW had been undertaking educational work on constitutional issues involving the federal division of powers for some time. The Liberal government's proposals to change the constitutional division of powers so that the provinces would control family law and divorce horrified many anglophone feminists, who envisioned a patchwork of different jurisdictions (as in the United States) and, consequently, even greater opportunity for men to evade supporting their families. Francophone feminists in Québec, however, generally supported the proposals. Neither group of feminists understood the position of the other. When conflict over constitutional matters finally erupted in NAC, it led to the departure of the FFQ from the organization for the first time. The equality guarantees were consistent with the founding coalition's philosophy, but many with NAC did not see them as worth spending much time on until it became apparent that there was to be a Charter of Rights, and that, unless women activists became involved, it would be as useless in securing women's rights as the existing Bill of Rights had been. Some NAC feminists, however, including Lynn McDonald, opposed the entrenched Charter altogether.

The discovery that it would require enormous effort for women to make their concerns matter in the constitutional-amendment process mobilized many women who viewed the guarantees, in the words of ad hoc committee member Linda Ryan-Nye, as 'not a hell of a lot to win, but ... a hell of a lot to lose.' For a number of reasons, NAC was unable to be an effective point of organization in the constitutional struggles. None the less, the ad hoc committee, with members in both Toronto and Montreal, tapped the enormous network of women and women's groups across the country. As Rosemary Billings, a member of the committee and past member of the NAC executive stated, 'NAC could have been on another planet but the people who were most active could do that role because of NAC connections ... If NAC had not existed, Ad Hoc could not have functioned' (personal interview with Chris Appelle, 26 November 1985). NAC's incapacity during the constitutional debates was a source of some bitterness within the NAC executive. Certainly, Lynn McDonald believed that NAC could have played a more effective role if it had been independent of government funding. Others believed that McDonald herself contributed to the breakdown. (The details of this conflict will be examined later in the chapter.)

Janet Boles's analysis (1979) of the failure of the U.S. lobby to achieve the Equal Rights Amendment (ERA) helps us see the matter of NAC's role in the Canadian constitutional process from a slightly different perspective. Although Boles attributes the defeat of the ERA to many things in the U.S. political environment that women could not have changed, she does identify one thing they could have avoided: the serious organizational splits that divided NOW from other segments of the movement. Women in Canada, in the course of their work together in numerous coalitions and in NAC, had developed a network that crossed partisan, ideological, regional, and sometimes even linguistic lines. Moreover, 'all vocal women's groups agreed on the mandate that role equality should be guaranteed' (Burt 1986b:16). Ultimately, then, the English-Canadian movement was able to work together towards common goals such as suffrage and achieving the establishment of the Royal Commission on the Status of Women. Another factor that worked to the advantage of the movement was the short duration of the campaign: right-wing groups did not have enough time to get their campaign in opposition to the equality guarantees off the ground.

For Lynn McDonald, the process of constitutional change proved NAC's organizational weakness. To many other observers, the process demonstrated the organizational strength of the movement, in which NAC's role, as the arena in which different factions could come together, was central – even if it was left to the ad hoc committee to orchestrate lobbying on the Constitution.

Two Coalitions Competing for the Future of NAC

In this section, we will explore in greater depth the issues that caused conflict between the two major coalitions in NAC. According to the minutes of 1 and 2 December 1979, at the beginning of the transitional period, NAC had a year-end balance of approximately $131,560 from all sources – more than double its 1977 balance of $60,000 – and a membership of 140 groups (85 per cent with dues paid up). By the end of the period, in 1982, the membership base had grown by only 50 groups (*NAC Memo*, 1982:5). The 'Friends of NAC' category of individual members, who could not vote at the AGM, was established in 1980 through a constitutional amendment.

This turbulent transitional period began in the final months of Kay Macpherson's leadership. At that time, NAC's increased funds were evidenced in the publication of the new, magazine-quality house organ, *Status*, and in the elaboration of its executive structure. The minutes of the 13 January 1979 meeting make note of six executive committees. Four of them were administrative (Editorial, Membership, AGM, and Finance); one, called the Social Services Lobby Committee, devoted its efforts to having the limits on the insurability of part-time workers removed from the revised unemployment insurance regulations; and one was entrusted with planning for the commemoration of 'Persons Year.'[6]

In this context, a major controversy erupted over the issue of membership for the group Wages for Housework. Three groups were being considered for NAC membership – Wages for Housework, the Lesbian Mothers' Defence Fund, and Employment Services for Immigrant Women. For the first time, NAC refused a group admission. The application of Wages for Housework was rejected because, according to the minutes from 24 February 1979, 'the principle of wages for housework has been explicitly rejected by NAC.' The other two groups were held back for further investigation because they seemed to have 'overlapping officers' with the rejected group.

We will discuss the policy implications of NAC's debate about Wages for Housework in Chapter 7. In terms of the struggle for NAC, however, the rejection of the Wages for Housework group may have been the first evidence of a leftist- and radical-feminist coalition around a policy issue, and it prefigured that coalition's ability to elect Lynn McDonald president at the 7 April AGM. This AGM was the occasion of an 'invasion' of organized 'poor women' (women on mothers' allowance and in public housing) to demonstrate in favour of the idea of wages for housework. Ottawa author Dorothy O'Connell and other leaders of the welfare mothers' movement attempted to bring home the fact that not all women consider work to be 'liberating,' as the NAC position suggested, especially if the work is badly paid and boring. Despite support for these views from some left-leaning women, such as Marion Dewar, this group did not persuade the majority on the NAC executive to change its mind.

At the spring and summer meetings of the executive, the fragility of the new coalition's majority became evident. At the 26 May 1979 meeting, Lynn Kaye 'expressed her displeasure' at the decision of the table officers not to distribute a news release she had drafted for NAC protesting the conviction of Jean-Claude Parrot and setting out NAC's position of support for CUPW. It is also at this time that executive factions start to appeal to resolutions passed by the AGM (and often presented there by executive members to legitimize their positions) in their conflicts within the executive. Just as support from NAC as 'the most powerful lobby of women in Canada'[7] was becoming important to many causes, support by the AGM was becoming important for legitimizing policy positions internally. Clearly, executive members recruiting new groups were acutely aware of the balance of forces in the organization, and favoured groups most likely to support their own faction. The minutes of 23 June 1979 record two new members: the Progressive Conservative Association of Women and the Public Service Alliance of Canada (PSAC, the largest and most 'macho' of public-service unions). Also at this meeting, 'bottom-line positions' for affiliation with NAC were discussed. It was agreed (with one abstention) that a pro-choice position on abortion was such a bottom-line position. This had effectively been the case ever since NAC's founding, as evidenced by the withdrawal of the Catholic Women's League (CWL) and the IODE, both of which had been involved in the period of organizing, before NAC was officially founded. A pro-choice position now became an overt condition for membership.

Plans to improve NAC's regional representation proceeded apparently without rancour. (The rancour came later over how to pay for it!) A series of reports from the 'regions' that were represented by an executive member became a regular feature of executive meetings. At the 23 February 1980 meeting, Jeanne Gariepy, reporting of FFQ activities, noted the federation's position that divorce ought to come within the provincial jurisdiction. This raised no discernible ripple. Far more significant to the executive was the first funding debate, which was reported in the minutes not when it occurred but a year later, when it was announced that the movement's lobbying had resulted in a fourfold increase of the Women's Program's regular budget, to $4.1 million, and that further increases over a five-year period were also assured. It was in this context that the reasons for a majority decision 'for diversified funding' were outlined in the minutes.

The writer of the minutes reported that 'the debate in 1980–81 was one of where to get money.' The majority favoured 'diversified' funding – that is, government core funding and funding from other sources. The following reasons for accepting government funding were reported as having been advanced: (1) 'we are a women's issues group – we are good at that, not at fund raising'; (2) 'NAC gets the largest amount of government funding of all women's groups and sets the cap. Therefore, we have a double duty to argue for more government funding – for them as well as for us'; (3) 'fund raising can help us, but only in small amounts' (executive minutes, September 1981). The minute writer also noted that the executive had supported the 'Friends of NAC' category as a fund-raising effort, since it 'had the added value of building a network.' The bad news, however, was that NAC's 1980 fund-raising efforts had had only modest returns: Friends raised only about $7,800; a medallion-selling campaign brought in only $12,000, for an enormous outlay of staff and volunteer effort; and a successful fund-raising dinner in Toronto raised $3,500 – all of which represented only 1 per cent of the budget. To put this discussion in context, we should note that the Treasurer's budget submission for 1980–1 showed that 'diversified' funding meant $158,325 in government grants out of a total of $220,815 from all sources. Despite plans for an energetic fund-raising program, even optimistic calculations presumed only $37,500 income from a range of ventures (AGM Literature 1980, 'Financial Summary').

At the 1980 AGM, organized by Lorenne Clark, the new majority coalition pulled out all the stops. The delegates heard from political philosopher Mary O'Brien; from firebrand Rosemary Brown, who saw a major goal of feminism as 'the reform of the family'; and from President Lynn McDonald. McDonald is quoted by Paula McLaughlin (1980:4) in the *Ottawa Journal* as stating that 'the time for talk is over and the time for action is overdue,' which was reported under the headline 'Women's Leader Warns Militancy Will Combat Neglect.' Guided by a revised constitution, the AGM delegates elected three vice-presidents (none of whom was from Québec), five regional representatives, eight members at large, and five table officers (now explicitly elected to their offices). This twenty-four-member executive included eleven members from outside Ontario. It also introduced status distinctions within the executive between table officers and regional representatives. Few left-oriented or union-affiliated members were elected, although Lynn McDonald was returned as president. Business woman Jean Wood was elected treasurer, and academic Chaviva Hošek, secretary (both were eventually to become NAC presidents). The balance among the fragments had changed, and the effect would provoke a crisis in the next year.

The year 1980 saw the beginning of a serious role for the AGM structure in generating and approving policy. Organized into workshops, the approximately three hundred women in attendance dealt with old issues such as child care and unemployment insurance and new issues such as genital mutilation and the treatment of foreign domestics. The April/May 1980 *NAC Memo* covered the constitutional issue. It was reported that the Coalition for Family Law in Manitoba supported its government's opposition to the proposed transfer of jurisdiction over divorce to the provincial level. It was assumed that NAC would agree with this position, and the FFQ's opposing views were not noted. It seemed obvious, as the FFQ delegates were to note at the next AGM, that Québec francophone women's opinions were not understood in NAC.

With the election of Jean Wood to the executive, that body acquired an expert on the issue of pensions, and, at the 24 May 1980 meeting, an Income Tax and Pensions Committee was empowered to write to the Federal Human Rights Commission. The other two policy committees staffed at this meeting were the Immigration Committee and the Employment Committee. Some of the leftist fragment moved their activities entirely to the Employment Committee, which came to operate as a NAC voice almost independent of executive scrutiny. At this time, regional reports reflected extensive activity and outreach to nurses, Women's Institutes, dental hygienists, 4-H Clubs, and rural groups, in general.

Disruption over the Constitution

Until spring 1980, NAC was not preoccupied with issues concerning Canada's Constitution. In this, it resembled other women's groups in Canada: they tended to focus on a wide range of economic and social objectives and to pay relatively little attention to legal equality provisions (Hošek 1983; Vickers 1986). The broader crisis engendered by the constitutional debates of 1980–2, however, in combination with the existing internal conflict that we have been describing, placed NAC under severe stress. The constitutional debates sparked internal crisis in the CACSW and the FFQ as well, and these, in turn, affected NAC. Moreover, long-standing political institutions, such as the New Democratic party and the Liberal party, also suffered serious internal splits. In short, all omnibus organizations that brought together regionally, linguistically, and ideologically diverse elements went through some level of crisis. As we have already noted, the issue that provoked authentic interest in the constitutional debates among women's movements was the agreement of First Ministers in February 1979 to transfer jurisdiction over divorce to the provinces. This development threatened an immediate split between the majority of Québec francophone feminists, who considered the Québec state to be more progressive than the federal government, and the majority of anglophone women, who feared the practical consequences of different divorce regimes across Canada and who saw provincial governments as generally less progressive than the federal government.

The minutes of the 14 June 1980 executive meeting report that Justice Minister Jean Chrétien was unsympathetic to NAC's request for funding for constitutional research. The executive struck a subcommittee, including a member from the FFQ, to work on constitutional issues over the summer. It was reported that the CACSW was planning a national meeting of women's organizations for September, and hoped to hold regional meetings as well. The NAC executive planned a special *NAC Memo* to exchange views and educate member groups on fifteen topics, from entrenchment of the Charter to the appropriate jurisdiction for matters pertaining to the environment. The executive agreed to disagree on the issue of the jurisdiction over natural resources, understanding that 'unity was impossible.' On all other issues, however, it was assumed that they 'would speak out as a women's group,' that is, suppressing regional differences. It is perhaps ironic that the executive could understand the desire for provincial jurisdiction over natural resources (as expressed at the 14 June meeting by Ann Bell, from Newfoundland), but not the FFQ position on provincial jurisdiction over family law, an issue that prefigured the 'distinct society' debate that would dominate discussions of the Meech Lake and Charolottetown accords.

Also at the 14 June meeting, the executive engaged in a long session on planning, co-chaired by Pat Preston and Penny Allderdice. 'Goals, activities, priorities and success measures for 1980–1 were established and responsibilities and report mechanisms were assigned.' A 'planning matrix,' introduced by Treasurer Jean Wood, proposed an increased formalization of executive roles. Constitutional reform and organizational, budgetary, and funding issues were set as the top priorities by a majority of the executive at this meeting. Instead of the more feminist political process desired by women now in the minority, a management-by-objectives approach was imposed by the new executive majority.

Like other organizations faced with internal conflict over the issues raised by the constitutional debates, NAC eagerly awaited the Advisory Council's conference, planned for early September. Research papers had been commissioned; the topics to be covered included the following: the possible effects of an entrenched Charter on women, in general, and on affirmative-action initiatives, in particular; family-law jurisdiction; Indian rights for 'non-status' Indian women; and the effects of multiple jurisdictions on the provision of government services for women (Hošek 1983; Kome 1983; Doerr and Carrier 1981). An underlying issue, however, was the Liberal government's intention to have the BNA Act patriated and amended unilaterally if the provinces failed to agree with the federal proposals. Women's hopes for the CACSW conference were that partisan conflict would be avoided by virtue of the careful, academic approach that was being planned. Apparently because of a strike by translators – a group consisting largely of women seeking maternity leave (*Toronto Star*, 3 September 1980; *NAC Memo* [October 1980]:1) – the Advisory Council cancelled the conference planned for early September just before the First Ministers' scheduled 'last-ditch attempt' to reach agreement forestalling unilateral action by the federal Liberal government (Hošek 1983; Kome 1983). This meant that NAC's mid-year meeting, planned in conjunction with the Manitoba Action Committee on the Status of Women and to be held in Winnipeg, would become 'the major conference of women and the constitution' (*NAC Memo* [October 1980]:1). The October *NAC Memo* also reports that 'regional meetings .... [were] in the process of being planned by Alberta, Newfoundland, Ontario, and Nova Scotia Status of Women Groups.' It continues: 'Word then came from Government that NO MONEY was available for the Winnipeg Conference.' The ensuing crisis in NAC was so complicated by interpersonal struggles that it is difficult to reconstruct a clear story-line. NAC executive member Chaviva Hošek has written about the period, and others have given interviews. The tendency, however, is to tidy up the conflict or to blame particular individuals for 'irresponsibility.' We have concluded that we must rely on the documentary evidence for this account. Given, however, that some of the evidence is missing, we cannot provide anything like a complete account of NAC's activities as they pertained to the constitutional debates. We can only begin to show how this essentially external crisis 'played' within NAC, which was already in the midst of an internal organizational crisis.

In Lynn McDonald's view, government funding – or, in this case, its withholding – was being used as a tool of manipulation and co-optation, making NAC a pawn in the political agenda of the governing party. The October 1980 *NAC Memo* reports that NAC replaced its planned 'regional' meetings with a one-day conference, on 18 October, in Toronto. Given the fact that many of the opponents of an entrenched Charter were from Québec and the West, this contraction to a Toronto meeting would have a contingent that was better disposed to the government's position and, hence, more vulnerable to potential attempts by representatives of government to influence its views.

The minutes of the next recorded NAC executive meeting are

31 January 1981. They document a conflict arising from the 18 October 1980 mini-conference on the Constitution. The question raised concerned a comment in Elizabeth Gray's article in the *Globe and Mail* the previous day (Gray 1981:7). Gray's account alleged that, according to Lynn McDonald, conference chair Beth Atcheson had succumbed to pressure from Minister Responsible for the Status of Women Lloyd Axworthy's 'Winnipeg coterie' and had steered the meeting to a resolution that showed 'unequivocal support for the Government's position' on entrenchment.

A letter from Beth Atcheson, giving another version of the events, was also read into the minutes. It stated that a last-minute interjection from the floor 'linking support for entrenchment with changes to the Charter' diluted the 'unequivocal support for the principle of entrenchment.' Atcheson reported that she had redrafted the resolution, in part because of discussions with a group of seven or eight people, which had included Nancy Connelly, someone known to be associated with Axworthy. The group discussion had reinforced her own conclusion that the majority had clearly supported entrenchment. She denied individual contact with Connelly and claimed she had changed her draft of the resolution and submitted it, telling both Norma Scarborough, the recorder, and Betsy Carr, of NAC's Constitution Committee. She rejected McDonald's allegation that she had been a dupe of the government. In fact, McDonald's opposition to the Charter was in opposition to the views of many in NAC.

The *Globe and Mail's* report of NAC's November 1980 appearance before the Parliamentary Committee appeared under the heading 'Charter Would Enshrine Bias, NAC Says' and quoted Lynn McDonald as saying that the proposed Charter 'is insidious' because of 'the inability amongst judges to deal with inequalities to women' (Sheppard 1980:9). None the less, the 31 January executive meeting, presumably chaired by Lynn McDonald, passed motions that resulted in a letter to the *Globe and Mail* 'setting matters straight' and in letters of apology to Beth Atcheson and Nancy Connelly. McDonald apparently agreed to the apologies because she believed Elizabeth Gray had misrepresented her statements about *how* the government influence at the 18 October conference had been effected. She did not, however, change her view that government influence had been involved in the striking of NAC's position, with which she now disagreed. (It is worth recalling that feminist New Democrats were also divided on the question of the value for women of an entrenched Charter. Positions often changed over time, however, as the question came to focus more on the *nature* of the Charter). The meeting concluded with a motion asking the table officers 'to develop a notice of motion re accountability of the executive to the recommendations of the AGM.' This registered the executive's displeasure at having its president commit NAC to a position that many of its member groups apparently opposed.

On 5 January, the Advisory Council's rescheduled constitutional Conference was cancelled, and 'a statement was issued saying that regional conferences would be more appropriate' (Hošek 1983:288). (We will not attempt to explain here the issues pertaining to the cancellation that were in dispute.) Doris Anderson resigned as CACSW president on 19 January, focusing the attention of the press, and of many ordinary women, on the constitutional process from a woman-centred perspective. Within a few days, an ad hoc committee of women in Toronto and Ottawa emerged and quickly set 14 February as the date for an ad hoc women's constitutional conference. This small group of 'Ad-hoc'ers' included feminist lawyers who were concerned about the content of the draft Charter. They believed that the Charter was a *fait accompli* and that it was time for conflict among women over entrenchment of the Charter to give way to concerted efforts to get the best possible legal equality rights for women.

The minutes of the 31 January meeting record the beginnings of a long conflict over NAC's position on the future of the Advisory Council, provoked by the resignation of Doris Anderson. The ad hoc constitutional conference, scheduled for 14 February, would coincide with a meeting to consult with women's groups called by Axworthy for 16 February. It was agreed that Lynn McDonald, Ann Bell, and Lee Grills would attend the meeting with Axworthy. The key issue would be the future of the CACSW and its political independence.

The minutes of this meeting also illustrate the NAC executive's ambiguous attitude towards what they called the 'alternate conference.' It was stressed that 'this is an ad-hoc meeting' and agreed 'that NAC [would] support the alternate conference' but 'send no official delegates.' Concern was expressed that the executive's decisions as to attending the 'alternate conference' or the Advisory Council's rescheduled conference were 'being interpreted by politicians, media, political appointees, etc., as evidence of support or non-support of the Council, Doris Anderson, Lloyd Axworthy, the Tories, the Liberals, etc.' The entry concludes, 'NAC, like the rest of the independent women's movement, remains committed to the concerns of women and not politicians.'

The Funding Committee report in the 31 January minutes gives another clue as to the crisis in NAC and the close-to-six-month silence on the subject in the official record. An entry reading '1980, difficult year' on page 31 of the Funding Committee's report was changed to read 'In 1980–1 the finances were not adequate to allow publication of *Status*.' The inherent conflicts in the desires of the women represented by Lynn McDonald were becoming increasingly apparent. Bravely, NAC's press release on the meeting called by Axworthy on the Advisory Council meeting ended 'We will not be pushed into making the minister's crisis our crisis,' yet NAC's financial dependence on the government made its situation difficult. The press release called for the examination of six questions during the minister's meeting, all of which focused on the Advisory Council's alleged lack of independence from political direction. A press release dated 17 March reported that NAC demanded Axworthy's resignation. It stated that NAC 'expressed deep concern over a CBC national news report ... which described its newly elected executive as "pro-Axworthy,"' and went on to report that 'the NAC Annual Meeting this past weekend voted to call for the resignation of Lloyd Axworthy.' Spokesperson Pat Hacker is reported as having added that 'all 22 NAC Executive Members are elected on the understanding that they are committed to carry out the policies passed at the Annual Meeting,' and that 'if we are not committed to them, then we should resign.' In fact, it is not clear that all executive members shared the view that they must resign if they did not agree with AGM positions.

Throughout the period of the constitutional debates, there were two parallel political dynamics affecting NAC. The first was the process of internal struggle that we have already described between the two relatively evenly matched coalitions. The second was a process that began with Doris Anderson's resignation and the creation of the ad hoc committee. The ad hoc committee was formed, at least in part, to bypass NAC, because it was clear that NAC could not have reached a common position without a serious, and perhaps fatal, rupture. Since McDonald and some other members of her coalition were suspicious of or opposed to the Charter, they were perceived as obstacles to be circumvented. In fact, the ad hoc committee process more or less hijacked the meetings of most national women's groups held in 1980–1, including NAC's mid-year meeting and its AGM in March.

NAC's crisis over both the constitutional and the funding issues[8] came to a head at the 1981 AGM, held 13–16 March. (Unless otherwise noted, all quotations in the following discussion are taken from the minutes of this meeting.) The AGM minutes also make it clear that the 1980-1 executive had passed, and then apparently rescinded, a motion of non-confidence in the outgoing president, Lynn McDonald. In the early hours of this conflict-ridden AGM, Treasurer Jean Wood, the executive's pension specialist, was elected president. Her election was to be the focal point for a second crisis during the next year. The recommendations of the AGM Finance Workshop revealed the depth of conflict over funding issues now made concrete by the constitutional crisis. The AGM was polarized into almost-even camps. First, in a recorded vote, the motion 'that NAC take funds and actively solicit them from any source (government or otherwise) that is willing to contribute them' was defeated 55-54.[9] A second motion, which resolved that 'NAC aim at 75% self-sufficiency [from government] over the next three years' first produced a dead tie (65-65, with 12 abstentions). The minutes name those who spoke for and against the motion: Those recorded as speaking in support of 75 per cent self-sufficiency within three years were Swenarchuk (Canadian Union of Professional and Technical Employees [CUPTE]), Shaikh (CUPE), Mulhall (International Women's Day Committee), Kaye (CUPTE); those recorded as speaking against were Peluso (Montreal Business and Professional Club [Bs & Ps]), Macpherson (NAC executive), Hill (Federation of Women Teachers of Ontario), Preston (NAC executive), Joly (L'AFÉAS), Holmes (Status of Women, Regina). The polarization between the old coalition and the new is evident, although some votes would have been swayed by the constitutional issue. Kay Macpherson's call for a recount was supported and the second count showed 73 in favour of the motion to achieve 75 per cent self-sufficiency and 70 against, with 7 abstentions.

A final vote took place on the resolution that 'NAC decrease its dependence on government funding and explore all other possible sources for funds, including expanding the Friends of NAC, private foundations and all other sources of non-governmental funds.' This vote was more clear-cut than the others, with 87 for and 46 against.[10] In the end, however, the motion commanding self-sufficiency would not survive the inclinations of the newly elected executive. During the next year, the Funding Committee, led by Chaviva Hošek, successfully lobbied for a large increase in the government funds available to all women's groups. The new executive did not turn down 'its share' of this higher level of funding, arguing that NAC was an ongoing organization, with well-established functions to perform in both fat years and lean.

The recommendations from the Membership Workshop at this AGM displayed a desire to have NAC increasingly play the role of a parliament of women. Members wanted NAC to provide a forum for constitutional issues to be debated from a woman-centred perspective. The first recommendation sought to facilitate cooperation among NAC members in the regions. The second demanded that 'regional representatives organize regional pre-annual meetings in order that women across the nation will have informed input into the annual meeting.' The third proposed that NAC executive members attend meetings of member groups, that NAC recruit more members, and the NAC groups devote a column in their newsletters to NAC affairs and appoint a liaison person responsible for informing members about NAC issues. The workshop also resolved that 'it is the role of the membership to determine the policy of the organization and send direction to the Executive and that there should be no restriction on the number of resolutions from the workshops to be put forward unless this is done through the Constitution.' The AGM, however, was not to emerge as the power centre for policy making. Because of the deep divisions within the executive, few activists trusted the AGM process, which remained easy to manipulate. Instead, the executive developed policy committees. And, although the 'experts' on those committees would often find themselves in conflict with member groups, who based their positions on their lived experience, the committees none the less constituted a structural way of dealing with the ideological stalemate reflected in the series of tie votes that occurred at the 1981 AGM. Indeed, the policy committees would allow NAC to develop a policy agenda that went beyond the recommendations of the royal commission, without either coalition risking defeat in the AGM.

The executive elected at this turbulent meeting was the largest in NAC's history, with twenty-one members, ten from outside central Canada and only five from Toronto. The introduction of three vice-presidents, explicit regional representatives, and members-at-large changed the dynamic of the executive considerably. The partisan balance and the ideological balance of views on issues of feminist organization, however, continued to reflect the stalemate that was evident at the AGM. The fact that the meeting was organized in such a way that the executive was elected before the conflicts erupted led some observers to challenge the newly elected executive's legitimacy. Indeed, Jean Wood was dogged by this allegation throughout her presidency. To remedy the problem, the constitution was altered yet again to ensure that, henceforth, voting would occur after the balance of the AGM had transpired rather than before.

The controversy surrounding the issue of the Advisory Council continued at the AGM. The minutes show that motions flew thick and fast. First, since no workshop had been provided on the subject, a group calling itself the 'Advisory Council Special Interest Group' sought to have the agenda changed so that the meeting could deal with its recommendations. Gariepy of the FFQ and Joly of L'AFÉAS argued the these motions were out of order. The minutes record that their objections were voted down, and that the FFQ then resigned from NAC, 'because it considers all motions from the workshop on Advisory Councils to be out of order.' In this, the Québec representatives were reflecting Québec francophone women's lack of support for the position on the cancellation of the Advisory Council's conference taken by Doris Anderson and her supporters. The passage of a motion inviting the FFQ to return to NAC and to 'consult' did not prevent the following motions pertaining to the Advisory Council from being introduced: (1) a motion calling for the new council, led by Lucie Pépin, to resign, 'to restore the credibility of the Council'; (2) a motion calling for Axworthy's resignation; and (3) a motion requiring that NAC 'not co-operate with the Council's proposed internal review.'[7] NAC ultimately adopted the position of requiring an independent public review of the CACSW, but bad blood between the supporters and denigrators of the council, of Anderson, and of Pépin, would haunt the organization for some time to come.

After such heated debate, the President's Report would normally have provided a relatively peaceful ending. This was not to be the case with Lynn McDonald's report. After her report was moved, with a vote of thanks, by Madeleine Parent and seconded by Lynn Kaye, some members of the 1980–1 executive, represented by Kay Macpherson (who had been an active Ad-hoc'er), insisted on correcting the record. They took issue especially with the part of the report that read 'At the October 19, 1980, meeting of the NAC Executive, a motion of Confidence in the President was passed.' McDonald argued that she had answered the charges against her at that meeting and that a motion of confidence had then been passed. Dorothy Richardson read her original motion of non-confidence into the AGM minutes:

Whereas the President of NAC has contravened the committee structure of the organization; has not followed motions previously approved; has acted independently in presenting policies and strategies not brought before or approved by the executive or the appropriate committees; has presented an inaccurate picture of the financial situation of the organization; and has, in my opinion, generally undermined decisions made by the executive – I move that this Executive express a lack of confidence in the President of NAC.

Controversy then raged as to whether there had actually been a restorative motion of confidence at the 19 October meeting. (Then-secretary Chaviva Hošek claimed that there had not.) In the end, a motion by Lynn Kaye criticizing the previous executive 'for using a non-confidence motion against the President and the manner in which they did it' carried (31 in favour and 23 against, with 11 abstentions).

Issues arising in connection with the constitutional debates, Anderson's resignation, and Axworthy's actions continued to add an extra charge to the conflict between the two struggling coalitions. It resulted in NAC's being sidelined during a critical period in the history of the women's movement. Moreover, NAC's failure to understand or accept the position of Québec francophone women marks the beginning of the end of NAC's ability, through the affiliation of the FFQ, to provide a bridge, however fragile, between the French and English movements. Although the FFQ would return to NAC for much of the 1980s, it would leave yet again when similar issues arose in connection with the Meech Lake Accord. Many NAC activists would again be unable to comprehend or accept the view of the majority of francophone feminists from Québec that their liberation rested with the Québec state and with recognition of Québec as a 'distinct society.'

Accountability and the Crisis over Pensions

The issues of accountability and of the solidarity of the executive were to continue to plague NAC throughout the presidency of Jean Wood. Lynn McDonald (1981) stated her views in an article written for the June/July 1981 issue of *Canadian Forum,* in which she argued that NAC had been both less democratic and less effective than she would have wished for a feminist organization. This provoked intense anger within the new executive. The ensuing debate revealed that feminist norms of solidarity and consensus, rather than the norms common to non-feminist organizations, shaped most participants' views. The next twelve months were the most turbulent and murky in NAC's history. Hot on the heels of the constitutional crisis, which was to drain NAC of the energies of many able women, came the issue of pension reform, which, in the final trauma of this era, would rock the brief presidency of Jean Wood. As we will demonstrate in Chapter 6, the decade-old pension debate reveals much about the conflicting views within the English-Canadian movement. In this section, however, rather than addressing the substantive issues, we will focus on the organizational crisis they provoked. With McDonald's position on financial independence accepted by the AGM but not implemented, the pension issue, the constitutional issues, and the unresolved funding and accountability issues all converged. McDonald and Wood, and their respective supporters, continued to play out the conflict between the two competing coalitions.

Jean Wood, who had chaired the NAC Pension Committee in 1980–1, is quoted in a NAC press release dated 9 December 1980 as calling the Liberal government's proposal to allow home-makers to voluntarily contribute to the Canada Pension Plan (CPP) an 'inequitable and piecemeal' approach (*NAC Memo* [December 1980]:7). The press release informed NAC members that the Pension Committee planned to present its recommendations to the Ministry of Health and Welfare at a Pensions Conference scheduled for spring 1981. At the 11 April 1981 executive meeting, Wood and Lynn Sullivan reported having attended that conference, and laid out a plan for consulting member groups to revise NAC's Discussion Paper on Pension Reform.

The planning section of this first meeting of Wood's presidency saw a discussion as to how the AGM resolution on 75 per cent self-sufficiency was to be achieved. Regional representatives such as Jill Schooley wanted money for the regions for travel and telephone liaison. Farida Shaikh's opposition to the possible appointment of an executive secretary was recorded. Jean Wood reminded the executive that the total government funding requested ($296,000) would constitute 80 per cent dependence on government, in the face of the AGM-imposed goal of 75 per cent *independence* from government funding. She called for a strategy for fund-raising. Lynn McDonald and Farida Shaikh moved that NAC 'aim at 40% non-government funding this year, 50% for next year and 75% for the following year.' In general, most members seemed to sympathize with Caroline Ennis's view that the AGM had 'given us contradictory resolutions' that demanded that the executive do more things that cost more money, while warning it off the one source that could produce the funds required. Rakowski proposed having member groups undertake NAC's fund-raising as an alternative. A professional fund-raiser and a fund-raising committee were also proposed. In fact, a committee was struck to 'make preliminary investigations' into alternative funding sources. With this, the executive shelved the discussion.

The minutes of the 11 April meeting also document conflict over the internal division of labour resulting from NAC's new constitution. Shaikh objected to the status distinctions between table officers and other executive members, but most accepted the more complex structure, agreeing to elect committee chairs and to assign accountability for the resolutions and behaviour of committees to their chairs. Six organizational committees were struck (membership, Friends of NAC, AGM, permanent funding, finance, and editorial), with contested elections for three. Lynn McDonald was not elected to any committee. Five policy committees were listed and staffed (employment, social services, housing, justice, and constitution), and another, on dealings with the media, was listed but left unstaffed. Ironically, no pensions committee was struck, which would cause conflict at a later point. A systematic program to ensure executive members' accountability with regard to public statements was passed with some opposition. It required that (1) all communications and public contact be signed by three executive members; (2) all communications to ministers be signed by the president and co-signed by the chair of the relevant committee; (3) any communication developed outside the NAC office be submitted to it for the NAC files; and (4) the committees be responsible for answering policy questions 'in their fields.' Also at this meeting, a motion was passed to revise the mandate for NAC's house organ to something more in line with its budget, and the idea of seeking a grant to reinstate the magazine-quality *Status* was rejected.

Another debate at this meeting pertained to the status of AGM resolutions 'from the floor' and to the issue of the accountability of the executive to the member organizations through the AGM. The views of the majority were expressed in the following motion: 'should the legal opinion be that according to the constitution, AGM resolutions are *not* binding on the Executive, then we take immediate action to ensure that AGM resolutions are binding on the Executive.' Although there was an amendment outlining the procedures to be adopted when the AGM passed conflicting resolutions, the general motion on accountability passed with only two opposed (and two abstentions). (Farida Shaikh was to claim throughout the year that she represented and was answerable to CUPE and not to the AGM or to membership of NAC.) Conflict was also apparent in the discussion of the proper way of conducting executive meetings. Hacker and Porter suggested the use of a facilitator.[11] McDonald and Shaikh expressed the view that 'conflict is to be expected' and that it could be accommodated 'with goodwill.' The issue of conflict versus consensus would erupt through-out the year, as would the question of solidarity, understood as an adherence to certain norms governing public statements about conflicts internal to NAC.

The May and June meetings saw debate about the Advisory Coun-cil, which, once again, raised the question of the executive's account-ability to the AGM. According to the minutes of the 2 May meeting, the legal advice was that 'the obligation of the Executive is to deal with each [AGM] resolution/recommendation in some way,' but that that could mean 'anything from carrying it out to the letter to recom-mending no action at this time.' The executive was to resolve conflict-ing resolutions, accommodate realities of the budget, and so on. The executive concluded that it would not change the constitution to bind itself more tightly and, hence, that it had some room to manoeuvre in its relationship with the Advisory Council, despite the stringent AGM resolutions that banned contact with the council until it accepted an external review. It was decided that Jean Wood should join with presi-dents of other national women's groups to discuss how women ought to be represented to the government in the next decade. This approach would allow NAC to re-enter the federal arena of women's politics without appearing to go against the AGM resolutions.

Also at the 2 May meeting, the Permanent Funding Committee re-ported its plans to approach corporations and foundations for funding and to use the NAC Trust's status as a charitable organization for tax purposes to attract funds. (Neither plan was to bear fruit.) The report of a Pensions/Tax Committee was given by the president. (Since no such committee was reported in the 11 April executive minutes, it is possible that this was an ad hoc committee created by Wood.) The report outlined an extensive process of consultation, including re-gional pension meetings, for which funds had been requested from Minister of Health and Welfare Monique Bégin. The committee re-ported that it would also deal with non-pension concerns such as the tax system, child care, and disability 'on an issue and as-needed basis.' A territorial competition among executive policy committees was be-coming apparent at this meeting. Kathy Moggridge reported that the Employment Committee wanted to give the labour perspective on pensions. The tax issues also interested the Social Services Committee. It appeared that a conflict almost on the scale of the constitutional controversies could be in the offing. In essence, rather than being equally represented on all the committees, the two conflicting ideological groups had seized different committees, and hoped to use them as a basis for the claim to speak on behalf of the millions of women indirectly affiliated with NAC.

With the policy committees developing into a new ground for factional power plays, the fact that Lynn McDonald had not been elected to any committee responsibility marginalized her even further. The minutes of the 21 June executive meeting report that Jill Porter of the Constitution Committee protested on its behalf Lynn McDonald's statement in the June/July 1981 issue of *Canadian Forum*, which was quoted in the minutes as follows:

Women's organizations with their fragile inter-party compositions, have been sorely tried by the Constitution debate ... [NAC] was less effective than it could have been, not giving the leadership it might have in sponsoring public meetings, and lobbying only minimally. Thus it was up to an ad hoc group to organize the largest conference/protest on the constitution, after the Advisory Council failed a second time. Further ... [NAC's] Toronto Conference was the occasion of one of the worst abuses of the democratic process I've seen in organizational politics. [She then restates her version of the Connelly 'intervention.'] The Chairperson's version ... was subsequently adopted by the ... [NAC] Constitution Committee and executive, an action that raises even more questions.

Just as in January of that year, a motion to send letters regretting the event and 'setting the matter straight' focused the issues. This time, however, the motion included the executive's statement that it 'disassociates itself completely from the remarks of its Past-President and, indeed, not only does not endorse these remarks, but condemns them.'

The debate concerning solidarity around this motion illuminates clearly a division that now existed within the left- and radical-feminist coalition. Pat Hacker's view, addressed to McDonald, was that 'it violates our solidarity as an Executive [for you] to have done this, to have published this paragraph.' McDonald responded that she had simply stated the truth about what had happened: 'I think the dirty dealing should come out.' Shaikh stated her view that conflict was normal: 'Why should solidarity mean that we don't disagree with the decisions that the Executive makes. I am tired of hearing this. Anyone is entitled to say anything we damn well please.' Hacker then attacked what she perceived to be a double standard on Shaikh's part: 'If this were a labour union, we would not wash our dirty linen in public. I want a policy on this. This kind of thing cannot be allowed to go on. I want solidarity around this table.' Shaikh repeated her position: 'Anyone is entitled to say anything we damned please. We are not responsible to the Executive. We are responsible to our member groups. We have not signed any oath in blood.' Other members voiced their opinions as well: 'These paragraphs do not reflect the events as I recollect them' [Billings] and 'As a member of the Constitution Committee I feel I'm being made a victim ... this is not a private opinion, it's in print and in public; I feel that my character has been called into question' [Grills]. (It is worth noting that Hacker and Billings supported the entrenched Charter through the ad hoc committee and that McDonald and Shaikh opposed it.)

The motion to write letters correcting the record and to condemn McDonald's remarks was passed with eleven in favour, four opposed, and three abstentions. The debate raged on, however, with McDonald arguing, 'We need to protect minority as well as majority rights,' and 'why should the executive forbid you from talking when you've lost in the group?' Trudy Richardson's intervention suggested the classic position of cabinet secrecy and solidarity: 'We try to have a democratic procedure inside the organization. Everyone has a chance to say what they have in mind. After the vote is taken, the issue is decided. That is a democratic process.' Shaikh continued to reject a policy of silence and assured the executive her organization would also oppose it. The issue was closed, for the day, by a motion seeking to devise 'rules of conduct and behaviour' concerning executive members' rights to speak publicly about NAC. According to Billings, for her, this was 'an ethics issue; for others, a matter of political practice to be established by motion.' The profound differences on the questions of consensus, solidarity, secrecy, and the rights of a minority after it has lost an issue went far beyond the specific matters raised by McDonald's actions.

Over time, as the executive developed into a more organized body whose members represented NAC rather than the member associations that had nominated them, its political culture became more important. The collective view that Lynn McDonald had acted without due regard for executive solidarity would set the scene for the intense suspicion shown by some to Jean Wood's initiatives concerning NAC's pensions policy. The humiliation of McDonald and Shaikh would be avenged in the explosion that met Wood's presentation of her committee's position paper on pensions, which included a role for private pension plans. Also evident in the account of this conflict, however, is the fact that some members of the executive were beginning to care far more about the integrity of NAC and its political processes than about the factions represented or the issues in dispute. This commitment would be the basis on which the institutionalization of NAC could begin to take place in the years following this transitional period. It also reflected the emergence of integrative feminism as the intellectual basis for NAC's role as a parliament of women.

Another period of missing executive minutes veils events for much of the remainder of Wood's brief term as president. The June NAC Memo reports plans for a mid-year meeting in October in St John's, Newfoundland, on the subject of pensions, as well as a planned executive meeting for September and a fund-raising campaign. (The latter was necessary to alleviate the financial crisis brought on by expanded activities, especially in relation to regionalization, and by the attempt to diversify funding sources.) The parties to the conflict continued to be involved in their respective committees, and a new committee was announced – the Committee on Native Indian Women, to be chaired by Caroline Ennis. In fact, the picture that emerges is a hectic one, with too many stimuli in the environment for NAC to respond to properly without, at the least, striking priorities or, ideally, a larger, more professional staff. And that, in turn, would require more money.

A Past President's Report from McDonald to NAC Member Groups and Executive Members, dated 15 November 1981, saw McDonald taking her accumulated grievances to the membership. Identifying Jean Wood as 'one of the instigators of the non-confidence motion against me,' she states that, 'having made the commitment to work with Jean, I now feel I have to report back that there is no willingness on her part to work with me.' McDonald then lists her complaints: a cancelled executive meeting after the mid-year in October 1981: a 'mishandling' of the controversy over the 'notwithstanding' clause[12] in the constitutional debates; and the lack of 'a clear priority of pressing for the most crucial aspect of pension reform for women in Canada – improving the CPP to pay decent benefits.'

A series of other memos, now from Marilyn Keddy (Maritime representative), Lynn McDonald, and Kathy Moggridge (vice-president), carry the narrative. Their November memo, entitled 'An Urgent Memo to Member Groups on Pensions and Procedures,' expressed concern about the 'inability of the NAC Executive to function' and called for a special meeting to determine NAC's policy on pensions before the AGM. It attacked Jean Wood (placing emphasis on her position as an assistant vice-president of Manulife) for transmitting a discussion paper that 'takes no position on funding' (that is, CPP versus private pension funds) and challenged that this conflicted with the position of other feminist pension 'experts,' such as Louise Dulude and Monica Townsend, who consider 'that improving the Canada Pension Plan is the single most important thing that can be done to ensure decent incomes for women on retirement.' The memo accused Wood in only a thinly veiled way of conflict of interest for inviting the Canada Life and Health Insurance Associations to attend NAC meetings in Toronto and St John's, while not inviting unions with positions on pensions. It continued: 'Nor has the employment committee been invited. Nor were some of the speakers suggested by the employment committee ever approached.' The explicit allegation that 'two active people on the pensions committee work in the private pensions industry [which] opposes the expansion of the CPP' is the handle on which the three signatories (Keddy, McDonald, and Moggridge) called for a special meeting to be held on 9 January 1982 to allow for constitutional amendments to introduce conflict-of-interest guidelines for executive members. The agenda they proposed was to accomplish the following:

1. Establish NAC priorities on the pensions issue, especially the crucial issue of improvement of CPP ...
2. Consider conflict of interest regulations for the NAC executive (these would have to be made a Constitutional amendment at the next AGM);
3. Ask for an accounting by relevant executive members of breaches of NAC procedures ...
4. Establish a code of conduct for running NAC for the next while (including the same rules applying to all members, ending the incivilities and restoring impartiality in chairing).

Attached to the memo was a sheet with the heading 'Some Unpleasant Questions That Have to Be Faced,' followed by a long list of hurts and alleged wrongs, and this conclusion: 'There are rumours that NAC is about to collapse from its internal difficulties. Let's prove them wrong by frankly facing up to the problems and working out a constructive solution.'

The minutes of the Special Meeting of the Executive held on 20 February 1982 show that those who had called for a special meeting were not present. (Lynn McDonald did, however, join the regular executive meeting the next day.) Regional Representative Jill Schooley reported, 'We feel we were all used by members of the Executive. There was a motion re Special Meeting. The meeting request was withdrawn.' Terry Padgham asked 'What is the worst possible case of what can happen at the AGM? Will we be defending ourselves against a tribunal? I think it's inappropriate in a voluntary organization to do that. There's no place on the floor of this AGM for personal complaints.' Jean Wood and others expressed concern about the possibility that the upcoming AGM, which was to celebrate NAC's tenth anniversary, could turn into a debacle. Bev LeFrançois felt that 'we were always being watched in our committees and the message was that we never did enough.' She believed that 'there were personal agendas to disrupt the group this year,' and that 'those people will want a big fight on the floor of the AGM.' Rakowski argued that the issue was the executive – 'who it's elected by and who it's responsible to.'

The minutes show that the participants of this special meeting tried to develop an understanding of the crisis the organization was undergoing. Hošek expressed concern about the politicization of all issues, many of which she believed were not inherently partisan at all. She concluded, 'I have problems with the Right/Left analysis. It simplifies/ distorts issues and if this organization is hospitable only to women with a specific political perspective, it should say so openly.' She also lamented the growing tendency to view middle-class or successful women as not legitimate participants in NAC. Others commented on the problems that arose from the tendency to equate disagreement with a breach of solidarity. With regard to the combined issues of government funding and the limits of volunteerism, the participants of this meeting decided to tell the AGM delegates that they had 'created an impossible task.' The fact that delegates could impose positions on the executive but did 'not perceive themselves to have any accountability to NAC for issues they vote for' was a cold shower of reality. Wood believed that many executive members had 'been timid for fear of being labelled.' She urged other women to take responsibility for their own positions at the AGM.

Gradually, the group also began to comprehend the contradictions in the organization they had attempted to steer. Grills expressed the following opinion: 'We are nominated by one group but elected by the whole organization. So we are responsible to *all* member groups, not just to the one which nominated us. Once elected, our responsibility was to the Executive for executing matters and to AGM policy decisions for policy.' Wood contributed this: 'My understanding of the role of President is to see that policies of the AGM are executed through the committee structure – in the interim, my job is to manage the process.' This was summarized in a motion to be transmitted by the president to the AGM: 'That the Executive of NAC is responsible to AGM on policy issues and resolutions and to the democratically taken consensus of Executive as a whole on operational and policy matters between AGMs.' The issue of executive solidarity, however, remained unresolved.

The conflicts erupted again at the regular executive meeting held the following day (21 February). The minutes report discussion of the fact that, constitutionally, Lynn McDonald, as past president, should be in charge of the elections process at the AGM, but that most of the executive did not trust her in this role. At the 1981 AGM, several resolutions pertaining to elections had been passed. One of them prohibited voting before noon on the Saturday of the weekend meeting. Technically, the regulations embodied by these resolutions had been passed unconstitutionally, because no notice had been given to the membership, as required by the constitution. Hošek and others were determined none the less that they would be observed. However, the 1981 AGM had also voted to allow a limited form of campaigning. McDonald had drafted guidelines that permitted candidates one mailing 'to ensure a reasonable dissemination of information to member groups at a cost that will not prohibit potential candidates from seeking a position.' Although this resolution was no more 'illegal' than the vote-timing resolution, the executive passed the motion that 'in order to adhere to our constitution, we will continue [the] policy of no campaigning.'

The group had, in effect, decided to take charge of the AGM process in order to prevent a repetition of resolutions from the floor that could bind the organization. Indeed, they agreed that there would be 'no resolutions from the floor. No Amendments from the floor, just acceptance or rejections. Committees will move acceptance of their whole report, and move support of their recommendations.' McDonald and Shaikh closed the meeting with a restatement of their grievances: 'I really resent the implication that I can't do my job' (McDonald) and 'I agreed to do media for the AGM. I cleared 10 days from my job to do it. I got here Friday and was told by Betsy [Carr] I was taken off the Media Committee. I am very irritated at this and resent it. I want to register a protest' (Shaikh).

Denouement

The 1982 AGM had two things going for it. First, it was to celebrate NAC's tenth anniversary, which would allow the survivors of the era of trouble and strife to emphasize the ceremonial and minimize the old conflicts. Founding mothers and ex-presidents rallied around to celebrate and to ensure NAC's survival. Second, some of the founding mothers had recruited Doris Anderson to assume the presidency. Her new status as a popular hero of the English-Canadian women's movement was sufficient to inhibit other challengers. In Laura Sabia's words, 'She was chosen for a particular reason ... she had done a magnificent job (at the CACSW) ... she was controversial ... and we knew she was good' (personal interview with Chris Appelle, 10 January 1986). She was also acceptable to both factions because she had had little to do with the organized movement before joining the Advisory Council, having concentrated her efforts as a feminist on *Chatelaine*.

At the AGM, outgoing president Jean Wood reported that four pensions seminars had been held across the country; the discussion paper on pensions had been revised to include a discussion of CPP improvement; and a very successful and popular pensions kit and slide show had been produced. Louise Dulude entered the NAC policy arena promoting the concept of pensions for home-makers. The AGM passed a resolution (which bypassed the Pensions Committee and emerged from the Employment Workshop) that would reform the Canadian pension system as follows:

a) to include all homemakers (whether or not they have young children) in the C/QPPs; if the homemaker is taking care of a child less than seven or dependent disabled family member, this inclusion should be subsidized by all participants to the C/QPP; if there are no young children or dependent disabled family members, this should be paid for by the homemaker's spouse;
b) to amplify the C/QPP so that its benefits would amount to 50% rather than 25% of previous earnings up to the average industrial wage;
c) employers should be encouraged to provide supplemental coverage over and above that provided by this expanded system; they should not be allowed to opt out of any part of the C/QPP.

The policy implications of this victory for a fully pro-statist NAC position on pensions will be examined in Chapter 5.

NAC had survived its internal conflicts and would develop into a more firmly based institution under the leadership of Anderson and, later, Chaviva Hošek. Some of the survivors from the McDonald and Wood executives continued to be active in NAC and began to apply the lessons they had learned there as new issues threatened to revive old conflicts. One of those lessons was that no single ideological faction or coalition of factions was strong enough to take NAC over completely. Women from different partisan and feminist points of view learned that they had to find ways to work together within the organization, or abandon the dream of a parliament of women. That dream, moreover, was beginning to take on a life of its own. Despite all the conflicts, at the end of the transitional era, NAC was to emerge larger, more skilled, and better supported than it had been at the outset. Although only a few of the questions raised during this era were resolved definitively, NAC had moved to a new organizational plateau. A new generation of feminists were entering the movement, and they took for granted the existence and functioning of NAC. It was at this point that the process of institutionalization truly began.

Notes

1 The role of regional representative was, however, instituted; it was based on the overambitious assumption that one woman could represent an area the size of France or Germany.

2 The minutes for some meetings from this period read as if two different executives were operating. For example, on the first and second days of a two-day meeting, the executive was often composed of different personnel, with some overlapping of key figures, and discussed different issues.

3 In a TV interview conducted by Jill Vickers at the 1987 AGM, Joanne Doucette of the Disabled Women's Network (DAWN) made the comment that 'They ought to have translation to render NAC policies into words of one syllable.'

4 The ad hoc committee on the constitution, with no public funding, was free of the restraints that might have been imposed on NAC if the funding had been granted.

5 Since institutions, in this view, are seen as invariably bureaucratic, the notion of a feminist institution is a contradiction in terms. Ferguson (1984:215), however, provides an understanding of a representative hierarchy in which members at each level would be selected and empowered from below.

6 Because some executive members were opposed to the honouring of individual women in commemoration of this anniversary, the ad hoc committee was formed to determine what NAC's member organizations considered appropriate.

7 This claim appeared on NAC brochures and on the cover of *Status*.

8 The minutes of the next executive meeting record a meeting on 13 February before the conference convened by the ad hoc constitutional committee with Huguette Labelle of the Department of the Secretary of State to discuss NAC's funding.

9 The rationale appended to the motion included the comment 'By taking government funds, we are simply drawing on the account to which we contribute [as taxpayers] on a regular and extensive basis.' (AGM Minutes, 13–16 March 1981).

10 Although they received far less attention, two other motions from the Finance Workshop were passed. The first committed NAC to an expenses pool for all meetings 'in order to lessen the financial burden on groups and individuals outside of central Canada.' The expenses to be pooled would include travel, accommodation, and child-care costs. The second resolved that 'the NAC executive allocate portions of the budget (in % terms) to each activity provided for in the constitution, so that limited funds do not entirely eliminate a function of the organization' (AGM Minutes, 13–16 March 1981).

11 The 2–3 May 1981 meeting of the executive saw Carmen Paquette acting as facilitator on the second day.

12 Having won in April 1981 a satisfactory wording of an equal rights clause (Section 28) in the draft Charter of Rights and Freedoms, Canadian women were appalled to learn that the federal government, compelled by the Supreme Court in September to reach agreement with the provinces prior to patriation, had traded away their equality guarantees to gain provincial consent. In the November accord, a notwithstanding clause was introduced that would allow provincial legislatures to override the provisions of the Charter, including Section 28. Another extensive lobbying effort, coordinated by the ad hoc committee, was required to force the premiers to remove the override from Section 28 (Hošek 1983; Kome, 1983).

4 A New Parliament of Women: Institutionalizing NAC, 1982–1988

In this chapter, we explore the institutionalization of NAC. In the process, we try to uncover how NAC, which entered the decade weakened by internal conflicts and external crises, could have become, by the end of the 1980s, the central organization of the women's movement facing the federal state – as Susan Phillips (1990) puts it, the 'one superordinate federation' able to coordinate, if not to control, the movement's activities. Phillips argues that the integration of the English-Canadian movement into a single network facilitated by NAC 'is a basis for movement longevity and political power because the potential for coalition formation is extensive' (95). We argue that NAC was able to play the role of central coordinator and facilitator because it had crossed the threshold of successful institutionalization with the recognition that no single ideological group or coalition could dominate it. The forces set in motion within NAC during its period of conflict combined with the general political environment in which NAC operated made the institutionalization of NAC as the stable focus for a multi-generational movement the best possible option for the English-Canadian movement.

During the period of institutionalization, NAC had to come to terms with four organizational initiatives inherited from the 1970s. First, in order to make good on the claim that it represented women better than any other political institution, it had to develop regional representation, an initiative that proved to be far more expensive – and far more effective – than originally anticipated. Second, it had to try to re-establish relations with the FFQ and Québec and to undertake measures such as simultaneous translation at AGMs in order to become more 'francophone-friendly.' These two mandates put an end to the view that dedicated volunteers could, with hard work, carry out all NAC's activities, and revived the goal of employing paid staff to perform 'professional' tasks, such as lobbying and producing the NAC magazine. The fourth issue inherited from the 1970s was that of NAC's dependency on government funding: As its activities and obligations grew, its dependency grew. This dependency would continue until the end of the decade, when the Mulroney government greatly reduced NAC's funding. The organization then developed what was to become an effective program of direct-mail fund-raising.

There were also important changes in NAC's environment that posed new challenges. A rapid mobilization of new segments of the female population across Canada, including groups as diverse as racial minorities, immigrants, prostitutes, and women with disabilities, doubled NAC's membership virtually overnight. The politics of equality seeking, moreover, quickened in tempo as the Charter of Rights and Freedoms provided a new focus for mobilization. The infrastructure of the women's movement expanded throughout the country, with rape crisis centres, battered women's shelters, and women's centres appearing in small towns and rural areas and within ethnic communities. This new mobilization and rapid expansion meant a greater general dependency on government funding and new controversies about NAC's purposes and modes of operation. At the same time, with the election of a Progressive Conservative (PC) government in 1984, the long Liberal era during which NAC had developed came to an end. The activities of right-wing backlash groups such as REAL Women and attacks on NAC by groups such as the National Citizens' Coalition and One Hundred Huntley Street created a context for defensive mobilization.

As we have stated, it is our thesis that achieving equality for women is a multigenerational project. We have also argued that the key strategy emerging from this premise is the creation of coordinating institutions to link the successive waves of women that are mobilized over time and space. Historically, it is clear that the only structures capable of achieving political objectives over time are institutions. And although the notion of the power of the individual is sanctioned by our culture, power is in fact typically exercised by people collectively. As Danielle Heb (CSN Status of Women) has argued, the important thing about women's power is that it be understood as a collective phenomenon (CRIAW 1987).

In this analysis, we use the term *institution* in reference to an instrument of social organization that exercises collective power over a number of generations. Most of us grow up seeing our society's major institutions as natural or inevitable. Indeed, a major part of feminist analysis has been devoted to deconstructing those institutions and revealing them to be arbitrary human creations that have oppressed women. Given this perspective, why would women even consider the creation of institutions to serve feminist purposes? Mary Douglas (1986:112) provides a clue: 'A pattern of given complexity, once stabilized, uses less energy than was required to bring it into being.' Institutions, seen as stabilized 'patterns of given complexity,' permit the perpetuation of social groupings, and of their 'legitimizing' ideas, over time and space with a minimum expenditure of energy. In their stability and seeming permanence, they become 'naturalized.' As Douglas puts it, 'What is excluded from the idea of institution ... is any purely instrumental or provisional practical arrangement that is recognized as such' (46).[1]

Distinguished Canadian feminists Mary O'Brien and Dorothy Smith have contributed important insights for deconstructing powerful patriarchal institutions. To O'Brien (1981:33), institutions are structures invented by men basically to transcend death by permitting their purposes to outlive them: 'Men have always sought principles of continuity outside of natural continuity.' O'Brien saw women as 'not needing' artificial devices for continuity, because they could send their purposes into the future directly through the children they bore and reared. She also observed that most of the institutions we have experienced have been structured on principles of men's exploitation of women and children (and of other men). Dorothy Smith (1979:13) identifies institutions even more explicitly with domination and oppression. To her, institutions are 'a complex of relations' forming 'part of the ruling apparatus, organized around a distinctive function.' She states that 'institutional structures are set up to organize and control and they do it well' This negative connotation of 'institutionalization' is encountered frequently in analyses of the women's movement. In some instances, institutionalization becomes synonymous with co-optation: Nancy Adamson and her colleagues (1988:181) define it as 'the way feminist demands for change are reconstructed and couched in terms of the existing institutions and ideologies,' and express the concern that 'the women's movement has become overly institutionalized and that this may undermine our ability to achieve change in the future'(20). In other instances, *institution* becomes synonymous with *bureaucracy* or *oligarchy*. In short, institutions have a bad name with feminists, and this has made the task of developing strategy for a multigenerational movement more difficult.

Douglas's analysis of how institutions are stabilized and Gerda Lerner's account (1986) of the centuries-long process of the creation of patriarchal institutions have begun to challenge such reactions against building feminist institutions for a multigenerational movement. In the past two decades, feminists have had the experience of themselves creating structures that have become institutions rather than being passive inhabitants of those created by others. They have witnessed new members coming into the organizations that they helped create (and shed ideological blood over) and accepting them as 'natural.' They have also seen younger women rebel against features of the structures they created, and they have begun to understand more profoundly the process of organizing women's collective power over time and space.

In this account of the institutionalization of NAC, we will stress two things. First, we will identify the patterns of interaction that were being established, especially as NAC's trajectory as a lobby group came into conflict with its development as a movement institution. Second, we will explore the legitimizing ideas that participants in NAC built up over this period, especially around the claim of being the group most representative of Canadian women – that is, of being a parliament of women.

Getting NAC 'Back on Track'

The energies of the executive during the early years of this period were spent getting NAC 'back on track.' Its various crises and conflicts had shaken confidence in NAC within government. According to the minutes of the executive meeting of 17–18 April 1982, the Women's Program, in particular, considered 1982–3 a 'make or break year for NAC.' Doris Anderson describes the situation she found within NAC in 1982 as follows:

When I became president, the organization had gone through an awful lot of turmoil and both sides thought I was acceptable. They were looking for someone from the outside who was not from either camp. One camp comprises the 'expansionists' who were accused of left-wing political union domination, while the other group were considered old liners and contained more business women. There were still people on the executive from both camps. (Personal interview with Chris Appelle, 17 September 1985)

Perhaps it was just as well that Anderson did not fully understand the nature of the conflict when she took NAC on. Certainly, her actions in the first year, as recorded in the minutes, suggest that she did not believe she was 'taking sides' when she supported funded regional representatives in all provinces, undertook to pay professional staff, sought to move the NAC office to Ottawa, pursued government funding well beyond the 45 per cent target, and downgraded *Status* and eventually transferred its production to staff who were not represented on the executive at all. Rather than worrying about ideological sides, she chose to apply her considerable personal skills to implementing constitutional reform in NAC and reorganizing the NAC office. In short, she was the first NAC president who was forced by circumstances to care more about the organization than about any substantive issue. She brought to NAC significant personal resources, including a pragmatic style, a good rapport with the media, sound management skills, a knowledge of how Ottawa worked, and a commitment to equality without an obvious involvement in any of the ideological camps – a quality that inspired a sense of trust and a belief in her authenticity.

Anderson had little sense of NAC as an emerging institution. To her, its role was to influence governments and to educate women. But she did not have a doctrinaire view of the best methods to use in either task. Her experience as editor of *Chatelaine* gave her an understanding of the transformative approach aimed at by some of the younger feminist women. Her experience within the Liberal party had soured her on official politics enough that she did not naïvely trust 'the fellows on the inside' to always deliver what they had promised. The defeat of the Liberals made Ottawa a new ball game in any event.

Anderson's first concern was to get a revised NAC constitution in place, to develop a plan for NAC activities that would allow her to seek increased funding from the Women's Program, and to develop structures that would protect NAC against future repetitions of the troubles it had just gone through. In order to achieve the latter objective, Anderson enhanced and formalized the roles of the AGM, the policy committees, and the regional representatives. The recrafting of the AGM was intended to establish it as the body to approve policy positions in NAC. Neutral chairing was to be ensured; resolutions and election materials were to be circulated well in advance. Only emergency resolutions would be received from the floor. Formal rules of procedure would be stressed in order to avoid the manipulations that had characterized the period of conflict. According to the minutes of

17–18 April meeting of the executive, regional meetings to discuss policy and a professionalized AGM office were discussed. Efforts were also made to improve the atmosphere of the executive meetings. People's needs were of concern. Anderson and Macpherson organized a series of Saturday night executive dinners, often at their own homes, to improve human relationships. As president, Anderson became ex officio chair of a burgeoning number of committees, although particular committees remained places of refuge for dissidents from both camps.

The minutes of the 3–4 December 1982 executive meeting show that, by that time, many of the newcomers were convinced that NAC's future effectiveness depended on moving its base to Ottawa, away from the fractious Toronto movement and to the site of the federal government. Two motions were recorded: one, 'that the recommendation that NAC move to Ottawa and reorganize [the] office to include an executive co-ordinator be put before the next AGM,' and the other, 'that consideration be given by the AGM to an alternate proposal to have a bilingual liaison base with one or more staff in Ottawa and that the main office be outside Ottawa.' An extensive discussion throughout the fall suggests that Anderson's concerns included the inadequacy of the existing staff, especially the office's lack of capacity in French. Anderson pushed for a more professional (some said bureaucratic) approach. The debate at the 23 October meeting saw some arguing that 'grass-roots representation and lobbying are equally important considerations,' while others saw 'the possibility of co-option' as a danger in the move. Concerns were expressed about the jobs of individual staff members and about the diminished role for volunteers if there were a professional office in Ottawa. Anderson's informal tally for the minutes of that meeting was thirteen executive members in favour of a move to Ottawa, and seven opposed or undecided. A schedule was developed for constitutional changes and both the office changes and the constitutional amendments went to the 1983 AGM. (The crisis at the previous AGM had been so serious that some constitutional changes had been forgotten – simply lost in the shuffle.)

The efforts of the 1982–3 executive to get NAC back on track were largely successful. Great care was taken in preparing for the AGM. The *NAC Memo* was used to signal planned constitutional changes, and the NAC Constitutional Review Committee, under chair Wendy Lawrence, operated an open process that received much positive feedback. The executive's plans were successful in that significant constitutional changes to stabilize the organization were achieved at the AGM. Some of the old fire was roused, however, over the issue of moving the NAC office to Ottawa. With a team of neutral parliamentarians chairing, the executive steered through amendments to the constitution that gave recognition of two official languages, broadened the statement of purposes, noted that organizations needed to support NAC policies to be eligible for membership, established a 'co-operating organization' category, specified that only individuals could be Friends of NAC, gave an initiating role to the executive in setting fees, and altered the structure of the executive and the AGM.

The new statement of purpose and objectives read:

The purpose and objectives of NAC shall be to initiate and work for improvement in the status of women by:
1. actions designed to change legislation, attitudes, customs and practices;
2. evaluating and advocating changes to benefit women, including measures proposed by the Royal Commission on the Status of Women and those adopted by NAC;
3. encouraging the formation of, and communication and co-operation among, organizations interested in improving the status of women in Canada;
4. exchanging information with member organizations and other interested persons or groups, and providing information to the public about the current status of women and recommended changes for improvement.
(NAC Constitution, March 1983)

The breadth of these objectives shows clearly that NAC had emerged from the shadow of the royal commission. NAC's constitution makers saw it as an organization that would stimulate activity on all fronts of women's politics.

Two regional representatives (one from Southern Ontario and one from Northern BC/Yukon) were added to the executive, reducing the percentage of the executive from the Toronto area. (NAC had still never elected a president living outside Ontario, and most officers were Toronto-based.) The AGM's activities had been been expanded and clarified. The executive's role was clearly to 'execute' and 'coordinate,' but only the AGM was to approve policy, legitimizing NAC's self-image as a parliament of women. The policy process was to allow member groups the opportunity for input and debate, and committees were specifically to be held tightly responsible to the organization by having an executive member as chair. In short, the twin demons of partisan conflict and excessive ideological contest had been put back into the bottle for a few years with a tighter structure, more clearly established lines of responsibility, and a better sense of accountability. Anderson's plan to move the NAC office to Ottawa received a rougher ride than the other constitutional changes. The meeting at which the resolution appeared ended up completely deadlocked, with a tie vote that no recount could dislodge. The second plan, already developed within the executive, was put in play; a satellite office with a bilingual 'government relations officer' and a part-time secretary would undertake lobbying in Ottawa. The main office, soon with an enlarged and upgraded staff, would remain in Toronto. It would be easy to see this decision as a resurgence of the old fractious spirit emerging to thwart Anderson's plans. In fact, our observation of that meeting identified three concerns that tipped the balance: (1) a concern about job loss for Toronto-based staff who could not move; (2) a concern that NAC's individuality would be obscured in Ottawa, especially since there were plans to share facilities with other feminist organizations; and (3) a concern that the newcomers did not understand that NAC was about much more than lobbying and that its ability to coordinate the movement and respond to developments among grass-roots groups would be diminished if it became too preoccupied with day-to-day responses to the federal government. The first two are normal human concerns. The third, however, reflected a sense that NAC needed to be constantly refreshed from the grass roots if it was to play a vital role over a long period of time. One speaker argued that the office needed to be in a centre 'where there are a lot of feminists.' While some took this simply as an apologia for the self-regarding view that Toronto is the centre of the world, its message for an institutionalized NAC was clear.

The remainder of Anderson's tenure as president and the period during which Chaviva Hošek held the office were years of expansion, organizational stability, and relative affluence. In 1982, NAC had 200 members. In 1986, there were 458 organizational members, with 900 Friends of NAC. A budget of $296,000 in 1982 (more than four times the 1977 budget) increased to $679,476 by 1986 (*Status of Women News/ Status* 1973–85; *NAC Memo* 1980–5; AGM report 1986). A region-by-region breakdown of NAC member groups also portrays a picture of a healthy organization from 'sea to sea to sea' (see Table 4.1). With more than 60 member groups in British Columbia, 47 in the three Prairie provinces, 40 in Québec, 50 in the Atlantic provinces, and 5 in the

TABLE 4.1
Breakdown of NAC member groups, 1985–6

Total group members 458*

National groups 70

Breakdown of regional groups:

Yukon	3	Ontario	186
Northwest Territories	2	Québec	40
British Columbia	60	New Brunswick	5
Alberta	28	Nova Scotia	20
Saskatchewan	13	Prince Edward Island	4
Manitoba	6	Newfoundland/Labrador	21

Source: Membership Committee Report, AGM, 1986

* In 1987, the total rose to more than 500 member groups.

North, NAC had very quickly become one of the most throughly representative women's organizations in Canada (Membership Committee Report, AGM, 1986).

What did NAC look like on this new organizational plateau? The Program Submission prepared for the Women's Program of the Secretary of State for 1985–6 gives one picture. (As anyone who has solicited a government grant will know, there is some measure of inflation in all such plans, and applicants may request what they know funders to favour. None the less, the submission will help give a general picture.) The preliminary statement identifies several significant features of the organization. First, regional representation, as well as its heavy costs, is stressed. Doris Anderson had budgeted for regional travel and communication in 1984–5. It was becoming apparent that the true costs of regionalization were far greater than had been expected and that the results, in terms of new members, were extraordinary. Second, the plan reports that a personnel committee to deal with staff issues had been added, making five standing administrative committees. Also reported for 1984–5 were nine policy committees: justice, employment, Indian women, survival, social services, health, pensions, pornography, and a committee to supervise activities related to the federal election.

The 1984 election had provided NAC, under Chaviva Hošek's leadership, with the opportunity to stage a high-profile event on national television. NAC organized a bilingual televised public debate, which took place on 15 August, in Toronto. Notables of the women's movement asked questions of the three leaders, and feminist issues were seen to be 'on the agenda' of the three parties in the election campaign. The debate and NAC's two high-profile presidents had begun to change the nature of the organization's activities. First, more and more women's groups sought to join. Second, NAC was swamped with media requests for commentary. The lobbying focus that was proceeding quietly in Ottawa came to be overshadowed by NAC's new public face.

The Program Submission for 1985–6 argued the need for more-extensive and more-sophisticated staff support. Using a fund-raising consultant, NAC had begun direct mailings in 1984, keeping true at least to the spirit of financial independence, if not to its letter. Money was being shifted to regional activities and membership solicitation, usually using executive members as speakers. The mid-year meetings were now seen as a way to ensure 'that women from regions other than Southern Ontario become more familiar with the working of NAC and that NAC work with women of the different regions of Canada around current and specific issues identified by these women' (NAC Program Submission to the Secretary of State for 1985–86:21). The budgetary allotment proposed for regional activities (including the mid-year meeting) was $62,875, with more than half going to regional representatives. The comparable budget for all of the policy committees and the lobbying program was set at $70,000. (The explosion of issues being dealt with at this time will be explored in detail in Chapters 6 and 7.) The submission proposed an executive coordinator, an administrative assistant for committees, an administrative assistant for regions and membership, a publications/bookkeeper position, a Toronto receptionist/typist, a parliamentary liaison officer, and an Ottawa secretary. The amount of $498,987 was requested from the Women's Program, and $411,000 was received. (Translation money for a bilingual AGM was received from another branch of the department.) The salaries proposed were not 'flat'; that is, there was to be a significant difference between the salaries of 'professional' staff and those of 'support' staff. None the less, they were all below the going rate for either Toronto or Ottawa, suggesting that an element of mandatory 'volunteerism' persisted.

The NAC that emerged under Doris Anderson's direction was organized, very active, growing constantly in membership, high profile, and effective in both public education and lobbying. None the less, a new set of contradictions also seemed to be developing at this new level of expansion and activity. NAC now had executive and staff members who cared more about the organization and its health than about any specific policy goal. NAC's new prominence in the media also made it a target for the many groups of newly mobilized women who 'wanted in,' as well as for right-wing groups who wanted to stop NAC, stop government funding of feminism, and, if possible, stop feminism.

The Great Leap Forward: The Expansion Examined

From the 1984 to 1987, NAC underwent the most rapid expansion of the period under study. Our analysis of the groups that joined NAC during these years reveals the trends in the broader women's movement and in the official political system that contributed to this expansion. We will consider several of the basic trends within the English-Canadian women's movement first, starting with that of networking among women's service and advocacy groups. Such groups had started to expand beyond the metropolitan centres and into smaller communities and rural areas, and many of them could not survive without funding from the state. Some of the groups from smaller communities joined NAC on their own; others joined or helped form networks, which then joined NAC. (In some cases, both the close-to-home group and the network joined NAC.) The development of such networking umbrella organizations to link small service and advocacy groups within a region or province was an important trend. In the 1970s, 'Network Nellie' was formed to link women's centres across the country, alleviating some of the isolation suffered by the centres in small communities and allowing for an exchange of information. The notion that grass-roots groups can operate without much structure is essentially an urban view. Although women in a collective in a city might not be officially linked to like-minded women in other groups, they encounter one another informally all the time. In more sparsely settled regions, feminists can feel much more isolated. They may find themselves sharing services such as battered women's shelters with non-feminists or even anti-feminists, and may even become visible targets for their feminism. In such circumstances, the value of networking organizations is especially important.

Another major trend in the English-Canadian women's movement that led to increases in NAC membership was the increased involvement of women's caucuses within labour unions. This reflected the continuing rise in women's participation in the paid workforce and their formation of sex-specific structures within unions and occupational groups. As Heather Jon Maroney (1987:87) has argued, 'By the end of the seventies, working-class feminism in Canada had become a distinct current in the women's movement.' Feminists involved in trade unions, often on the staffs of established unions, also developed cross-union structures, such as Organized Working Women (OWW) and the Equal Pay Coalition (EPC), which have joined NAC. Maroney explains that 'Trade union feminists are caught in a contradictory situation. Their position inside the labour union is vulnerable and their room to manoeuvre depends upon the extent of feminist radicalization and trade union militancy of women in the rank and file' (91). The support by NAC leaders of many high-profile women's strikes and NAC's new-found prominence under Anderson and Hošek made it attractive to union-based women as a point of affiliation with the expanding movement.

Susan Phillips (1990:94) has noted the absence of pan-Canadian organizations with an explicit ideology of socialist or radical feminism. She also argues that 'there are relatively few ties between women's organizations and unions' (124), and concludes that the movement fails to represent the interests of working-class women. By contrast, many observers of and central participants in NAC argue that NAC makes economic issues, which are so central to working-class women, a high priority. Our study of NAC membership in 1987–8 revealed the following member groups: eight inter-union associations (such as the Equal Pay Coalition), two labour federations, the women's section or bureau of seven major labour federations, three additional national unions, nine provincial and local unions, and five francophone union caucuses and inter-union groups from Québec. Such affiliations clearly facilitated the involvement of union women in the movement. In addition, NAC's involvement in numerous policy coalitions with the Canadian Labour Congress (CLC) suggests that the middle-class label so often pinned on NAC by academic feminists may be unwarranted. Moreover, many women with left-feminist views were visible and influential within NAC during the period studied.

At this time, another major trend in the women's movement was the progressive radicalization and involvement of organizations representing traditional women's occupations such as nursing and home economics. The Registered Nurses' Association of Ontario and Nurses for Social Responsibility are two examples. Some women teachers' associations, both provincial and local, had been radicalized and had become involved much earlier, but a number of new and local groups were now becoming affiliated. (This trend was uneven, taking some time to work its way through the entire profession. Its progress has perhaps been most rapid in Québec.)

As noted earlier, a dramatic mobilization of women was also taking place during this period around the issues of sexual harassment, sexual violence, pornography, and the representation of women in the media. New groups, often involving young women, and networks of groups, were forming at a rapid rate. The high level of anger that surrounded these issues came into the NAC arena with the entry of these groups during the expansionary period. Service, self-help, and advocacy groups dealing with child sexual abuse and incest were also on the rise.

Yet another trend was the involvement in the movements of segments of the female population that had been little touched by feminist organizing – for example, immigrant women, visible-minority women, prostitutes, and women with disabilities. Jon Leah Hopkins, who was instrumental in leading NAC to begin to recognize its own racism, began attending meetings of the executive in 1984 as an observer. Groups that had joined previously, such as the Canadian Congress of Black Women, now demanded real participation. Ethnic associations with feminist caucuses joined. Some of these groups would not have existed without government funding; certainly, the Disabled Women's Network (DAWN) found it difficult to operate even with government support. In many instances, these groups had to fight a battle on two fronts – that is, to establish their right to participate fully, first within NAC and then within society at large.

A final trend contributing to membership growth was the increased visibility of lesbians. Lesbians had always been present in NAC, but the formation of groups such as the National Lesbian Forum began the process of their demanding explicit support from NAC for lesbian rights.

Some important counter-trends were also developing during this period, and they are evidenced to some degree by the following: Although 140 new groups affiliated with NAC in the period 1986–8, the same years saw the departure from NAC (or the complete disappearance as organizations) of 25 groups. Several factors were drawing women away from activity in autonomous women's groups. First, the issue of self-government was becoming the primary goal of many native women. Achieving reform of the discriminatory features of the Indian Act seemed to signal the end of a common cause between native and white women. Women of colour had begun to force white women in NAC to face up to their racism, but there were few native groups within NAC to explain what their new path would be and how NAC could help. Phillips's study (1990) depicts aboriginal women's groups as largely isolated from the women's movement.

A second force drawing women away from autonomous women's groups was the growing visibility of women as activists in partisan politics. NAC's non-partisan orientation in relation to the official political system made women from all the political parties uncomfortable. None the less, NAC remained a channel through which many women passed before gaining partisan office, and there was little evidence that this trend would threaten to rob NAC of potential political talent.

The final trend was the development in Canada of a vocal and often effective anti-feminist movement. The significant expansion of involvement in NAC as this movement became active, moreover, suggests that its activities will further expand NAC's membership base as groups feel the need for solidarity. Some groups of stay-at-home mothers, such as Mothers Are Women (MAWS), began to define themselves as participants in the feminist movement at least in part to avoid association with anti-feminist groups.

The expansion of NAC's membership, activities, office, and resources continued smoothly until 1988, when accumulated stresses linked directly to the extent and speed of the expansion erupted in another period of conflict and crisis. The problems centred around the fact that NAC could not meet the expectations of many of the newly affiliated groups. For example, the costs associated with ensuring full participation in the AGM or the executive for francophone women[2] (simultaneous translation, document translation, bilingual staff) and women with disabilities (signing, hearing loops, physical access) were very high, and NAC was already coping with various other new expenses and organizational pressures (rapid regionalization, travel and communications subsidies, pressures for committees to become participatory, and so on). The political expectations of some of the newly affiliated groups also taxed the organization. Many of the new recruits had high expectations about what NAC could do for them, but their reactions were also tinged with suspicions about racism and élitism.

We devote the remainder of this chapter to an account of two conflicts that illustrate the effect on NAC of some of the trends we have described. One was the conflict with anti-feminist forces over the issue of state funding. The second was the conflict within NAC over a process known as the organizational review.

Opposition on the Right

The struggle to institutionalize NAC has revolved around its claim to represent the women of Canada better than any other organization. This claim rested on the size of its membership base,[3] the partisan and ideological diversity of the groups represented, its regional representation, and its links, fragile as they were, with the women of Québec through the FFQ. NAC's claim committed it to expansion and the constant integration of newly mobilized groups of women. Politicians, who saw political parties as the only legitimate tools of political aggregation, resisted such claims by social-movement organizations. None the less, NAC's representational claims enjoyed increasing legitimacy in the 1980s.

Ironically, it was attacks by the Right that solidified NAC's claims to represent at least those women interested in advancing the status of women. By making NAC the chief target of their campaign, anti-feminist groups established its claims while exposing it to further attack. Beginning in 1985, the newsletter of the National Citizens' Coalition, *Overview*, carried 'exposés' about NAC. The REAL Women newsletter, *REALity*, carried a barely Canadianized version of the U.S. New Right analysis cheek by jowl with attacks on PC feminists such as Flora MacDonald and Maureen McTeer. In a well-orchestrated and well-funded campaign, REAL Women staked out its claim to 'equal time' with NAC as an equivalent group representing 'pro-family' women. The campaign culminated in an attack on the prevailing nature of state funding and on the 'bias' that REAL Women believed existed against its band of 'simple housewives.' (That members of REAL Women were 'simple housewives' was the journalistic peg on which everyone from *100 Huntley Street* to *Saturday Night* hung their stories. In fact, its spokeswomen usually had professional training.)

The mandate of the Women's Program of the Secretary of State was up for review in 1988. The position of REAL Women was that it had been denied funding because the program funded only radical feminists and 'we do not share the radical feminist point of view' (REAL Women pamphlet no. 6 [1985]:3). During this time, an error originating in a REAL Women press release was promulgated by the press – namely, the government was giving NAC $13 million. In fact, this was the total Women's Program budget, distributed among seven hundred groups, including the Girl Guides, the Catholic Guides, the Federated Women's Institutes, and many other traditional groups and services (Emergency Consultation of Women's Groups 1986). This factual error persisted and some of the new groups that joined NAC in 1987 believed it had $13 million instead of the $400,000 that it actually received in that year.

The review of the Women's Program mandate was approached with some apprehension. Although women's groups achieved some success before the Tory-dominated Boyer Committee on Equality Rights, this was clearly not the Liberal era. The parliamentary committee included only one woman and was dogged throughout by several unofficial 'members' from the PC caucus ('Tory neanderthals,' as some PC feminists called them) who 'sat in' on the committee's deliberations. The committee convened in five cities, heard from 144 groups, and received 265 written briefs. REAL Women's supporters had their day, but the committee nevertheless reaffirmed the program's mandate. The committee's report, entitled *Fairness in Funding: Report on the Women's Program*, stated that 'advancing the status of women,' which was key to determining who and what would be funded, was to be interpreted in relation to the equality provisions of the Charter of Rights and Freedoms and the U.N. Convention on the Elimination of All Forms of Discrimination against Women.

Committee members Jim Jepson and Ricardo Lopez issued a minority report that described the process as a sham: 'Although the Committee heard from a large number of groups, 85 to 90 per cent of these groups were members of NAC. It is difficult to see how the presentations made can be considered a cross-section of the views of Canadian women' (Crittenden 1988:34). NAC had acted effectively as an organizational centre, ensuring input to the committee and coordinating efforts among its member groups. Jepson and Lopez, however, in suggesting an image of NAC directing its affiliates as if they were homogeneous and subordinate chapters, failed to understand that NAC's member groups were not subject to 'direction.' What the anti-feminist elements and most of the press also failed to see was the role NAC played in achieving cooperation between its members and more traditional groups, such as the Women's Institutes, which also supported continuing the Women's Program and its mandate. Indeed it is because of umbrella structures such as NAC that efforts to drive wedges among different elements of the women's movement have been less effective in Canada than in other countries.

After the re-election of a Conservative government, significant cuts in the Women's Program did occur and reduced NAC's funding back down to the level that had prevailed in the early 1980s. In addition, the FFQ was threatened with a change in its own funding because its affiliation with NAC was deemed inconsistent with its status as a 'national' organization. (The FFQ was to leave NAC again in 1989, motivated primarily by NAC's position on the Meech Lake Accord.)

Attacks from the Right and funding cuts both harmed NAC's ability in the short term to function at the heady levels of 1986–8, but they did not create deep schisms within NAC. The conflicts within were being created by the contradictions inherent in the organization as it proceeded through the process of institutionalization.

Organizational Review

The growth and increased regional, racial, and class diversity of NAC's membership; its effective lobbying; and its visibility as the main target of anti-feminist attacks all led it 'to be identified as the voice of feminist women in Canada' (NAC Organizational Review Document [April 1988]:3 [cited hereafter as NAC ORD 1988]). But demands for an organizational review began in 1987, reflecting the frustrations of several distinct categories of NAC participants. First, the newly mobilized groups (visible minorities, immigrant women, and women with disabilities) and francophone women were frustrated because NAC could not readily supply the resources necessary for their full participation in all of its structures. Some women from outside central Canada still found NAC distant and inaccessible. A third category included women who, because of a lack of education or money found NAC inaccessible, since in many respects the organization conducted its activities on the basis of an assumption that participants had education and access to resources. A fourth category included women from small collectives, who found NAC's operating style alien and who wanted to develop within it a feminist decision-making process. Finally, many white, ablebodied women, accustomed to seeing themselves as victims, were experiencing guilt and frustration after having been compelled to face their own racism, ethnocentrism, able-bodied bigotry, heterosexism, and classism. In some instances, women were experiencing frustration for more than one reason. Clearly, these segments were all seeking different things from an organizational review. In some instances, what they were seeking was not to be found in an organization such as NAC.

The concept of the politics of accessibility best characterizes the dynamic of this period. For many women, the issue was 'fairness of representation' rather than feminist process. Both issues were explored, however, in the two reports produced for the 1988 AGM. The 1987 AGM had established an Organizational Review Committee with a broad representative membership and sufficient funding to cover some travel and translation costs, but, in the end, it was decided that the Québec membership would engage in a separate process and produce a separate report. The committee chose to work through consultants in both cases. The NAC Organizational Review Committee chose Ottawa consultants Lynn Tyler and Joan Riggs. According to a NAC document summarizing the 1988 report of Nicole Lacelle, the francophone groups in Québec obtained special funds to conduct their own consultation and organizational review 'due to the fact that there was considerable discontent, resulting in the possibility of a withdrawal from NAC.'

The Québec Consultation involved the discussion of three scenarios: (1) the restructuring of NAC on the basis of equal participation for francophones or of a federative model, with each province/region having a federation that would in turn be part of a federation; (2) an independent Québec feminist organization to interact with the federal state; (3) Québec women to stay within NAC but to pose certain minimum requirements. Scenario (3) was adopted, based on the premise that scenario (1), while desirable was not unattainable. The possibilities explored involved two presidents, equal representation of the Québec movement on the executive, different voting procedures, and a changed role for representatives. A federative structure was rejected because it was believed it could 'endanger the autonomy of Québec groups to the extent that ... [the FFQ] would be one link in a pan-Canadian organization.'

The debate focused more on traditional concepts of concurrent majorities and on the constraints of NAC's claims to 'represent' the Québec movement than on issues of feminist process. However, Noëlle-Dominique Willems, a member of both the executive and the Organizational Review Committee, associated doing things 'the feminist way' with doing things 'the way we do in Québec.' She believed that Québec feminists had dispensed with many formalities of political process and had developed a feminist way of proceeding that fell somewhere between 'the male model' and the consensus approach of the small feminist groups. Unfortunately, no concrete examples of this modified process emerged. Furthermore, the real issue of structural equality within NAC between national movements was not raised for serious debate.

The Québec Report, (according to NAC's summary of Lacelle's report) outlines the 'minimal requirements' to ensure meaningful participation by francophone women in NAC, including improved and expanded translation services, the mandatory wearing of translation devices by anglophones, orientation sessions for new participants, workshops to allow more discussion of issues, clearer and fairer rules of order,[4] and anglophone and francophone co-chairs in all sessions. The core issue was francophone women's sense of being excluded and feeling handicapped in participation. Although most of the improvements represented increased structure, it was clear that the Québec members viewed them as bandaid measures. Noëlle-Dominique Willems likened francophones trying to participate on an anglophone executive or committee to women with disabilities facing physical barriers to access. Ironically, many anglophone participants were feeling good that NAC had elected its first francophone president in Louise Dulude. They were uncomprehending when Québec francophones pointed out that she lived in Ottawa and did not represent the Québec movement in many of her views (not least, in her views on the Meech Lake Accord).

For the reasons we have already explored, NAC's structure was not initially devised to achieve representative input on matters of policy from across Canada. NAC's increased visibility, however, and its claim to be 'the voice of feminist women' made the politics of accessibility increasingly important. Clearly, if it retained its structure and its funding base, NAC would not be able to afford all the measures that would have to be taken to eliminate the various existing barriers to full participation. Nevertheless, greater accessibility appeared to be a prerequisite of becoming fully institutionalized as a parliament of women.

The Organizational Review Document (ORD) produced by the anglophone consultants identified some problems facing NAC: the rapid growth and diversity of the English-Canadian movement, the complexity of issues facing NAC, the development of an anti-feminist attack, and 'the increasing perception that NAC is politically partisan, and linked to one political party' (NAC ORD 1988:7). The thrust of the consultant's report was to propose that member groups should undertake many of the activities currently handled by the executive, that the policy-making process should be opened up to more participants, and that norms of accountability should be developed.

The five working assumptions outlined in the report revealed the philosophical orientation of its authors:

1. The principle of accessibility and representation of the diversity of women's experience in Canada. The emphasis here was on removing barriers to participation rather than on ensuring representation through, for example, structural changes to accommodate the Québec movement or internal affirmative-action programs for marginalized groups.

2. The principle of democracy, conceptualized as everyone having 'an equal opportunity to influence and make decisions if they so choose, regardless of geographic or other factors.' This reflected a concern about the inadequate representation of women who were distant from the centre, less well educated, or economically disadvantaged, with respect to equal access to the full decision-making process, including participation on committees.

3. The principle of accountability, conceptualized in terms of having clear 'lines of decision-making, implementation and accountability' rather than of any sense of the collective responsibility of executives or the holding to account of officers through an open election process.

4. The principle of 'ownership by member groups', reflecting a rejection of NAC's claims to being an institution that was greater than the sum of its parts, but also a desire for member groups to undertake certain NAC activities, such as lobbying, and for NAC to provide backup services to help them do so.

5. The principle of empowerment, stressing sovereign individuals 'finding their own voices' and 'being able to create their lives as they choose.' Empowerment was understood as pertaining to the individual more than to the collective.

Politically, the Organizational Review Document produced considerable controversy and another AGM that frustrated many member groups because no 'real issues' were decided. (The CORP delegate described it as a gigantic 'bitch session.') The legitimacy of the report was questioned because of the very low rate of return for the questionnaire on which it was based in some membership categories. Perhaps not surprisingly, return rates were highest where there was most dissatisfaction. Thus there was a 45 per cent return rate for the questionnaire in British Columbia compared with a 15 per cent return rate in Southern Ontario and a 7.2 per cent return rate from NAC's affiliated national groups. A contested election for the presidency pitted college instructor and Organizational Review Committee member Lorraine Greaves against labour lawyer Lynn Kaye. For the first time in NAC's history, a full debate about visions of the two potential presidents took place, although it eventually displaced onto other issues.[5] The ideological aspects of this conflict were from the realm of second-wave feminism, with leftist feminists being unwilling to see member groups 'assume ownership of NAC' and thereby pursue the path of decentralization. Women of colour and other women who had felt marginalized essentially wanted to be fully accepted within NAC's decision-making centres, but few shared Lorraine Greaves's vision of a decentralized entity based on the norms of feminist process. Furthermore, many of those pursuing the goals of feminist process were hostile to party politics and saw NAC's multipartisan approach as threatening in times of right-wing backlash. In short, the old themes were being replayed, but with a considerably different spin. (The 1989 AGM received yet another organizational-review report, including proposals for internal affirmative action. Most of these proposals were implemented.)

Conclusion

The development of NAC towards institutionalization occurred in a political environment that responded to the organized women's movement in English Canada in several ways. While many women remained alienated from structures such as political parties, others were encouraged by the increased representation of women in state institutions, especially in the court system. The election of a woman as leader of the NDP reflected a long campaign for equality by women in that party. Women in the governing party had their own base of power and believed they had prevented the implementation of most anti-feminist policies. Despite some improvements with regard to the presence of women in official politics, however, governments have undertaken little positive action to improve women's lives. While equality seeking had become a major dynamic in federal politics, the existence of the Charter has diverted a large part of women's energies to the courts rather than to legislatures. Within Canadian conservatism, moreover, neither the anti-feminist New Right nor the pro-feminist 'red Tories' represent a majority. The majority view, rather, is that of the neoliberals, who are dedicated to gender-neutral policies (which tend to disadvantage women and other weaker, more marginalized people).

Sandra Burt (1986b:49) has argued that, until 1985, the federal government's response to movement demands had four characteristics: a developing commitment to role equality (but not the fundamental transformation of women's roles); incremental policy making; the segregation and dispersion of women's issues; and continued support for voluntary groups. Although it is premature to evaluate the Conservative era in federal politics, it would appear that Burt's assessment will be very little changed when such an evaluation is concluded, except perhaps to revise the description of the first characteristic to read 'a commitment to symbolic equality appointments.'

Clearly, there was little in this political environment to challenge our conclusion that the equality project will take several generations to complete. The increased pace of mobilization of women who were previously marginalized and the development of an anti-feminist movement both suggest at least another decade of intense activity before the next lull. As in the labour of delivering a baby, we must assess NAC with this multigenerational 'push and rest' strategy in mind. It is now clear that the process of NAC's development into an institution of Canadian women's movements involves cycles of expansion, conflict, and consolidation. As new elements of the female population become active within NAC, the structures created by previous waves creak and groan under the weight of new expectations and obligations. The role of leadership in the constructive reformation of NAC's structures was evident in our account of Doris Anderson's tenure. In the next chapter, we examine theories of leadership as they have developed within an institution in which politics is conducted as if women mattered.

Notes

1 In the early days of NAC, its 'instrumental' character was clear to all: It had been created for specific purposes. But new generations came along who 'could not see the strings moving the actors' – in other words, not recognizing it as a 'purely instrumental or provisional practical arrangement,' they related to it as an institution.

2 The FFQ resumed its membership in NAC in 1984 and remained a member through 1988. As our examination of the organizational-review crisis will demonstrate, however, the affiliation was largely symbolic.

3 Structurally, NAC's membership base included pan-Canadian, chapter-based groups; pan-Canadian groups based on individual memberships; umbrella groups, which like NAC, regroup other organizations and represent them to the provincial/territorial state; national federations of local groups; networks of service groups, either national or provincial/regional; single-issue coalitions; and local groups, collectives, centres, and services.

4 The rules of order used in Québec are from the *Code Morin*, while NAC follows the American *Robert's Rules of Order*. Although different from *Robert's Rules*, the *Code Morin* is not more feminist.

5 In Chapter 5, we will explore Lorraine Greaves's conception of how NAC might work. Here, we must note that the AGM was deprived of the opportunity of choosing between the two visions because Greaves withdrew from the presidential race after motions to extend the organizational-review process and begin implementation were lost.

5 Agency, Leadership, Representation, and Democracy in NAC

In this chapter, we will explore some thorny questions that emerged as NAC increasingly came to be considered the parliament of the English-Canadian women's movement. In the founding era, answers to the questions 'Who acts for NAC?' and 'For whom does NAC act?' were not complicated. The founders assumed that executive members represented the views of their groups; that NAC's voice was decided within the coalition by its leaders; and that NAC represented the views of women who were members of their groups. This clarity about agency in NAC faded when member groups stopped sending their presidents to NAC, when women on the executive began to see themselves as part of NAC rather than as delegates of their nominating organizations, and when the executive came, eventually, to include women from only a fraction of the affiliated groups. Moreover, as NAC succeeded in grafting on a radical grass roots, its activists no longer shared a common understanding of the nature of leadership, representation, or democracy. Many in the new generation of feminists were quite willing to share a commitment to concrete policies with women of the alliance between traditional and liberal feminists, but they were unwilling to share their views on leadership, agency, representation, or democracy. Nor did they share a common theory of social change. Finally, NAC's success as an organization led to the development of representational claims beyond the women in NAC member groups. NAC was able to hire staff (beyond secretarial help), and this led to questions about the areas in which staff should be to act as agents for NAC – a debate that culminated in the mass resignation of all but one of the staff members at the 1988 AGM.

Increasingly, NAC's legitimizing claim to be 'the voice of feminist women' and the body in Canadian politics that represents women better than any other opened up the issue of the validity of that claim to outside scrutiny. NAC was also subject to heavy criticism from within regarding the authenticity of its representational claims. The FFQ rejected any suggestion that NAC represented Québec women. Since it could never give women from small grass-roots groups the sense of primary attachment they got from involvement in those groups, NAC would always disappoint them. Since it could never afford all the translation services, bilingual staff, signing, hearing loops, office modifications, travel subsidies, executive stipends, and child care needed to allow all women to participate directly, NAC would always disappoint some women. Although the president could report in 1985–6 that a significant percentage of the year's one hundred new member groups were groups of minority women, NAC could never eliminate racism (or able-bodied and heterosexist bigotry) fast enough and so would continue to disappoint some of the new recruits.

As NAC assumed the enormous task of both leading and mirroring the English-Canadian movement, it also became a lightning rod for fear, anger, and conflict within the movement. As NAC was attacked by anti-feminist forces in the media day after day, the growing tendency of some of its members was to blame it for those attacks – that is, to 'blame the victim.' In the 1988 Organizational Review Document, for example, NAC was seen as unable to repel right-wing attacks, unable to shed the image of being 'extremist and fringe,' and 'no longer an equal negotiator with politicians,' because it wasn't sufficiently feminist as an organization (NAC ORD 1988:7). There was an examination of NAC's behaviour to determine whether it had indeed provoked the attacks. The notion that if NAC had been an authentically feminist organization these bad things would not have happened was an example of a kind of displacement that had been seen in NAC before. Many of the new generation of feminists projected onto NAC (and other feminist organizations) all of their negative experiences with male-dominated organizations. Perceived 'abuses of process,' 'élitism,' and 'exclusionism' were unforgivable in NAC because it was supposed to be a model feminist organization. To claim that there wasn't enough time or money was 'not good enough'; any failure to remedy such perceived problems immediately was seen simply as 'a matter of priorities.' The critics assumed that the structures and processes found in NAC had been *chosen* by its founders, and did not consider relevant the fact that their choices had been limited by the realities of Canadian economics, geography, and politics.

Barbara Sinclair Deckard argued in 1983 that one response of feminists to the inadequacy of patriarchal institutions was to set up counterinstitutions that were 'intended to serve as models for structures in the future good society' (468). One of the key issues raised in this chapter is that of the constraints imposed on NAC by its role as a counter-institution. Many women became active in NAC with some model of an ideal feminist organization in mind – often that of the small consensual group writ large. For some, it was preferable to have no organizations beyond the small group if such organizations could not be true to the small-group model. For many, however, the goal was a compromise structure, a cross between the ideal of the small group and the larger, more formally organized group. According to Vickers (1990b), Noëlle-Dominique Willems argued that the main problem for NAC was finding a middle path between the consensus model of the small group and 'the male model.' Vickers (1991) has referred to this process as learning to 'bend the iron law of oligarchy' by finding ways to achieve greater internal accountability and accessibility within an evolving institutional structure.

We explore these themes in four sections. First, we identify the member groups of NAC. Working in part from the analysis in the 1988 Organizational Review Document, we consider the question of whether member groups are (or could potentially be) agents of NAC. We also look at the problems resulting from the desire among some member groups to see NAC's basic unit as the individual rather than the group. Second, we turn to the question of leadership and examine the NAC executive and its presidents in the context of feminist concepts of leadership. Third, we analyse the concept of representation from a feminist perspective, and consider the question of NAC's representational claims. Finally, we outline the understanding of democracy that emerges from our knowledge of NAC as a woman-centred political institution.

In considering this final theme, we argue that contemporary feminism has thus far failed to develop a concept of democracy that goes beyond a simple egalitarianism. We also posit that feminist theories of leadership, representation, and democracy have, to date, been shaped by women's reactions against their experiences in mainstream, patriarchal institutions. Rarely having experienced female leadership, women tend to assume the 'maleness' of all leadership and, therefore, to reject it as inappropriate in a woman-centred institution. We argue that although this is an understandable feature of the movement's growth as each new wave is mobilized, it hampers the development of woman-centred institutions and norms for governing them. An institution such as NAC needed norms of operation that would reflect how women ought to practise politics when they are in charge. As we will show, it is a matter of particular urgency for NAC to develop mechanisms to ensure the accountability of agents and the protection of minorities.

A Revolution of Rising Expectations: NAC Member Groups

In the 1981 president's report to AGM, a telling phrase was used to explain one result of an early experiment with regionalization. Lynn McDonald explained that regionalization had resulted in a 'lack of executive members in Toronto to do the work.' By 1987–8, the NAC executive had thirteen regional representatives and responsibility for twenty-two committees. The perception of the problem had changed little, however, with overworked executive members, committees, and staff still unable to do all of the things necessary to perform NAC's minimum functions. What had also changed little was the role of NAC's member groups. A few were active in providing executive members and committee members (five presidents came from the Ontario Committee on the Status of Women). Most simply provided the participants for the AGM and the annual lobby, and the numbers for NAC's membership claims in its literature. That is, until the 1988 organizational review, it was assumed that action by NAC was undertaken mainly by the executive and its committees, with the AGM ratifying that action. It was also assumed, however, that NAC acted on behalf of the women of Canada, or at least the progressive majority of them. It was far less obvious to most NAC activists that they were acting on behalf of some five hundred different member groups, each of which had particular needs and expectations.

In this section, we examine the character of the NAC membership in 1987–8, a period of full institutionalization (See Appendix B). We are less interested in the 'numbers game' (How many women does NAC really represent?), than in understanding NAC's actual members, which are its groups. (The nine hundred Friends of NAC, unable to vote at the AGM or be elected to the executive, remain an unknown element.) We will examine NAC's membership from the following perspectives:

group purposes, origins, organizational philosophies, and expectations of NAC. Finally, we explore the question raised by the Organizational Review Committee in its 1988 report: Were NAC's member groups agents of NAC's objectives or were they largely the passive objects of NAC's agency, which was located at the centre and away from the grass roots?

NAC's umbrella structure was designed to facilitate coalition management for lobbying a centralized federal government. A membership based on groups ensured it a broad ideological spectrum. A contrasting structure is that of NOW, with uniform chapters at the local, state, and national levels, based on individual memberships. (NOW also has offices at all three levels, although local services depend on the financial resources in the area.) NOW's structure also makes it a competitor with other organizations for funds and human resources. NAC was consciously designed to minimize such competition, with the founders seeing its purpose of coordination and coalition management as secondary and functional as compared with the primary purposes, such as service provision, of its member groups. What interfered with the workability of the original design was the vast expansion of NAC's membership base and the growing expectations about what it could achieve. In the Organizational Review Document, for example, the consultants recommended that NAC adopt a 'full regional structure,' which would include meetings, services and staff 'in the regions,' research, leadership training, and more sophisticated communications (a feminist news service, video production, and so on). It also argued that NAC should use its member groups far more extensively as agents acting on NAC's behalf. It was clear that the expectations of some of the groups that supported this full institutionalization of NAC far outstripped NAC's original design and, under current circumstances, its resources.

A central point, which we have noted earlier and shall consider more closely here, is that NAC contains a significant number of small grass-roots groups operating according to radical-feminist principles of organization, and that these groups must co-exist in an umbrella structure with larger, traditionally structured organizations. These grass-roots groups are different from the small chapters, caucuses, or clubs that often exist within larger organizations. They retain their autonomy and can pursue methods quite different from NAC's in their internal operations. Recent analysis reveals that, unlike traditional women's groups, most small, ad hoc women's groups usually worked on the basis of consensus and are internally unstructured, with no formal rules for membership, so that women can be involved on a flexible, 'do what you can when you can' basis that fits their lives well, especially during child-bearing years (CRIAW 1987; Vickers 1988a). Few of these groups are interested in mobilizing large numbers of other women into the group. Each tends to find its optimal size, and then to encourage potential recruits from neighbouring areas to create their own group. The more structured a group becomes, the more 'expensive' participation becomes in terms of the time and money women have to invest. The participation costs for individual women increase directly with group size even in groups that operate within a single town, but they increase sharply when being part of a larger group means that meetings are held away from home. Other than voting, then, participation in small, ad hoc groups is the most common way in which women participate in politics in the liberal democracies.

A CRIAW research project conducted in 1987 and funded by UNESCO studied ten groups, some of which were affiliated with NAC. Two were pure collectives – Women of the North, in Fort McMurray, Alberta, and Pandora, a publishing collective in Halifax, Nova Scotia. Women in these groups were asked what constrained and what facilitated their involvement in public life. The factors they identified as constraining their involvement were time, money, distance, and the risks of partisan politics, such as losing a job or public housing. They attributed their ability to be involved in the collectives to structural flexibility and procedural accommodations. They reported feeling comfortable and empowered in their primary groups, while in the other groups, they often felt uncomfortable and inadequate (CRIAW 1987:57–66).

It is important to consider the effect of this experience in primary groups or collectives on a whole generation of women active in NAC member groups. Certainly, we know that unstructured groups are far more dependent on and responsive to particular individuals who can 'make or break' a group. Larger associations are less likely to be radically affected, either for good or for bad, by individuals. As we will see, women's experience of leadership in these groups is quite unique. Sandra Burt in her research (1986a) has identified another aspect of activist feminists' experiences in such groups: 'most of these women were so caught up in their group activities that the more general political issues were not very important to them. Their main concern was the status of women' (67). The CRIAW research suggests that such women will undertake some involvement in official politics only out of a sense of duty. The experience of NAC, then, represents a relatively uncommon success story of involving women from such primary groups in a wider political context – one that eventually interacts with the official politics of the federal state.

An orientation package for members of the new 1987–8 NAC executive told them this: 'Essentially you are an unpaid MP for women in your region of Canada. You are elected to do this without much local office support, with a small budget and in addition to your paid work and/or homemaking responsibilities' (quoted in NAC ORD 1988:15). The fact that NAC was now expected to play a role far more complex than its founders had intended for it reflected its institutionalization and its members' rising expectations. The claim that NAC was 'the voice of feminists' was true in the sense that it included far more groups representing a wider range of women than any other comparable structure in Canada or elsewhere in the liberal democracies. In relation to organized feminism in Canada generally, however, NAC's member groups were concentrated in certain areas of activity, while other areas were only marginally represented (see Figure 5.1, on page 162). (The minimal structure required for NAC membership was ten members, a group name and address, and minimal fees.)

There are several major areas from which NAC drew little involvement. First, there were few groups from the quality-of-life movements for peace and environmental protection.[1] Second, both health and religion were relatively underrepresented areas considering the great importance of the feminist spirituality and well-being movements in English-Canadian feminism. Some advocacy groups, however, involved health-related issues such as midwifery and abortion. (We have categorized them as advocacy rather than health groups because they were organized primarily to seek relief from legal restrictions that inhibited women's choices rather than to deliver services.) Finally, there were few groups concerned with Third World feminism, although the number of affiliated groups dealing with race and immigrant status grew markedly during the 1980s.

Status-of-women action committees and single-issue advocacy groups made up a large segment of NAC's membership (ninety-seven groups). Basically designed to lobby for change, these groups came the closest to representing NAC's core. Some, such as the Vancouver Status of Women Action Council, predate NAC. One, the Alberta Status of Women Action Committee (ASWAC) was an early provincially based structure (founded in 1974) with purposes similar to NAC's and with a membership in 1986 of roughly 550. ASWAC, like most of the other action groups, was also funded by the Women's Program. Profiled in the 1987 CRIAW research study, ASWAC went through a 'de-structuring' process in 1982. The women interviewed differed sharply as to whether the results of the de-structuring (featuring a self-selected board, no

FIGURE 5.1

NAC member groups by type or main area of activity, 1987–8

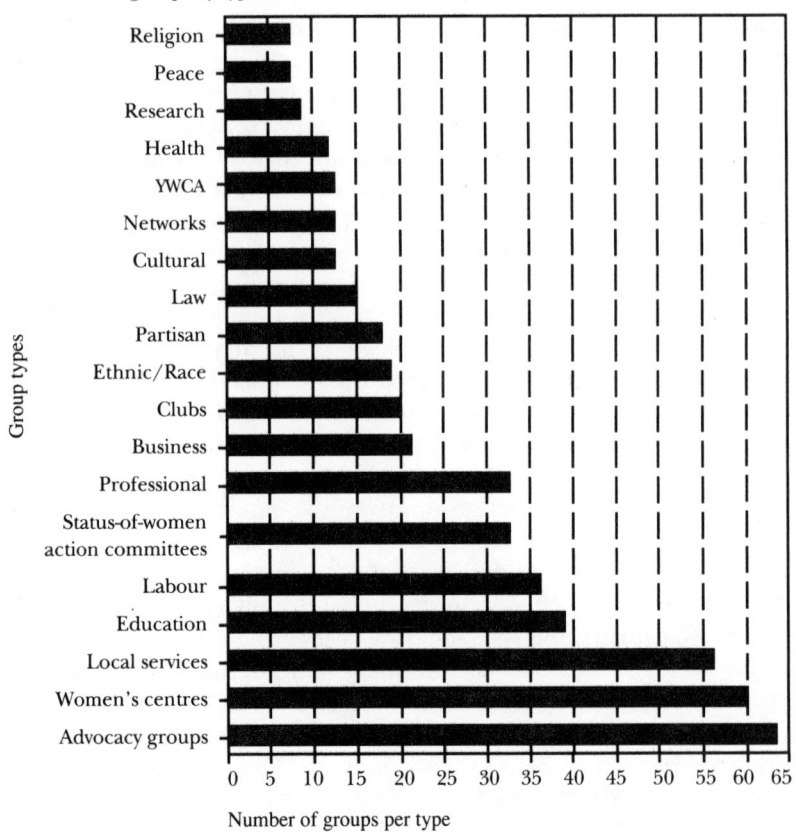

Number of groups per type

Source: NAC Membership Report and Brochure, 1987–8; see also Appendix B

rules of order, no formal reports, and so on) were positive or negative (CRIAW 1987:17–21, 63).

The richness of NAC's ideological spectrum was rooted in the diversity of its membership base in the often conflictual sectors of business, labour, the professions, and partisan politics. Unlike the single-issue advocacy groups or the action committees designed to pursue feminist objectives across a broad range of issues, groups from these sectors involved women in efforts to achieve equality *within* our most powerful and recalcitrant institutions. Not surprisingly, women from these areas were often the least sympathetic to demands for decentralization and feminist process. The environments in which they sought equality for women were tough and conflictual, and they wanted NAC to be engaged in more than moral critique – to be 'professional and effective,' not 'vague and touchy-feely.' In some instances, the member groups to which these women belonged were caucuses or committees within unions, parties, or national associations. The brilliance of NAC's original umbrella structure was to permit such affiliations just as it permitted the affiliation of chapters of the more traditional groups that felt solidarity with NAC's purposes. In both business and labour, women also derived strength from networks they created across organizations. These were sectors in which women understood that the stakes in equality seeking were high. Most did not see their involvement in their member groups as volunteerism. Almost a quarter of NAC's member groups (123) were from these sectors. A higher percentage of the groups in these sectors were national groups, and they affiliated larger numbers of women than did groups in the other sectors. Few of the groups in this category received government funding for their activities, and some were deeply opposed to this practice for NAC.

A second major source of NAC's ideological richness was its large segment of small groups organized around the women's-centre model of the 1970s or as service collectives. There were at least 116 member groups that fit the category of the small, primary group organized collectively to provide services, a context for self-help, and an opportunity to share experiences and raise consciousness. In many sparsely populated areas, women's efforts were not split up into several groups; instead, women's centres provided the range of services that would be specialized in most cities. Even in sparsely populated areas, however, crisis centres for the victims of male violence had developed as the single most-needed service that women provided to other women (Walker 1990).

As we have seen, the development of service-oriented groups operating on a volunteer basis was fostered in Canada partly through policies of government funding. Being dependent on government in this way led some services to create network organizations (of which 13 were member groups of NAC in 1987–8) and advocacy groups, such as Action Day Care, Ontario, to lobby on their behalf and to permit an exchange of information. Women from these groups saw NAC quite differently from women in groups organized around the workplace.

For the most part, they saw their activities as volunteer (although some services were grappling with problems of paid staff), and many of them clearly valued the control of the decision-making process the group gave them. Influenced by theories of feminist process, they were often uncomfortable with conflict, favouring consensus decision making or group splitting if conflict could not be transcended. Many were inexperienced in the processes of large organizations and lobbying. Some expected NAC to provide training to make its processes accessible to them.

We will examine in some detail the ideological basis of the collectivist or unstructured group in the next section. Here, we simply observe that it is the 'organization of choice' for a large number of women, especially those who have been mobilized around issues of sexual violence – that is, rape, incest, battering, and pornography. It was not uncommon in such groups to make little distinction among activities such as consciousness raising, advocacy, self-help, and the delivery of a service. One of the main problems with this cell-like structure, however, was that, except in large urban centres, it tended to result in groups operating in isolation from one another and lacking links to activity elsewhere. One of the purposes of affiliation with NAC was to provide such links.

Another important segment of NAC's member-group population was composed of sixty-one member groups (53 local, 8 provincial/national) that had their origins in the first wave of mobilization – that is they were formed before 1950. There were more groups of the first-wave origin in NAC than from the unions and the NDP combined (of which there were 46). There were also more groups from the first-wave than there were groups organized around issues of violence (57). Many of the women in the traditional groups supported NAC out of sisterly solidarity. One such group provided NAC with its first president (Sabia), and women from first-wave groups have often been stabilizing influences in times of internal crisis. However, the influence of this sector in NAC, and in the movement generally, will wane over the next decade. It is therefore important for us to assess both the agency of these groups and their understanding of leadership.

The final sector of member groups that we must note includes the groups organized on a pan-Canadian basis (although often not within Québec). Including both pan-Canadian and Québec national groups, there were some sixty groups we can designate as national in scope. (Five others were caucuses of national groups.) Some were federations of provincial organizations, some had local chapters or caucuses, and some were based on individual membership. Several were themselves umbrella organizations like NAC. The 'nationals' were also often members of NAC for reasons of solidarity. With their own complex and challenging structures, many did not provide personnel for NAC. Often competitors for government funding with NAC, there was none the less a common bond of some importance. From the point of view of many of the women coming from the 'nationals,' NAC's path paralleled that of their home organization. These women generally had experience with processes in large organizations and required little from NAC in terms of service, except in the crucial areas of lobbying and coordination.

Until recently, NAC had few member groups representing women from rural areas, low-income women, immigrant women, and racial-minority women. Although the most recent wave of expansion began to draw groups of women who had previously been marginalized into NAC's arenas, Conservative government strategy was to drive a wedge between groups affiliated with NAC and other women's groups considered less radical in their demands for equality. Government's courting of groups representing visible minorities and groups of organized rural women was quite intense under the second Mulroney government.

In 1988, the organizational-review consultants reported that 'some women feel excluded from and lack ownership of NAC. It is viewed as élitist, racist, classist and not addressing the needs of many women (e.g., women with disabilities, lesbians, rural women, francophone women outside Québec and many women outside Central Canada)' (NAC ORD 1988:3). Because of the importance of these claims to NAC's legitimacy as a movement organization, the views expressed in this report require scrutiny even if most of the committee's proposals were not accepted by the 1988 AGM.

Although lobbying had been NAC's original function, successive waves of women attempted to broaden its activities to encompass policy making, representation, and political education. The wave of newly mobilized women of the late 1980s tried to extend NAC's mandate even further. Underlying the Organizational Review Document was the premise that a parliamentary institution such as NAC should do more than create a 'level playing field' that would allow any women who wished to participate to do so on an equal basis. Specifically, the ORD envisioned that (1) NAC would assume the participation costs for meetings beyond a fixed minimum affordable by all (the level set was

$100, which would still have excluded many women); (2) NAC would reduce the complexity of its policy process by de-emphasizing 'experts' and involving more 'ordinary members'; (3) NAC would compensate for the geographic barriers to participation by further decentralization; (4) NAC would provide training for women who wished to participate but didn't have the education or skills. This proposition saw the individual woman from the small group (consisting of nine or ten other women) as the basic unit of the movement NAC was to serve. This view of the individual rather than the group as the basis of NAC was also reflected in the ORD's concept of democracy, which would permit only the most limited role for representatives. Equality of condition was to be achieved for potential participants through the removal of all barriers of education, distance, disability, language, and skill. (The ORD did not explain how any of the proposed measures would deal with the barriers of prejudice and racism. This may explain why women from marginalized groups decided to follow the traditional option of pursuing executive places rather than supporting the destructuring envisioned by other feminists – a decision that led to the breakup of the organizational-review coalition. The Québec francophone element had already broken from the coalition with its separate report, which required more, rather than less, structure in NAC.)

In understanding how an institution recruits participants, a useful model distinguishes between supply-side barriers and demand-side barriers (Randall 1987). On the supply side, socialization and situational constraints (such as distance or having young children) affect the availability of women, especially for élite roles. On the demand side, by contrast, available women are excluded by institutions through the actions of gatekeepers, structural barriers, and discriminatory effects of supposedly gender-blind rules. This framework was designed to understand women's problems in gaining access to 'male-stream' institutions; it can also be useful to our immediate purpose of identifying aspects of the Organizational Review Document to which NAC had to respond if it was to become stabilized as a woman-centred political institution.

Looking first to the demand-side barriers to participation in NAC, we know that women of colour and immigrant women believed there were gatekeepers in NAC excluding them from office and preventing their issues from receiving priority. These women represented groups that identified racism as the central barrier to the full involvement of their members in society at large. In general, most of these women wanted full access to NAC structures and demanded relatively little change in those structures, except to incorporate a determined attack on racism. The changes proposed by the Organizational Review Committee, however, offered a weak response to racism and other demand-side barriers. It advanced an equal-opportunity model in a context in which an affirmative-action program would have been more effective. A second set of women also fell within the category of those who faced demand-side barriers. Lesbians had been present in NAC from the beginning, but there had always been a sense that to identify themselves as such would mean their exclusion from posts on the executive. Until the formation of the National Lesbian Forum, most separate lesbian organization was of the small group, service type, and few such groups belonged to NAC. Since no electioneering was permitted under NAC's constitution, except for a very brief statement to the AGM, being elected as an acknowledged lesbian would have required a woman to 'come out' to an audience of five hundred women. As with the barrier of racism, the barrier of homophobia would have been little diminished by the changes proposed by the organizational-review group. Two other groups in the coalition were affected by structural and other demand-side barriers: Both francophone women and women with disabilities experienced clear physical barriers, as well as barriers of money, priorities, and attitudes.

As we have seen, the real structural barriers to representing two national movements of equal importance were not addressed in a serious way by the organizational-review process. In 1987–8, there were only twenty-seven francophone groups represented in NAC directly, and the FFQ, which represented many others indirectly, was treated as an ordinary member. While it was clear to us that only a co-president, concurrent-majority structure with an absolute commitment to full bilingualism would have offered a chance of creating in NAC an institution that genuinely represented both language groups, this option was viewed as unattainable by the Québec groups. The ORD addressed the issue of removing barriers to francophones in only a minimal way. It recommended that the executive become 'more accessible' through bilingual executive meetings. The possibility of French/English co-presidents was presented in the document but was modified at the AGM by the committee chair, who added rotating gay/straight and able/disabled co-presidents in her presentation. The questions of the bilingual functioning of twenty-two committees, regional meetings, and mid-year meetings and of the need for bilingual staff were not addressed. Discussions of the barriers to be removed for women with disabilities were also limited to the question of AGM accessibility. The question of full accessibility for all meetings and facilities was not addressed. Furthermore, the costs of removing some of the demand-side barriers facing both francophone women and women with disabilities were not addressed.[2] (There was no dispute about the acceptability of government funding in the organizational-review coalition. It represented groups that both expected government funding and often could not exist without it.)

Most of the 1988 organizational review focused on supply-side barriers to individual women's participation in all areas of NAC. To rectify the geographic disparities resulting from the location of the AGM and lobby in Ottawa, a travel-subsidy system was proposed 'to reduce travel cost as a barrier to participation,' at an estimated cost of $100,000 per year. Most of the committee's recommendations depended on the notion of moving many individual women to a single spot in an equitable way. Far more inventive were the suggestions that envisioned NAC member groups becoming agents responsible for some of the activities that were being performed by the executive, committee members, and staff. Women's centres, for example, with their demonstrated effectiveness in getting women in isolated regions to communicate with one another, could, it was thought, become the information nodes for a more decentralized NAC structure. With twenty-two committees, much of NAC's committee work could also be decentralized, as it has been in some other women's groups.

As institutionalization increased the demand for NAC to have a significant regional capacity, the grooming of member groups as actors in lobbying, policy making, and local administration would become essential. Important though these very tentative steps towards a more fully realized grass-roots operation would be, however, major problems concerning agency and accountability had to be addressed first to avoid risking NAC's growing capacities as a multigenerational institution. For example, decentralization could hamper institutionalization if it diverted resources from the various centrally maintained record-keeping functions that facilitate the retention of a collective 'memory' of the measures and initiatives that have failed or succeeded over the years. Institutionalization, however, also posed the dangers of bureaucratization in the course of maintaining the collective memory and undertaking other functions of continuity. We will return to the role of a central memory in successful institutions in Chapter 8.

The Ideological Spectrum within NAC

We now turn to a further examination of the ideological spectrum within NAC. A snapshot survey undertaken at the 1984 AGM gives us an opportunity to examine more closely the range of ideas that NAC activists brought to its meetings. The survey tapped the views of a self-selected group of 125 anglophone delegates (see Appendix A). It showed a high degree of agreement (68 per cent) among the delegates on many key feminists beliefs and issues.[3] It also showed a strong continuity in beliefs across the generations. Where the respondent group disagreed, however, is also important. Factor analysis showed that the disagreements among respondents (an overall 32.1 per cent variance) resolved into four opinion forces: strong feminist, traditional feminist, economic, and liberal/reform.

A strong feminist force, accounting for 10.2 per cent of the variance, represented support for more-confrontational and less-conventional tactics, along with the view that one could place 'little trust in any political system to bring about change.' All of these items associated with this factor represent 'role transformation' rather than 'role equity' or 'equal opportunity' issues. These values express less support for narrowly defined (instrumental) groups, political or otherwise, and more for 'organic' organizations, such as collectives, which do not involve the internal structuring and hierarchical management often associated with traditional organizations. (The rapid expansion in NAC since 1984 has included a significant number of such 'organic' groups.)

A traditional feminist force represented 9 per cent of the variance. Loyalties here were to particular organizations, with no strong commitment to feminism *per se* or to any particular policy issue. The value of service dominates. This orientation has been a consistent and stable part of NAC since its founding days.

An economic force accounted for 7.2 per cent of the variance, which seems low, given that many considered NAC to behave 'as if the economic concerns ... [were] the most urgent' (Chaviva Hošek, personal interview with Chris Appelle, 17 September 1985). This force reflects something more broadly based than what could be attributed to the influence of working class/union feminists[4] within NAC alone. It also shows the influence of academic socialist-feminists. This orientation emphasizes collective rights and involves the following beliefs: that housework should be shared by the sexes; that job security should be ensured for new mothers; and that working mothers can have just as secure relationship with their children as non-employed mothers. We should also note that the distinctions on various questions of women's status are becoming increasingly blurred as more women of child-bearing age enter the paid workplace and experience at first hand the difficulty of separating 'private' and 'public' roles. The economic force in NAC is therefore likely to grow even without an increase in the union sector.

At 5.7 per cent of the variance, the liberal/reform force was the smallest. It involved a commitment to influencing the existing political system in specific conventional ways. The delegates who conformed to this profile tended to trust in the political system to bring about change and to show a desire to take part in the existing power structure. Women of this orientation are more likely to be involved in party work than in movement institutions, although a significant minority of women so committed considered an involvement in both arenas to be important, perhaps seeing NAC as a good training-ground for official politics.

This snapshot of a self-selected group of anglophone delegates in 1984 can only hint at the ideological complexity within NAC. Since 1984, a large new wave of women has entered the organization, and many of the new groups, such as the Rape Relief and Women's Shelter of Vancouver and Local 3 of the Canadian Union of Education Workers, Women's Caucus, of York University, would bring strong feminist values. Other groups, representing racial minorities and other marginalized women, might constitute an entirely new force if the survey were to be repeated today.

NAC's institutionalization was born of successive waves of expansion and the inability of any single ideological element to dominate the organization. We must therefore assume that, in the stalemates that ended each period of conflict in NAC, stabilizing forces surfaced in the form of women who cared more about the survival of NAC as an institution than about the outcome of any particular ideological debate. In both of the periods of conflict we have considered, the question of the future shape of NAC was a critical part of the debate. In the transitional period, the key issue was dependency on government funding; in the organizational-review debates, the issues of agency, decentralization, and accessibility, summed up in the concept of 'feminist process' were key. In the latter case more than in the former, the antagonists all assumed that NAC would serve as the movement's focal institutions 'for the duration.' The view of many activists that 'if NAC folded, we'd just have to reinvent it' was one of the elements that allowed these debates to resolve into plans for a structure that could survive and serve much of the movement over a long period of time.

Leadership and Accountability: Is Anyone Here in Charge?

Many of the problems NAC faced in developing enduring structures reflected conflict about the role of leadership in woman-centred politics. Others related to the difficulty of establishing mechanisms to ensure the accountability of agents. In this section, we examine some general theoretical propositions drawn from both feminist theory and feminist practice that may shed light on these related problems. In general, we will argue that the reluctance of many women, especially those influenced by the ideas of radical feminism, to develop an understanding of leadership suitable for a woman-centred practice has seriously hampered the movement's ability to operate. At the core of the dilemma is the rejection of leadership *per se* (rather than of male models of leadership only), which reflects an emphasis on equality at the expense of other democratic values. So few examples of woman-centred leadership exist in official politics that the evidence from which to draw insights for a new theory is limited. Moreover, some of the examples of women leaders in official politics (consider Margaret Thatcher) make many feminists even more determined that leadership must be rejected outright. Our approach will concentrate on the *practice* of leadership within NAC and, in particular, on the rejection of electioneering (on grounds of egalitarianism) as a symptom of the leadership/accountability problem. The Organizational Review Document urged NAC to 'accept the leadership of its groups' and to empower them to speak both in the name of NAC and in their own voices. We will examine this approach to the leadership/accountability issues along with several others.

So difficult is the subject of leadership within feminist groups that it hardly even exists as a category of analysis. In the extensive literature on feminist theory and feminist organizations, the subject of leadership rarely rates a single chapter or even an entry in an index. And any references that are to be found are usually negative. The underlying conceptions about leadership in feminist analysis rest on a view of power as a fixed quantity. The assumption is that, if an organization selects a cadre of leaders, there will be little left in the power 'pot' for others once the leaders have taken their share. On the subject of leadership, most contemporary feminism consists of a 'reactive negation

... of [the practices of] existing society and politics' (Miles 1982:15). As we have shown, the origins of such 'reactive negation' lie in part in U.S. radical feminism, but its tenacity as an approach lies in its confirmation of the lived experiences of most women who have participated in existing organizations. Until recently, few women could experience leadership from a woman. Moreover, few women experienced leadership as a phenomenon that could empower them. Most women and many men in our society experience leadership primarily as something that drains their resources in the aim of achieving the goals of others, not their own.

Theories about and experiences of leadership make evident the importance of the twin forces of power and accountability. Before examining in more detail the cultural-feminist vision of reconstituting leadership in NAC, we will explore some of the recent feminist analyses of these forces. In 1980, observing that many of the conflicts arising in feminist organizations resulted from differences in feminists' views of leadership and decision making, Jill Vickers (1980) suggested that feminist theories be reassessed through an examination of the nature of leadership in some of the pre-state societies that flourished, for example, in Africa and America before European colonial rule. In such contexts, leadership exercised by women in the area of work was based on respect, affection, talent, capacity to pass on skills to others, wisdom, or superior physical skills. That is, such evidence as we have suggests that before the establishment of patriarchal state societies, the leadership of women by women was not necessarily based on domination, oppression, and exploitation. There are relatively few arenas within patriarchal, state-organized societies, however, in which women can lead other women and be chosen for their aptitudes. The relationships among women in kin groups may provide some insights, but models of female leadership among unrelated women are rare.

Nancy Hartsock (1983) expanded on this approach and conceptualized power as having two faces. The first, as in Vickers's account, involved power being exercised in ways that resulted in empowerment and benefit for followers and, potentially, in costs for the leaders. Here, power was understood as a renewable capacity, not as a commodity in a zero-sum game, wherein a leader gains power only by depleting the power of others. Rather, a leader's powers (strength, capacity, energy, skill) would increase and foster the power of others. The second profile of power Hartsock identifies is more familiar: in it, power is seen as a currency of fixed quantity, and leadership involves legitimized exercises of power that can result in dominance, oppression, and subordination. Accurate though Hartsock's second profile of power and leadership is in its general outlines, there are certain aspects it fails to consider. First, the processes of liberal democracy modify the power/leadership profile by establishing some structures, however inadequate, for representation and participation. Second, leadership in official arenas may also be based on skill, capacity, energy, and strength. The skills of mediation and consensus building,[5] for example, create leaders in labour relations. Leadership in this area is based on an individual's capacity, energy, and skill, as well as on the trust people place in his or her abilities. Finally, Hartsock's general profile leaves no real place for the charismatic leader whom we may follow because of his or her force of personality, skills and capacities, or qualities that inspire love. In our analysis of leaders within NAC, we identified several examples of women who were chosen to lead because of their ability and skills of mediation and because they inspired respect and allegiance.

Radical- and Cultural-Feminist Critiques of Leadership

Where, then, does contemporary feminism's view of leadership have its roots? In 1971, Juliet Mitchell described feminist small-group organizations that undertook collective work as being opposed to systems of leadership and representation. These groups, in her view, sought to eliminate the 'dangerous development' of 'powerful expertise' and 'the rise of ego-tripping leaders' (58). The 1969 manifesto of a New York group called 'The Feminists' (previously known as the 'October 17 Movement'), a radical offshoot of NOW led by Ti-Grace Atkinson (Willis 1984:96), reflects the underlying premises of such collectivist organizations:

THE FEMINISTS is an organization without officers which divides work according to the principle of participation by lot. Our goal is a just society, all of whose members are equal. Therefore, we aim to develop knowledge and skills in all members and prevent any one member or small group from hoarding information or abilities.

Traditionally official posts such as the chair of the meeting and the secretary are determined by lot and change with each meeting. The treasurer is chosen by lot to function for one month.

Assignments may be menial or beyond the experience of a member. To assign a member work she is not experienced in may involve an initial loss of efficiency but fosters equality and allows all members to acquire the necessary skills for revolutionary work. (Reprinted in Koedt et al. 1973:372)

Rothschild-Witt (1979:513) argues that social control in such groups is maintained on the basis of 'personalistic and moral appeals' that are effective only when 'the group selects members who share their basic values and world view.'

Freeman (1979:565), observing the U.S. movement, noted that 'the very ideas of "leadership" and "organization" were in disrepute.' Ellen Willis (1984) has described her involvement in the Redstockings group, which she and Ottawa's Shulamith Firestone started in 1969 as a spinoff from New York Radical Women. As she recounts, the group's model of struggle was that put forward in *Fanshen* (1966), William Hinton's popular account of revolution in a Chinese village. Willis and Firestone translated that model into a vision of 'direct confrontation between sexual classes [that] put an enormous premium on unity among women' (100). Any emphasis on leadership privilege would have weakened the unity required to sustain the day-to-day militancy of direct confrontation. None the less, as Willis explains, these groups did have leaders (she and Firestone were the leaders of the Redstockings; Atkinson and Koedt, of The Feminists).

Willis attributes the disintegration of radical feminism first to the fact that 'radical feminist ideas caught the attention of large numbers of women, especially educated, upper-class women, who had no radical perspective on other matters' (107). These women seized on the idea of women's oppression as the primary oppression and concluded that other struggles were 'male' and could be ignored as such. Willis describes the less political cultural feminism that emerged out of radical feminism in the U.S. context as anti-leftist. The second aspect of the disintegration of radical feminism that Willis identifies, however, relates to conflict over issues of leadership and structure:

The first issue to create permanent rifts was equality in the movement. Partly out of rebellion against hierarchical structures ... [and] partly because consciousness-raising required informality, radical feminists, like w.l.m. as a whole, had chosen the putatively structureless small group as their main form of organization. Yet every group had developed an informal leadership, a core of women ... who had the most to do with setting and articulating the direction of the group. Women who felt excluded from equal participation challenged not only the existing leaders but the concept of leadership as a holdover from male-dominated organizations. [These] debates ... began to dominate meetings to the exclusion of any engagement with sexism in the outside world. (108)

These issues became the staples of many cultural-feminist groups. Since it was impossible to equalize power in the institutions of society at large, the emphasis was put on equalizing power within feminist groups. This emphasis on direct democracy colours most feminist discussions of leadership.

Joan Richardson (1983) studied the women who led (in fact, if not officially) the small collectives in the anglophone movement in Montreal, and her research provides us with a rare glimpse of feminist leadership within 'structureless' organizations. She noted that groups that survived over a period of several years usually did so because of the moral force and commitment of the particular women who led them, regardless of group dedication to the values of direct democracy. She identifies three main characteristics of these women. First, they all displayed energy, defined by Richardson as an unfocused commitment to organizational activity, manifested in their membership in various groups and their willingness to accept a wide range of responsibilities. Second, they all displayed selflessness, as reflected in their almost unlimited availability and willingness to take on any aspect of the group's activities. Third, there was an absence of passion in their own personal relationships (including a tendency towards celibacy) as well as an attenuation of all relationships not related to the group in which they functioned as leaders (362–3). This profile bears an uncanny resemblance to the image of the 'good mother' in the patriarchal family: energetic on her children's behalf, selfless, and without apparent sexuality, exhibiting passion only in the cause of her children.[6] Such a profile has certainly been evident in some of NAC's executive members through the course of its history.

Most of the objections made to the collectivist form of organization have been practical: Such groups have been seen as inefficient. Freeman (1974, 1979) argued that in the United States, they were unable to join together in nationwide action and that they failed to tap fully women's different skills and talents. Others pointed to a 'tyranny of structurelessness' that permitted informal leaders and élites to prevail and offered no means of holding them accountable (Freeman 1974). Still others argued that 'sisterhood can become a coercive consensus which makes it emotionally difficult for women to say what they feel' (Rowbotham 1979:40).

Despite these critiques, the collectivist organization had become the organizational form of choice for a significant number of contemporary feminists. It meant that women's experience within collectivist groups would have an influence on any umbrella organization that sought to affiliate groups dealing with a range of major issues, especially issues of male violence. Although ill suited to the manipulation of the mainstream political system, these groups helped create a new context in which women could produce a political agenda and analysis out of their lived experience.

Without the tremendous mobilizing capacity of the small group experience, which gave women the opportunity to be 'in charge' of the process, the movement's pace would have slowed significantly. It is important, therefore, to understand why and how the small-group process mobilized women and allowed them to operate collectively as a creative force. It was the rejection of authority – the statement that no leader and no expert could tell a woman what she felt and what she had experienced – that had the potential to release women's energy and ignite the creative spark. This does not mean to say that all collectivist groups realized that potential. Ellen Willis (1984:102–3), in her description of the radical-feminist group The Feminists, reveals a different experience: 'The Feminists were idealist, voluntarist and moralistic in the extreme. They totally disregarded what other women said they wanted or felt, and their idea of organizing was to exhort women to stop submitting to oppression by being subservient or participating in sexist institutions like marriage.' But the groups that were able to tap the positive potential of authority-rejection often showed remarkable results. Analysis of the progress of women in the MUMS (Mothers United for Metro Shelter) group in Halifax illustrates the power of small-group experience even for women who were severely marginalized and apparently without resources (CRIAW 1987). The success of the self-help dimension of the MUMS collective experience may have been attributable to the substitution of concrete actions for moralistic exhortations.

It is important to understand that their experience within collectives affected the expectations of leadership and accountability that women brought to NAC. There was, for example, a general sympathy for any mode of operation that would empower inexperienced and less skilful women. Although this rarely meant choosing tasks by lot, it often did mean the rotation of functions such as chairing and recording. The core purpose of these practices was to develop knowledge and skills in all, in order to achieve an equality of condition. There was also the purpose of preventing any individual or group from hoarding information or abilities. Similar motivations accounted for a desire to avoid the development of 'media stars'; hence, there was resistance to dealing with media and outside agencies except in a collective manner. One consequence of these tendencies was to privilege the 'close-to-home' and to favour decentralization. Another was the rejection of formal elections and electioneering, which, it was assumed, permitted money and articulateness to win. Finally, policy making with the aid of 'experts' or reliance on expert authority in general was often rejected. Rather, the thesis was that women's views existed to be 'discovered' and that policy *per se* was needed by government more than it was needed by women.

We are fortunate that Lorraine Greaves, one of the women who led the organizational review process in NAC from 1986 to 1988, wrote about that process. Greaves is part of a generation of women who were not involved in NAC's founding and who view it as the focal institution of the English-Canadian movement. Greaves (1991:101, 103–4) has stated that 'NAC was regarded as the official voice of the women's movement in Canada' and that 'it was variously regarded as the formal women's movement in Canada, the official women's opposition, and the public voice and symbol of feminism in Canada' (see also Michell and Greaves 1988). Greaves describes her own background as focused in the grassroots endeavours of 'creating services for battered women' and establishing various health services. She writes that three characteristics of the NAC executive puzzled her: (1) 'the apparent lack of interest, experience in and attention to social and cultural issues affecting women'; (2) 'the dominant emphasis on economic and employment issues'; and (3) 'the rigidity and impersonality of the process used to debate and decide on the business of NAC at both the executive and the annual meetings' (1991:102). She concluded that NAC was 'the most "male" organization I had ever participated in.'[7]

In fact, the impersonality and rigidity that Greaves attributes to the NAC executive and the AGM reflected some of the norms established by Doris Anderson after the troubles of the transitional era. Greaves came into NAC with no exposure to its history and rebelled against its nature, which clashed with her vision of how a feminist organization should operate. In that, she was treating NAC *as an institution*, not comprehending that some of its norms of operation, such as the very formal meeting style, had been established a mere three years earlier and that they had been born of the experiences of a previous group attempting to overcome a particular set of problems. The earlier group had sought formality to minimize the damage done by the unregulated conflict aimed at individuals and had imposed measures such as the schedule of elections and the restriction on resolutions from the floor in an attempt to prevent the manipulation of the AGM. Greaves attributed NAC's 'neglect' of 'social and cultural issues' (especially issues of health and of violence against women, which were of particular concern to her) to the absence of feminist process in the organization. She believed the latter would result in a precise reflection of the views of all women in the movement and lead to the valorizing of the issues she considered most critical. At the heart of Greaves's call for a more open way of setting NAC's priorities was the vision of an active, decentralized organization in which all women could participate (presumably with the aid of much more extensive government funding):

By 1986 it was clear to me that NAC was a feminist organization without a feminist process. Its executive formed a hierarchy, with the President and a few table officers at the top. Robert's Rules were used routinely in decision-making at the executive and annual meetings, and voting was always the method of resolving conflicts. The importance attributed to the Presidential role, while comforting for the public and government, and convenient for the media, was rather a traditional approach for a feminist organization. (1991:104)

The fact that members of NAC's policy committees were largely self-selected and that the committees were dependent on executive members willing to chair them was of concern to another actor in the organizational-review process. Greaves notes that Megan Ellis of the Vancouver Women's Research Centre also felt frozen out of the process of striking NAC policy and priorities (1991:105). When NAC was founded, of course, the report of the Royal Commission on the Status of Women served as its blueprint; by the mid-1980s, a fairly extensive policy system had emerged, driven by women with expertise and a determination to have their issues 'count' in NAC. The Employment Committee, dominated by academic and labour women, was a particular target of suspicion and anger. Energetic and possessed of considerable political skills, this cohesive group of women (mainly from the 'golden triangle') of Southern Ontario and Montreal) advanced feminist economic analysis considerably. Greaves believed that these committees operated with 'only informal structures' and that such 'vague processes are open to abuse' (105). Informal agenda-setting was believed to be occurring as executive members jockeyed for budgets for 'their' committees.

The committees operated as part of the executive structure, meeting at the same time as the executive did, until 1987, when the Health Committee extended its net through the use of conference calls, and the Lesbian Issues Committee became Canada-wide through the use of corresponding members. Devices such as this had been in use in other national organizations, and Greaves and Ellis were correct in their supposition that the executive did not wish to let the committee process out of its hands entirely. Still smarting from the experience of having a Pension Committee that some women believed had tried to promote private over public pensions (Louise Dulude, interview with Jill Vickers, 17 May 1989), the executive had established clear-cut accountability, with an executive member chairing or co-chairing each committee to ensure that committee policies remained within the broad guidelines of NAC policy. These broad guidelines reflected the ideological statement of the early 1980s, and it was feared that reopening them would again threaten the fragile coalition.

To Greaves, the executive and committee members were guilty of 'hoarding information and abilities' and preventing others from being involved in the policy-making and agenda-setting processes. She suggested decentralization as a remedy for alienation. Her vision was of NAC's becoming fully 'representative' of the women's movement, and something more than 'simply a political organization responding to the strongest and most articulate pressures from various lobbies within the women's movement' (1991:107). Greaves saw the main business of NAC as creating equality of condition, so that all women who wished to could gain access – that is, could participate directly in all of NAC's processes. She did not seek to establish rules about the relationship between representatives and those represented, arguing instead that correct process would resolve issues of representation. It is our opinion that Greaves underestimated the difficulties of mediating among represented sectors to sustain an ongoing coalition. While a further extension of NAC's grass roots would be an important step in the process of institutionalization, it is not clear to us that even extensive decentralization would eliminate some women's alienation from an organization as complex and as large as NAC.

NAC's Leaders Profiled

In this section, we will discuss the role that leaders, mediators, coalition builders, facilitators, elders, and founding mothers play in an institution such as NAC. Because NAC's members are groups, the pool of available women from which it draws activists is beyond its control. Many groups, especially the small collectives, rotate their delegates to the AGM. This means a very high year-by-year turnover. (In some years during the 1980s, the parliamentarians who chaired the AGM plenary sessions found that close to two-thirds of the delegates at the AGM were first-time attenders.) Groups with the same representative for a number of years can achieve their objectives far better than those that send a new delegate every year. In such a context, those women whose commitment is to NAC as an institution must provide leadership to ensure that the processes are not manipulated as they were in the transitional years. In short, NAC needs leaders with energy, skill, and commitment to NAC as an institution and to fair process.

In NAC, during the period of institutionalization, there was both a formal leadership, elected by the AGM delegates according to the constitution, and an informal leadership, composed of women who were highly respected in the movement because of work in their own sector, women who were previous official leaders or founding mothers, and women who were 'experts' or activists on particular policy issues. NAC's historic resistance to an election system in which campaigning is allowed meant that member groups could not easily identify the program that a candidate for an official leadership position would pursue if elected. This was a major weakness in NAC's structure. To achieve an equality of condition among potential office holders, electioneering was forbidden, on the assumption that it would favour the articulate and those with resources. (Only a brief written statement and a speech of a few minutes were allowed.)

Within NAC, this group of formal and informal leaders played several critical roles. One of the most important was the task of managing a complex coalition of distinct ideological forces and mediating disputes that threatened the coalition. Individuals unable to transcend their own ideological orientation and those for whom a particular issue was so important that it overshadowed organizational survival were the least successful NAC leaders. The most successful leaders, whether official or informal, were integrative feminists who could comprehend NAC's function beyond the purposes of their own ideological segment or group and who could make common cause with women from other segments. Despite critiques of NAC as being 'male' in structure and operation, its executive traditionally reflected the influence of radical-feminist ideas about political process. As Carden (1974) pointed out with regard to NOW, while actual effects may be hard to measure, the belief in this 'feminist difference' clearly had an impact on the organization. Within NAC, most of the leaders we interviewed described features they believed demonstrated the ways in which NAC's operation differed from that of nonfeminist organizations. With regard to the character of NAC's leadership, however, our account will be impressionistic.

Although no typologies of leadership within woman-centred organizations are available, there are three typologies of styles of women legislators that may be useful. Two are based on women in the United States: Jeane Kirkpatrick's study (1974) of women in state legislatures and Irwin Gertzog's study (1984) of the evolution of women's legislative styles in the U.S. Congress. The third is Elizabeth Vallance's typology (1979), based on women legislators in the United Kingdom. Several of the categories from the Vallance and Kirkpatrick typologies provide insights for us here. It is important to remember, however, that these typologies were constructed from the behaviour of women who were not necessarily feminists and who operated in male-dominated and male-created political institutions.

Kirkpatrick identifies four styles among women legislators: the leader, the personalizer, the moralizer, and the problem solver. She sees the leader as seeking authority and influence in order to exert her will on the entire policy process. The moralizer seeks out the moral aspects of questions and concentrates on the moral/ideological issues in what amounts to a 'struggle against evil.' The personalizer seeks approval (even affection) and behaves in such way as to win it. Finally, Kirkpatrick's problem solver has an instrumental view of politics as a device for achieving community goals and seeks to get on with her colleagues in order to achieve her goals. More than half of the state legislators in Kirkpatrick's study are problem solvers (1974:174–7).

Vallance's typology also consists of four categories: the pragmatist, the moral reformer, the committee woman, and the 'imperator.' The pragmatist parallels Kirkpatrick's problem solver. In a parliamentary system, she is not a strong partisan and rejects the value of grand strategies in favour of issue-by-issue achievements. The moral reformer corresponds to Kirkpatrick's moralizer battling against 'evil'. These women are motivated by a strong sense of social justice. The committee woman is an organizer, fixer, and manager of 'schemes dreamed up and hotly debated by others.' The imperator (think Margaret Thatcher), like Kirkpatrick's 'leader,' is ambitious, opinionated, and interested in power for its own sake (1979:79ff.).

Although we cannot assume that all of these styles would develop within a woman-centred institution such as NAC, many of the women who played leadership roles in NAC developed their styles in other organizations. If we compare any of these styles with the 'good mother' style Richardson (1983) observed in woman-centred collectives, we can understand why leadership is as problematic in practice as it is in theory within feminism. As we discuss NAC's presidents, it might help us understand their leadership styles better if we identify the organizations in which they were active before serving NAC. We will also be alert to several additional categories of leadership that have emerged in the Canadian context. For example, the category of facilitator, or 'process person,' whose efforts direct a group to consider *how* decisions are being made rather than *what* decision should be made, has emerged out of the interaction between feminism and male-dominated institutions. (Audrey McLaughlin, the leader of the federal New Democrats, has been described by many in the party as a process person.) Finally, we should keep in mind Angela Miles's category of integrative feminists.

The effectiveness of NAC's official leaders hinged on factors of the style and personal resources they brought to office, their networks of community support, their longevity and status in the movement, and the political milieu within which they functioned. NAC's first three elected leaders were high-profile women, each of whom had an established public image before becoming chair of NAC. Each could also draw considerable organizational backing in her home group. Finally, each represented a distinct and different position in partisan politics: Laura Sabia later ran as a candidate for the Progressive Conservatives, as Grace Hartman did for the New Democrats, and Lorna Marsden was appointed as a Liberal senator. In this early period, therefore, the organization sought leaders who, collectively, could draw women into NAC from all three major parties.

NAC's first chair,[8] Laura Sabia (1971–4), with her forceful personality and fearless style, fits the profile of Kirkpatrick's 'leader.' She performed the miracle of formally establishing NAC at the 'Strategy for Change' conference as though by sheer force of will. In fact, Sabia also possessed formidable skills of coalition building and mediation. She saw herself as the 'front-woman' for the effective coalitions of the late 1960s and early 1970s: 'I was the mouthpiece backing those intelligent, quiet women who had their own degree of acceptance and public visibility grounded in organizational structures that were highly respected in the community' (personal interview with Chris Appelle, 10 January 1986).

Sabia had a clear image of the NAC she chaired: Its purpose was to lobby the federal government to implement the recommendations of the royal commission's report. Sabia's activism had spanned several decades before NAC was formed, and her base support among traditional women's groups was solid. Her connections to the Canadian Federation of University Women (CFUW) were useful in NAC's early days. Other 'founding mothers' tapped the resources of their home organizations as well. Sabia's experience in coalitions before the founding of NAC had clearly developed her skills as a mediator among groups that had strong partisan differences. Her accumulated experience and abilities helped her to embrace all of the women's groups in NAC and to establish norms of cooperation and negotiation. Sabia made herself available for NAC throughout the 1970s and early 1980s. Her daughter Maureen, however, has expressed bitterness about what she considers the 'pirating' of NAC away from her mother's original vision by radical forces (private communication to Jill Vickers, June 1987).

Sabia, often seen as a maverick, was an independent thinker. While her views on particular issues did not always find widespread support within NAC, she insisted that a feminist could be a free-enterpriser (and that a free-enterpriser could be a feminist). She was no less comfortable as a member of the Progressive Conservative party than of the Roman Catholic church. A practising Catholic throughout her life, she was none the less actively pro-choice, explaining her long-standing views on abortion as 'part of my fury at the Church for being so chauvinistic' (personal interview with Chris Appelle, 10 January 1986). Her campaigns to fight against discrimination and inequality did not always endear her to her party, which did little to find her a winnable seat. She was not a 'red' Tory, however, and spoke out against paid maternity leave 'at public expense' (that is, through the unemployment-insurance system). She rejected state interference with the free-enterprise system, but supported state action to guarantee women equal rights and to implement the recommendations of the royal commission (*Status* [Winter 1981–2]).

Grace Hartman, who followed Sabia as the chair of NAC (1974–5), was deliberately chosen as a contrasting figure in terms of partisan affiliation, a strategic move that reflected the early concern within NAC that it be multipartisan. Hartman was part of a long line of labour women who contributed leadership to NAC. Union organizer Madeleine Parent served for almost two decades on the NAC executive. Labour lawyer Lynn Kaye would be president from 1988 to 1990, after a long stint on the executive. Union activists Laurel Ritchie and Monique Simard are also part of this line. Hartman's support was grounded in the public-service unions and the NDP. Simultaneously chair of NAC and secretary-treasurer of CUPE, she was constrained by the two concurrent roles. As a result, her leadership was more important in symbolic than in practical terms. A 'pragmatist' in style, Hartman was a clear representative of working-class feminism. She began her career as a secretary in the North York Board of Education in 1954, was elected president of the National Union of Public Employees (NUPE) in 1959, represented the Canadian Labour Congress (CLC) on the Committee for Equality for Women (CEW), and became the 'first woman' in many national and international union offices. Hartman also served two terms on the Canadian Advisory Council on the Status of Women (CACSW).

As both chair of NAC and recognized leader of several hundred thousand trade-union women and men, Hartman bridged important ideological and class barriers in the English-Canadian women's movement. As NAC chair, she provoked consideration of the royal commission's recommendations within unions and the CLC. Fostering the development of a cadre of working-class feminists within the unions, she facilitated and encouraged their active involvement on the NAC executive. Despite the profound differences between unionists and many feminists in the early 1970s, Hartman's leadership helped make NAC a more broadly inclusive institution in class and ideological terms from the beginning. Hartman enjoyed a high degree of personal respect and gained cooperation from the memberships of both CUPE and NAC. In her view, cooperation between working-class and middle-class feminists was possible in Canada because of the relatively small size of the movement compared with that in the United States (in actual numbers, not relative to population) and, consequently, the relatively easy access for members to movement leaders. As she explains it, 'We were able to handle the issues because we were able to talk with one another ... a fact which highlights the manageability of the relatively small network of groups and their leaders which formed NAC during the early years' (personal interview with Chris Appelle, 10 January 1986). After her tenure as chair, Hartman remained active on NAC's Survival Committee. In 1985, she finished her second term as vice-president of the Public Service International, having been the first woman representative to that body in its seventy-five year history.

On the heels of this working-class unionist came Lorna Marsden, who might be said to have straddled generations: She had been a 'Strategy for Change' conference delegate and was also a member of the younger generation of feminists. Marsden (1975–7) was an academic and a committed Liberal. Her support network consisted of contacts in the Liberal party, the Ontario Committee on the Status of Women, and the academic world. (She is now a university president.) A professor of sociology, she was the first woman to become head of the University of Toronto's sociology department, associate dean of graduate studies, and vice-provost of the university, all during the late 1970s. She was the first chair of NAC to focus on its organizational needs. The executive had worked within a very loose structure in which resolutions were passed and actions initiated, but there was no strong sense of program or sustained plan of action. Elsie Gregory MacGill, who had served on the royal commission and on early NAC executives, and whom Marsden respected and admired, was the author of NAC's first constitution. In her leadership of NAC, Marsden concentrated on: (1) strengthening NAC's structure; (2) developing its 'national character'; and (3) establishing stronger links with government (*Status* [May 1977]). In order to implement these goals, Marsden and other members of the executive visited many parts of the country, recruiting 45 new groups and building the membership base to 120 groups by the 1977 AGM. Marsden recruited aggressively from among the new women's groups that were forming throughout the country at that time, many of which initially wanted little to do with structures such as NAC.

In 1976, Marsden devised the form that the annual lobby would take for more than a decade, personally leading the first NAC delegation from the Beacon Arms Hotel in downtown Ottawa onto Parliament Hill to 'interview' representatives from the three main parties. The highly visible annual lobby became an attractive selling-point for many newly created feminist groups, who saw it as a form of direct action that could help to focus government attention on their concerns. As a sociologist, Marsden (1980) wrote about NAC's role in facilitating the development of equal-pay policies in Canada. A liberal feminist as well as a Liberal, her view of NAC's role was that it should lobby more privately, as well as help activists to access the structures of the government party, the bureaucracy, and the opposition parties. Marsden plugged NAC firmly into the women's network of 'femocrats' in the Ottawa bureaucracy. She also initiated the establishment of an office for NAC by hiring Pearl Blazer, who was to become the keeper of

NAC's organizational memory and its mainstay for close to a decade. Marsden's style might be seen as a combination of the 'problem solver' or 'pragmatist' and the 'committee woman.' More in harmony with the institutions of the official political system and with the ideology of the governing party than were her predecessors, she readily admits that her contacts as a party insider helped establish channels of communication that allowed NAC's requests to be heard with greater interest and regularity. Marsden remained available to NAC throughout the 1970s. She became the Policy Chair of the Liberal Party of Canada and, in 1984, was appointed to the Senate of Canada.

Ironically, Kay Macpherson (1977–9), who followed Marsden, had previously been considered 'too radical' to chair NAC. A socialist who later ran for the NDP, Macpherson was active in the peace movement and in the Voice of Women. She proved, in fact, to be a unique bridge, both personally and philosophically, between the old and new generations of feminists and between old and new styles of radicalism. Macpherson is described by her colleagues as an 'eclectic' individual, combining maternal qualities and a strong moral orientation with many of the values of radical feminism. A self-described 'bridge between the long white gloves and the hob-nailed boots,' she had played a leadership role in the Association of Women Electors (starting in 1957–8), the VOW, the CEW, and the National Ad Hoc Committee on the Status of Women. In 1972, she organized independent candidates for the newly formed Women for Political Action (WPA) and personally ran in three federal campaigns – first as a WPA independent, in 1972, and then as an NDP candidate, in 1978 and 1979. Macpherson's tenure as chair of NAC led some to believe that NAC was 'in the NDP camp' and perhaps raised expectations about a possible dominance of NAC by the Left – expectations that fuelled the fires of conflict in the transitional era.

Macpherson's wide and diverse involvement created a network of colleagues, friends, and resources that was as eclectic as the woman herself. Born in England, she had originally worked as a physiotherapist, and was married to the late C.B. Macpherson, whose position as a distinguished political philosopher and professor at the University of Toronto allowed her to work full-time at chairing NAC. Macpherson's executive was open to the issues of the new generation of feminists. The issues of rape, pornography, and battering jostled successfully for agenda time with economic issues, constitutional reform, and Macpherson's analysis of militarism. Very much a 'moral reformer' in style and an integrative feminist in approach, Macpherson travelled frequently and combined recruitment for NAC with efforts to encourage women's groups throughout the country to raise their issues with candidates during the 1979 federal election. NAC began to play a role in disseminating information and strategy proposals pertaining to the election to its affiliates (*Status* [Fall 1979]). Partly as a result of these efforts, women's issues were given far greater public exposure than they had ever received before in a federal campaign. Knowing she had no chance of winning, Macpherson viewed her candidacies as part of the multipartisan campaign by WPA to get more women to run for office. Although NAC's role was non-partisan, many people, both within and outside NAC, assumed mistakenly (though understandably) that because Macpherson campaigned as a partisan candidate in a federal election, NAC, too, must be partisan.

Macpherson also used her office to help mobilize support for strikes by working women by participating in their picket lines. Not having to be in the paid workforce allowed Macpherson to devote more time to her role than some other NAC leaders could; in fact, she worked for NAC virtually full time. (We should note that the presidency of NAC is now, in the 1990s, a paid, full-time position.) The Fleck strike was just one instance in which active support on the picket line by NAC executive members consolidated links with working-class feminists (Executive Minutes, 24 June 1978).

Macpherson is an important historical figure in the English-Canadian women's movement not only in her capacity as a NAC leader. She was instrumental to the success of the ad hoc constitutional lobby by making available to the committee her own personal network of contacts, as well as NAC's. When Doris Anderson was recruited as president, Macpherson was 'recycled' as acting past-president in the absence of Jean Wood because of her reputation as a conciliator. Today, despite serious visual impairment, Macpherson remains deeply committed to the peace movement and has remained an active member of the NAC Survival Committee.

Assumptions about the nature of leadership in NAC began to change during the transitional period. Lynn McDonald was the first NAC president (1979–81) to acquire a political profile through her involvement with NAC rather than bringing a profile gained elsewhere to the role. Although she was one of the Toronto-based presidents, some of her views on NAC as an organization may have come from her involvement in feminist activities in Halifax. McDonald assumed 'the presidency' (as it was now called) with a program of reform for NAC in hand. She sought independence from government funding, as well as an expansion of membership to include senior, Indian, immigrant, and other as-yet unorganized women (*Status* [June 1979]). She hoped to improve relations between the NAC executive and office and the member groups. She advocated a system of regional representation to make NAC a more pan-Canadian institution. She supported the NAC Trust, a Friends of NAC membership category, and the production of a magazine-quality publication. Although she was not the originator of all these proposals, McDonald hoped to implement them as a package in the aim of turning NAC into the voice of a more representative, more unified, more independent, and more leftist women's movement.

McDonald, like Marsden, was a professor of sociology. Unlike Marsden, however, she was not a senior administrator at a university. If she hoped to succeed in implementing any of her objectives, McDonald needed to lead NAC to accept the proposed structural changes. In NAC, however, proposals for structural change generated great conflict. It would have taken either a very forceful leader – say, of the imperator type – or a consensus builder who could exercise great patience in persuading all parties that the changes were for the good and avoid disrupting the internal balance of power. McDonald was neither. She had developed no discernible leadership style in other contexts. A strongly committed socialist-feminist,[9] moreover, her leadership of NAC involved an attempt to build a solidarity of the Left that provoked a year-long disruption within the executive.

The events surrounding the constitutional debates taxed NAC's collective leadership. This situation would surely have tested any president, as the many cross-cutting political issues threatened NAC's affiliation with the FFQ and jeopardized the organization's very survival. After McDonald led NAC's delegation before the Special Joint Committee of the Senate and of the House of Commons in the fall of 1980, she and NAC lost control of the process, being supplanted by the ad hoc group, which used NAC networks but operated independently of the executive. It is unlikely that NAC could have formulated a common policy on the constitutional issues, even without the crisis with the FFQ. Executive members and NAC member groups held different views on patriation, the amending formula, and the strategies employed by the ad hoc committee. Certainly McDonald, whose own views on constitutional issues were not shared by many NAC activists, had difficulty knowing how to lead an organization that did not share a common purpose and, indeed, that had several conflicting objectives. McDonald's term of office spanned three federal governments and two general elections rife with partisan conflict that spilled over onto other issues. Nevertheless, the ad hoc constitutional conference and lobby were a major accomplishment for the English-Canadian women's movement.[10] It had come as a great shock to many Canadian women 'to discover that equality for women still had to be negotiated, fought for and defended at every stage' (Hošek 1983:291). McDonald was not among those who were surprised. She had never doubted that the achievement of women's liberation, as she understood it, would require struggle, which was the reason she had sought to transform NAC into a more independent and vigorous actor for change.

Many of the changes McDonald proposed for NAC were eventually achieved. Her plan for financial independence, however, while passed by the AGM, was never implemented. (Ironically, cutbacks in government funding in recent years have forced the same outcome.) McDonald's tenure in NAC gave her important political training and support, and she eventually won the NDP nomination in the federal riding of Broadview-Greenwood (she held that seat from 1982 to 1988). Her best-remembered legislative achievement is in the area of non-smokers' rights.

Jean Wood (1981–2) is in many ways the mystery woman among the early NAC presidents. Like McDonald, she came to NAC without an already-developed leadership profile. As we have seen, she joined the executive as treasurer, having come from the business world, where she was an executive with a life-insurance company. She was also active on the Ontario Committee on the Status of Women (OCSW). The executive minutes show that Wood operated on a leadership model familiar to business women, especially those in large organizations. For example, during McDonald's second year as president, Wood, as treasurer, introduced a 'management-by-objectives' program to get the executive organized. As president, she improved salary and benefits arrangements for the NAC staff. Her work on pensions for NAC was energetic and successful, despite disputes about its ideological orientation.

After the founding era, leaders in NAC tended to be women who had a low public profile before they assumed the job. Chaviva Hošek has argued that NAC needed leaders with 'strategic minds' after the experience of the constitutional lobby, and she believed that such women were more likely to be found in behind-the-scenes jobs (personal interview with Chris Appelle, 17 September 1985). An exception was Doris Anderson, who assumed the task of leading NAC after Wood, and came to the job as the closet thing to a charismatic leader NAC has ever had. Rendered a hero for many Canadian women by her resignation from the Advisory Council in the face of what she judged to be political interference, Anderson was a Liberal whose position at the helm of the council had been a patronage appointment. She readily admits that she had not thought of herself as a feminist leader before this point. Instead, she had followed a somewhat more traditional career path. She was editor-in-chief of *Chatelaine* magazine (from 1958 to 1967) and raised three sons in her marriage to a prominent Liberal party insider (who later became a judge). Journalist Michele Landsberg (1982:49) described the impact Anderson had in furthering women's equality through the pages of *Chatelaine* as follows: 'so level-headed and realistic was Doris' approach that she almost single-handedly made possible the advance of feminism in Canada. The most cautious and conservative women were willing to listen to an argument for equality when it came wrapped in the reassuring package of the magazine they could trust.'

Undoubtedly, the fact that Anderson's was a patronage appointment to the Advisory Council made some Liberals assume she would be a tractable president. Her willingness to stand up to the government that had appointed her and her role as catalyst in creating the ad hoc committee on the Constitution rendered her a hero well beyond feminist circles. Her high visibility and her reputation as a non-ideological conciliator led to her recruitment as the only president of NAC with no prior experience in the organization.

Anderson, who was president from 1982 to 1984 demonstrated a range of noteworthy characteristics: a non-ideological, pragmatic style that brought support from a wide range of groups; a good rapport with the media and excellent communication skills; good management skills from years of experience in the publishing business; and a commitment to equality issues that inspired a sense of trust in all but the most hardened partisans and made people believe in her authenticity. Using these skills and attributes, she undertook a period of healing and reform. Ironically, she completed much of the program that McDonald had initiated, although she accepted government funding as 'a fact of Canadian life.' Both constitutional reform and some reorganization and professionalization of the NAC office were achieved through her skills as a manager and conciliator.

Anderson's leadership lent an aura of competence and authority to NAC that was conveyed to both member groups and the public. The projection of this new image was facilitated by Anderson's own experience with the media. The overall effect on NAC was significant. Louise Dulude, NAC's first president from outside Toronto, argues that 'before Doris, NAC was not high profile – it wasn't insignificant, but the Advisory Council was higher profile ... but then this reversed itself, particularly through Doris and then through Chaviva and the leaders' debate' (personal interview with Chris Appelle, December 1985). Evidence of NAC's increased public stature was reflected in membership growth, more-frequent contact with cabinet ministers, unsolicited and regular coverage by the media (though not all of it was friendly), and enough activity to justify the existence of offices in both Toronto and Ottawa (Mary Lou Murray, NAC Government Liaison Officer, personal interview with Chris Appelle, 4 January 1984). After her tenure as president, Anderson remained on the NAC executive (which continued to benefit from her steadying influence) until the spring of 1986. Her skills as a conciliator were also employed when she was asked to step in, as past-president, to replace Hošek, who did not complete her term as president. Like Sabia, Anderson's leadership style allowed her to transcend partisan and ideological perceptions, and her temperament made it possible for her to foster cooperation among individuals who might have been at war under other circumstances. Also like Sabia, she was not closely attuned to the ideological divisions within new feminism and was consequently relatively little influenced by them.

Chaviva Hošek (1984–6), like McDonald, was relatively unknown to the general public when she came to NAC. She was a professor of English and American literature at the University of Toronto, chaired the Women's Studies Program, and then became the first woman to chair the prestigious Academic Affairs Committee of the Governing Council. She served on the Steering Committee of the Ontario Committee on the Status of Women (OCSW) from 1974 to 1982 and on the NAC executive for four years before becoming president. Hošek was one of the very few members of NAC's formal leadership group to survive the turmoil of the transitional era. This experience made her very sensitive to the possibility of ideological and tactical splits.

In her own words, Hošek focused on a more strategic leadership and developed a number of high-profile actions for NAC. With her executive, she capitalized on the federal election campaign of 1984, organizing the first leaders' debate on women's issues ever to occur in

Canada. Within women's circles, the debate 'electrified' electoral politics and displayed NAC and its leader in a positive light. The staging of this event highlighted particular characteristics of Hošek's leadership style. Having no obvious partisan leanings, she could get along with everyone without appearing to undermine her principles. This was true both in planning the debate and in developing strategy for later lobbying efforts. She was almost instinctively comfortable with politicians and the media, communicating her intelligent grasp of public issues in a non-threatening way. In fact, Hošek became something of a media star. Although a story in *City Woman* (Finlayson 1985) that stressed her affluent lifestyle and expensive taste in clothes did not endear her to some NAC activists, rave reviews of the televised debate on women's issues – one of which, appearing in the *Montreal Gazette*, claimed that 'The case for equality has been put as it never has before' (Lynch 1984) – attracted many new member groups.

Political spin-offs for NAC from this new, high-profile leader included the opportunity to have important issues aired. NAC gained cross-country exposure. Most of her colleagues were surprised and delighted by Hošek's apparent impact on government leaders and the media and by her success in recruiting new member groups. In Lorna Marsden's view, 'She's exceeding everything I thought could be accomplished' (Finlayson 1985). Some within NAC, however, doubted whether the strategy of getting party leaders to commit themselves publicly to equality measures and then assessing their performance during the next election campaign would continue to work for NAC.[11] Indeed, many were simply very uncomfortable with a media-star president, despite recognizing the advantages of the situation.

Hošek's pragmatic, 'committee-woman' style was facilitated by the fact that she appeared to be non-partisan. After her term of office, she was elected to the Ontario legislature as a Liberal, and served briefly as a cabinet minister. She was defeated in 1990. Her emergence as a media personality and her acceptance of a high-profile job in the insurance industry during her term of office in NAC (but before her election to the provincial legislature) puzzled and disappointed some. It also left to her successor the task of finding some solution to the problems that accompanied her success as a recruiter of new member groups (the costs of rapid expansion) and her ability to gain media exposure for NAC (which made it a central target for right-wing groups).

Hošek's successor in 1986 was Louise Dulude, a lawyer and pensions expert originally recruited by Lynn McDonald. Dulude had been part of the NAC executive since 1982, concentrating her energies on policy making. In many ways, Dulude's presidency was a watershed for NAC. Her election marked the first time NAC had chosen a leader who was not Toronto-based. Even more significant was the fact that Dulude served as NAC's first (and, to date, only) francophone president. During her tenure, she worked to increase the organizational voice of Québec and of francophone women outside Québec within NAC. While Dulude's own interest and considerable expertise in the area of pensions helped NAC make significant progress in dealing with this issue under her leadership, her term also coincided with a broadening of NAC's policy agenda. Anne Molgat (1992) describes Dulude's executive as taking action on 'abortion, aboriginal issues, sexual orientation, affirmative action, the proposed law on pornography, child sexual assault, unemployment insurance, the federal budget, midwifery, child care, the rise of the new right and fathers' rights groups, fiscal reform, free trade, refugees, and the Meech Lake Accord.' Dulude's presidency also spanned a period in which NAC's organizational-review committees wrestled with the growing tensions over regional representation, funding, and decision-making practices within a rapidly expanding NAC.

NAC's presidents during the period of study were always surrounded by both a formal leadership group on the executive and an informal group of leaders active on committees and at the AGM. Because NAC's members were groups, many of the women who stepped into the NAC arena had experience of some form of leadership within their own group. In some cases, women played an informal leadership role in NAC for a number of years before agreeing to serve on the executive. In other cases, 'founding mothers' and other notables or known conciliators were asked to rejoin the executive in times of crisis. Informal leaders included the following types of women: notable women who had outstanding achievements in their field, which caused them to command respect within the group on matters touching that field; partisan or ideological leaders who had followings of like-minded women; policy experts whose knowledge of particular issues gave them the ability to lead; spokeswomen for issues, who were identified with particular campaigns; women who had become symbols of a shared cause; and the founding mothers. In addition, NAC's informal leadership cadre included conciliators, women who were identified as the representatives of a region, and delegates of organizations who acted as message carriers, usually to exert influence on NAC's policy direction.

Representation: The Heart of the Matter

It is commonly argued that the interests of particular groups will best be served by their representation in the political system. This argument is made with regard to women's interests and the official political system. It is also made with regard to diverse women's interests and the political system within NAC. The parallel between the two situations is not exact, of course, because the first relates to male-dominated institutions, whereas the second relates to a woman-centred structure. None the less, the concepts of 'interests' and 'representation,' which apply to both, require some detailed examination. Since there has been little research concerning the representation of diversity within woman-centred institutions, we begin by examining some of the discussions of these concepts that pertain to official politics.

The concept of representation seems quite simple on the surface but, in fact, constitutes one of the more complex aspects of Western theories of democracy. In this analysis, we rely first on the work of Hannah Pitkin (1967), who outlines the four major meanings assigned by political theorists to the term 'representation' and then proceeds to develop her own understanding of the concept, which transcends the limitations of those definitions. The four major theoretical views of representation are as follows: (1) authorization, (2) accountability, (3) descriptive representation, and (4) symbolic representation.

According to Pitkin, the schools of thought that adopt the first two views see representation primarily as a formal process. The view of representation as authorization defines a representative as someone who has been authorized to act for another (or others). This is similar to the legal view of agency, in which anyone who authorizes an agent to act on her or his behalf must assume responsibility for the representative's consequent actions. In this view, the electoral process depends on representation as authorization, based as it is on a transaction of authority and representation. An examination of NAC's constitution reveals that its founders viewed representation in this way, as there is no provision for motions through which the members' confidence in leaders could be challenged or leaders recalled. The accountability theory sees the relationship between representative and represented as involving only a partial transfer of authority and responsibility. The representative can be held to account if she or he exceeds a mandate. Pitkin considers this view of representation a device for achieving responsiveness on the part of the representative. It was the notion of the accountability of the elected representative that moved

Anderson's executive to amend the NAC constitution in 1983. But the continued absence of statements of intent or electioneering by potential NAC leaders meant that the full process could not be realized. (Two criteria must be met before the represented can hold their representatives accountable: first, those who wish to be representatives must have the opportunity to state what they intend to do if they gain office and, second, there must be devices for removing officers who fail to act constitutionally or according to stated and approved intent.)

Descriptive representation theories involve the requirement of an accurate correspondence in legislatures and bureaucracies between the representative and the represented; in other words, the representative 'stands for' others in the same way that a sample stands for the whole population in a statistically valid survey. Rather than acting on behalf of others, representatives simply state their own views and, if the correspondence is accurate, they are by definition also stating the views of those they represent. In the context of an institution, then, it can be assumed that the representatives will collectively arrive at a correct policy or decision. This view of representation comes closest to the one that was held by many of the players in NAC's organizational-review processes: They saw the representative as a figure whose only role was to mirror her group's views. The representative was, consequently, to play no role in transcending limited or ideological views by creating alliances or persuading people to accept compromises. The fourth theoretical view of representation – that is, as a largely symbolic act – also sees the representative as a mechanical figure. Here, representation is seen as a symbolic ritual essential to legitimization, but without substance beyond that role. This view may be reflected in gestures made largely for effect, such as the appointment of token women in some institutions. The opinion of some NAC executives that the AGM was simply a troublesome ritual to be endured also reflects this view.

Pitkin's own view of representation is much broader than any one of these four views, and incorporates aspects of each. She sees the act of representing as acting in the interests of the represented in a way that responds to their own perception of their interests. To her, representative government involves institutional devices that ensure that representatives are controlled by those they represent, and not vice versa. Although this does not always require that they be delegates instructed and recallable by those they represent, it does necessitate a system of trusteeship (1967:221–2). The question of understanding the nature of women's interests as *they* understand them is not addressed by Pitkin. A recent survey of the debate concerning women's interests (Jónasdóttir 1988) reveals that it continues to revolve around establishing (in opposition to traditional political thinking) that women qua women are indeed a group with 'representable interests' rather than exploring what women's conception of their interests in a woman-centred institution might be. As we have already seen, women in NAC were clearly concerned that their interests as *different kinds of women* from different places be expressed, as well as that views on their *shared* 'representable interests' be formulated.

The ideological opposition of many new feminists to leadership and representative structures in general has meant that these women have done little to develop structures that would ensure the control of representatives by the represented. First-wave feminists, by contrast, were very concerned with this issue. They campaigned for the use of the devices of direct democracy, such as the initiative, referendum, and recall, to enforce the people's control in the systems of official politics that they had just entered. Within their own organizations, they saw the formal devices of representative government as protections for the represented. The 'official' disdain for anything short of direct and fully participatory democracy among many second-wave organizations left NAC at a great disadvantage. The original assumption that each delegate would represent the views of the group that sent her to NAC in whatever way the group saw fit proved to be more fiction than fact. All this led to NAC's facing major problems with regard to representation on several levels. First, NAC claimed that, through the device of group affiliation, it 'represented' a significant proportion of Canadian women who held progressive views on the status of women. The fact was, however, that NAC itself had no way of ensuring that the women who were sent by its member groups did what their organizations wished or that executives consulted other women in their groups concerning the positions they should take. Consequently, although NAC really did represent, through group affiliation, several million Canadian women, the devices to ensure fair representation lay outside its control.

The second level of NAC's representational problems lay in the selection of women to act within NAC's executive and committees and, at the same time, to represent the interests of some definable segment of the population of women. Only geographic interests were systematically represented in NAC through the executive's system of regional representatives. Linguistic interests were represented in a limited way in the position of a Québec vice-president. There was no method for ensuring sectoral or ideological representation on the executive, or sectoral, linguistic, ideological, or geographic representation on the committees.

The third and final level of NAC's representational problems was rooted in the question of how NAC was represented in the broader processes of official politics, which entailed the problem of how to enforce accountability in the actions of official leaders in the absence of formal devices to ensure, and later enforce, statements of intent. NAC did not use devices of direct democracy such as initiative, referendum, or the recall of its elected leaders by the membership.

A time-honoured method of holding representatives to account is through the location of financial control. Many groups reserve the approval of budgetary plans to an annual general meeting. In NAC, however, budgetary control always rested with the executive and officers in combination with the government funding agency. It should be noted that, in comparison with organizations based on direct, individual membership, NAC had to keep its affiliation fees very low. In any event, the device of withholding dues as an ultimate measure of control was rendered ineffective for NAC's member groups by government funding, which would have enabled NAC to continue most of its activities in spite of such action (unless, of course, the withdrawal of a large number of groups as a concerted act undermined its legitimacy in the eyes of the funding agencies). NAC was not alone in evolving as a structure without a serious system of fiscally based accountability. The internal accountability of many groups, feminist and otherwise, has been hampered in the same way. In essence, these groups have been more responsible to government than to their members for the spending of money. As we discussed earlier, observers have often expressed concern about the dangers of co-optation inherent in government funding. We would argue that the most serious negative impact has not been that of co-optation but of the inhibition of mechanisms to exercise accountability through the budget-setting process.

Sandra Burt (1986a), in her analysis of the differences in male and female conceptions of politics, stresses that the women in her survey were more concerned about the responsibilities and responsiveness of representatives than the men. Women working for feminist goals in the status-of-women groups expressed the most concern for more direct contact between representatives and the people they represent. CRIAW research (1987) also showed that women accustomed to small, intimate groups were the most cynical about the real purposes of representatives, doubting that they were committed to the needs and the interests of the represented. All indications are that women will need to develop a far more complex understanding of representation than they currently possess if feminist institutions are to be developed successfully.

NAC has often been portrayed as representing Canadian women better than any other political structure. Groups of anti-feminist women have, of course, challenged this claim, arguing that NAC does not represent their interests or views. Other women, while not anti-feminist, have had difficulty accepting NAC as their voice because some of the policy positions NAC advances conflict with their religious or other views. Many francophone women in Québec, moreover, have rejected NAC's claim to represent them at all. In short, NAC's representational claims are not likely to be accepted at face value in the future. For the purposes of both responding effectively to feminist requirements and effectively conducting politics in general, then, NAC must strengthen its theoretical grounding on the subject in order to develop new modes of achieving representation (especially in the policy-making process) and new devices to ensure the accountability of representatives once they have been selected or elected.

Process and Democracy in NAC

As we pointed out earlier, contemporary feminist conceptions of political process, organization, and democracy evolved in opposition to many of the institutions and practices of the liberal democracies. Although feminism now barely exists in its original form,[12] all of the new forms of feminism have been influenced by its views on the nature of organization. Radical feminists chose equality as their touchstone, rejecting organizational forms other than the collective as unacceptable to the extent that they failed to ensure absolute equality of participation in consciousness raising, theorizing, and agenda setting. Contemporary cultural feminism, which has as its goal 'freeing the women from the imposition of so-called "male values," and creating an alternative [woman-centred] culture' (Willis 1984:91), valorizes the choice of equality in the collective as 'female' and rejects all manifestations of leadership, representation, and so on, as 'male.' Hence, creating a feminist process is seen as a moral cause in itself, not as an instrument for achieving an equal society. The equal society has become the feminist collective writ large.

This emphasis on equality to the exclusion of all other values important to liberal-democratic theory and practice poses serious problems for the development of feminist theories of politics. Taken to its extreme, the goal of equality in political process requires the direct involvement of every member or citizen in each decision – a requirement that precludes the possibility of any representative structures. Short of that extreme, only a completely accurate mirror in which all representable interests are equally voiced, and voiced in the particular way in which the represented understand their interests, could suffice. The emphasis on accessibility in recent NAC debates demands, in practice, the exact mirroring in decision-making bodies of all representable interests. In principle, however, representative structures continue to be rejected as hierarchical and élitist, because those in the centre (the representatives) are seen as knowing more and having more influence in the decision-making process. As a result of this normative rejection, no rules for making representatives accountable have been developed. Nor have rules been developed specifying how instructed delegates are to behave – for example, when they are to consult with their constituencies and when they are to compromise or transcend the views of their constituencies. Rejection of representation in principle has meant that practices to ensure responsible representation have not emerged. In short, feminist principles have stunted the development of feminist practices of responsible and accountable decision making.

Having experienced the exclusion, alienation, and sense of powerlessness that is the lot of those 'on the bottom,' many marginalized people have tried to avoid élitist ways of operating in the groups they have created for themselves (Janeway 1981). A classic discussion of the possibility of developing genuinely democratic organizations is that of Robert Michels ([1915] 1962). Observing European working-class movements, Michels developed the hypothesis that elected leaders and paid officials would always eventually constitute an oligarchy in any organization, regardless of the strength of the organization's ideological commitment to democratic control. He argued that those at the centre/top (even if they are not intent on consolidating power) develop more knowledge and expertise than those at the grass roots, and that this advantage constitutes the basis of their power. Michels thus formulated his *iron law of oligarchy*, which holds that the tendency to top-down control is an inherent characteristic of organizations.

Ironically, what Michels attributes to the nature of the organization itself, many radical feminists, in their formal ideological explanation of causes, attribute to male nature. Hence, when cultural feminists describe organizations, including NAC, as a 'male,' they are attributing their negative characteristics as much to the male creators of organizational forms as to the forms themselves. One of the key questions for contemporary feminism, however, is whether women could build complex organizations (that is, larger and more complex than the collective) that do not repeat the oligarchic tendency described by Michels in the male, European tradition. It is our view that it is not only possible, but, also necessary, to bend the iron law of oligarchy in order to build movement institutions that are able both to endure and to transmit norms of feminist process to new generations of women. To bend Michels's iron law in woman-centred organizations, it is necessary to develop ways of incorporating the insights about political process that have been drawn from the simple, collectivist organization. Although a movement institution cannot simply be the collective writ large, it can encompass aspects of its operation.

As we have seen, several key norms of liberal democracy are rejected in the operation of radical-feminist groups. In addition to the critiques of representation and leadership that we have already examined, the conception of democracy often described as feminist process or 'the feminization of politics' also involves the rejection of majority rule, of voting as the means of reaching decisions, and of representation by population (one person/one vote). The practice of majority rule has emerged as a key issue of contention in the debate about feminist process.

Majority rule is rejected by many feminists in favour of consensus decision making because it recognizes conflict and resolves it through a formal process in which there are winners and losers. To some, 'the major advantage of consensus over majority rule is that no one becomes committed by others to a decision she cannot live with comfortably' (Hawthurst and Morrow, 1984:73). The method of achieving consensus involves extended discussion until something 'everybody can live with' has emerged. (It should be noted that this process resembles the one practised by many of the First Nations.) The idea that any conclusion reached must be one with which everyone can be 'comfortable' reflects the importance in feminist politics of 'taking things personally.' From this follows the view that 'feminist process also implies the abandonment of politically correct, unitary positions on issues, the ideological categorization of ourselves and each other' (Greaves 1991:17). In this analysis, seeing politics in terms of majorities and minorities involves accepting dichotomous yes/no positions on questions that are too complex for such simple oppositions:

There are not two sides to questions when approached using a feminist process, but many. Instead of mountains of policies largely unknown by the NAC membership, there would be 'bottom lines', guidelines ... Within these limits, women could decide to join and support NAC if they could at least 'live with' its aims. Feminist process would abandon the dogged search for a unitary position on issues. (Greaves 1991:19)

Turning NAC into a consensus-based organization has the allure of what has been called 'the Icelandic solution.' Women from the Icelandic Women's List (who rejected the very word *party* in their name) have been invited to visit Canada frequently in recent years (on one occasion by NAC), reflecting the hope of many English-Canadian women that the Icelandic experience could be repeated here. In Iceland, a woman-centred political program based on women's personal experiences was developed through a process of consensus building that allowed the women involved to arrive at common positions that they could all 'live with.' The original group consisted of twelve members; other women became part of the group if they could support the main ideas that had been established. This structureless, consensus-based process was possible in Iceland because of that country's homogeneous, small population and its small, compact territory. In NAC, women come together as representatives of other women belonging to groups and organizations that vary widely in size, character, and aim. To some, the emphasis on personal experience that 'the Icelandic solution' involves 'makes it difficult to communicate ideas which have been gained from the women's movement in the past or from other forms of radical politics' (Rowbotham et al. 1979:40).

The demand for consensus is seen by some feminists as the prelude to a suppression of the expression of differences. *Feminist process* is often seen as a code-name for a politics that 'takes homogeneity as its standard' and perpetuates a 'myth of sisterhood [that] is oppressive when it rules out [political debate over] differences of race, class, ability, language, political perspective and sexuality' (Jones and Stevens 1988:5). This is perhaps the deepest schism within feminist body politic. On the one hand are those who consider conflict something to be talked out and bridged, or transcended; on the other are women who believe politics to be conflictual, about making choices, and about defending the choices made. The feminists committed to consensus processes believe there should be no winners or losers. The vision that agreement can always be reached with the requisite time and will is based on the experience of homogeneity and the ideology of sisterhood in small groups. It does not realistically accept the existence of differences that cannot be transcended or talked out.

Too often, feminist debates concerning political process and organization become reduced to a matter of either/or. The case is often put that feminist organizations can *either* be efficient (and surrender the dream of an authentic politics) *or* engage in intimate political debate in impotent isolation from the forces of change. It is our view that emerging practices within women's movement as a whole provide the basis for transcending this 'either/or' dilemma. Few contemporary feminists would settle for replicating the operational modes of male-dominated groups, and there is no reason for woman-centred institutions such as NAC to surrender women's desire for a more inclusive and less alienating way of operating. The aim should be at least to *bend* the iron law of oligarchy, if it cannot be broken.

Our examination of agency in NAC has revealed many ways in which its processes could become more clearly democratic and representative. The first involves a recognition that NAC is an organization of organizations and that those organizations are composed of women who are currently not being represented fairly. The rejection of representation by population within NAC reflects a conception of representation that sees the rights of the women who are representatives as more important than the rights of the women represented. The vast underrepresentation of the large, generally national organizations and the overrepresentation of the small-group collectives in NAC seriously distort its voice and hamper its ability to maintain its complex coalitions with some degree of stability. The difficulty experienced by many women in NAC in working out what it could mean to represent a group resulted in considerable chaos in the evolution of NAC's policy-making processes. Energetic individuals have been able to pirate the policy process away from NAC's formal leadership and from the influence of groups with significant experience in the area. The goal now must be to strike a balance between the values of representation, on the one hand, and of accessibility, on the other. The policy process is, in fact, the main expression of efforts to do just that.

Notes

1 Clearly, the degree of influence in NAC is not always determined by the volume of group membership. The Survival Committee, for example, which links environmental and peace issues and reflects the influence and leadership of women like Kay Macpherson and Betsy Carr, has clout in NAC far beyond the number of member groups in the organization from these areas.

2 It should be noted that few Canadian institutions short of Parliament can afford translation on the scale NAC would require. If NAC is to become a movement institution anchoring women's efforts over several generations, however, it is crucial that this be a matter of high priority.

3 Again, we must stress the paradoxical nature of NAC's structure. Individuals completed the survey questionnaire as individuals. We have no way of knowing if these women mirror the views of other women in their groups. Had the same survey been conducted the year before or the year after, it might have revealed a different profile. Lack of money for translation of the survey questionnaire prevented Chris Appelle from including the francophone delegates (of whom there were about twenty) in what was a student research project.

4 Although female representation in trade unions in Canada has jumped in recent years, it rose from 24 per cent to only 30 per cent in the 1972–82 decade (Briskin and Yanz 1983). NAC's great fortune in having Grace Hartman as president created links of some importance. As Hartman said, 'links between feminists and unionists were very weak in the early seventies' (personal interview with Chris Appelle, 10 January 1986). She and Madeleine Parent have been important leaders and symbols within NAC for working class feminists.

5 It is interesting that many of the new generation of feminists attribute the capacity to achieve consensus to the absence of certain procedures (such as vote taking and rules of order) and to the presence of others (such as check-ins, agenda modification, and process notes). Few see the capacity to foster consensus as a quality of leadership.

6 Dorothy Dinnerstein's hypothesis that we fear female power because we experienced the patriarchal good mother in the nursery is suggestive here. It is worth noting that Richardson's leaders did not exercise authority in the sense of telling other women what to do. They were like the good mothers in a patriarchal household: they were the ones who made things possible, but the father was in fact the authority.

7 Greaves's Manichean projection of maleness onto all of the negative features of NAC was a common element of the cultural-feminist critique in this debate. It was as though describing NAC as male or its processes as based on the 'male model' was the most profound charge that could be made against it. This Manicheanism is a feature of experience in collectives, in which women have difficulty dealing with conflict that cannot be bridged or transcended.

8 Kay Macpherson notes that the term *president* was not typically used in NAC until after her term in office.

9 See Chapter 1, note 3.

10 In hindsight, however, we can see that the ad hoc process prevented English-Canadian feminists from understanding why the Charter of Rights and the issue of patriation were provoking a crisis within the FFQ. This, in turn, meant that they failed later on to understand the importance of the Meech Lake Accord to most francophone feminists in Québec.

11 In the 1988 election, no leaders' debate was held and NAC's calling-to-account appeared as though it were anti-government rather than part of a well-developed strategy. Hošek views about the strategy reflected her support for a liberal-feminist program of getting more women elected in official politics.

12 Today, many women who call themselves 'radical' feminists are best described as cultural feminists. Willis (1984:91) describes cultural feminism as 'essentially a moral, countercultural movement aimed at redeeming its participants, while radical feminism began as a political movement to end male supremacy in all areas of social and economic life, and rejected the whole idea of opposing male and female natures and values as a sexist idea.' Others would see cultural feminism as more consistent with first-wave 'social feminism' (Black 1989). See the Glossary for our attempt to clarify these terms.

6 The Policy Process: Structures for a New Parliament of Women

On 7 April 1972, a letter to the editor under the heading 'Women's Conference Discriminatory' appeared in the *Toronto Star*. Writing about the impending conference at which NAC was to be formed, Gwen Landholt pointed out that a $15,000 federal grant was being used for financing, but that anti-abortion groups 'have been refused permission to send representatives to the April Conference.'[1] On 10 April 1972, the *Globe and Mail* ran a report on the 'Strategy for Change' conference headed 'Abortion a Non-Topic but Keeps Coming Up' (Kirkwood 1972), which described the conference as having lurched from controversy to controversy. Radical feminists and women opposed to abortion were the noisiest dissenters from the seventy-eight 'hard-line demands' that were drawn up by assembly participants after an explosive debate. A bit of foreshadowing was provided by a controversy that erupted between sculptor Maryon Kantaroff, who favoured a women's party, and some first-wave 'big guns,' such as Florence Bird and Thérèse Casgrain, who wanted women to work within existing political structures. This birth of NAC in conflict and disagreement over both policy and political practice led to the initial strategy of supporting the recommendations of the Royal Commission on the Status of Women. York University professor Esther Greenglass was quoted as saying that 'it was assumed the women agreed on the recommendations of the status of women report: It was now time for action' (Hamilton 1972). The royal commission's report and its 157 recommendations were generated through a process of nationwide consultation with women's groups, supplemented by extensive research, and many women were willing to accept them as a blueprint and proceed with action to gain implementation. This strategy had far-reaching consequences for the development of NAC. It meant that attention was focused in the early years on the 'how' of implementation more than on the 'what' of concrete policy issues.

As we have illustrated, debate in NAC about the relative value of the 'lobby-and-brief' method as opposed to educative methods and more-confrontational direct actions was intense from the outset. The acceptance of the royal commission's report as NAC's focal policy document meant that little thought went into designing a policy process. Rather, the policy process was left to develop randomly, with little conscious planning about the nature and role of policy in feminist politics. However, it also enabled NAC to survive its founding period, as well as the process of grafting on a radical grass roots. It is quite likely that NAC would not have survived at all, or would have survived only as a more narrow coalition of traditional and liberal feminists, if the policy process had been wide open during the formative years.

In this chapter, we examine the policy process in NAC during the three periods that we have defined. During the founding era, the emphasis was on action, especially lobbying. The report of the Royal Commission on the Status of Women represented the centre of the process, with conflict revolving around issues of strategy and tactics and of priorities among the many policy recommendations. Policy was largely the responsibility of the executive and the AGM, and action was undertaken largely by the executive and annual lobby. No need for policy 'experts' emerged. When the royal commission recommendations proved insufficient in some areas of policy, member organizations were consulted as knowledgeable sources in their particular areas of interest. The first major eruptions of conflict around policy issues occurred during the transitional phase. The executive developed an internal committee structure, which began to initiate policy and advocacy rather than simply dealing with resolutions that came from member groups through the AGM. In particular, the NAC Left (working-class/union feminists and socialist-feminists) began to develop the Employment Committee as a virtually independent base for policy development, responses to government, strike support, and participation in various coalitions. Conflict over strategy predominated during this period, underwritten by ideological and partisan debates that cut across a number of issues. None the less, most of the major actors agreed on the nature of the policy process and on the fact that it involved the development of feminist 'experts' and a feminist mode of analysing the legislation and other initiatives generated by governments.

During the era of institutionalization, conflict over the nature of the policy process itself came to predominate. To many new feminists, the notion of feminist expertise was objectionable, and policy, as a product of expertise, was seen as 'male.' Positions on which women might take action were seen as properly generated through a decentralized process of gathering opinions worked out by women in small groups. Constructing a political agenda in this way would involve all the women of the movement equally as 'the experts,' and the problem for NAC would be how to tap into that diffuse knowledge. In this chapter, we therefore focus primarily on conceptions of policy, expertise, research or knowledge, and opinion, on the one hand, and on the structures of the policy process within NAC, on the other. In particular, we explore the ways in which emerging feminist conceptions of the policy process differed profoundly from government conceptions of that process.

We have argued that the long-term success of the English-Canadian women's movement will depend on its ability to develop an institution capable of organizing women's efforts over several generations. Such an institution, therefore, has political objectives at two distinct levels: concern for long-term goals affecting several generations of women and concern for short-term goals affecting women within our own lifetimes. It is, in fact, difficult to distinguish between the short-term and the long-term issues.[2] To describe an issue as short-term or long-term, moreover, does not necessarily indicate its relative importance; it suggests only the likely time-span for the achievement of a particular goal.

The other component of the policy process that will occupy us in this chapter is agenda setting and the establishment of priorities among problems, causes, and issues. In her article on the organizational review, Lorraine Greaves (1988) suggested that, to date, NAC had acted as an 'ordinary' political organization, in which the loudest, largest, and most articulate voices captured its policy agenda and got NAC action on 'their issue.' In this chapter, we test her hypothesis as we examine the policy process in several concrete cases.

Our exploration of policy making in this chapter enables us to see the transition from status-of-women issues as NAC's main policy focus to the incorporation of a more holistic feminist analysis that challenges the private/public 'split' and seeks to achieve both short-term goals and long-term objectives of fundamental change. The ability of the state institutions to which NAC relates to even comprehend long-term change is in decline. Hence, the process of setting goals, devising solutions to problems, and testing programs designed to achieve change relies heavily on the initiative of women themselves. In this chapter, therefore, we also pay heed to the ways in which changes in governmental processes have affected NAC's understanding of the broader policy process.

Our analysis will proceed in four sections: (1) changing conceptions of the policy process in NAC; (2) the evolution of structures to develop policy, set agendas, and choose among action goals; (3) NAC's interaction with government on short-term issues; (4) NAC's treatment of long-term issues.

Changing Conceptions of the Policy Process in NAC

NAC was designed to educate and lobby with a 'set-piece' document in hand. At the 'Strategy for Change' conference, Florence Bird, who had headed the Royal Commission on the Status of Women, called for 'Action now!' on the recommendations contained in her commission's report. Despite Gwen Landholt's complaint, Laura Sabia's brave vision was to take 'every group possible, from traditional to radical' even though 'we knew we were running a calculated risk' (Hamilton 1972). Officially, NAC's approach was to be balanced; most of its effort was to be devoted to gaining action on the recommendations of the royal commission, but the NAC coalition could generate new policies as well. Clearly, such an approach was necessary if the groups of newly mobilized feminists were to play any role in NAC at all, since the royal commission's recommendations left untouched large areas of their concern.

Although the founding mothers wished to emphasize action rather than the study or the debate of policy, they were also familiar with the rich tradition of the many organizations of the first wave of women's mobilization and of the voluntary or service organizations women established to 'get things done.' Certainly, first-wave women assumed they could undertake both the political analysis of an issue or problem and the formulation of a program or policy to deal with it. It rarely occurred to them that they would require 'experts' to tell them what ought to be done to alleviate the problems they identified. The development of the helping professions, such as social work, however, began to create a distinction between the views of grass-roots women and those of women 'educated to help,' lending a greater authority to the latter (Walker 1990). This professionalization was the first step towards challenging the legitimacy of ordinary women's policy ideas.

Most of the areas in which women's groups were active would now be categorized as areas of social policy rather than the so-called hard areas of economic, fiscal, military, scientific, and technological policy or industrial and labour policy. The political strategies women's groups most frequently employed involved the presentation of briefs and resolutions to governments,[3] as well as direct action, often in the form of creating services. During the first wave, visiting nurses' orders and children's aid societies were created in this way, as, more recently, were rape crisis centres and shelters for battered women. Communities depended on women and women's associations to identify problems, provide interim services, and solicit legislation and programs from government for permanent solutions.

The role of women as direct policy generators, then, initially grew out of the rich traditions of women's political culture that had developed before suffrage and that had been further elaborated in the period up to the 1960s. Women's experience as initiators of policy (rather than as passive consumers) declined as the helping professions developed (leaving little room for 'amateurs') and as 'hard' policy areas came to dominate political discourse at all but the local levels. The norms involved in women's traditional policy debates were also frequently at odds with the norms that prevailed in public institutions. Women's concerns were usually for social justice and security. (Such gender-gap analysis as is available for the first half of this century suggests that women in Canada displayed a stronger level of support than men for welfare-state institutions such as medicare.)

Women have generally tended to measure the success or failure of a program by whether it actually achieves its desired objective rather than by its efficiency in the abstract. After the Second World War, a renewed ideology of pronatalism and the privatization of women (Sapiro 1983) made it increasingly difficulty to persuade people that the private/public 'split' was a myth of male-centred ideology. As the Canadian political system became more centralized and more bureaucratized, the policy processes of the state became more professionalized and were purported to draw more extensively on the knowledge of experts. Since relatively few women became the 'experts' and fewer still became mandarins in the public service, public policy was not constructed 'as if women mattered.' Indeed, until the 1970s, the notion that policies might affect women differently from the way they affect men would have been ridiculed. And, although it is now more clearly understood that apparently gender-neutral policies can have a differential and negative effect on women, the indicators of appropriate policy choices still depend on male-centred values that parade as universal.

The process adopted by the Royal Commission on the Status of Women established a pattern in Canada of allowing policy recommendations to be guided by both expert research and grass-roots individual and group knowledge and testimony. Within the NAC community, however, there were two positions on the nature of the policy process. One stressed feminist expertise and non-sexist knowledge in developing a policy-making process that took women seriously (Eichler 1988). The second stressed the importance of revealing the knowledge of their situation that women already had, and presenting it in ways that would allow them to identify strategies for change (including interventions in the public-policy process, where that was appropriate).[4] The concept associated with this orientation to policy making is that of action research. Local groups would engage in action research, and use its results as the basis for their issue positions within NAC. We devote the remainder of this section to a closer look at each of these orientations.

The 'Lobby-and-Brief' Approach to Policy

The first of these positions on the nature of the policy process operated within the framework of interest-group liberalism, which held that the public-policy agenda was properly to be shaped by the society's organized interests. The keys to women's having a serious impact on public policy were seen as (1) persuading the policy élite that their sexist research base must be changed and (2) developing feminist experts who could bridge between the public-policy process and the women's movement. Control of policy by feminist experts in NAC was therefore seen as a permanent feature of the policy process. In terms of government policy making, control over the federal policy process was concentrated in the party system and the bureaucracy until the late 1970s but, in recent years, there has been increased involvement by the Prime Minister's Office (PMO) and the Privy Council Office (PCO). These changes, along with Parliament's reorganized and strengthened committees (Aucoin 1979),[5] increasingly meant that 'experts from non-traditional backgrounds' (*read* 'women') became a necessary component. As Findlay (1987:37) states,

Both the under-representation of women in the bureaucratic decision-making process and lack of expertise on women's issues made it difficult to argue that the state could act in the interests of women's equality. The bureaucracy's task was to correct this situation, both by increasing its own expertise and by appointing women to decision-making positions who would be seen to understand and represent the issue.

Although Findlay argues convincingly that the bureaucracy remained largely resistant to feminist policy analysis, other actors, especially within the parliamentary-committee system and the political parties, did become more open to feminist expertise in some areas. (They became more open to anti-feminist expertise as well, as Parliament's Special Committee on Child Care was to show.)

The lobby-and-brief framework usually reflected this traditional view of policy making in NAC. In 1976, the AGM recommended that NAC seek funding to recruit 'resource people' and that it solicit the services of the newly formed Canadian Research Institute for the Advancement of Women (CRIAW). Lorna Marsden's belief in the importance of expertise is evident in her interview with Cerise Morris (1983:100) in October 1978:

First, many issues of the women's movement are too complex to be put forward in a useful way to influence public opinion; e.g., 'crummy pay' is OK to talk about but strategic considerations of equal pay for work of equal value are too complex ... more fundamentally, if you look at the way social change occurs in Canada most impact comes from influence on institutional authorities challenged in a quiet, straightforward way – not from populist protest.

Elsie Gregory MacGill constructed NAC's Index of Policy Recommendations for the period 1972–8 (which was later updated to 1982).[6] The index shows considerable policy activity beyond that recommended in the royal commission's report. The recruitment of 'experts' or consultants to advise the executive is also apparent during this period. For example, in 1977, Toronto lawyer Mary Eberts advised the executive with regard to family law (Executive Minutes, 20 March 1977). Also available to members of the executive during that year were political scientist Ruth Bell; Lorenne Clark, Canada's foremost feminist expert on rape; economist Marjorie Cohen; sociologists Lorna Marsden and Lynn McDonald; and labour specialists Lynn Kaye and Laurel Ritchie. Political expertise was also provided by Bell (PC) and Marsden (Liberal). During this period, NAC recruited feminist expertise directly onto the executive rather than using that structure for representation. Workshops held during the combined conferences and AGMs also permitted the recruitment of policy experts. In fact, until the development of policy committees attached to the executive, workshops at the AGM were the main mode of debating policy options outside the executive.

The first evidence of the development of policy committees in the executive appears in 1978 with the creation of the Social Services Committee. Lorenne Clark (Toronto Rape Crisis Centre) is reported as explaining Bill C-52 as it dealt with prostitution (Executive Minutes 12 August 1978). The Employment Committee was created at the 26 May 1979 executive meeting, following extensive activity in the Employment Workshops at the 1979 AGM, which created a policy agenda for the new committee.[7] The first task assigned to the committee by the executive was to 'organize a delegation to meet with Sylvia Ostry on the Economic Council of Canada study on women in the economy' (Executive Minutes, 26 May 1979). By April 1981, the executive had struck six policy/action committees: employment, social services (including health and reproductive rights), pensions (tax, and so on), justice, media policy (communications), and constitution. The ideological breakdown of the committees of the executive at this time was as follows: radical feminists, under the leadership of Lorenne Clark, primarily on the Social Services Committee; leftist feminists, primarily on the Employment Committee, with Marjorie Cohen as the ongoing element of continuity; and liberal feminists, on the Pension Committee, with Jean Wood, and on the Constitution Committee.

Conflict occurred in each of these broad policy areas, but all of the elements, as then represented, seemed to share a common view of the nature of policy, the role of expertise, and the appropriateness of NAC's actions *vis-à-vis* the public-policy process. The Employment Committee had a busy and detailed agenda throughout the transitional period. A variety of new items, such as occupational health, were brought to the executive through the expertise of its union members. The developing socialist-feminist critique of mainstream economic analysis was also apparent. Moreover, as the usefulness of the report of the royal commission as a policy guideline faded with new members and new issues flooding the arena, the evolution of real policy structures began. We analyse those structures in some detail in the next section. But, first, we examine the other major orientation to the policy process in NAC – the position based on grass-roots knowledge and action research.

An Alternative Conception of Policy: Strategies for Change and Action Research

The conventional policy framework, even with the addition of the feminist experts, remains fixed on the belief that governments can deliver the changes required to improve women's lives or to make women equal. We have already discussed the ideas of some new feminists who rejected this proposition out of hand. For those who saw a complete social and cultural transformation as the ultimate goal, the issue of policy development often seemed irrelevant. In fact, however, many of those who espouse complete transformation and oppose a policy approach that focuses only on the state do not necessarily avoid or ignore the state and its institutions altogether. As one feminist involved in the Vancouver Women's Research Centre argues,

Notwithstanding our recognition of the state's role in perpetuating women's oppression, the fact is the state exists and its institutions have direct power over women's lives. We believe that if part of the mandate of feminism is to improve the conditions of women's lives, then as feminists we have no choice but to work with the state and to try to influence how state power is exercised. To turn our backs on the state, to refuse to deal with 'our oppressors,' is to abandon women in the interest of purism. We can and must seek to change what the state does in women's lives and how it does it. (Price 1988:8–9)

The assumption that state institutions have direct power over women's lives is an important element of the integrative feminism that permits the complex coalitions within NAC to exist. Feminists of the Left and some radical feminists have adopted the approach of developing effective 'strategies for change.' Rather than assuming that state action, and especially legislation, is always the most effective route however, these sceptics pursue a more strategic approach, examining courses of action other than getting the law changed. They recognize that institutions other than Parliament affect women's lives, and that attempts to educate or pressure those institutions might be a necessary element of other, effective political strategies.

Two examples of feminist groups using action research and the strategies-for-change approach are the Women's Research Centre in Vancouver, and Relais femmes, in Montreal. The Vancouver Research Women's Centre, for example, facilitated a campaign by Women Against Violence Against Women (WAVAW) to educate the police department in that city about women encountering male violence and to challenge the ideas the police had about women. Price (1988) argues that institutional change may often involve change less in *what* people do than in *how* they do it. Pointing to a change in British Columbia's policy on wife assault in 1983, when the attorney general directed the police to arrest battering men, she argues, 'There was no change in the law; what was changed was the policy of enforcement and the procedure for laying charges under the existing law' (18). Megan Ellis (1987) links the strategies-for-change approach to action research in her discussion of professionalism and expertise. She explains that, to 'experts,' crime is defined not by the victim's experience of harm but by the measurement of an activity against an abstract standard. By contrast, action research, which grew out of the consciousness-raising and theoretical work of feminist groups formed during the second wave and out of the experience of small groups providing services, assumes that the information necessary to choose among strategies for change is possessed by the women who are seeking change for themselves – that is, that they do not need experts to interpret their experiences for them. The goal here is research *by* the people who hope to benefit from its findings. The role of the Women's Research Centre in Vancouver [8] is to facilitate women's research and to educate them about the research methods that are available to them.

This approach echoes the reports of grass-roots experience and women's testimonies about their lives that gave the Royal Commission on the Status of Women such legitimacy. Action research, unlike academic or expert research, is not theory driven. Existing theories are often flawed by being constructed on the basis of male experience only or by using male experience as the norm. Moreover, 'If the action strategies are to serve women's interests, then it is clear that research and analysis building must begin with women. Research that begins, for example, with institutional decision-makers and with their questions, concerns or experience will serve their interest' (Women's Research Centre 1987:5). From this perspective, even feminist experts have interests that diverge from their subjects' interests.

To those who pursue this approach, the term *policy* itself is something of a misnomer. Some feminists have taken the action-research orientation farther by seeing the very process of reaching decisions as the definitive quality of feminism. Lorraine Greaves (1991), for example, believes that NAC should stop 'reacting' to government calls for policy proposals. She argues that:

There are not two sides to questions when approached using a feminist process, but many. Instead of mountains of policies largely unknown by the NAC membership, there would be 'bottom lines,' guidelines, lots of background information, strategies, educational pamphlets, and 'how to' manuals ... NAC's long tradition of clarifying and sharpening for public consumption a singular feminist position on legislative issues is less appropriate in a more representative, diverse women's movement facing increasingly complex issues. Singular positions serve the media's interests best in its [sic] search for succinctness, and serve the membership the least, in ignoring the texture and evolving nature of feminist opinion. (114)

These two orientations to the policy process and to the media have operated within NAC almost from the beginning. NAC's original *raison d'être* was action, based on the policy positions of the royal commission. As NAC's membership base increased and became more diverse, however, the development of policy became important, and structures such as the AGM, the lobby, and the committees evolved to create policy, determine priorities, and strike agendas. As NAC became institutionalized, it began to take on characteristics of a parliament of women; that is, geographic, sectoral, and linguistic representativeness rose on the NAC agenda. The organizational-review coalition showed influences both from the strategies-for-change approach, which would downplay the public-policy process, and from those who take the public-policy process very seriously but wish to ensure the involvement of member groups in the policy, priorities, and resource-allocation decisions. In the consultants' report on organizational review, a distinction emerged between reactive policy requirements and proactive policy or strategy developments. This suggests that a NAC institutionalized 'for the long haul' would continue to devote some of its energies and resources to responding to government demands for briefs and position papers, while reserving some for the development of broad, in-depth political surveys on a long-term work plan as well as for the development of feminist political process (NAC ORD 1988:19). This sense of reserving a significant portion of NAC resources for long- and medium-term policy suggests a much more strategic approach to change. It also emphasizes the capacity of NAC member groups to engage in action research and to share their experiences in dealing with institutions, so that long-term strategic knowledge can emerge.

Evolving Policy Structures in NAC

As a parliament of women, NAC's lack of structures for setting priorities has been it most serious weakness. As NAC moved from a narrow status-of-women approach to public policy to a broader feminist politics, its structures came to be increasingly ill suited to the heavy demands being made on them. The Annual General Meeting, which worked well as a structure for policy debate with fifty delegates, was an alienating nightmare with five hundred. The executive, which had dealt effectively with resource allocation when it and NAC's resources were small, became ineffective when twenty-five women each tried to capture her committee's or cause's 'share' of time, money, attention, and energy. Committees that began as devices to co-opt the energies of policy experts into NAC came to be seen as élitist groups pursuing their own agendas in a largely unaccountable and inaccessible way. In this section, we examine the policy structures that emerged during NAC's development, remembering that NAC was originally intended to be an *action committee* that would campaign for the implementation of policies already developed by the royal commission.

The NAC Lobby and Lobbying

We begin by delineating the structures developed to lobby the federal government for implementation of the recommendations of the Royal Commission on the Status of Women. We believe it is important to begin here, because the AGM and the executive were designed for the lobbying activity and took on other functions only more recently. In fact, it is our contention that their weakness as policy structures is attributable to the tacking on of new functions over time.[9] In 1975, the current structures of an Annual General Meeting and an executive were finalized. The format of a formal lobby following an annual general meeting held in Ottawa was introduced by Lorna Marsden in 1977.

During the 1972–8 founding period, extensive lobbying occurred, conducted largely by the officers. With the establishment of the AGM lobby, which required that the AGM be permanently based in Ottawa, the initial structures for NAC lobbying were in place. The one-woman, Toronto-based office, staffed by Pearl Blazer, was part of this structure; it was a far cry from the specialized structures developed in the 1980s, which included an Ottawa office and a parliamentary liaison officer. NAC's lobbying activities took two major forms: (1) the mass lobby of the three main political parties by NAC delegates after the AGM, and (2) the ongoing lobbying effort, consisting of briefs and presentations to the prime minister, cabinet ministers, working committees of the House, and parliamentary task forces. The ongoing lobby was least effective at the level of the bureaucracy, although some chairs and executive members did establish useful links, especially with the network of feminists within the public service. Some structures, such as the Women's Bureau in the Department of Labour, have provided access consistently for a long period of time. Others, such as the women's program in the Public Service Commission, survived only briefly.

The functions of the AGM lobby were:

1. for NAC delegates to see at first hand how the parties behave and how the top decision-makers respond to the issues of the day;
2. to provide education and new skills for the individual delegates in questioning their elected representatives – skills that could carry over to the provincial and local levels;
3. for NAC to exercise and experience its own strength as a lobby organization that wields political clout and to persuade new or wavering member groups of that clout;
4. for NAC to gain media coverage (ideally, a clip on the national news to highlight the key issues and the stature of NAC).

When the format of the AGM lobby was designed by Lorna Marsden, the politicians 'receiving' the lobby for the government were often briefed in advance and were frequently supportive. To some degree, the results could be stage-managed to enhance the apparent success of the event. Such a symbiotic relationship was of short duration, however, and later AGM lobbies rarely resulted in concrete policy achievements. Instead, they continued the century-old tradition among Canadian Women's groups of commanding the attention of the powerful, but only for one day a year.[10] The AGM lobby's public and sometimes combative character made it controversial in an era of Conservative government and anti-feminist backlash.

The desire for direct action, which the AGM lobby reflected, also declined in an era in which politicians felt free to express anti-feminist positions or to stonewall because they believed that women were divided. (NAC ORD 1988). The willingness of the Mulroney government to simply ignore the AGM lobby and to risk whatever consequences such a tactic might produce could force a change in its format.[11]

NAC lobbies the federal government on an ongoing basis throughout the year. To a significant degree, the government set the agenda. The basic problem for NAC has always been what issues to neglect, since almost any government initiative will rouse the concerns of some groups within NAC's large and diverse membership. The resolutions and emergency-resolutions process at the AGM has typically involved groups pressing their claims on NAC's time, money, and energies, usually in a bid to have NAC respond to some government initiative or other. Some groups have joined NAC with an emergency resolution concerning impending legislation in hand. The Canadian Organization for the Rights of Prostitutes (CORP), for example, joined NAC seeking support in opposition to legislation that threatened the rights of prostitutes. Other long-standing member groups, such as VOW, have wanted NAC to respond on international and military issues.

Lorna Marsden (1980) highlighted characteristics of NAC's ongoing lobby in her account of the lobby for federal 'equal pay for work of equal value' legislation. Focusing on the importance of experts and technical preparation, she noted that there was no attempt on NAC's part to gain broad public support for the issues. Rather, it was pursued through a 'quiet process' of accommodation between policy makers and lobbyists. She argued that 'Any attempt to draw into detailed debate a mass movement with demonstrations, the private sector with its enormous resources and vested interests or particular industrial or occupational groups will only decimate attempts to discuss such complex issues as equal pay for work of equal value, and lead to failure' (258). Marsden's approach has a limited value for a movement institution organized to achieve long-term as well as short-term goals. Governments come and go, and they view the world in short chunks of time. Fundamental changes in societal values (and the notion of equal pay for work of equal value represents just such a change) will take decades, not months, to establish. Although Marsden may be correct in her opinion that, in the case of the equal-pay issue, getting the principle established in law could have occurred only in the absence of extensive public scrutiny, there has been little concrete implementation as a result of this 'quiet' achievement. Moreover, partly because of this approach, when neoliberal and New Right opponents began to describe the principle as reverse discrimination and as 'equal pay for unequal work' (REAL Women brochure, 1988), women's movements had not developed an analysis of the principle sufficient to defend it effectively to the public. The legislation remained 'too technical' for many women's groups to defend and for popular political discourse to incorporate. It took Judge Rosalie Abella's analysis in the 1984 report of the Royal Commission on Equality and Employment to begin to develop a justification that women's movements could use.

In the 1980s, new conditions emerged that further shaped NAC's reactive lobbying approach. They included the following:

1. an increase in the number of organizations representing public interests in all sectors of society, including many coalitions of the NAC type, as well as a number of other equality-seeking coalitions that emerged in response to Section 15 of the Charter's equality guarantees;
2. the increasing complexity of government structures including the growing involvement of supplementary entities such as political staffs, public-affairs firms, and paragovernmental research and opinion-polling agencies;
3. the structural development of the English-Canadian women's movement, including many new lobbying devices such as networks and single-issue coalitions, as well as a significant rise in women's political awareness.

As a result of the first two new conditions, NAC had to begin both to collaborate and compete with more organizations on issues that were gaining increased public visibility. At the same time, it had to spread its resources over a much broader area in order to influence an expanding government network. With far more professional 'opinion shapers' in the field, the activity of influencing government became both slick and expensive. NAC's capacities in the reactive-lobby area, however, had come to be much stronger than they were in the 1970s. Indeed, NAC came to mount a comprehensive lobby on women's issues and to place an increased emphasis on coalition building and participation in coalitions with many other equality seekers.

NAC's ability to deal with an extended lobbying framework was limited by its scant resources. Only during the 1984–8 period was it possible for NAC to have a professional profile on Parliament Hill, through the Ottawa office. Most of the time, however, the Ottawa office was able only to monitor some of the main occurrences on the Hill and to keep the executive and members groups up to date on impending legislative action. In the past, the ongoing lobby had also included some largely symbolic events, such as budget lobbies with the finance minister and the nationally televised leaders' debate on women's issues of August 1984. Despite limited resources, however, the Ottawa office and the executive and officers were able, in some instances, to work together in well-organized campaigns. Mary Lou Murray, NAC's parliamentary liaison officer from 1985 to 1988, recounts NAC's efforts in relation to changes in the Indian Act:

With the Indian Act, we went door to door and lobbied everyone in the Cabinet and then staff and lots and lots of M.P.s. NAC's Indian Affairs Committee [*sic*] had presented numerous briefs to government ... the issue then became part of the election lobbying, and a question of native rights was included on the national television debate on women's issues ... I monitored daily the working of the Indian Affairs and Northern Development Committee of the House and reported back to NAC as well as to native groups across the country [*sic*, see following commentary] ... The bill finally passed in June 1985. (Personal interview with Chris Appelle, 4 December 1985)

Murray's account demonstrates both the strengths and the limitations of NAC's day-to-day lobby during this period. In the construction of policy, NAC's attention to issues was limited by the scope of its membership. The groups of aboriginal women that joined NAC in the 1970s largely represented women who had lost their status as Indians because of the discriminatory Indian Act. Leaders such as Mary Two-Axe Early participated in NAC and other organizations, such as CRIAW, to gain the support of the white women's movement. Within NAC, the advocacy of Madeleine Parent kept the issue fresh and NAC's support constant. What was lacking was the point of view of those Indian women who *had* Indian 'status' and whose concerns were focused on collective rights and equality among races more than on the rights of individual women. From their perspective, NAC's position amounted to advocacy of continuing the 'right' of the federal government to determine who was an Indian. It is unlikely, then, that NAC advocates of 'Indian rights for Indian women' understood the point of view of 'native groups across the country,' as Murray suggests. They had either taken the views of the disinherited women to represent the point of view of all Indian women or discounted the conflicting views of Indian women who wanted the First Nations and not the federal government to have the right to determine Indian citizenship. (That the latter was a just position is not in dispute; the point here is that NAC was not fully aware of it – or of other positions that may have been just but were not represented in its membership.)

NAC's effectiveness with regard to public policy has been enhanced by its involvement in advocacy coalitions and its ability to access parliamentary tasks forces and committees in a systematic way. We examine the latter ability in the final section of this chapter, in the course of our assessment of NAC's capacity to pursue long-term goals. Here, we will simply note one instance of NAC's involvement in advocacy coalitions – specifically, in the alliance that emerged in the fall of 1985 as a result of the proposed de-indexing of family allowances. The Family Allowance Coalition included groups such as the National Anti-Poverty Organization, the Canadian Labour Congress, the Conference of Catholic Bishops, and the Canadian Council on Children and Youth (*Status* [January 1986]). Modelled on the coalition that had successfully defended old age pensions against the Conservative government's attempts to de-index them, this coalition was in fact unsuccessful in its actual policy objective. It did, however, establish a firm coalition among groups fighting against the government's program of rolling back welfare-state entitlements. It also established NAC as an equal partner with the CLC and the Conference of Catholic Bishops.

The involvement in this coalition clearly confirmed the view of NAC as an organization that had to act strategically with long-term as well as short-term goals in mind. Participation in coalitions, sometimes with odd partners, was an approach troublesome to many women involved in small primary or organic groups. Although such groups may have been willing to join together in coalitions with like-minded groups at the local level, they were more suspicious of NAC joining high-profile national coalitions. Some wanted NAC to 'go it alone,' in order to avoid 'contamination' from non-feminist coalition partners. Moreover, such concerns were reinforced by the feeling among many of these groups that they could not exert control over the decisions of the executive and the committees as to which coalitions NAC would enter.

The third new condition that affected NAC's approach to lobbying – that is, increased support among women for more aggressive political tactics – emerged from NAC's experiences in relation to the ad hoc constitutional group's lobby. Political analysts have stressed the importance of this factor to the success of the lobby (Kome 1983; Bashevkin 1985). After that event, there appeared to be a broader acceptance of a wide range of strategies for influencing public policy. In part, this reflected the realities of the Conservative era. There was no longer a Conservative equivalent of Lorna Marsden in NAC urging a 'quiet conspiracy to do good,' although there were many PC feminists acting within the party and within state institutions to moderate the government's policies when they threatened women's status or well-being. Non-Conservative women supported the coalition strategy. Marjorie Cohen, for example, argued that 'not enough is known about government to make definitive statements about how it actually works ... my sense is that we have to work harder at building bases, expanding coalitions ... and really press our views towards government' (personal interview with Chris Appelle, 10 January 1986). What largely disappeared from NAC's discussion of its lobbying/advocacy function was the view that NAC alone could have an impact on bureaucracy and government sufficient to achieve its goals. This was partly because most of the groups NAC represented had needs requiring fundamental changes that could be achieved only in the long term. It was also because, to build up the clout required to gain access, a single lobby group would need extensive funding to maintain a larger lobby staff, as the National Organization of Women did in Washington, and to hire professional opinion polling and advice, available only on a professional basis.

It was also clear that the Conservative government had set ideas about appropriate lobbying behaviour for women's groups. A former minister responsible for the status of women, Barbara McDougall, through Janet Smith, her deputy minister for privatization, convened a workshop of some groups of the women's movement (broadly understood to include non-feminist but not anti-feminist groups) in April 1988. The objective was 'to improve the quality of communications and the consultative process between women's groups and policy makers in the interests of improving the status of women in Canada' (Canada, Secretary of State, Women's Program 1988: documentation kit). Deputy ministers were invited, and a few of them (mainly women) attended. The workshop was run by the Public Policy Forum, with well-respected feminist Jan Mears acting as facilitator. Although the ostensible purpose of the workshop was a two-way exchange of information between 'the leaders of the women's movement' and deputy ministers, the main business was an attempt to educate the movement in effective ways of entering into 'the consultative process.'

The overwhelming message was that there was a technical 'fix' that would improve communications between the movement and government – namely, that the movement should adapt to the pace and workings of the public-policy agenda, with its windows of opportunity' (usually created on the basis of pollsters' advice) that permitted little time for consultation between leaders and the grass roots. The message conveyed was that movement groups that wished (and could afford) to compete for time on the government agenda and that would accept the short-circuiting of the consultation process could achieve some short-term policy objectives if they behaved in 'appropriate' ways. Similarly, the workshop stressed that the government was not willing (or, perhaps, able, in terms of comprehension and attention span) to attend to views that deviated from these norms. This message was familiar to women within NAC, who had been attempting to influence public policy for several decades. The approach NAC *could* pursue, if it had the resources, was a full-dress lobby operation similar to that mounted by NOW in Washington. NOW's choice of approach, however, reflected fundamental differences in the political systems of the United States and Canada. In the former, the congressional system of government leaves individual legislators wide open to lobbying, because they are able to influence the public-policy agenda directly; the Canadian parliamentary system, by contrast, operates with strict party discipline, making individual MPs less desirable as objects of lobbying efforts.

The overall effect of lobbying at the federal level by NAC and other groups, however, was that women's issues did come to be firmly established on the public-policy agenda, even if effective government responses to those agenda items were not often achieved. Before the election of the second Mulroney government in 1988, NAC was consulted on a number of social-policy and economic issues. It participated in pre-budget consultations with the finance minister, as did the NCWC, the National Council of Jewish Women (NCJW), the Canadian Congress of Learning Opportunities for Women (CCLOW), the National Association of Women and the Law (NAWL), the FFQ, and AFÉAS. (Note that, with the exception of the NCWC, all these groups were affiliated with NAC.) NAC, along with the CACSW, the National Anti-Poverty Association, the National Council of Social Welfare, and the Canadian Association of Social Workers, also regularly advised the Social Policy Reform Group of Ministers. In 1986, NAC met with the prime minister on several occasions to discuss a full range of 'women's issues.' When NAC began to address what the Conservative government saw as general (or men's) issues, such as free trade, unemployment insurance, and immigration, however, it was criticized as being anti-government rather than pro-women. Indeed, NAC's increasing efforts to expose the gendered consequences of supposedly gender-neutral policies were strongly opposed by government, which wanted it to stick to 'women's issues.'

In the 1980s, NAC focused more heavily on getting a feminist analysis of many issues important to women into the public-policy arena. A major stumbling block to this effort was the gatekeeping role played by the media with regard to the introduction of new issues into the political agenda (Nelson 1984; McConney 1985). None the less, NAC and its member groups played a critical role in helping to restructure the public discourse on issues such as pornography, wife battering, incest and child abuse, rape, prostitution, day care, and pensions.

They did so by being available as 'authorities' who could offer the media different analyses of some of these issues from those they would obtain from professional and government experts (Stone 1992). The task of interpreting these issues and articulating satisfactory solutions is enormous and not something that can be accomplished in the short term. Efforts by NAC to introduce feminists analysis into all public-policy debate, including that pertaining to 'hard' economic issues, must be understood as even more long term.

The AGM and NAC's Policy Agenda

In the 1970s, the AGM functioned as a conference, at which there were some workshops that generated resolutions, and as a business meeting, at which such resolutions were adopted and became NAC policy, meant to direct the actions of the executive. As long as the size of NAC and its policy/advocacy agenda were such that a three-day annual meeting could deal with the business, there was some sense that member groups *could* steer the policy process through the AGM. Indeed, during this period, certain member groups and executive members argued that AGM decisions existed to control and constrain the activities of the executive. In the 1980s, the explosion in NAC membership made the AGM far larger. The agenda became so crowded that not all resolutions could even be considered, let alone seriously discussed. The AGM structure staggered under the increased burden, and many resolutions were simply referred to the executive, with no great faith on the part of member groups that they would be debated. In fact, resolutions originating in executive committees *were* more likely to receive attention. In this, the NAC AGM began to resemble a political party's policy convention, but without the accompanying steering devices, such as policy review committees.

Thus, two routes existed into the policy mill of the AGM: the route in from the committees, including the executive, and the route in from member groups. The AGM workshops became less effective as arenas in which member groups could debate policy. First, they were squeezed in terms of time by the expanding organizational business agenda. Second, they increasingly had to compete for agenda time with skills workshops and workshops that introduced delegates to the policy initiatives of the executive committees. Useful though the workshops were, especially to many first-time delegates, they did not serve the function of policy discussion and initiation that the earlier AGM workshops had served.

AGMs in the 1970s and early 1980s were structurally able to process policy recommendations and establish some sense of the delegates' priorities for the coming year, even if delegates did not exercise control over resources. A ten-year (1972–82) survey of NAC policy recommendations[12] revealed that a wide range of policy, advocacy, and action resolutions were passed. The approximately 290 resolutions passed by AGMs during this period would work out to a stately pace of about 30 resolutions per AGM. Since many were uncontroversial 'motherhood' statements, reassertions of support for royal commission recommendations, and calls for NAC advocacy or action, it is unlikely that more than several resolutions provoking conflict and controversy arose at any single AGM. The first seriously conflictual AGM occurred in 1979, when a number of controversial issues, including wages for housework, regional representation, and travel subsidies, racked the assembly.

By 1986, AGM included ten skills workshops, seven workshops to overview NAC issues, and thirty policy and/or advocacy workshops on everything from incest to free trade. The names of the skills workshops listed below give a sense of the range of activities at the AGM:

What is NAC and How it can work for you;
Dealing with the Right;
How to meet your MP;
How to write briefs, press releases and petitions;
How to reach uninvolved women;
Fundraising and Secretary of State grants;
Building alliances and making friends;
How to use humour ... to promote feminism;
How to attract and keep volunteers;
How to organize public meetings.
(AGM Briefing Book, 1986:12–13)

In addition to these activities, crammed into a day and a half, the delegates were expected to debate sixty regular resolutions, five amendments to the NAC constitution, and seventeen 'emergency' resolutions[13] in the next day and a half. Finally, exhausted delegates were expected to attend a workshop to prepare them for the AGM lobby the following day.

In 1984, after the crises of the transitional years, Doris Anderson introduced the practice of having plenary sessions chaired by neutral parliamentarians. (Strategy sessions were still being chaired by NAC officers.) This well-intentioned move, by releasing executive members from responsibility for the conduct of the AGM, actually freed them up for political wheeling and dealing. Like the AGM committee and the staff, the parliamentarians had responsibility, but no power to control the AGM format. Tensions heightened as single-issue groups lobbied for their causes; grass-roots groups tried to get new issues on the agenda; francophone women lamented poor translation (and the lack of any in committees and workshops); immigrant, disabled, and poor women pursued greater visibility and inclusion; 'rule jockeys' attempted to highjack the proceedings; the executive tried for efficiency, usually at the cost of fewer groups being heard; and everyone complained about the food. These tensions heightened the mood of the proceedings but also strained the AGM structure, which could not accommodate policy debate except in favourable circumstances. Although some issues were resolved, more were referred to the executive for resolution after the AGM than it could handle.[14] Moreover, the election process was also threaded through each AGM and, in the absence of electioneering, which would have linked candidates to policy positions clearly, many policy debates were prolonged by candidates' attempts to get their positions across to the voters in the course of the debate. The resolutions committee that attempted to sort out the resulting tangles was viewed with suspicion, especially by newcomers, who criticized the process as élitist.

There was frequent conflict when delegates, especially the majority of first-time delegates, believed their concerns were not given adequate attention. At the 1986 AGM, for example, delegates from a housing group felt that more time should have been devoted to women's pressing housing needs than to the issue of international peace, where they perceived NAC could have only a limited impact. Successive AGM committees attempted to devise methods to make allocation of time to subject areas 'fair.' Such methods usually included some kind of lottery process, which could mean that a new group joining NAC specifically to present its case might not get the opportunity to do so.

Clearly, the AGM structure worked more effectively when there was cohesion and cooperation among the groups. Regional umbrella groups, for example, could negotiate priorities in advance, at regional meetings, and then press for the achievement of a few important goals at the AGM. Delegates familiar with the operation of large meetings always enjoyed an advantage, no matter how dedicated the parliamentarians were to assisting the less experienced delegates. Women from small primary groups rarely had large-meeting skills and were often frustrated and angry about being made to feel incompetent in the process.

The Organizational Review Document of 1988 stressed the importance of having the AGM set priorities and policy and determine resource allocation in order to ensure that member groups rather than the executive or the committees would control NAC. A combination of regional meetings and a 'formal priority-setting procedure' was proposed,[15] along with an annual budgeting process in which member groups, through the AGM, could establish 'clear financial guidelines for the executive and staff.' These were activities that even a large and cumbersome AGM could accomplish. However, the real financial guidelines for much of NAC's spending were being established by the government funding agency, and this limited the ability of member groups to succeed in having their priorities met. Although it is true that other organizations dependent on government funding involve their memberships in the budgeting process through general-meeting structures, it is no less true that real budgetary control can be achieved only by a membership that funds the majority of the group's spending. In fact, some of the executive cynicism about the AGM came from the perception that the member groups really didn't 'pay the freight in NAC.' As a result, the executive, which had to raise the bulk of NAC's funds from government grants, may have felt justified in paying less attention to the AGM's views on matters of policy and priority than member groups might have wished.

The Organizational Review Committee's concern was as much with controlling the executive as with designing an effective policy-setting process. The document called for 'fewer resolutions at the AGM [in an attempt] to focus discussion and avoid leaving the executive with resolutions to be considered after the AGM.' This recommendation evaded the issues of deciding whose policy concerns would be ignored or deferred and of devising effective methods for policy setting in large groups. If the annual lobby had been attached to a smaller meeting in Ottawa and the AGM freed from the lobby, it might have been possible to structure a policy conference that could have both travelled across the country and met for a sufficient length of time to allow for serious debate. An ongoing policy-review structure, large enough to be representative, could have coordinated policy work in the committees. Potential restructuring aside, however, it was clear that the AGM, as it existed in the late 1980s, could not serve as an effective policy-making body. The main danger of an unreformed AGM structure in NAC was not that it alienated delegates who found the process unacceptable (although that *was* a damaging result), but that it made the organization vulnerable to co-optation by an organized subset of groups bent on a particular political course.

Executive and Committees

We have examined the development of the executive as a decision-making and representational structure in some detail. We now move on to a discussion of the role of the executive and its committees in the processes of policy making, priority setting, and resource allocation. In the absence of effective AGM mechanisms, both priority setting and resource allocation took place in the executive, with a role also being played by the staff. In this section, we use a number of sources, including the NAC program submissions to the Secretary of State Women's Program for 1984–5 and 1985–6, to help us re-create the operation of the policy process. Documents prepared for government funding agencies can be misleading, because they often inflate an organization's activities, particularly in categories favoured by governments. None the less, they give an adequate general picture. We also employ an analysis of the activity reported in *Feminist Action*, which succeeded *Status* as NAC's house organ and use Lorraine Greaves's published account (1991) of the political process within NAC and its committees as she perceived them during her tenure as an executive member.[16]

As we have seen, NAC's committees emerged out of the executive's involvement in policy once the shadow of the royal commission had faded. To call the committees then or since *policy committees*, however, would be to misrepresent their usual nature. According to the evidence to be found in the executive minutes and reports in NAC publications, committees functioned primarily to accomplish the following: respond to governments; decide if governments should be responded to; identify new policy areas; solicit or undertake research; recruit experts; construct and engage in coalitions; debate policy options; engage in advocacy; and educate NAC members and the public. In the 1984–5 program submission to the Women's Program of the Secretary of State, we find requested a total amount of $62,375 for NAC's 'policy committees.' (The amount actually received and allocated to committees was $35,000.) Given the fact that $445,780 was requested overall, it is clear that the policy committees were considered a minor part of NAC's operation compared with the staff function, for example, for which NAC requested $101,200 to cover salaries and benefits.

In fact, policy development also occurred in member groups, whose 'experts' or activists were subsequently, if infrequently, recruited onto committees. The fact that many groups felt excluded or were unaware of this practice is largely explained by its relative rareness, attributed to limited resources. In 1984–5, for example, only $1,500 was requested for travel for two free-standing committee meetings. Given the size of the country and the cost of travel, attendance by one member from Yellowknife or Vancouver would wipe out a committee's entire travel budget at a single meeting. The problem, essentially, was that the primary interest of many members of the executive was policy and the advocacy of policy; consequently, the executive was unwilling to relinquish much in the way of freedom or resources to policy committees.

The 1985–6 program submission made the distinction between NAC's reactive role in responding to government initiatives and its proactive role in helping member groups initiate policy. It made it clear that the actual balance between these two roles would depend on the number and nature of the government initiatives that emerged to which NAC felt it had to respond. In this submission, a role for ad hoc committees for specific issues was noted and plans for eight committees were presented: survival, social services, health pornography, justice, pensions and benefits to families, employment, and native women.

The plan for 1985–6 was disrupted by the creation of many more policy committees than those proposed by the AGM. In fact, fifteen policy committees were struck by the new executive in July 1985 in an attempt to respond to the wave of new participants seeking input into the process. New committees were established, each with an executive co-chair, to initiate and coordinate policy and advocacy in the following areas: lesbian issues, services to victims of violence, training, Third World women, and visible minorities. Existing committees also found it necessary to create subcommittees. The Health Committee, for example, had subcommittees on choice, reproductive hazards, and reproductive technology. Even if NAC had received the full $70,000 requested for the eight committees it had originally planned, it could not have supported the activities of fifteen committees. The most stable committees – employment, social services, justice, and pensions and benefits – which had well-established agendas (and whose mandates were partly accomplished), did best in the competition within the executive for the very scarce resources. The very large portion of the budget that went to support two national offices seems not to have been questioned at this point. Instead, resentments developed between the newcomers and the old stagers on the executive and in the committees. Lorraine Greaves (1991:106), chairing the unscheduled Services to Victims of Violence Committee, saw the informal resource-allocation processes as particularly objectionable:

... executive members would compete, posture, bargain and trade at the first executive meeting of the year to establish as much money as possible for their favourite committee. Inexperienced executive members were often less successful at this, not realizing that cooperation and openness were likely to render them 'losers' in the budget allocation process. Consequently, in 1987–8, for example, the committee budgets ranged from $500 (disabled women's committee) to $16,000 (employment and economy committee).

An analysis of the policy and advocacy activity as reported in *Feminist Action* in selected issues (July 1985; October 1986; February 1988) shows a heavy weighting of the newcomers' issues in the area of policy debate (prostitution, Third World women, lesbian issues, visible minority issues, violence, midwifery, anti-racism, AIDS). Also, in reports of advocacy (lobbying and actions), many of the newcomers' issues are involved. The space devoted to issues relating to the established committees does exceed that relating to issues associated with the fledgling committees. The established committees' issues, however, appear most frequently in the Responses to Government Initiatives section, with the Employment Committee's response to the Unemployment Insurance (Forget) Taskforce Report, responses on free trade, Meech Lake, the new Divorce Act, and the Parliamentary Committee on Equality Rights taking up much of the allotted space. The established committees, with the exception of the committee on violence, tended to involve the executive's ongoing reactions to government initiatives. As such, the activities of these committees are well lodged in the offices and in NAC's lobbying pattern. Greaves's account captures the fact that the struggle to gain time, space, and money on the executive's agenda for the new issues often meant challenging the centrality of NAC's responses to government initiatives in favour of paying more attention to long-term and equity issues.

Staff

NAC was created as a volunteer organization, with the assumption on the part of its founding mothers that the work of policy generation and lobbying would be done by volunteers. Contemporary feminists have a highly ambivalent view of volunteers and volunteerism. On the one hand, volunteerism was associated with old-fashioned feminine self-sacrifice and was to be avoided. On the other hand, many feminists were opposed to the development of hierarchy, structure, professionalism, and expertise that they associated with the introduction of paid staff. Many had experience with much larger office estabilshments, such as unions and teachers' associations, that employed professional, technical, and secretarial staff. In the period studied, the NAC staff was given no formal voice in committees, on the executive, or at the AGM. As a result of feminists' unresolved conflicts about volunteerism and professionalism, therefore, NAC re-created for its staff a familiar pattern for women – lots of responsibility but little power.

In 1988, there were five and a half staff positions in Toronto and two in the Ottawa office. An article written by a group of NAC staff members at the time contains a description of their work situation: 'the executive had great difficulty determining priorities, which led to conflicting and contradictory directions to staff from a very "hands on" executive' (Campbell et al. 1988:7). The staff felt 'invisible and undervalued,' and the authors of the organizational-review report believed that 'the skills and expertise of staff [were] often under-used' (NAC ORD 1988:21). By 1988, the two professionally staffed offices planned in Doris Anderson's era to manage a lobbying operation were in existence. The alternative of a volunteer organization that would not be dependent on government funding was now a defunct vision. The apparent contradiction, then, of a staff that was simultaneously underused and overworked reflects a lack of clarity about the role of the staff in policy functions and a history of ambiguity about the staff role.

The staff positions outlined in NAC's program submissions to the Women's Program for 1984–5 and 1985–6 offer some insight into the views of the NAC leadership on the roles staff should (and should not) play. In the 1984–5 submission, the plan was for a consolidated office in Ottawa with four staff members: a government-relations officer, a communications co-ordinator, an administrative coordinator, and a receptionist/typist. A part-time editor was to coordinate the production of the *NAC Memo* and *Status*, with the technical and production work contracted out (as translation functions had always been). Except in the case of the position of government-relations officer, the job descriptions included only support work for the policy function (for example, maintenance of the NAC policy index).

A brief examination to two job descriptions from this period will make the problem more concrete. The new position of executive coordinator, with the responsibility of coordinating the activities of the president, the executive, and both offices, was created; it was filled by Judy Campbell. The job amounted to serving as NAC's 'wife' or 'mother.' The job description allowed for no role in policy making and no official voice in the executive or at the AGM, although heavy responsibilities relating to these areas were involved. The position was to include staff evaluation, but not the power to hire and fire. With double the number of committees seeking time, resources, and attention, the offices were pressed to provide a level of support for committees that they simply could not meet. The executive coordinator, like any good wife and mother, was expected to stretch the resources to fit the needs.

The job description for the parliamentary-liaison officer in the 1984–5 program submission had been revised from an earlier version to reflect increased demands from committees. An explicit relationship with the committees was specified, making the position holder the 'eyes and ears' of all the committees, as well as of the executive. Responsibilities included monitoring government publications, such as Hansard, and news-clipping services, as well as tracking the legislative agenda and the activities of parliamentary committees and task forces. Added to the job description, as given in the 1985–6 program submission, were the following responsibilities: to 'make all necessary arrangements for the executive to come to Ottawa to lobby,' 'inform all executive members of the daily business of the house,' 'respond to requests for specific pieces of information,' 'distribute press releases to the national press,' and 'arrange press conferences.'

It is easy to conclude that NAC's executive, committees, and AGM generated far more policy and advocacy work than even a much larger staff could perform. The large professional staff maintained by NOW in Washington responds to the same range of issues and approximately the same level of legislative activity as NAC would encounter in Ottawa. The difference is that we have only about a tenth of the population and enjoy only a tenth of the resources available in the United States. The size of the staff during this period was far too small for NAC to imitate NOW.

What was apparent from our investigation of the NAC staff function was the absence of ways to utilize the volunteer resources of member groups. Individual volunteers on the executive or committees were included in the plan, but those in the member groups were not. There seems, for example, to have no inventory of the skills that individuals or groups could contribute to NAC's operation. Thus, while government funding had the apparent effect of eroding the traditional attachment of Canadian women's groups to self-help and volunteerism, there was a simultaneous suspicion of paid staff, as evidenced by the pattern of assigning staff members responsibility without power and of trying to limit their involvement in the policy area to support functions. The suspicion was never strong enough, however, to explore the alternative of a more efficient utilization of group resources across the country. Government funding seemed a permanent feature of the political landscape, with most of it consumed by a staff that the organization did not wish to utilize fully except in support roles.

Publications

NAC publications generally played a minor role in policy development. In 1973, however, when few feminist publications existed for English-Canadian women, *Status of Women News* offered women insights into such issues as equal pay, day care, and changes to family and property law. The policy debate was neither deep nor profound, and it focused primarily on well-established issues. The period of the magazine-quality *Status*, by contrast, fostered the emergence of interest in a number of policy areas that would help develop a feminist approach to public policy. New feminist issues around violence and women's culture were addressed in its pages. It also promoted a coherent feminist analysis. The Winter 1979–80 issue, for example, focused on the theme of the built and unbuilt environments, including the North, and covered areas such as urban planning, transportation, the pipeline, surviving the suburbs, woman-centred internal space design, women in the housing market, and spatial aspects of power. This issue introduced readers to a coherent, holistic, feminist analysis that linked together in a meaningful way of many aspects of their lives. Instead of the avalanche of issues and themes that usually characterized NAC publications, *Status* in this period encouraged a deepening of thought by devoting each issue to a single central theme.

The *NAC Memo* was introduced in 1980 as a reporting device that was required because the magazine-style *Status* carried little NAC news. Published after each executive meeting, *Memo* highlighted topical issues and actions planned. No in-depth analysis of policy was offered. *Memo* also included reports from regional representatives and updates on conferences and workshops. It played an important support role in networking, but was rarely detailed enough to engage women on policy.

(During the time of the ad hoc constitutional lobby, however, *Memo* was used to educate member groups and to alert them to the importance of pressuring provincial leaders to exempt Section 28 from the override clause).

In 1985, the existing publications were replaced with a new one of a different format.[17] *Feminist Action*, replacing *Memo*, was geared to outlining (but not developing) NAC policy positions. *Action Bulletin* was a single-page release published six or eight times a year, when issues arose that required immediate and concerted action by the membership, usually in support of executive actions. *Action* contained detailed and specific directions for ways in which groups and individuals could act. The likelihood of mobilization was considered greater when member groups were provided with a concise summary of the issue and direction on how to approach the issue, including the names and addresses of people within whose jurisdiction the issue or legislation fell. It was hoped that, through this informational process, individuals in each region would emerge who would know the subject matter and, therefore, be in a strategic position to mobilize local resources.

Apart from its formal publications, NAC also produced kits on pay equity, the 1984 election, and pension reform. The pension-reform kit, produced initially under Jean Wood's direction, was especially effective, canvassing the policy debate in an extensive and understandable way. Although the publications were useful for newsletter communication, they were not effective in developing the policy debate (except during the era of *Status*). (Much of the necessary communication and mobilization could be achieved with a combination of electronic mail, fax, and telephone trees. Aboriginal women across the North have organized such networks.)

NAC's structures for the generation and development of policy displayed a number of weaknesses, which we have already identified. None the less, NAC enjoyed some important successes in terms of both short-term policy goals and long-term issues. In the final portions of this chapter, we trace the evolution of several of these success stories.

NAC's Ability to Deal with Short-Term Policy Issues

In NAC's first decade, developments in the area of women's rights to employment generated a large number of policy resolutions that we can categorize as responses to short-term issues, although the overall category of women's employment encompasses a long-term endeavour. We have selected one aspect of the employment portfolio, unemployment insurance, to illustrate the character of NAC's responses to short-term issues. (The issue of maternity benefits was piggybacked on the U.I. program.) Twelve resolutions were passed during the period 1977–82 concerning unemployment-insurance benefits for women. The following list of the subjects of these resolutions (or parts of resolutions), taken from NAC's Index of Policy Recommendations (as amended to 1982), depicts a history of linked, short-term issues:

- *UI Act*, maternity benefit time restriction ('Magic' 10 week rule), 1977;
- *UI Act*, pregnancy benefits for adoptive parent, 1977;
- *UI Act*, claimant's right to part-time job without disentitlement, 1977;
- *UI Act*, literature to be translated (other than French and English where numbers warrant), 1977;
- *UI Act*, claimant's right to be informed re. statements against her/him, 1977;
- *UI Act*, oppose general eligibility change 8 weeks to twelve, 1977;
- *UI Act*, either parent to be eligible, 1977;
- Oppose UI claimants disqualified re. child care, NAC brief, 1978;
- *UI Act*, maternity benefits, new scheme proposed, NAC brief, 1978;
- *UI Act*, rescind special qualifying conditions for maternity benefits, benefits to become available at any point in a claim, continue to be based on individual not family attachment to the workforce, part-time workers to be covered, rescind reduction in benefits 1/1/1979, 1980;
- NAC prepares brief to educate government that parental leave benefits are for the care of the child, not for 'incapacity', restating NAC positions re. inadequacy of maternity/parental leave provisions, 1981;
- [re]state positions on UI paid maternity leave: (a) extend coverage and increase benefits under UI, (b) remove magic 10 rule, (c) pay two weeks waiting period, (d) benefits available during a strike, (e) guaranteed right to return to work; (f) up to 2 years unpaid leave/right to return guaranteed, NAC to call on Government to amend UI Act to remove discriminatory provisions to conform with Charter, 1982.

These twelve resolutions flow from the combined factors of the movement's success in getting paid maternity leave for women in the paid workforce and constant efforts by governments (whether Liberal or Conservative) to reduce UI benefits and impose more-restrictive entry requirements. Each of these responses to short-term issues advanced the process towards a goal, but a short-term goal none the less, since we must assume that full employment and a guaranteed minimum income would have been the long-term goal of feminist economic analysis. The other subject areas under the general heading of employment were benefits (primarily pensions), equal opportunity, equal pay, inflation control, job training and techniques, minimum wage, and the rights of part-time workers. The pattern of many linked, short-term issues is evident in these areas as well.

These issues do not reach final resolution in the period studied. Rather, they recur in a cycle in which NAC, along with other equality seekers, struggles to protect the gains already made and to inch forward to new benefits wherever possible. In 1986, for example, Employment Committee co-chair Madeleine Parent reported on the Forget Taskforce on Unemployment Insurance, warning that 'Forget favours removal of the 15-week paid maternity benefits from the Act.' Arguing that 'these benefits constitute insurance that women earned and paid for,' she explained that 'if the benefits become part of a social welfare program, they could be subject to means tests and to cuts, as happened with family allowances and almost happened with the old-age pension' (*Feminist Action* [October 1986:8]). The changes feared did not take place and, no doubt, NAC's *Action Bulletin* and Madeleine Parent's analysis and tireless efforts played a role in this result.

In its responses to short-term issues, NAC operated within a framework that reflected the understanding of economic issues developed by the Employment Committee, which was NAC's bastion of union or working-class feminism and academic socialist-feminism. Similarly, other committees developed shared policy frameworks on the basis of which they worked out NAC's responses to short-term issues.

NAC's Approach to Long-Term Policy Issues

The English-Canadian movement's capacity to advance long-term policy issues in the public arena has been handicapped by a number of factors, including women's lack of background in policy making, women's continuing lower rates of participation in disciplines such as economics and political science, women's near invisibility at the élite levels of politically 'relevant' occupations, and, finally women's poverty, both individual and collective. Canadian women have no equivalent of a Club of Rome, an Institute for Public Policy Analysis, a Fraser Institute, or a Conference Board of Canada. The Canadian Research

Institute for the Advancement of Women operates on a shoestring budget. An ingenious 'institute without walls,' it draws on the talents of feminist academics and policy specialists in various fields to stretch the shoestring. None the less, it has not had the resources required to devote itself to the development of long-term policy issues. The Canadian Advisory Council on the Status of Women is better funded and has developed a good research capacity, but efforts by some of its members to engage the long-term issues have usually failed to gain the needed approval of the government-appointed council. While most council members accept an issue-by-issue, status-of-women approach, fewer accept a holistic feminist approach that sees most public-policy issues as gendered. NAC has begun the process of developing a capacity for long-term policy analysis. Its structural approach, however, is far different from that of the think-tanks developed by men. While Doris Anderson has stated (at a 1986 AGM workshop) that 'one way government keeps you on the ropes is to ask groups to write briefs all the time,' she none the less believes that NAC has done well in its dealings with parliamentary committees (Vickers 1990b). Although it is tempting to believe that it is the parliamentary-committee structure that enhanced NAC's performance, that notion may be misleading. The performance of NAC and other movement groups before the 1988 Parliamentary Committee on Child Care was excellent, for example, but the committee did not produce a report that could make the movement consider its efforts a success. It has also been argued that the method of combining research and hearings characteristic of the royal-commission structure is particularly well suited to the treatment of long-term issues such as pornography, prostitution, and reproductive technologies. (On this ground, a coalition of women led by Margrit Eichler fought to get the Conservative government to establish a royal commission on the impact of new reproductive technologies.) We believe it is unwise to assume that there is a particular structure for policy generation that is necessarily more favourable than others for dealing with long-term women's issues. The beacon of the Royal Commission on the Status of Women owes as much to the presence of feminists on the research staff and on the commission as to the structure and methods adopted. Parliamentary committees or royal commissions that are woman-centred, as the Bird Commission was, tend to be excellent settings for the development of feminist policies, but when the same structures are impervious to feminists analysis, they can freeze hostile analyses into 'truth.' The royal-commission option for subjects on which feminists are divided is particularly problematic, since the recommendations contained in royal commission reports can hold sway for a generation.

NAC's ability to be an effective participant in the constitutional debate was limited, as we have seen. In the post-Charter era, however, NAC made an important contribution to the development of our understanding of the equality rights guaranteed in the Charter. That it was able to do so in a parliament dominated by a Conservative government with the largest federal legislative majority in Canada's history is especially remarkable. When the Charter was passed into law, the equality sections were suspended until 1985 to permit the federal and provincial governments to 'get their houses in order' through statute audits that would eliminate or replace discriminatory laws. At the federal level, many women were concerned that the new government was not undertaking this process. Their worst fears seemed to be confirmed with the appearance of the Discussion Paper on Equality Issues in Federal Law, which was tabled in the House of Commons on 31 January 1985 (Canada, *Sessional Papers*, 1985). The document took a 'majoritarian approach' to equality rights, in that it argued that 'if there is something in the present law then this indicates that it is acceptable social practice and therefore should be immune from Charter challenge' (16:115). On 16 February, the discussion paper was referred to the Parliamentary Committee on Equality Rights, chaired by Conservative MP J. Patrick Boyer. The parliamentary committee was composed of five Conservatives, one New Democrat, and one Liberal. It contained three women, including Liberal Sheila Finestone, who had been president of the FFQ. The committee was to 'seek the views and opinions of Canadians, both individual and organizations, on the subject matter of the Discussion Paper' and to 'review federal statutes ... in order to ensure their conformity with the letter and spirit of equality and non-discrimination guarantees in the Charter' (Canada, Parliamentary Committee on Equality Rights, 1985:v).

In a now familiar pattern, the English-Canadian women's movement used the period following the enactment of the Charter to develop or strengthen effective coalitions. Several organizations that played a central role in shaping the approach to equality rights that the Boyer Committee adopted were formed by women lawyers who had 'earned their spurs' during the Charter debates. Among such organizations were the Charter of Rights Education Fund, the Charter of Rights Coalition (Vancouver and Manitoba chapters), the Legal Education and Action Fund (LEAF), the Manitoba Association for Rights and Liberties, and the National Association of Women and the Law (NAWL), with its numerous chapters.[18]

The majority of the seventy-odd women's groups that presented briefs to the Boyer Committee were NAC affiliates. Indeed, NAC established (and gained government funding for) an equality-rights project to assist its members in developing an understanding of the long-term issues involved. In her report, project coordinator Marian Bloom noted that 20 per cent of the 250 verbal presentations made to the committee in twelve major centres came from NAC members. Of the 550 written briefs received by the committee, about 7 per cent came from NAC affiliates, except in Ontario, where the figure was 30 per cent, and Nova Scotia, 16 per cent (*Feminist Action* [December 1985]:11). NAC's pragmatic role was to ensure that the various equality-rights claimants among women were heard.

The issue of the kind of equality the English-Canadian women's movement seeks is of some importance in understanding why its trajectory has been quite different from those of the U.S., U.K., or Québec movements. To understand NAC's approach to long-term issues, therefore, it is important to understand the kind of equality its members sought to have the Boyer Committee uphold.

The equality-rights section (Section 15) of the Charter, with its explicit permission for affirmative-action programs, does not contain a clear-cut definition of equality. Indeed, it has often been argued that equality seekers fill an empty concept of equality with the contents of their own experiences (Vickers 1986). In order to ensure that a concept of equality that took women's experiences of inequality into account was accepted by the parliamentary committee, it was essential for NAC to ensure that the committee heard from a variety of groups offering different approaches to equality seeking.

Although NAC saw to it that the committee heard about experiences of a wide range of women, Bloom's report notes two key failures: the committee did not hear about the experiences of sole-support mothers or women on social assistance (*Feminist Action* [December 1985]:11), nor did it hear from collective-rights advocates.

Almost without exception, movement groups urged the Boyer Committee to look beyond a formal equality approach that aimed at always treating men and women the same in sex-blind 'gender-neutralizing' legislation, to achieve 'equality of results in the application of the law and programs [as] the yardstick of success in equality-oriented actions'

(CCLOW Brief, cited in Kee and McDonnell 1986:2). Although fewer traditional feminist groups participated, their briefs advanced similar views on equality, urging 'Action now: no more consultations!' 'Equality for women [is] non-negotiable,' and 'Equality is [a] fundamental Canadian right.' The University Women's Club of Ottawa argued that 'Equality [means equality] of opportunity, access and result' (cited in Kee and McDonnell 1986:4).

If NAC found itself on the sidelines during the constitutional debates, it was at its most vigorous during the Boyer Committee hearings. As well as gaining the funding for the project to help member groups participate, it acted as an organizational centre and clearing-house, able to tell groups speaking to the committee in one city what others planned to present to it in the next. Other institutional centres of the movement were also prominent in terms of the education of groups and the presentation of briefs. For example, the CACSW and the advisory councils of Newfoundland and Labrador, Prince Edward Island, and Nova Scotia made presentations. The alienation of Québec from the whole process of constitutional 'renewal,' however, limited the number of francophone groups that participated. Gay-rights activists in search of the explicit inclusion of sexual orientation as a prohibited ground for discrimination and people with disabilities arguing for a clear federal responsibility to ensure their equality were among the most moving witnesses of the hearings.

For the first time in the formal equality-seeking dynamic, some women's groups – REAL Women; Women for Life, Faith and Family; and the Alberta Federation of Women United for Families (AFWUF) – argued against the Charter's already-enacted equality guarantees. Women for Life, Faith and Family saw Sections 15 and 28 as a 'total attack on the foundation of a good stable country – the family' (cited in Kee and McDonnell 1986:3). Three chapters of the Catholic Women's League made presentations about the Charter from a 'prolife' (anti-abortion) perspective. The discussion paper 'call[ed] on the public to demonstrate that inequality exists in legislation that makes distinctions under the mentioned categories.' The Charter of Rights Education Fund brief argued that 'the burden is too heavy, distinctions in Canadian legislation [are the results] of decades of sexist, racist, and classist attitudes – all distinctions should be regarded as inherently suspicious.' (cited in Kee and McDonnell 1986:1).

To the surprise of many, the Parliamentary Committee on Equality Rights produced a unanimous report in less than a year, with eighty-five recommendations for changes in federal government practice, legislation, or policy. Forty-one dealt with issues solely or primarily related to sex-equality guarantees. The committee recommended changes to comply with Charter guarantees in all of the following areas: maternity benefits, marital-status issues, equality issues in pensions, family violence, women and the armed forces, part-time workers, employment-equity programs, and order-in-council appointments for women (including the judiciary). The committee supported positive action, such as contract compliance (Recommendation 63), to achieve equality goals. Certainly, the committee went far beyond the formal, sex-blind understanding of equality that many feminists feared might prevail. And in the area of lesbian and gay rights, the committee argued for a new era of official recognition and tolerance despite the homophobia emerging from New Right groups such as REAL Women.

Many women's groups were disappointed that the committee declined to make recommendations about pornography (an area under scrutiny by the Justice Department) or about the abortion law (which would soon be struck down by the Supreme Court). Others were concerned that several of its recommendations about parental rights seemed to support the positions of some men's-rights groups on mandatory shared custody. In fact, the outcome of the process in terms of entrenching equality seeking in the federal political agenda was highly successful. The English-Canadian women's movement had been given a 'mini' version of the report of the Royal Commission on the Status of Women to use as a focal document in lobbying and developing a strategy for litigation. Although the government's document did not accept all of the committee's recommendations, it (perhaps grudgingly) recognized that the Canadian public supported the equality project to a far greater degree than a poll of government backbenchers would have suggested. The government's introduction of free trade and the Meech Lake and aboriginal self-government debates seemed to diffuse the focus on the equality-seeking dynamic at the federal level. In fact, in NAC and in the country at large, the issues of equality came to seem far more complex than they had before. Québec and the First Nations demanded the right to equality as collectivities. The working-out of many of the concrete recommendations of the Boyer Committee continued, however, as the movement regrouped for the next phase. In the period leading up to the 1992 referendum on the Charlottetown Accord, NAC played a highly visible role in opposition to the accord. Moreover, most observers agree that women's equality has become a central issue in the public's understanding of constitutional politics.

Summary

In this chapter, we have explored the question of whether the structures that evolved within NAC to generate policy have proved to be adequate to the task. On the whole, our conclusions are positive. Although NAC has not developed the infrastructure necessary to realize the vision of a widely participatory process for developing policy and setting priorities, it is none the less able to respond to a diverse range of policy challenges. With so many different groups wanting input, however, and with little aggregation of policy demands taking place among member groups, much of NAC's policy activity continues to be reactive crisis-management. Nor has NAC been able to take enough time from responding to government initiatives to develop long-range strategies. Faced by pressures from government and member groups to formulate policy on short-term issues, NAC is almost always forced into an incremental, issue-by-issue approach, although some NAC policy committees do manage to develop more systematic analyses over time. Finally, we can only be encouraged by the ease with which NAC has been able to enter into and sustain policy coalitions with actors such as the CLC and the Conference of Catholic Bishops, who are well beyond the ambit of women's politics as it is normally defined. While a detailed analysis of the dynamics of these coalitions is beyond the scope of this text, the fact that NAC's policy-making and agenda-setting structures permit such developments bodes well for NAC's further institutionalization as a major centre of feminist policy ideas.

Notes

1 Gwen Landholt was chair of the Right to Life Committee, Toronto. Reports show that anti-abortion groups did attend the conference. The Catholic Women's League, for example, was represented, although it had left the planning coalition three months earlier. Conference funding was facilitated by Freda Paltiel, a senior public servant.
2 For example, many of the issues dealt with by the NAC Survival Committee, such as pollution and disarmament, are clearly of a long-term nature. Others, such as whether women should be admitted to combat roles in

the Canadian military, are less clear. Still others, such as obtaining political rights of assembly and free speech for wives of military personnel on bases, are short-term issues.

3 The tradition of having delegations petition the government goes back to the period before women enjoyed the right to vote. In fact, the traditions of public education and direct action also go back to the pre-suffrage period.

4 The Vancouver Women's Research Centre and its activists, such as Megan Ellis, Cheryl Dahl, and Helga Jacobson, have been the most closely associated with this approach in contexts that have affected NAC. The Québec group Relais femmes plays a role similar to that of the Vancouver Centre, and CRIAW's 'Institute without Walls' project shares its basic values.

5 These structural changes in the policy process, however, were not the only factors opening it up to feminist (or non-sexist) expertise. The enormous rise in women's participation rates in higher education in Canada (now at parity at the undergraduate level, although still lower than men's at the graduate level and in 'hard' areas) increased the pool of young women who would move into the public-policy area. The research staffs of most parliamentary committees now include women of this generation.

6 The index includes ten original categories of recommendations: child care; education/training; employment/human rights/anti-discrimination; family law; family planning/birth planning/abortion; international; NAC; status of women; taxation/income support; violence. The category containing by far the largest number of recommendations is 'employment/human rights/anti-discrimination.' Ninety-eight recommendations appear in this category for the 1972–8 period, and most of the employment recommendations involve newly determined positions rather than recommendations of the royal commission.

7 Its membership included those who volunteered at the AGM: Laurel Ritchie (Canadian Textile and Chemical Union), Carole Swan (Manitoba Action Committee on the Status of Women), Farida Shaikh (CARAL), Annette Legault (AFÉAS), Jeanne Gariepy (FFQ), Marjorie Cohen (Ontario Committee on the Status of Women), Lynn Kaye (CUPE), and Pat Preston (Alberta Status of Women Action Committee) (Executive Minutes, 26 May 1979; *Status* [June 1979]:7).

8 The Women's Research Centre works on five assumptions: (1) social/political action is necessary to end the oppression of women; (2) the

initiative for change in women's situations comes from women themselves, especially as organized in community-based groups; (3) the theories and research on which conventional expertise is based have excluded women's perspectives; (4) it is necessary to develop methods, structures, and research processes that will include women's perspectives; (5) an analysis of issues based on a description of how those issues are actually experienced by women is essential to the development of effective strategies for social political change (Women's Research Centre 1987:1–2).

9 NAC's Rules of Association were changed almost annually from 1972 to 1978.

10 Doris Anderson tells of attending the AGM lobby and seeing that 'Slasher' Erik Nielsen, part of the cabinet delegation representing the Conservative government, was 'shaking' as he awaited his turn to speak (Vickers 1990b). Whether Nielsen was shaking because of nervousness, as Anderson supposes, or because of anger at the fact that a fiesty and unruly group of women presumed to call him to account is unclear. Anderson, however, clearly found the AGM mass lobby empowering.

11 Annual lobbies are organized by other sectors, such as higher education, as well. They meet intensively with many individual MPs and cabinet ministers on a small-group basis. The entrée is always the presence of at least one person from the member's riding, and an ongoing relationship is established, which is continued within the riding. Disrupting the AGM lobby format would have the effect of freeing up the AGM geographically. It could move across the country, with local and regional groups bidding for its presence, as occurs with other feminist organizations, such as CRIAW. A mid-year meeting in Ottawa would be quite sufficient for a redesigned lobby. Certainly, other highly effective lobbies are conducted with relatively small numbers of participants.

12 The following chart shows the number of AGM recommendations made during the period of 1972–82 in each of the ten original categories and the five new categories added in 1982:

Child care	17
Constitution	1
Education/training	7
Employment	73
Fiscal arrangements	2
Human rights/anti-discrimination (includes 6 re. native women)	30
Family law	23

Family planning/reproductive rights	35
Immigration	4
International/peace	9
Media	2
NAC (internal)	30
Status of Women	7
Taxation/income support	35
Violence (including pornography, prostitution)	14

13 One such emergency resolution, drawn up in the course of addressing an emergency relating to impending legislation, would establish as NAC policy the view that 'given the problems inherent in the current world commodity system, prostitution is as valid an occupation as any other' (Emergency Resolutions file, June 1988). As this illustrates, the range of resolutions at any AGM increased considerably after 1982.

14 In fact, many of these resolutions were reaffirmations of existing NAC policy and should have received no time on the agenda. Because of the lack, since 1982, of a compilation of AGM resolutions that could be made available to member groups, repetitions were frequent.

15 NAC's reluctance to use postal-ballots to establish priorities prevented it from realizing the potential effectiveness of the AGM structure.

16 Unfortunately, no committee minutes were available to us. Indeed, it is not clear that such minutes exist, at least not within NAC's organizational control. Rather, it seems likely that any committee minutes that have survived are languishing in the basements or bottom drawers of successive chairs. As a result, our ability to analyse the functioning of the policy process *within committees* is limited. Instead, we will look at stated intentions, conflicts, and outcomes – a poor substitute for the actual political analysis that we hope this work will stimulate.

17 Doris Anderson, who had been editor of *Chatelaine*, was especially dubious about the magazine-style *Status* (personal communication with Jill Vickers, May 1988). Others were concerned that many of the views expressed by contributors to *Status* were not necessarily those of NAC but reflected the broader English-Canadian women's movement.

18 Most of these groups received at least initial funding from the federal state, and the Boyer Committee accepted the case for extending state support for 'citizenship activities' to the funding of cases before the courts on Charter equality issues. Since 1978, the Court Challenges Program, administered by the Human Rights Directorate of the Secretary of State, had provided financial assistance to individuals and groups

initiating litigation relating to Canada's official languages, to facilitate court rulings clarifying language rights. (Once again, the affirmative-action programs launched by the Royal Commission on Bilingualism and Biculturalism paved the way for comparable programs for other equality seekers.) In fiscal year 1984–5, the program's budget was $200,000. While the Boyer Committee's report was in preparation, a modified, expanded, and enriched court-challenges program was introduced to cover both language and equality-rights litigation. The program was eliminated in the 1992 budget.

7 Feminist Ideology and Policy Making in NAC

There are many ways of being feminist in NAC, especially since a critical third wave of mobilization brought previously marginalized women into the movement. It is the fact of this diversity within feminism as represented in NAC, that best justifies NAC's claim to be a parliament of women. The institutionalization of structures of the women's movement such as NAC facilitates the emergence of a new level of debate both within feminism and between feminism and 'male-stream' politics. English-Canadian women have had the advantage of a woman-centred, woman-controlled arena within which debate shaped by the diversity of experiences of member groups could occur. The English-Canadian movement has also been sufficiently pro-statist in orientation that women active in NAC have developed feminist approaches to conventional political issues that transcend the more-limited status-of-women approach. The inclusion under the NAC umbrella structure of many small, more-radical groups not primarily oriented to the state ensures that significant debate also occurs within NAC on feminist issues arising directly from women's experiences as women.

In this chapter, we survey two ideological dimensions that we have identified in NAC's policy process.[1] First, we should note that we are using the term *ideological* in its most simple sense to describe trends of thought or points of view. In NAC's founding period, the generally liberal-feminist perspective embodied in the report of the Royal Commission on the Status of Women was the starting point. As NAC developed its capacity as a parliament of women, however, the full range of positions that arose as critiques of 'male-stream' thought came into play, including conservative feminism, liberal feminism, and left feminism. A second grid of positions has also emerged, generated by women from their lived experiences as women encountering structures of oppression, including radical feminism, lesbian feminism, and the feminisms of women of colour and women with disabilities. (We have attempted to define these terms with greater precision in the Glossary.) We will explore the rich debate within NAC concerning such bench-mark issues as wages for housework, home-makers' pensions, women's role in military combat, prostitution, and housewifery, using these issues to contextualize our insights about the existence in NAC of these two ideological dimensions and the interactions between them.[2]

Our analysis in this chapter proceeds in three parts. First, we review some ideas about the ideological trends within feminism and present evidence concerning the presence and absence of these trends in NAC. Second we examine NAC debates concerning several issues within the feminist ideological spectrum. Third, we analyse several NAC debates that demonstrate the development of a holistic, feminist approach to public-policy issues on what has traditionally been understood as the 'male-stream' political agenda. (We will not explore feminist debates concerning political structure and process further, although aspects of these debates interact with the two ideological dimensions on which we will focus.)

Throughout this text, we have argued that some feminist demands cannot be integrated into liberal-democratic politics at this point in time. NAC has consequently been forced to focus on both the politics of the state and women's politics primarily from the perspective of women's experiences as embodied people defined largely by their sexuality and capacity to reproduce. In small groups and safe spaces, it has also been possible for women to explore the actual experience of oppression from rape, child sexual abuse, incest, sexual and racial harassment, homophobia, and the humiliation and danger of pornography. Women have constructed a political agenda out of their shared analysis of these experiences and the agenda of what ought to be changed is widely shared. Women have begun to infiltrate the public agenda with evidence of oppression, 'making an issue' of some men's crimes against women and children. It has been harder to construct scenarios of how things can be changed. Feminists disagree, often fiercely and intensely, about ideology, policy, and the research findings used to support policy choices (the debate around pornography and censorship is one example of this). In our analysis, we explore the complex political process that characterized NAC's efforts to make women's experiences matter in the world of formal politics.

In Search of a Framework:
Understanding the Ideological Trends in NAC

Most accounts of the nature of feminist ideas rely on formal works of theory; such as Shulamith Firestone's *The Dialectic of Sex* (1970) or Mary O'Brien's *The Politics of Reproduction* (1981). In this analysis, we are interested in feminist ideas contextualized in the political arena in debates about what can and should be done in an actual country at a particular time. Women acting in the political arenas of NAC are certainly not ignorant of major works of feminist theory, but they also rely on their own experiences and the experiences of other women as they construct their views on issues. And they rely on their understanding of both the feminist political systems in which they are operating and of the male-dominated political system of the local or national state. All of these understandings (and misunderstandings) together constitute what we have described as ideological trends.

Adapting a framework developed first by Gayle Yates in 1975, Micheline Dumont (1986) identifies three major feminisms that we will describe as (1) feminisms of equality, (2) feminisms of difference, (3) feminisms of androgyny. Table 7.1 summarizes several aspects of these ideological branches to help clarify Dumont's analysis.

Feminisms of equality tend to work with an absolute-equality concept that requires that legislation, programs, and policies be sex-blind and gender-neutral. Arguing that 'matter doesn't matter,' feminisms of equality do not recognize significant differences between women's and men's experiences, except with regard to the physical aspects of reproduction. All other differences are seen as the result of socialization. Legislation providing for protection of women or for any treatment of women different from that accorded to men would be considered unacceptable as either inherently undesirable or potentially dangerous, because it could be used against women. In legal terms, 'any differentiation on the basis of sex would be subject to the strictest scrutiny, which would allow almost no distinction to stand' (Ontario Statute Audit Project Advisory Committee Memo, 29 February 1984, as cited in Charter of Rights Coalition [BC] 1985:41–2).

Feminisms of difference are associated with a gender-specific approach to equality that regards women's unique experiences and qualities as desirable and worthy of advancement in society. They adopt the premise that if legislation perpetuates women's oppression, it is unacceptable, but if it contributes to redressing the inequalities between

TABLE 7.1
Ideological schema of three major feminisms

	Feminisms of equality	Feminisms of difference	Feminisms of androgyny
Ordering principle	Women as equal to men	Women over and against or separate from men	Women and men equal to each other
Source of standard	Established by men; adopted by women	Arrived at by women	Arrived at by men and women together
Primary focus for change	Political	Social	Cultural
Enemy	Socio-economic attitudes and institutions	Men; other women; capitalism; the family	Cultural value orientations and institutional structures
Strategy	Pressure	Conflict	Conversion

Sources: Dumont 1986; Yates 1975, as cited in Dumont 1986

men and women, it is desirable. 'Protective' legislation would be subject to scrutiny to determine whether it could be used to exclude women from, say, employment and whether it recognized women's needs as different from men's without defining those differences as unchangeable or natural. This gender-specific approach focuses on achieving equality of results and therefore recognizes that different inputs may be required to achieve identical results (Ontario Statute Audit Project Advisory Committee Memo, 29 February 1984, as cited in Charter of Rights Coalition [BC] 1985:42–3).

Feminisms of androgyny are associated with a sex-specific/gender-neutral approach to equality.[3] This approach would have legislation take into account sex-specific experience (for example, that women are overwhelmingly the victims of rape, battering, and so on) but at the same time use neutral terms such as 'spouse' or 'parent' and extend benefits and protection equally to men and women in the same situation. Conflicting positions on shared custody, for example, reveal conflict over the goal (advanced by feminists advocating an androgynous approach) of having fathers become more active in child-rearing. A sex-specific/gender-neutral analysis would comprehend that while *voluntary* shared custody could reflect the gender-role transformations that have been achieved by relatively few families, *mandatory* joint custody laws would impose responsibilities on the majority of mothers who remain the primary parent, without giving them the power to make decisions (Ontario Statute Audit Project Advisory Committee Memo, 29 February 1984, as cited in Charter of Rights Coalition [BC] 1985:43–4).

To contextualize the differences among these three approaches within feminism, we will examine the NAC debate on the 'spousal deduction' issue. The Spring 1983 issue of *Status* carried an interview with Margrit Eichler on the subject of the spousal income-tax exemption (also called the 'spousal deduction' or the 'married exemption'). Eichler's view, as presented in the article, was that spousal deductions are 'regressive' and should be abolished, and that the money saved should be put into 'progressive' programs such as the family-allowance program. (Note that, in 1983, the issue of same-sex spousal claims had not yet arisen.) Eichler's reasons for wishing to abolish the spousal deduction were that (1) it 'defines women as dependents [because] the money does not go to the wives themselves but to the husbands'; (2) 'women who are only servicing a husband are performing work that is useful for the husband and therefore, if anyone pays for that, he should; (3) women at home looking after small children are engaged in socially useful (rather than privately useful) work and should be remunerated directly through an expanded system of family allowances; and (4) money freed up from paying men for their 'privately useful' spouses can be transferred to mothers, including single parents, who are performing 'socially useful' work (*Status* [Spring 1983]:8). The approach Eichler proposed combines an absolute-equality mode of analysis with some elements of a sex-specific/gender-neutral approach in the remedy. While she did not state that full-time home-makers without small children at home are 'parasites,' her view was clearly that they are not engaged in 'socially useful' work. The 'servicing' of adults in the home was viewed as a private benefit whether those adults were old or young, rich or poor, or engaged in money-making ventures or urgent national business.[4]

Not all feminists accept the absolute-equality approach inherent in this analysis. For example, many lesbians argued not for the elimination of spousal benefits but for the extension of 'married-equivalent' benefits to same-sex couples. (An Ontario court recently ruled that denial of benefits to same-sex partners is discriminatory. At the time of writing, however, federal tax law has not been changed.) Some stay-at-home mothers have also organized within NAC. The group MAWS (Mothers Are Women) is an Ottawa-based group of women who have chosen (and admit they can afford to choose) to stay at home with their children, despite education and training (mainly for professional occupations). Most consider themselves feminists but do not consider that the absolute-equality approach reflects either their views or their interests. MAWS argued for a NAC day-care policy and taxation policies that would recognize the differential effects of things like state-supported, universally accessible child care on one-earner as well as two-earner families. They also argued for the retention of the 'married-equivalent' benefits.

As we will see in our examination of the home-maker issues, NAC's orientation has included both a critique of the family, including the role of home-maker, and policies supportive of the home-maker's needs and rights. As feminists have pointed out, we can critique institutions such as motherhood at the same time that we devise policies to aid those women caught in the institution's quagmires (Levine and Estable 1981). An absolute-equality approach, however, is based on the premise that the integration of women into the public sphere of paid work is the appropriate, ultimate goal. As we will illustrate in our analysis of the wages-for-housework debate in NAC, when the issue was first raised in 1979, both liberal and leftist feminists in Canada pursued an absolute-equality approach, resisting policies they believed would enhance the attractiveness of the home-maker's role as a chosen occupation.

Dumont's framework classifies objectives into four distinct areas – the body, employment, developing a separate voice, and power – all of which are relevant to all three types of feminisms. Under the crucial category of the body, Dumont (1986) includes contraception, abortion, pornography, battering, rape, control of one's own health, feminist intervention against sexism in therapy, self-defence techniques (wendo), support for pregnant women and single mothers, and lesbianism. Under employment, she includes sexual discrimination in jobs, salaries and promotions, access to all training programs, maternity leave and day care, sexual harassment in the workplace, the status and rights of women who work with their husbands, the impact of new technology and women's access to non-traditional occupations, work in the home, and the financial support of women in the home. Under the category of developing a separate voice, Dumont includes women's endeavours relating to consciousness-raising groups, publishing houses, bookstores, plays, shows, films, publications of all kinds, research groups, magazines and scientific journals, symposia, courses, programs of study, associations, training sessions, religious expression, and language itself. Finally, under the heading of power, she includes the vote and women as mayors, as MPs, as presidents of labour unions and corporations, and as holders of any other seats of power in our society, including those within 'the fortress' that is the Catholic church.

Some of the issues discussed in NAC, such as international affairs and global survival, the environment, immigration, and fiscal arrangements, are difficult to place in Dumont's scheme. Also hard to locate are feminist approaches to the issues that dominate mainstream politics, such as the Constitution and free trade. Although Dumont does not construe such issues as being part of the feminist political spectrum, NAC has made efforts to develop feminist approaches to all public-policy issues.

Despite possible omissions, Dumont's four broad categories do succeed in identifying the basic elements of women's experience that have gone into the construction of a feminist political spectrum. The latter includes the range of issues on which women have developed positions on the basis of their experiences of discrimination, oppression, or exploitation, as well as the range of responses or remedies that flow from the different feminist positions in each case. Women's responses might range from proposing state action to advocating a separatist, cultural solution involving women's self-help or creativity. We should again warn against assuming internal consistency in the ideas of individual women or groups. Women who reject an analysis of oppression and exploitation with regard to employment may accept such an analysis where it pertains to spirituality and women's position within their church. This 'split-spectrum' is perhaps evident in the responses of some conservative feminists, whose conservative position on economic issues may be balanced by a radical stance with regard to matters of religion. The idea of a split spectrum is certainly not new or particular to women: it has often been evident in men's politics, as in the example of well-to-do U.S. Republicans who hold conservative positions on economic issues but are tolerant or even radical on issues of race, and who, at least prior to Reagan, supported the ERA. (In Reagan's terms, these were members of the hated 'Eastern liberal establishment.') Similarly, women who accept legislation or state programs as effective or appropriate in one area may reject them in another.

It is possible to predict, in a very preliminary way, the sorts of issues that will cause division within feminism. To do this, we have constructed a grid that tentatively locates a few benchmark positions in the spectrum of feminist ideology and policy. The issue of women in combat, for example, which falls within Dumont's power category, sparked conflict in NAC between women who adhered to a feminism of equality and those who committed to a feminism of difference. Feminists who pursued a goal of absolute equality favoured the extension of women's activity into the realm of military combat, linking women's claims to equal citizenship to their willingness to bear arms in defence of their country. Feminists committed to a feminism of difference argued that women's role as 'moral mothers' and peacemakers precluded their supporting military involvement.

As we noted above, the issue of joint custody provoked significant conflict in NAC between women committed to a feminism of difference and those who endorsed a feminism of androgyny. Issues of surrogacy, erotica for women, and wages for housework have also brought this fault line within feminism to light.

One problem that quickly became apparent in the course of our analysis was that feminist positions on certain key issues, such as abortion, appeared to be held in common for the sake of solidarity in the face of rising anti-feminism, and that potential differences were consequently obscured. Clearly, far more unites women in NAC than divides them, but it is none the less useful to try to understand the full range of positions in play and the nature of the differences among them.

We are a long way from understanding all the elements that contribute to shaping women's ideas, causing them to become feminists as opposed to non-feminists or anti-feminists or to prefer one variant of feminist over another. In a survey in the United States, Alice Rossi (1982) found, for example, that 'low religiosity' was a highly significant and independent factor contributing to women's endorsing feminist beliefs in the four areas, or indices, she specified (marital equality, economic rights, child care, and 'bottom-line' feminism). In other words, it was possible to predict the nature of a woman's position on issues in these areas by knowing her 'level' of religiosity. In Appelle's 1984 survey of anglophone NAC delegates (reported in Appelle 1987), by contrast, religiosity proved not to be a reliable predictor of attitudes on the same indices for the English-Canadian women surveyed. There was a similar difference in the results of these two surveys with regard to age: Rossi's U.S. study revealed a clear generation gap between younger and older delegates, especially in relation to marital style and definitions of who could be considered a feminist, whereas the NAC study showed no such gap (this might not have been the case if francophone women had also been surveyed [Maroney 1988]).

What these preliminary studies of women's views about their lives as women demonstrate is the error of trying to infer women's positions on issues on the basis of demographic characteristics alone; that is, we must assume that women are political agents capable of constructing ideas about their experiences that may well transcend those experiences. Ideology can organize women's views on a range of issues in a way that a scrutiny of demographic factors could not explain.

The Development of a Feminist Ideological Spectrum in NAC: Some Benchmark Issues

In the early years of NAC, the status-of-women approach to issues identified by the royal commission prevailed. For the most part, the commission's recommendations reflected a feminism-of-equality approach. The commission's belief, however, that society and the state had obligations to women because of their role as mothers took its recommendations towards a feminism of difference as well. The liberal feminism that characterized the ideas of most of the commissioners and key staff proved, in fact, to have some radical overtones, which provided a bridge to the feminism of difference accepted by many of the new generation of feminists. To understand more clearly how the feminist policy spectrum has evolved over several decades, it is useful to look at some of the benchmark issues within NAC, including wages for housework, pensions for home-makers, child care, lesbianism, prostitution, and women in military combat.

The wages-for-housework issue created an alliance between liberal feminists and leftist feminists, revealing them to be equally committed to the feminism of equality where issues of employment were concerned. As we saw in our earlier organizational analysis, the wages-for-housework issue was the first to challenge the fairly comfortable agreement between liberal and leftist feminists about the way 'liberated' women ought to live. Liberals and leftists agreed that women's participation in the paid workforce was the key to their liberation and that the unpaid activities of child-rearing and housewifery for one's own family were not acceptable full-time occupations for liberated women. They had all kinds of good, substantive reasons for their views: stay-at-home women were unpaid, denied pensions, vulnerable because of economic dependency on their spouses, and generally denigrated by society (as evidenced by the common expression 'just a housewife'). Clearly, the position of many women in NAC was such that the bid of groups organized around the wages-for-housework issue to join NAC was viewed in 1979 the way an application to join by REAL Women would have been viewed in 1986 or 1987. (In fact, the campaign by the Wages for Housework [WFH] groups to join NAC was perceived, probably correctly, as an attempt at infiltration, disruption, and manipulation, which made it easier to maintain alliances opposing them.)

Ironically, the concept of wages for housework was originally devised by an Italian Marxist feminist, Mariarosa Dalla Costa. It was promoted by black feminist Selma James in the United Kingdom and ultimately taken up by Peggy Morton and others in Canada. Dalla Costa's purpose was to challenge the view of the Italian Left, which was based on Marxist analysis, that what women did at home was not productive work, and, consequently, that stay-at-home women were not 'workers' and could not be mobilized as workers. The analysis held that because such women were isolated in their individual homes, they were structurally prevented from developing a 'correct' consciousness that would allow them to be mobilized in the struggle against capitalism (Costa and James 1972). Recognizing that Marxist theory's conception of 'productive work' had in fact been absorbed from capitalism and liberal economic theory, Dalla Costa reconceptualized the household as a social factory, with a product (worker-power, in the form of the children and adults that were 'serviced' there) and exploited workers (unpaid housewives). She also explored the collective nature of women's domestic work, much of which took place in communal spaces in warmer Italy, rather than in private households. Laundromats and markets could be seen as women's shop floor. What women lacked for doing this 'real' work was a wage – hence, the mobilizing concept of wages for housework. Dalla Costa's goal was to convince the Communist party in Italy to begin to mobilize housewives, traditionally suspect as potential class enemies and strike breakers. In view of the small percentage of Italian women who were in the paid workforce in the 1970s, she believed housewives could no longer be ignored.

The strategic origins of the wages-for-housework concepts were probably not known to the NAC women responding to WHF groups in

1979. Neither did they understand the ways in which Selma James had adapted the campaign in the United Kingdom to highlight the interaction between issues of sex and race. James found the reconstruction of Left analysis around the issue raised by Dalla Costa to be useful in the struggle of black women in the U.K. as well. The fact that black women were often hired – for very low wages – to clean the houses of white women raised the central question of whether work is 'real' and 'liberating' because it is paid or because it is productive and enjoyable. At the NAC AGM in 1979, Dorothy O'Connell, then a leader of the Ottawa Tenant's Council and author of several humorous books about the views and the organizing of poor women, spoke on women and poverty. Raising the question of why women on welfare or mothers' allowance were urged to 'get work' instead of being paid adequately for the work they were already doing in their homes, O'Connell accused NAC feminists of 'downgrading women in the home' (*Status* [June 1979]:2). Like James, O'Connell highlighted the contradiction revealed by the wages-for-housework analysis, but whereas James linked it primarily to issues of race, O'Connell focused on issues of class.

The central contradiction revealed by the wages-for-housework analysis was one that the Left had inherited (and failed to challenge) from capitalism, namely, the notion that what is 'real' work is what is paid. In other words, whatever receives paid remuneration usually counts as work. Both liberal feminists and leftist feminists (at that time) accepted this conception of work and believed in work's liberating effects. The fact that the majority of women who left their homes were white and that many of the women who then entered and cleaned them were non-white was ignored. Also ignored was the fact that the women of colour who did the cleaning (and were poorly paid for it) did not usually find the work liberating. Another reality that remained unrecognized was that the level of pay offered by women to other women for the replacement of their work in the home was low, partly because the employer women were themselves paid less and partly because other women were providing the same services in their own homes without pay. O'Connell did explore the fact that poor women, who were not paid for doing housework in their own homes, were being encouraged to go to other women's homes and to offices to do cleaning for which they would receive low pay.

In her presentation of these issues in an article entitled 'Politics within the Women's Movement' (*Status* [June 1979]:6), Kay Macpherson stated that the 'NAC executive believes that the WFH goal ultimately reinforces the stereotype of women in the home and the current division of labour by sex.' Describing a meeting between the WFH group and the executive she observed that

> ... while NAC and the WFH group did not disagree on short-term goals – daycare, job training and improved support services – we had fundamental differences in philosophy and strategy. What NAC is aiming for in the long run – equal opportunities, equal pay, and [an] end to sex role stereotyping – appears to be in contradiction to the basic goal of the Wages for Housework groups; pay for housework, even the activity of keeping oneself clean and fed.

WFH activists argued that their campaign could effectively mobilize immigrant women and poor women, whose view of the value of full-time housewifery might well be different from the views of white, middle-class women. Macpherson's response was that NAC was already deeply involved in briefs, resolutions, and lobbying on behalf of such women. But she concluded that NAC remained committed to the position that the only way to solve the problems of immigrant and poor women was to 'end sex role stereotyping and to achieve full participation [by women] in all areas of society.' The tactics employed by the WFH groups at the 1979 AGM (including slick video presentations, meeting 'crashing,' and press releases and reporting that 'reached as far as California') alienated many NAC delegates and made it more difficult for them to hear any part of the WFH message. In the long run, however, the solidarity between liberal and leftist feminists on the issues involved would be challenged by women who endorsed feminism-of-difference and feminism-of-androgyny approaches. By the time MAWS again challenged NAC's views on the stay-at-home mother in 1987, NAC's understanding of women's work at home had been broadened, and MAWS was admitted and subsequently succeeded in having a task force established to consider the issues involved.

Despite having rejected the WFH groups as members, NAC absorbed many elements of their analysis. In the 1980 resolution on domestic labour, for example, NAC urged the government to change the Statistics Canada questionnaire to eliminate discriminatory assumptions about women who worked in the home. They urged, for example, that the question 'How many hours did you work last week?' be replaced by 'How many hours did you work for pay last week?' (Index of Policy Recommendations, March 1980). NAC positions on pensions for home-makers and on marriage breakdown recognized the value of the work women did in the home. However, campaigns to give Canadian mothers equal rights with fathers in conferring citizenship on children (Bill C-20), as well as equal status as 'breadwinners' under the Immigration Act (Bill C-16), were fresh in the minds of NAC women. Each of these campaigns had been based on arguments of absolute equality in the public sphere, which seemed to be undercut by the demand for wages for housework. Furthermore, the Canadian WFH groups had not presented the concepts on which they based their cause simply as educative tools, but had used them to lobby for the introduction of a state-funded social program. Consideration of the practical details of such a program further complicated the debate. Would housewives who participated in the paid workforce also be paid for the housework they did at home? Who would inspect the work? What rates of pay would be involved? Whose standards of cleanliness (and so on) would be employed?

The wages-for-housework controversy was a blip in the evolution of a feminist policy spectrum within NAC. The issue flared up in a short blaze of publicity (which had as one result the unfair labelling of NAC by the press as anti-housewife and unsympathetic to women in poverty), and soon gave way to other issues. The solidarity between liberal and leftist feminists in their analysis of wages for housework was also quickly disrupted by disputes over other issues. The process of grafting a radical grass roots of local groups organized primarily around feminisms of difference onto the founding NAC alliance was well under way, and it would significantly alter the nature of debates in NAC on issues such as wages for housework in the future. None the less, the wages-for-housework debate revealed a fault line in NAC around questions about how liberated women should live. This area was full of controversy, whether the debate revolved around work, sexuality, or a combination of the two (as in the case of prostitution). Such debate ultimately led to the creation of a feminist ideological spectrum, with positions on such issues as housewifery, child care, and military combat, all of which involved aspects of how women define themselves through work, and on such issues as lesbianism, which involved aspects of how women define themselves through sexuality. Prostitution, which combined work and sexuality, provoked significant debate in NAC in the late 1980s. The remainder of this section is devoted to outlining the development of this feminist spectrum through an examination of some of these benchmark issues.[5]

Margrit Eichler (1986), in her critique of the anti-feminist, 'pro-family' movement, argued that 'it is feminist organizations and individuals who have drawn attention to the unpaid work performed by women in the home as socially necessary and important work that should be recognized as such, and that upgrading the status of wives and mothers have been feminist concerns [*sic*] since the very beginning of the movement'(5). Eichler recognizes the existence of 'incisive' critiques of the patriarchal family within feminism, but downplays their prominence in NAC debates. It is true that the English-Canadian movement, as represented in NAC and as compared with the U.S. and U.K. movements, has not generated extreme critiques of the family. None the less, Eichler's account failed to convey the complexity of debate that did exist in NAC on the question of the family and, especially, on the status of stay-at-home wives and mothers. In her analysis of NAC policy up to 1982, Eichler identifies five categories of policies under the heading 'Feminist Positions concerning the Family': (1) the rights of mothers; (2) marriage and the status of the wife; (3) maternity, paternity, pregnancy, and adoption benefits; (4) maintenance and custody; and (5) introducing housewives into the Canada Pension Plan, credit splitting, and drop-out provisions. Only one of these five categories – that of pension reform – relates exclusively to positions concerning the stay-at-home wife and mother; the others relate to positions on all wives and mothers, regardless of whether they are in the paid workforce or work in the home. Thus, it is the debates on the subject of pensions for housewives that will best reveal the development of the feminist ideological spectrum around the issue of work.

Eichler argues that NAC has been consistently concerned with the status of housewives in old age. As part of her documentation of this conclusion, she identifies this resolution: 'Be it resolved that NAC support, as an immediate and interim objective, the concept of introducing housewives into the Canada Pension Plan through the splitting of past accumulated credits on the breakdown of marriage' (1986:8). What Eichler's analysis does not show is that delegates to the 1976 NAC AGM also debated the possibility of including the home-maker, *independent of* the income earner, in the C/QPP; that is, they debated the right of the home-maker to a C/QPP pension regardless of marital status or of the spouse's ability to earn the home-maker's pension credits. Furthermore, Eichler fails to note that NAC's 1976 position was weaker than that represented in the royal commission's recommendations. Of the twenty-seven voters on the inclusion issue at the 1976 AGM, eighteen reserved their position, reflecting the high level of uncertainty that existed around this issue. Only three voters supported inclusion, while six opposed it (Minutes of the third annual meeting 23 April 1976).

In fact, it took close to a decade of debate and struggle for NAC to reach the conclusion that home-makers ought to be included in the C/QPP pension system because of the work they were doing for society. The debate and struggle revolved around two central issues, both of which are important for us to understand. The first was whether husbands or society benefited from the work home-makers did at home; the second, intertwined with the first, was whether a mixed private/public pension system or a primarily public system could best achieve women's pensions needs.[6]

The long debate raised by the pensions-for-home-makers issue involved conflict over mixed private/public versus public delivery of pensions that saw leftist feminists being opposed by liberal feminists. The debate also involved a distinction made by feminist 'experts,' such as Eichler, between work of private benefit (home-making for husbands and adult children) and work of social benefit (home-making for dependents, including the aged and infirm, and for pre-school children). In the heat of the conflict over Jean Wood's commitment to a mixed system, which would retain a role for private pension provision and a responsibility for corporate and institutional employers, Louise Dulude, who had pioneered the CACSW's position of pensions for home-makers came 'to the rescue.' She managed to get the NAC AGM to accept a home-maker's pension provision in 1980, with no specification that public funding of the premiums would be dependent on home-makers' performing 'socially beneficial' work. NAC's position in 1982, by contrast, slipped back to the distinction made by Eichler that if work is of private benefit, the husband pays, and if it is of social benefit, the state pays.[7]

NAC's current position supports the right of home-makers to publicly funded pensions. Eichler's view that there is 'accumulated evidence of long-established, ongoing efforts by NAC to raise the status of housewives' is also supportable, as long as all women with children are described as housewives, even if they are in the paid workforce. Her conclusion that 'it seems patently absurd to charge NAC with trying to denigrate housewives,' however, is hardly self evident (1986:9). Most of NAC's positions are supportive of mothers, regardless of whether they are in the paid workforce or work at home; fewer are supportive of the stay-at-home housewife who is not a mother. Eichler herself is quoted as saying that the work of the home-maker without dependent children is only of private benefit. There is little doubt that part of the ideological struggle within NAC has been against the patriarchal evaluation of being 'only a housewife.' Just as leftist ideology absorbed the capitalist evaluation of work not paid for as not work (but a labour of love), many feminists absorbed the patriarchal belief that you are what you do. The fact that many women clean toilet bowls whether they are lawyers or full-time home-makers is key to the ideological contradiction. The struggle within NAC to come to terms with house-wifery as a way of being a woman at work is important to our under-standing of the development of the feminist ideological spectrum.

The fate of the home-maker's pension issue in NAC illustrates the importance of committed groups and individuals, such as Louise Dulude, in the policy process. Lacking a strong contingent of groups that reflected feminisms of difference and feminisms of androgyny during the early years, NAC had difficulty dealing with challenges that cut across the private/public divide, which most liberal and leftist feminists pursuing absolute-equality goals accepted. Both wages for housework and pensions for home-makers challenged that traditional divide.

Like the pension issue, the development of child-care policy in NAC reflected two dimensions: discussion about home day care and profit-making services versus a state-funded, school-like system, and discus-sion about who should pay and benefit between working parents and stay-at-home mothers. (Through the debate, there was little discussion of workplace child care, which was frowned on by many of the anglophone delegates as being bad for children and as tending to tie a woman to her employer.) NAC had come to support a position de-veloped by the Day Care Advocacy Association that 'tax benefits given directly to parents are a waste of money and the least effective way of developing a system of quality child care services in Canada' (*Feminist Action* [February 1988]: 1). It was this position that MAWS opposed.

In fact, there was little debate about the nature of the child-care program NAC policy would support through most of the 1980s. The membership of the day-care advocacy groups in NAC included few op-erators of for-profit centres, few representatives of workplace (as opposed to neighbourhood) centres, and few 'independents' provid-ing child care in their homes. Most NAC groups favoured a public model that would offer good care to children and decent wages to child-care workers. Women providing for-profit care were stereotyped by many in the feminist community as purveyors of 'Kentucky-fried children.' Home care was often presented as 'incompetent and unsafe.' There was no conservative-feminist defence of for-profit centres to parallel Laura Sabia's position on state-provided maternity leave (see pages 269–71). MAWS simply supported the right of the stay-at-home mother to receive the financial support towards the care 'of her choice' that the government's proposed program offered. Although MAWS was not excluded from NAC as the WFH groups had been, the position taken by its spokeswomen led to debate and conflict. MAWS did not oppose public child care, as did many anti-feminists. They did ask why NAC would support a policy that extended public support for child care to women in the paid workforce but not one that extended similar support to women who worked at home.

Issues surrounding the status of housewifery and of the stay-at-home mother continue to point to a fault line in NAC, despite the many positive contributions it has made to improving the status circumstances of women at home. Moreover, NAC's ability to deal with issues along this fault line is basic to its ability to cope with the New Right challenge. As Lorna Marsden argued, 'Only if we abandon the homemaker do we abandon ourselves to the possibility of REAL Women' (personal interview with Chris Appelle, 19 March 1985).

There has been relatively little conflict in NAC over the issue of lesbianism, which suggests a tolerance of different, non-traditional ways of being a woman. There has never been the sort of crisis concerning lesbianism in NAC than there was in NOW (where lesbianism was referred to as the 'lavender menace') (Ferree and Hess 1985; Deckard 1983). Kay Macpherson has explained that 'no one openly questioned the fact of whether lesbians belonged or not ... they were simply included' (personal interview with Chris Appelle, 10 April 1985). Jeri Dawn Wine, a founder of the National Lesbian Forum, has argued, however, that lesbians within NAC have largely been silenced in terms of their own rights (Vickers 1990b). She maintained that NAC avoided the sort of split that NOW suffered in 1968 only at the cost of a decade of silence of lesbians. The conflict within NOW over lesbianism was divisive and damaged NOW's organizational strength, with founder Betty Friedan opposing the inclusion of lesbian rights in NOW's agenda. But, as Wine observed, this conflict had positive results in the sense that lesbian rights subsequently became an up-front part of the NOW platform.

Appelle's 1984 survey of anglophone NAC delegates (Appelle 1987) included two questions on the issue of lesbianism. The availability of similar data for the United States in Alice Rossi's 1977 study (Rossi 1982) allows us to consider the issue comparatively. The two sets of responses to these questions are represented in Table 7.2. A far higher propor-

TABLE 7.2
Survey responses to questions about lesbianism

		Strongly agree	Not sure	Strongly disagree
Lesbian issue does more harm than good to women's movement	NAC	15.2%	27.2%	53.6%
	U.S.	38.9	27.4	33.7
Not feminist if will not work for lesbian rights	NAC	11.2	8.8	73.6
	U.S.	15.5	12.1	72.5

Source: Appelle 1987; Rossi 1982

tion of the U.S. sample believed that the issue of lesbian rights could damage the women's movement. Nearly three-quarters of the women in each sample, however, disagreed with the proposition that they could not consider themselves feminists if they were not willing to work for lesbian rights. Moreover, disagreeing with the view that support for lesbian rights harms the movement was strongly associated with the belief domain we have described as 'strong feminist.'

These responses, however, mean that lesbianism *per se* sits on the fault line generating the feminist ideological spectrum. Donna Stephania's 1985 report as chair of the Lesbian Issues Committee in NAC in *Feminist Action* (December 1985:10) illustrated the effectiveness with which NAC organized to support lesbian rights before the Boyer Committee on equality rights. The Boyer Committee's recommendations on sexual orientation were without doubt the most surprising in the committee's report (especially in view of the primacy of the issue of gay and lesbian rights in the literature of anti-feminist groups such as REAL Women, in which homophobia had overtaken opposition to abortion as the main issue.) Stephania acknowledges 'the work of the women at the 1985 AGM who successfully advocated the inclusion of lesbian issues on NAC's agenda at the Federal Lobby and as a committee in its own right.' Thus, many years after NOW's high-profile 'lavender menace' conflict, NAC explicitly included lesbian issues in its agenda. Although it did so only after after the entrenchment of the

Charter of Rights and Freedoms, it was in the context of a high-profile and successful campaign in connection with the parliamentary committee. Certainly, the homophobia of right-wing groups is increasingly apparent, and this may make lesbian rights an issue of solidarity rather than dispute in NAC in the 1990s, just as abortion rights were in the 1980s.

Prostitution emerged in the late 1980s in NAC as an issue that challenged many women's views about this combination of work and sexuality. Many feminists had regarded prostitutes as victims, and prostitution as part of a way some men oppressed women. In 1986, a resolution was passed that argued that prostitution was as valid an occupation as any other under the circumstances (that is, in a capitalist society that offered few good job opportunities for women). This signalled a departure from the position that prostitutes were victims, who, because of poverty or negative childhood experiences, had to do for money something that other women did without pay. It asserted instead that prostitutes were agents whose 'choice' of their occupation was at least as free as that of women who 'chose' marriage and motherhood. Introducing her committee's 'Forum on Prostitution,' chair Lorraine Greaves stated that 'It is apparent to all of us that the more questions we ask about prostitution and related issues, the less black and white our ideas and opinions become' (*Feminist Action* [December 1986]:7). She argued that the women's movement had progressed because women were able to listen to others who expressed their experiences and to 'honour' as authentic both those experiences and the accounts of them. She suggested that this was what had enabled women to come to terms with the experiences of rape victims, housewives, mothers, battered women, incest survivors, poor women, visible-minority women, and women with disabilities. She insisted that the same ability to listen and honour now had to be applied to prostitutes as well.

An article on pimping by Val Scott and Ryan Hotchkiss of the Canadian Organization for the Rights of Prostitutes (CORP) accompanied Greaves's article. In it, the authors explored the position that advocated 'Leave the poor girls alone, but come down hard on the pimps.' The authors stated that 'In popular mythology, a pimp is a man, usually black, who coerces, assaults and extorts money from a younger, white, female prostitute.' But, they argued, pimping laws could convict friends, lovers (male and female), spouses, or even adult children who 'live off the avails of prostitution,' which is itself a legal activity. They suggested that victim analysis, which sees the prostitute as a victim and, consequently, the pimp as a villain, was 'insulting to whores.' Drawing a parallel between husbands who batter and pimps who assault, they argued that since the law convicts men for battering, not for being husbands, it should convict pimps for assault, coercion, extortion, or exploitation, not for pimping (*Feminist Action* [December 1986]:7–8).

This focus on different aspects of prostitution and the laws against pimping followed passage of NAC's policy, and was an attempt to develop solidarity between prostitutes as represented by CORP and the women's movement as represented in NAC. Making NAC women aware of the way some women viewed their sexuality and their work in the context of prostitution challenged women's assumptions by breaking one of patriarchy's most ancient taboos – the one forbidding interaction between 'decent' women and whores. It also raised the question of how to treat as authentic women's experiences that apparently involved free choice but that were viewed by some as threatening to the general liberation of women and girls. In this sense, the issue of prostitution caused conflict in NAC for perhaps the same reasons that the issue of the status of stay-at-home housewives did: Both were watershed issues around which feminist ideological positions were being generated. Those coming from feminisms of androgyny tended to be the most accepting of attempts to reconceptualize prostitution, as it affected both sexuality and work, and to consider questions of sexual 'servicing' of women, the aged, and people with disabilities as part of the debate. The contempt expressed by prostitutes for the 'housewife who denies us yet is silently thankful we had sex with her husband so she can be left in peace' illuminated the full complexity of the debate that this issue raised. (*Feminist Action* [December 1986]:8).

Ironically, one of the other landmark issues comparable to house-wifery and prostitution in terms of the extent of controversy it engendered was that of women in the military and, especially, of women in military combat. This issue was of particular importance for two reasons. First, it involved convictions developed by many feminist in the first wave of the movement that women are 'naturally' pacifists and that their role in the political sphere is to be 'moral mothers,' nurturing, protecting, and opposing war. Second, the issue was central to New Right campaigns against equality measures such as the ERA, which, it was argued, would have required U.S. women to give up their protected status *vis-à-vis* military service and, in particular, combat. The

U.S. anti-feminist group STOP ERA, led by Phyllis Schlafly, used the danger of girls' being drafted, along with the possible loss of alimony after divorce, as the two key mobilizers of anti-ERA sentiment among women. That the issue was also conflictual in NAC reflects its importance as a benchmark issue.

NAC feminists were forced by the equality-seeking processes of the Charter to examine the largely unquestioned anti-military positions inherited by second-wave feminists and brought into NAC by groups such as the Voice of Women. In 1985, the Canadian armed forces sought an exemption from the Charter of Rights and Freedoms equality provisions, especially in relation to the service of women, gays, and lesbians. Long-time peace activist and former NAC executive member Carole Wallace argued as follows: 'I believe there is a place for the military in Canadian society in terms of peacekeeping, natural disasters and national sovereignty. Then one must go to the next step and say there is a role for women in the military and it should be an equal role' (*Feminist Action* [October 1985]:4). Survival Committee member and long-time NAC activist Betsy Carr responded that 'NAC is against the arms race and the social deprivation and oppression that result from militarism. Feminists who would integrate women into the armed forces do not question the present system' (*Feminist Action* [October 1985]:4). The debate between these positions in NAC demonstrated the existence of a strong alliance between first- and second-wave women operating from a feminism-of-difference position that stressed women's role as 'moral mothers' in opposing war and militarism. The compromise resolution adopted by the executive began with a restatement of NAC's 'anti-military stand' but also argued that 'Under no circumstances should there be an exemption [for the military] to Section 15 of the Charter. As a result, all trades and classifications in the Armed Forces should be open to women.' The remainder of the resolution addressed the issues of fair treatment for women who are involved in the military, while 'not advocat[ing] women's involvement in the military.' Similarly, the rights of gays and lesbians in the services and of wives of military personnel on bases were supported in a resolution that, none the less, critiqued the military as 'destructive' and 'the last bastion of overt male supremacy' (*Feminist Action* [October 1985]:4).

This issue demonstrates again the importance to the NAC policy process of committed groups and individuals. In this case, the issue itself mobilized relatively few women either within NAC or outside it.

Even a ringing endorsement of the military by NAC would not have stimulated many new recruits for Canada's small military. In this case, Marjorie Cohen, chair of the Employment and Economy Committee, acted as the developer of a compromise position that stressed both NAC's feminism-of-equality approach to matters of work and its feminism-of-difference approach to the issue of militarism and the military. Grass-roots opposition to 'militarization' (as represented by the presence, or absence, of military bases and defence industries in a community) was evident in regional reports published in *Feminist Action* (for example, the PEI Report, April 1986, and the report of the Innu of Labrador at the 1988 AGM). Whether the Charter might open up the possibility of drafting women for military service, however, was not an issue for NAC as it was in the United States for NOW, in conjunction with the ERA. Certainly, the Canadian movement never pursued a strict feminism-of-equality approach that could have resulted in the drafting of women for military service through the Charter. Indeed, it intervened to ensure that the Charter's equality guarantees permitted consideration of difference and of affirmative-action programs. An absolute-equality approach, in which women's right (or duty) to equal involvement in combat and the military would have superseded feminist values concerning peace, did not prevail in NAC. Nor was there any serious reconsideration of the 'moral mother' stance from the perspective that such things as peacekeeping, defence of sovereignty, and action in natural disasters might represent a modern equivalent of 'moral mothering.'

From a Status-of-Women Approach to a Feminist Politics

In the first decade of NAC's operation, its approach to public policy could best be described as a status-of-women approach. NAC undertook responsibilities for general public-policy issues to the extent that they had a clear status-of-women dimension. In the 1972–82 period, status-of-women issues vastly outnumbered general public-policy issues (peace and war, taxation, immigration, fiscal arrangements) on which women had a unique position or which affected women in a different way than they affected men. In this section, we distinguish between the status-of-women approach to general public-policy issues and the approach of a holistic, feminist politics. We examine several concrete issues both before and after the basic watershed, which is the debate over patriation of the Constitution and the Charter of Rights and Freedoms. In the early period, the policies that NAC developed on status-of-women issues were very much influenced by partisan political positions, especially when it came to matters of whether the state should be involved in legislating or providing services. The example of maternity-leave policy permits us to explore several varieties of conservative feminism that were present in NAC before 1982.

After 1982, there was less evidence of a full spectrum of partisan positions in NAC, with Conservative feminists becoming less active than they had been during the era of Liberal government. The federal Conservative government drew some Conservative feminists into government, diminishing the representation of this segment of the spectrum in NAC. In addition, NAC's increased sophistication in feminist policy analysis made it more threatening to the Conservative government, which also faced with a virulent anti-feminist backlash. To date, there has been no explicit change in NAC's commitment to being multipartisan. None the less, the increasing importance of the feminist spectrum has blurred partisan positions within NAC and made them less important. What has also changed is the government's view of NAC. It became easier for the government to label the NAC of the late 1980s as 'an NDP pawn' than for Progressive Conservative feminists to join the debate within NAC over issues such as the government's child-care policy. The front line for Conservative feminists has been to oppose the anti-feminists in the party, causing their influence in NAC to decline.[8]

As we have seen, NAC was created organizationally by an alliance of women from the three major political parties. In the first decade of NAC's operation, a conservative feminist voice was present on the executive, in policy debates, and in the pages of *Status of Women News*. It must be remembered that, except for the brief period of the Clark government, the Trudeau Liberals dominated Ottawa, making NAC an important arena for Conservative feminists. For example, a debate between Laura Sabia and unionist Jean-Claude Parrot was provoked by the decision of the Supreme Court in the case of Stella Bliss (1978), in which Mr Justice Ritchie argued that Bliss was not entitled to maternity benefits under the Unemployment Insurance Act on the grounds that 'Any inequality between the sexes in this area is not created by legislation, but by nature' (*Status* [Winter 1981–2]:9). (This case was one of several that persuaded feminists of the importance of the Charter. The Charter effectively overturned Bliss.) Sabia outlined her understanding of the state's responsibilities *vis-à-vis* women's equality in the *Toronto Sun's* debate column in July 1981. The *Status* editors then solicited the debate pieces, which illuminate Sabia's ideas clearly.

Just as English-Canadian socialism is different from its counterparts elsewhere, conservatism within the institution of the federal Progressive Conservative party is also different from its U.S. or U.K. counterparts. In 1981, conservative feminism in Canada had two main types: the 'red Tory' strain, which is uniquely Canadian, and the neoliberal/libertarian strain. The latter is now described as 'conservative' because of its relative lack of enthusiasm for state intervention in people's lives and because of its belief that there is a limit to the number of positive-action programs government can and should undertake. Both strains support government action to strike down barriers against women's equal opportunity to participate in the paid workforce. Both support reproductive freedom for women. The 'red Tory' feminists are more supportive of positive programs to create a 'level playing field' in the 'equal opportunity sweepstakes'; neoliberal feminists apply libertarian principles in attacking any governmental barriers to women's freedom in matters such as abortion.[9]

In the *Toronto Sun* debate pieces (reproduced in *Status* [Winter 1981–2]:6), Laura Sabia expressed her opposition to state-funded maternity-leave programs sought by working-class and liberal feminists in neoliberal terms:

(1) Wherever we found 'protective' legislation, we found discrimination ... Our restrictive divorce and abortion laws started out as 'protective' legislation.

(2) I don't believe in the almighty power of the state. I'm a private enterpriser from way back. I believe in the supremacy of the individual. I believe in the individual assuming the responsibility for his/her actions.

(3) Having a baby is not an illness. It is not a fatal disease. It is a conscious choice made by two people. Have they no responsibility for that conscious choice?

(4) [Parrot of the Postal Union] said: 'It is time to recognize that bearing children is a social responsibility.' Is it? Do women want the state to control their wombs? Have we gained control of our bodies only to turn them over to the state? What's to stop the state from ordering women to procreate at the dictates of the state and be paid for it too?

(5) Business establishments, both big and small, will be loath to employ young women knowing that a pregnancy will force them to pay two salaries for 17 weeks or more ... 'Paid' maternity leave is a subtle plot to keep women from ascending the ladder of success and keeping the best jobs for the sex with the penis.

(6) We are creating a new expensive social program for the private and public sectors without cost estimates when our economy can ill afford it.

Sabia's analysis of paid maternity leave, like Jean Wood's support of a mixed-economy approach to pensions for women, represented a position that questioned whether women could or should trust the state or expect the state to provide services for them. In NAC, an alliance between leftist and liberal feminists committed to positive state action prevailed in both cases. The feminist agenda itself, however, revived the question of how far feminists should trust state action in the issues of censorship of pornography and of the control and funding of services for victims of male violence. None the less, in the period after the watershed of the Charter, there has been far less debate about the movement's pro-statism and a diminished presence in NAC of neoliberal feminists.

The equality-seeking dynamic has changed the face of English-Canadian politics since the 1960s. Opponents on the Right have identified this as a fundamental shift in public policy. Harry Antonides (1986:4) writes that this shift

means adopting the following changes in the purposes of the state and of law:
(1) Instead of being a passive instrument, the law becomes an active one;
(2) Instead of ensuring equality of opportunity, the law is designed to ensure equality of results;
(3) Instead of protecting citizens' freedoms (over and against the state if need be), the primary purpose of the state is to provide certain social and economic 'rights' (or entitlements).

Without accepting all of Antonides's analysis, there is little doubt that the changes we identified showed a maturation of the politics of equality-seeking in Canada after the entrenchment in the Constitution of the Charter's equality guarantees. The effect of this on NAC was to change the character of its approach to public-policy issues. In one major area, abortion, feminists wanted freedom from the state but simultaneously expected the state to provide services. But, in all cases, the language employed was the language of rights (reproductive rights, lesbian rights, the right to maternity leave). A whole range of new issues raised questions about the rights of women to use their bodies as they chose. Should women who 'choose' to be 'surrogate' mothers be free from state interference? Should prostitutes who 'choose' to do so be free to earn their living with the sexual parts of their bodies? Should adult women who 'choose' to engage in military combat or 'erotic' dancing be free to do so? (Each of the words we have enclosed in quotation marks represents disputed terrain.) Although the old debate about an activist state tied to 'male-stream' political labels and political parties has largely been closed in NAC, a new feminist debate concerning what it is like to be an autonomous woman is just beginning to take shape. The questions about responsibility that a feminist theory of freedom must encompass are just beginning to be asked.

In the period before 1982, NAC was often reacting to positions developed by male-dominated political parties. After 1982, debates began to originate *in* NAC around issues concerning freedom and the state, and the debates were rooted in feminist terrain. Ironically, the analysis of theorists such as Catherine MacKinnon (1989), who characterized the state as unremittingly patriarchal, appears to have dampened the enthusiasm of women in NAC for state involvement very little. What has emerged is an increased belief in the possibility of an unaligned feminism. This tendency to withdraw from engagement with the official politics of the state is, once again, ironic, given the success English-Canadian feminists have had in changing the basic political agenda of the federal state to include equality as a major feature of our constitutional regime. The leadership of NAC during this period has been deeply engaged in trying to develop an integrative-feminist approach to public policy. In this final section, we will explore two examples of this: the debate about free trade and the debate about the Meech Lake Accord.

The debate about whether Canada should enter into a free-trade agreement with the United States could have threatened NAC with partisan conflict. After all, in this debate, women could not be represented simply as seekers of rights: They had achieved a significant framework of rights, and they were now exploring them. They were increasingly coming to see themselves as equal partners in the process of making choices about Canada's future. The free-trade debate illustrated a fundamental problem inherent in developing a feminist policy analysis that moves beyond the equality-seeking dynamic. To what issues will such a feminist politics respond? Will it respond to those women who have begun to enjoy the benefits of equality in our society or to those who continue to suffer the disadvantages of inequality (still, in all likelihood, the majority)? Or will it somehow respond to both?

NAC's response to the prospect of free trade was spearheaded by economist Marjorie Cohen through NAC's Employment and Economy Committee. It was also shaped by the strong positions of union feminists on the committee, especially Madeleine Parent, who represented women textile workers threatened by the proposed free-trade deal. In her analysis, Cohen claimed that many Canadian women would be hurt by free trade through loss of employment, inability to relocate, and the potential loss of hard-won social services. Her analysis entered into the public-policy debate, forcing the government to respond with literature about the gains women could be able to make under free trade in other sectors, especially small business, and as consumers. Analysis that focused on threatened social services and state programs was presented in a feminist context, showing women (and children) as more dependent on social services and women as more frequently employed by state agencies than men. Few women who are involved in 'moving up' the corporate ladder, who were entrepreneurs, or who saw opportunities in free trade as consumers were in organizations represented in NAC. The anti–free-trade position developed by Cohen and the Employment and Economy Committee, therefore, came to be the position associated with NAC. It assumed that the liberation of women required state programs and that these were threatened by the proposed Canada–U.S. Free Trade Agreement (FTA).

A significant gender gap in opinion emerged on the free-trade issue, at least in part because of Cohen's analysis and NAC's insistence that the proposed deal was an important feminist issue (Gidengil 1992; O'Neill 1992). Provoked by feminist critics, the Royal Commission on the Economic Union and Development Prospects for Canada had admitted knowing that the negative effects of trade liberalization would fall disproportionately on women workers, because of their predominance in textiles and light industry. The commissioners felt this was not something that should cause serious concern, however, because adjustment assistance would give women workers the chance 'to leave low-wage declining sectors of employment for expanding ones'. (Canada, Royal Commission on the Economic Union ... 1985: 2:629). The commission ignored the fact that, because of family responsibilities, women are far less able than men to relocate and to gain access to retraining programs. Cohen's very detailed discussion (in an article entitled 'The Macdonald Report and Its Implications for Women') showed that the consequences of these supposedly gender-neutral recommendations of public policy for the majority of women workers were little understood by the commissioners (*Feminist Action* [December 1985]:13–15).

Canada's chief document of neoliberal policy originated in a royal commission appointed by a Liberal prime minister and chaired by a former Liberal cabinet minister and was finally implemented by a

Progressive Conservative government. The irony was that the Liberal party, now in opposition, opposed the FTA. NAC joined the coalition to oppose the agreement. NAC's opposition, based on sound feminist analysis concerning its impact on the majority of women workers, was then severely criticized by the Conservative government as being partisan. (Subsequent significant cuts in NAC's grants are viewed by many as punishment for this position.) In fact, NAC's 'sin' in the eyes of most men in the public-policy process, from Macdonald Commission researchers to irate free-trade negotiators, was that it had strayed outside the bounds of the more limited status-of-women framework expected of it. By daring to engage in the key debate about Canada's economic future, NAC, the CACSW, and Cohen herself had in fact provided Canadian women with an analysis of economic policy 'as if women mattered.' Clearly, many women accepted the analysis, as the gender gap in support for the deal shows.

Ironically, the free-trade agreement edged out of the 1988 election agenda the issue of the government's child-care policy, which for a few brief weeks seemed likely to become one of the top three issues of the campaign. The election then became a single-issue affair, with the free-trade agreement crowding out all other concerns. The two main opposition parties picked up aspects of the feminist analysis of free-trade issues, which had come to represent an important element in the debate.

The debates in NAC about the Meech Lake and Charlottetown Accords also showed its evolution towards a full-fledged feminist politics. At the heart of both of the accords was an attempt by the political élites to respond to Québec's demands for greater autonomy and to other provincial leaders' insistence on equality for all provinces (and for provincial leaders) by creating a more decentralized constitutional regime. Many anglophone feminists in NAC, who so often rejected centralized structures in favour of the 'close-to-home' and the grass roots, opposed the accords because they feared that greater provincial powers would weaken the federal system of social services and put those services at the mercy of provincial governments, which most feminists considered to be less progressive. In NAC, member groups of women with disabilities, women from visible minorities, and immigrant women, for whom a weakening of federal powers was especially threatening, also opposed the accords. Most francophones feminists in Québec, by contrast, believed they could ensure that the Québec state would be progressive in the way it wielded its powers as a distinct

society. All feminist organizations with significant Québec membership were forced to grapple internally with the conflict between Québec
feminists' support for the Meech Lake Accord, which recognized their
distinct society, and anglophone and allophone feminists' desire to
retain a strong federal role in the social-service system. Furthermore,
there was intense reaction to any possibility that the Charter's equality
rights, fought for so recently and with such tenacity by English-Canadian feminists, could in any way be diminished by the accords. The
response of partisan politicians tended in the early stages to be 'don't
worry your heads about this.' Just as those whose focus was economic
policy had reacted violently to the intrusion of feminist analysis into
their domain, lawyers and politicians reacted with hostility to women's
groups who expressed concern about the potential effect of the accords
on their rights and services.

Although events within NAC surrounding the Charlottetown Accord
are too recent for us to do more than report the public manifestations
of the debate, it is clear that the divisiveness NAC experienced over the
Meech Lake Accord was largely avoided in its response to the referendum on the Charlottetown Accord. Only a month after the Meech
Lake Accord was released, there was a controversial debate at the
AGM. The lines drawn were classic: Québec francophones opposed a
resolution by President Louise Dulude that rejected the accord because of its probable effect of weakening the social-service system on
which women relied so heavily. Poor translation, the displacement of
a Québec resolution, and the inability of anglophone delegates to
understand the conflict between Dulude (an Ottawa-based francophone) and the Québec francophones rendered the debate a nightmare. Only a last-minute agreement that created a special committee
to develop a compromise prevented the withdrawal of the FFQ from
NAC at that meeting.

The NAC special committee allowed for the development of a position that was acceptable to both the FFQ and the NAC executive. It was
presented to the Special Joint Committee of the Senate and of the
House of Commons on the Constitution on 16 August 1987. The position accepted the basic importance of recognizing Québec as a distinct
society. Indeed, 'NAC representatives testified to the Special Committee that it was fundamental to their position to avoid any damage
to this clause. NAC's Québec representatives explained that the well-
established women's movement would be among the institutions protected by the distinct society' (Roberts 1988:14). More than any other

debate, the one surrounding the Meech Lake Accord showed the profound difference in political consciousness between Québec francophone feminists and feminists in English Canada. Québec francophones expressed confidence that they could achieve what they wanted best through the Québec state. Anglophone feminists, faced with intense anti-feminist forces in their provincial states, could not afford to accept a weakening of federal involvement and protection. The NAC compromise position was to give Section 28 of the Charter both protection from legislative override and symbolic prominence: 'Although some NAC members personally favoured proposals of a more Draconian nature, the organization's position was that shared with the FFQ' (Roberts 1988:15).

Had the government accepted the sort of compromise worked out by the NAC/FFQ special committee, that compromise might have held within NAC. Most of NAC's member groups, however, presented positions to the Special Joint Committee on the Constitution that were far less understanding of Québec feminists' aspirations. As they did not trust their provincial governments, their belief as feminists in decentralization remained, in this case, strictly theoretical. Most NAC affiliates came to argue against the Meech Lake Accord and many actively lobbied federal and provincial politicians against its implementation.[10] The child-care issue came easily to hand to illustrate their belief that no new programs with 'national standards,' such as medicare, could ever again be implemented if the accord were ratified. At the next NAC AGM, the revived ad hoc constitutional group sought to disrupt NAC's compromise position and to persuade the AGM to adopt a position that rejected the accord. In a painful session in which ad hoc activists marshalled minority women and women with disabilities as speakers, the compromise that had been struck in 1987 began to unravel. Newly mobilized groups of women presented reasons for their concern about the accord's potential decentralizing effects, especially in terms of immigration policy and services and facilities for people with disabilities. They voiced anger at the fact that a compromise between the old established groups (French and English) should interfere with their right to express their own concerns to government. Once again, a special committee was struck, which worked out another compromise within a few hours. But the damage had already been done. When the FFQ withdrew from the NAC, it was ostensibly for reasons other than the lack of comprehension of the FFQ position that most of the NAC delegates displayed at the AGM. In fact, it had become apparent to most of the women who had struck the compromise that the day for settling such issues by élite accommodation in NAC was long gone. And the day when anglophones and Québec francophones could debate the issue easily and fully with each other had not yet arrived.

NAC's role in the Meech Lake debate was none the less an important sign of its progress towards the development of a full-fledged feminist approach to public-policy issues. The ability of NAC and FFQ leaders to develop a compromise that recognized the legitimate aspirations of both Québec francophone feminists and English-Canadian feminists was most impressive, despite the fact that NAC was not able to mobilize all of its affiliates around its official position. The development within NAC of a public-policy debate that took women seriously and that took public policy seriously represented one of the most important advances NAC had ever made as an institution of an enduring women's movement. Since 1981, NAC has faced four major public-policy challenges: entrenchment of the Charter in the Constitution, the free-trade agreement, the Meech Lake Accord, and the referendum on the Charlottetown Accord. Its capacity to develop a feminist approach to public-policy issues has clearly grown with each challenge.

Although NAC's involvement in constitutional politics around the 1992 referendum on the Charlottetown Accord goes well past the end of the time frame of our study of the NAC documentary record, a brief overview of what constitutes NAC's most public presentation of a feminist political analysis may be useful to readers. After the demise of the Meech Lake Accord and the outbursts of aboriginal anger expressed in conflicts such as the one at Oka, between the Mohawk Nation and the Québec state (through its police) and the federal state (through its army), NAC developed a 'three nations' constitutional position based on a vision of asymmetrical federalism. In this vision, the Québec nation and the First Nations would enjoy special status and decentralized powers, while the rest of Canada (ROC) would enjoy a centralized federation with significant federal power to create and maintain national social programs. This vision represented, finally, NAC's understanding of Québec's and the First Nations' aspirations.

When the Charlottetown Accord was presented to Canadians in a referendum, the NAC executive surprised (and shocked) many observers by quickly and unanimously deciding to oppose it and to encourage women to vote 'no' in the referendum. This seemed at odds with the 'three nations' position that had been developed. The NAC executive, which now had strong representation from the new force of immigrant and racial-minority women, women with disabilities, and lesbians, was reinforced in its decision by the fact that most Québec francophones, who had supported the Meech Lake Accord, opposed the Charlottetown deal. The issue of aboriginal self-government was more problematic. Because they maintained that the right of aboriginal peoples to self-government was *inherent* and not something the federal or provincial governments could confer or delegate, most aboriginal leaders rejected the application of the Charter to First Nations. This and the opposition to the accord by the Native Women's Association of Canada (NWAC), who had been denied status at the constitutional bargaining table, allowed NAC leaders to advance the position that, while NAC supported aboriginal self-government, it could not support a deal that would leave aboriginal women unprotected by the Charter.

The prominence of NAC's president, Judy Rebick, in the media coverage of the referendum campaigns was not matched by an analysis of the gender gap in opinion concerning the acceptability of the élite compromise that the accord represented. Although Rebick outlined the concerns of the women represented by many of NAC's member groups, male analysts focused more on the disagreements among women and usually failed to understand the underlying concerns Rebick was expressing. The fact that the women's movement, which was heavily involved in the constitutional conferences, was excluded in the final rounds of executive federalism persuaded many women that the deal was fatally flawed.

Notes

1 There is a third aspect of ideology apparent within NAC, which we have already discussed in earlier chapters. It is the spectrum of views within feminism on hierarchy, organization, leadership, bureaucracy, voluntarism, and the appropriateness of political, social, or cultural modes of achieving change. This process spectrum does not neatly or easily correspond with either of the other dimensions. For example, it is possible to find leftist feminists in NAC who support structure, organization, leadership, bureaucracy, and political modes of achieving change and leftist feminists who oppose structure, organization, and so on, and who support only cultural or social modes of achieving change.

2 We will not explore the important issues that divide feminists and anti-feminists (in particular, the issue of abortion, because it is an issue

considered to be resolved within NAC and, therefore, has not been a subject of debate).

3 The phrase *sex-specific/gender-neutral* was coined by Catherine MacKinnon to describe her proposals for legislative change in the area of pornography.

4 It is interesting that this issue is not included in Eichler's 1986 publication, 'The Pro-Family Movement: Are They For or Against Families?' in which she argues that NAC policy has defended home-makers better than have New Right groups. Eichler's support for an enriched program of family allowances is a sex-specific/gender-neutral solution. Since the financial support would be for the parent with primary responsibility for child care (whether she or he remained at home or not), the perpetuation of dependency by making it attractive (either for women or men) for women to stay at home would apparently disappear. In fact, it would transfer dependency of the primary parent (usually the woman) to the state.

5 As noted earlier, we do not explore here the key issue dividing feminists and anti-feminists – abortion. We should, however, note the existence of a small pro-life group of feminists, who are consistently pro-life on all issues from vegetarianism to pacifism, and who have been described by observers such as Karen Dubinsky (1985). These women appear to have played no role in NAC. The 'Strategy for Change' conference in 1972 was organized by Sabia (herself a pro-choice Catholic) in such a way as to avoid focusing on abortion as the defining issue.

6 The sequence of the debate, some of which we have already discussed in terms of its involvement in the partisan and ideological conflicts within the NAC executive at this time, was as follows:

1978: A brief to the Cabinet (17 March) called for 'a pension plan for home-maker spouses'; supported the government's adoption of a 'drop-out' amendment to the CPP for 'parents of pre-school children'; and called for provision for survivor spouses under 65, survivor benefits not to be terminated on remarriage, and the right of home-makers 'to contribute up to 50% of the year's maximum pensionable earnings, as long as a dependent child under the age of 18 is in the home' ('The Economic Outlook,' reported in the Index of Policy Recommendations).

1978: A resolution protesting the Human Rights Commission's 'intention to delay consideration of private pension plans,' seeking prohibition of the use of actuarial tables based on sex in calculating private pension benefits (resolution moved March 1978 by Merry Chellas and Louise Laporte, Index of Policy Recommendations).

1979:   Reaffirms opposition to Ontario and BC, which refuse to agree to the 'drop out' provision to permit inclusion of home-makers (Index of Policy Recommendations).

1980:   'NAC urges the federal government to provide universal pension coverage to home-makers under the C/QPP by means of publicly funded premiums' (Index of Policy Recommendations).

1980:   Support unisex mortality tables (Index of Policy recommendations).

1982:   'The Canadian pension system to be reformed in the following ways: (a) to include all home-makers (whether or not they have young children) in the C/QPP; if the home-maker is taking care of a child less than seven or dependent disabled family member, this inclusion should be subsidized by all participants to C/QPP; if there are no young children or dependent disabled family members, this should be paid for by the home-makers spouse' (Index of Policy Recommendations. This is not a complete record of the 1982 pension resolutions; the other aspects deal with general improvements to the plan).

7   Eichler's own analysis (1986) of REAL Women's pamphlets identifies a recommendation that the drop-out provision for home-maker's pensions be changed to cover the period of time until the child turns sixteen, suggesting the utility of debate concerning the age at which mother's activities cease to be of social benefit.

8   It is important to note here that another factor that changed the nature of NAC's debate on general public-policy issues was the Charter of Rights. Before the Charter, NAC was involved in advancing an equality-seeking dynamic. With the entrenchment of the Charter's equality provisions, NAC's efforts had to go into defending positions already attained, as in the case of the Parliamentary Committee on Equality Rights. The Charter also introduced a whole new strategy dimension in relation to women's equality; that is, the process of litigation to advance equality claims. New organizations such as LEAF emerged to plan a complex strategy and to raise funding to support it. Creations of the feminist legal professionals who played such an important role in getting the Charter guarantees, groups such as LEAF belong to NAC but are also somewhat aloof from it. (Scholarly analysis of 'L.A. Law feminism' has been limited to its impact on popular culture. The huge increase in the proportion of women in law schools and the legal profession, however, has certainly changed the face of the Canadian movement.)

9 The concept of neoliberal conservatism perhaps requires further discussion. Vickers has distinguished between neoliberal and New Right opposition to the welfare state (Vickers 1986). Neoliberals look back to the pure free-market model and support a libertarian stance in relation to private activities, including sexuality and reproduction. New Right Conservatives, by contrast, seek to increase government intervention in people's private lives, while 'freeing enterprise' from government control. Neoliberal feminists, then, support classical liberal protection of 'free competition' and a libertarian stance on sexual and reproductive issues.

10 See Roberts 1988 for a full account of the positions held by the various groups.

8 Conclusion

We began with the premise that women's movements represent values and demands that cannot be accommodated quickly or entirely through the official politics of liberal-democratic societies. As a result, we argued, women's movements must be seen as multigenerational projects that can be fully effective only if they become sufficiently institutionalized to steer women's collective efforts across time. Within this general framework, we have explored the role of NAC in stabilizing and legitimizing the English-Canadian women's movement through its own institutionalization and its resulting ability 'to co-ordinate, if not control' the wider movement (Phillips 1990). We have also sketched the stresses and strains endured by NAC in the course of its evolution from a largely liberal-feminist coalition aimed at lobbying the federal government to a parliament of women with a radical grass roots and waves of newly mobilized women to be integrated. Our discussion of NAC has described the quandaries that the organization confronted in its emerging role as a parliament of women – in particular, about how to represent women and how to devise policy in new ways that would reflect feminist values and commitments.

In this conclusion, we pose a series of questions about the future of NAC and women's politics in Canada's changing political environment. As readers will recall, it was also our desire to provide a model of conducting political analysis 'as if women mattered' – that is, using concepts and insights derived from a woman-centred perspective. To be consistent with this approach, therefore, we will present our concluding questions in a way that integrates women's political insights and their views on the purpose of institutions such as NAC. We begin by asking 'What is success?' from a woman-centred perspective.

What Is Success?

To evaluate the ways in which NAC succeeded (and failed) in its first two decades, we must understand more fully its position in Canadian women's politics and decide what we consider to be markers of success for social movements in Canada. Several measures of success have been proposed by those evaluating movements for change elsewhere (Gelb 1989:180–7). Success may refer to (1) the legitimization of group goals through changes in consciousness and through concrete public-policy outcomes; (2) the opening up of existing power structures to movement personnel; (3) changes in power relationships; (4) the creation of alternative sources and centres of power through new organizational forms; and (5) the survival of the group or the movement (187). Each of these standards of success has been derived from the study of womens' movements in other countries, none of which, however, has an umbrella organization such as NAC and none of which has movements that have depended so heavily on government funding. Furthermore, the movement we have studied indirectly through NAC exists in a multinational, multilingual, and multicultural state that imposes a significant additional test of success on all organizations claiming to be pan-Canadian – namely, their ability to incorporate participants of widely diverse backgrounds.

In general, NAC contributed to the success of its member groups in the period studied by legitimizing women's goals for change by getting them on the public agenda and, in many cases, elevating them to the political agenda as well. It helped directly in opening up power structures to movement personnel; indeed, NAC and some of its affiliated organizations have become a major alternative training ground for aspiring women politicians. Moreover, through the construction and institutionalization of an embryonic parliament of women, NAC has created an alternative centre of public-policy proposals, legitimized as representing the views of progressive women on both 'women's issues' and general issues of public policy. Indeed, apart from fielding candidates, NAC came increasingly to resemble an omnibus political party in Canada, with internal ideological wings and linguistic and regional conflicts. Its grafted-on grass roots, composed of many small, local groups, including radical groups, constantly refreshed its policy agenda by bringing the experiences of diverse women directly into many NAC debates. Certainly, despite many dire predictions, NAC both survived and become institutionalized, in the sense that many English-Canadian women now consider it as much a part of the political landscape as the political parties and, indeed, as an essential part in terms of expressing feminist views.

In terms of concrete policy outcomes, the impact of NAC's role as coordinator of efforts and aggregator of diverse points of view is harder to assess. By no means have all of the recommendations made in the report of the Royal Commission on the Status of Women been implemented, for example. Canadian women achieved our 'ERA' in the new Charter of Rights and Freedoms, but at a high cost. The constitutional process of 1981–2 and 1989 to the present refuelled Québec's movement for separation. Regional alienation, which has caused so much conflict in our formal political institutions, has also had an impact on NAC: as a parliament of women, it was constantly being confronted by vastly expensive representational demands that could not be met within its financial base. Furthermore, the constant presence of constitutional debate and the explosion of anger from First Nations people throughout Canada displaced issues such as child care, which the movement had finally, after decades of work, brought to the top of the public and political agendas. None the less, NAC is now able to work with new coalition partners beyond the women's movement to enhance its established voice in the public-policy arena. Moreover, the crippling effects of the divisions over constitutional issues experienced in the early 1980s have been overcome and NAC has proved itself at least as able to deal with the conflict generated by Canada's diversity as any other political institution.

Can NAC's Role as a Parliament of Women Continue?

We have described NAC as an institution in which diverse points of view within feminism can interact, develop policy, and comprehend the basis of one another's differences. We have also argued that NAC's claim to represent women better than competing political structures are able to rests on the number of diverse groups it has managed to include. It is necessary, then, to assess the likelihood that NAC will be able to continue along this course of development. We shall consider four dimensions of this question.

The first dimension involves NAC's limited ability to maintain its links with francophone feminists in Québec. Susan Phillips (1990) has examined the links among thirty-three organizations she describes as making up Canada's 'national' women's movement. In her analysis,

Phillips includes the FFQ not because it has a pan-Canadian membership, but because federal government agencies call upon it to 'represent' Québec women at national conferences and consultations. Phillips
found that it displayed linkages with the movement network she un-
covered only through its links with NAC. Indeed, Phillips's research
clearly established that NAC was the coordinating centre of an integrated network. As we have shown, NAC's relationship with its
francophone members in Québec (focused primarily on the FFQ), after the 'honeymoon' of the founding era, has involved only intermit-
tent interaction that was frequently fraught with misunderstanding.
Our first task of evaluation, therefore, must be to understand the
difficulty NAC has experienced in maintaining stronger links with the
Québec francophone component.

As we demonstrated in Chapter 2, relationships between anglophone
and francophone liberal and traditional feminists made an effective
bridge in the 1960s and early 1970s. The mode of cooperation that
developed in the process of gaining the royal commission and creating NAC to implement its recommendations continued to be evident
in NAC's publications and lobbying efforts. As the process of grafting
on a grass roots developed in NAC, however, the paths of the English-
Canadian movement, as expressed in NAC, and of the Québec
francophone movement diverged. As Heather Jon Maroney (1988) has
shown, francophone feminism in Québec developed institutionally
separate 'wings,' with revolutionary left and radical feminists resisting
organizational involvement with liberal-feminist groups such as the
FFQ. The FFQ's 'umbrella,' therefore, never incorporated these elements, although the organization was somewhat revitalized in the mid-
1970s and began to accept feminist purposes broader than those intended by its founders. Moreover, the development of a progressive
form of nationalism in Québec shifted the focus of many younger
francophone feminists to collective rather than individual rights claims.
(Such as a shift had also occurred among some First Nations women.)
These collective claims set feminism in francophone Québec on a
trajectory that anglophone feminists within NAC would take some time
to understand.

Despite a growing disengagement of intellectual viewpoints, there
was considerable effort to sustain the NAC/FFQ bridge. After the turmoil of the Charter period and the FFQ's first withdrawal, NAC developed a new constitution that recognized French as an 'official' NAC
language, mandating simultaneous translation at AGMs and transla-

tion of all official documents. Under Doris Anderson's guidance, NAC also increased the capacity of its staff to provide some services in French, although the continued presence of the main NAC office in Toronto limited this process. Between 1984, when the FFQ re-entered NAC, and the end of the decade, when it withdrew again, serious efforts to make the participation of francophones in NAC meaningful and not just symbolic had limited success, as the organizational-review process showed.

It is ironic to be evaluating NAC's performance as a parliament of women in relation to its Québec francophone minority at the same time as Canada's official political institutions are rocked by the same representational crisis. Although both NAC and the FFQ received government funding in part to sustain the bridge they constituted, there was never enough money to permit real communication between anglophone and francophone feminists, except in the most formal settings of an AGM that offered simultaneous translation. NAC executive and committee meetings almost always proceeded in English because the cost of simultaneous translation was prohibitive. Given the huge sums of money available to official political structures to facilitate French–English dialogue, we should not be surprised at the fragility of the links established through the efforts of a few bilingual women, mainly from central Canada. The fact that Phillips found surviving links in an integrated network almost twenty years after the 'honeymoon' era suggests that the record is one of qualified success rather than total failure.

A second aspect of our evaluation of NAC's ability to act as a parliament of women has to do with its limited success in developing the regional representation that would be appropriate to a woman-centred project. With the addition in the 1980s of explicit regional representatives to its executive, NAC recognized that organizing women across space is almost as important as organizing them across time. Given the fact that federal political parties in Canada have difficulty maintaining representation in all the provinces and territories, NAC's problems in this regard should come as no surprise. One basic problem has been the quite different contexts within which provincial and territorial women's movements must operate. In some provinces, such as British Columbia, for example, ideological polarization makes the movement's political environment more like that in Britain than that in the Canadian federal arena. In some cases, it has been difficult to sustain a belief in reform through the state. The longer anti-feminist governments prevailed in some jurisdictions, the more difficult it was for women's groups to pursue a coordinated provincial/federal strategy. In any event, it is clear that NAC must be more effective in making common cause with provincial and territorial (umbrella) action groups, where they exist, rather than continuing to rely on its regional representatives alone.

This, in turn, points to the problem of NAC's continuing its perhaps undue emphasis on the federal state. In order to retain its centrality, even as a coordinating body, NAC will have to ponder the implications of Canada's becoming a still-more-decentralized federation. At the very least, it will have to come to terms with the wish of its member groups to pay more attention to provincial, territorial, and local decision makers. This is especially likely in provinces in which NDP majority governments have become the focus of attention for many activists who previously paid more attention to Ottawa.

A third dimension of our evaluation lies in how well NAC has integrated the waves of newly mobilized women, especially those of racial and ethnic minorities. Although Phillips shows that the pan-Canadian groups of these minority women were somewhat marginalized in the late 1980s, our analysis of events within NAC suggests the prospect of a more optimistic future. The movement of NAC into anti-racist coalitions and the election of minority women to the NAC executive in more than token numbers suggest there is the political space within NAC to draw such organizations into its parliamentary orbit. As we have seen, however, these new elements of previously marginalized women further test NAC's ability to restore and retain its fragile ties with Québec francophones. On the issues raised by both the Meech Lake and the Charlottetown accords, for example, most women from minority and immigrant groups and most women with disabilities opposed the weakening of federal powers and the decentralization that the accords would have meant. Only the fact that Québec francophones also opposed the Charlottetown Accord permitted cohesion in the referendum campaign.

In general terms, we should ask, therefore, whether NAC can continue to incorporate and represent so many diverse groups. The high financial cost of regional and linguistic representation has been only vaguely possible to bear with the aid of government funding. If NAC wishes to continue to represent such a widely diverse spectrum, it will ultimately face the question of whether the groups involved value its coordinating role enough either to pay for the representational costs, since it is increasingly clear that governments are becoming less willing to pay for them, or to lower their demands for direct involvement in all decision making. An additional cost of representing many diverse points of view is the pressure it places on NAC's policy process. As we have seen, NAC has faced great difficulties in setting priorities in the past and is increasingly inundated with important, but often short-term, issues from both member groups and government. NAC's continued status as an originator of feminist public-policy analysis, however, depends on its ability also to deal with long-term and general public-policy issues, such as free trade, however challenging that may be. Because the NAC policy process is frequently overloaded, it cries out for a more effective agenda-setting process to establish autonomous priorities.

Evaluation of NAC as a parliament of women must also consider its difficulty in providing a forum within which First Nations women could develop their political voice in a relationship with other Canadian women. Important though NAC's support for the restoration of Indian rights to non-status women has been, most aboriginal women's groups were connected to NAC only indirectly, as, for example, through the YWCA (Phillips 1990). Throughout the 1980s, in fact, many aboriginal women came to pursue a more militant, collective-rights approach, which rejected white feminism for a number of reasons, including its stand on individual rights and its failure to defend aboriginal collective rights during the Charter negotiations. In the summer of 1990, these views finally became more apparent to white women through NAC's explicit support of Mohawk demands for self-determination. There is little prospect, however, of NAC's being able to include most aboriginal women's groups in its arena. Ultimately, as with the francophone movement in Québec, NAC will have to recognize as equals movements of aboriginal women, and develop coalitions with either or both of these co-equal movements when such an approach would be productive. While the vision of a multination, multilanguage, women's movement should not be abandoned, it is probably not achievable in this generation.

A final dimension of our analysis of NAC is its position as the key target for the anti-feminist Right. Because NAC is, in fact, the coordinating nerve centre, at least of the English-Canadian women's movement, it is highly visible and highly vulnerable to attack. As we have seen, NAC's representational role is very costly and the organization depends heavily on government funding, as do many of its member groups. The federal Conservative government, pressured by its anti-feminist wing, refused to participate in the NAC lobby from 1988 to 1992 and significantly reduced funding to women's groups (especially those like NAC, that it saw as opposing government policy). Regardless of the electoral fate of the Progressive Conservatives or the Reform party, the anti-feminist movement is most likely here to stay. NAC's unsought role as the chief target in the anti-feminists' demonology has had both positive and negative effects on NAC itself. On the one hand, it created a solidarity and a renewed basis for mobilization. The anti-statism and homophobia of groups such as REAL Women, for example, caused groups that might otherwise have wavered to join in solidarity with the progressive majority (Beaudry 1990). On the other hand, this creation of solidarity by attack from the ultra-Right also has the potential of stifling debate within feminism on some issues. In terms of NAC's ability to create new modes of discourse suitable for future generations, therefore, this limitation of debate by making some issues 'out of bounds' is potentially damaging. This is especially the case in terms of the English-Canadian movement's need to debate the framework of collective rights versus individual rights. Unless frank debate can occur about such things as reproduction and immigration as they are seen by feminists pursuing collective-rights conceptions of equality, little progress can be made to establish real understanding between the movements represented by NAC and the national movements in Québec and the First Nations.

Is Radical-Liberalism Outmoded as a Cultural Basis for NAC Politics?

It is important in this conclusion to ask whether it is reasonable for English-Canadian women to continue to support a strategy of reform by the state or whether its radical liberalism has become outmoded in an era in which pro-statist policies are generally under attack? While most NAC activists are unwilling to question the norms of radical liberalism, some have begun to question the trustworthiness of the state in some circumstances, such as the censorship of pornography. Cultural feminists within NAC have argued that its continued focus on developing common positions to present to governments prevents the development of a truly feminist political process (Greaves 1988:3). The problem with this argument is its failure to provide an alternative to NAC's current approach that would not lead to the fragmentation and frustration of the localized British movement (Gelb 1989).

Pro-statism has been accompanied in NAC by a dependence on state funding and a top-down organizing strategy. As we have seen, state funding can distort priorities and disrupt movement development. We have suggested that two features of NAC's political environment will force some change of approach – namely, continued cuts in government funding and the desire of feminists in Québec and elsewhere to focus on provincial states and more local campaigns. This suggests that NAC will have to develop innovative methods of communication and representation if it is to continue to play a strong coordinating role. In the period studied, NAC made limited use of modern technologies of communication (electronic-mail systems, for example) and did not succeed in developing a way of using member groups as agents of NAC activity at the local level. Another serious problem has been the lack of a collective memory in NAC. Its now reduced office cannot easily retain a common memory of the approaches and actions that failed and those that succeeded in the past. But, if it is to remain effective into the next century, NAC must serve as the movement's memory or, at least, ensure that the memory of its own development is not lost.

NAC's umbrella structure has served it well by allowing groups of diverse size, orientation, and philosophy to interact. As we have seen, however, NAC's group-membership base is largely a fiction, in that the organization behaves as though individual activists were its members. This issue of agency and representation will undoubtedly continue to plague NAC as it seeks new sources of funding and a new role for its large pool of individual, non-voting 'members' in the Friends of NAC category. Despite 'official' feminist views, leadership at several levels has been crucial to NAC's success as a parliament of women. The grooming and recruitment of NAC leaders, however, cannot be left to chance. We have argued that the movement itself must become institutionalized, because its goals cannot be achieved by the efforts of only one generation of women. The same holds true within NAC, which must increasingly compete with other groups and with the official political system for women with leadership skills. To the extent that NAC retains something of a pro-statist stance and a political culture of radical liberalism, however, it will continue to be a useful alternative forum for aspiring women to gain training in a woman-centred political institution before taking on the still male-dominated structures of official politics. At both the provincial and federal levels, Canadian women can only gain by having women politicians who have experienced woman-centred politics within NAC and its provincial counterparts.

Will NAC Survive?

Finally, it is important to contextualize NAC's future in terms of Canadian politics generally. Clearly, NAC experiences most of the same stresses as do the institutions of the dominant political system in Canada. The difference is that NAC is composed of women who have far less money, less security, and less time for politics than do their male counterparts. Ironically, the very fact that most women know that the changes needed to eliminate the poverty, violence, and degradation that often mark their lives will not come quickly makes it likely that NAC, like its model, the National Council of Women of Canada, will survive for many more decades.

What is less clear is how long NAC will be able to perform its current, crucial role as coordinator of and parliament for the English-Canadian women's movement. Some aspects of the current trend towards decentralization in Canadian politics may help NAC retain the vigour required to perform this role. Sadly, the separation of Québec would remove one facet of NAC's current representational dilemma. The development of supranational bodies in North America, however, could open the way for effective cross-national ventures among women's movements, as has happened in the European Community. Still, the prospect of more years of constitutional conflict holds real danger for NAC. As we have illustrated, most women's groups were negatively affected by the constitutional crisis of the 1980s. If constitutional questions, including those that pertain to the rights of First Nations and the destiny of Québec, dominate the public and political agendas through the 1990s, NAC's ability to maintain its internal coalition will be challenged constantly. In the process, the agenda generated by women's politics can become marginalized as women are forced to concern themselves with constitutional issues. None the less, the model of a parliament of women that NAC provides for us will remain crucial as long as the values and demands represented by women's movements cannot be fully or quickly integrated into the official political system, in whatever way that system is ultimately reconstituted. One thing that will not mark the future as it did the 1980s is the denigration of women's politics by male politicians. Certainly, no future Canadian politician, male or female, will fail to understand that rape, wife beating, abortion, pornography, sexual orientation, and child care are intensely political issues. In that, NAC and its member groups have experienced a stunning success in persuading Canadians that women's politics have a place on the public agenda. Similarly, we will not be likely to find women's groups urging, as some did in 1981, that the politics of the state do not matter to women. By linking women at the grass roots of the movement to the official political system and providing a woman-centred arena for policy debate, NAC will become an increasingly important part of the political system. Indeed, as Canadians reassess their political institutions, structures such as NAC may increasingly be seen as important supplements – or even alternatives – to political parties.

Afterword

Since 1988, when we concluded our study of NAC, a number of changes have taken place that deserve some brief comment for our readers. (Our vantage point for this latest period, however, is that of more-distant observers.)[1] As we sensed it would, the 1988 AGM proved to be a turning point for NAC. In the wake of that meeting, all but one of NAC's eight staff members resigned. Government funding cuts hit NAC especially hard, and the reorganized offices could be staffed by only four women. (A hasty move to a smaller office put many of NAC's records in storage, which made research difficult.) Although the staff complement had crept back up to six in 1992, NAC became dependent for some financial support on other organizations, as it had been in its founding era. The Federation of Women Teachers and several unions provided donations in kind, especially to maintain NAC's publications. NAC's loss of 50 per cent of its government grant between 1990 and 1992, moreover, made its fund-raising efforts more important and, out of solidarity, more successful. The Friends of NAC category of non-voting, individual 'members' grew, largely as a funding device. NAC now raises significant amounts through direct-mail appeals. Indeed, the vision of a more independent NAC may be realized in the future.

NAC in the late 1980s and early 1990s has been significantly more radical than it was during the period we studied. Although this might give some credence to the view that less dependence on government funding would radicalize NAC, other forces were also at work. The second Mulroney government pursued a more determined anti-statist agenda than the first. It involved cuts in the funding of many movement organizations, especially those engaged in activities deemed to be political or anti-government. The grants to women's centres, for example, were cut, as were grants to NAC. (Some women's centres were forced to close.) Even more radicalizing, however, were events such as the Montreal massacre, in which a man murdered fourteen engineering students, all women, explicitly because they were identified as feminists, and the Chantal Daigle case, in which the senior Québec court upheld (although the Supreme Court later denied) the idea that a pregnant woman's ex-lover had the 'right' to force her to bear his child. The eruption in 1990 of anger and violence between the First Nations and white Canadians also had a radicalizing effect on NAC. No less effective in this regard, finally, was the need to mobilize women to prevent the reintroduction of another law that would once again have criminalized abortion.

Increasingly, NAC came to operate as part of an extraparliamentary opposition to a federal government whose behaviour reflected an even more hostile attitude to the traditions of the Canadian welfare state and, indeed, to the progressive strains within its own party. The government's withdrawal from the NAC lobby and the diminishing influence in NAC of elements supportive of quiet lobbying heightened the membership's receptiveness to a more radical stance. (There was a tentative return to the lobby by a few government members in 1992, apparently because of the government's desire to get NAC 'on side' on constitutional issues. Ironically, NAC's focus on the lobby has diminished and, in the future, the AGM may be held outside the Ottawa region in alternate years.)

NAC now sees itself much more as part of the women's movement. It has also abandoned its early multipartisan stance for a more extrapartisan position, as fewer of its activists than ever before are involved in political parties. Instead of being concerned about the partisan balance of its leadership, NAC is now far more attentive to successfully representing women's groups within a framework that values feminist politics as much as regional politics. The second withdrawal of the FFQ has put the issue of language on the back-burner. The issues of the day are now primarily issues of race, disability, and sexual orientation. Furthermore, many of the representational issues raised by the organizational reviews eventually met with effective responses. Hence, affirmative action is now employed with regard to membership in the executive, in that several positions are officially designated for francophone and racial-minority representation.

This revitalized, more-radical NAC is the result of a second period of conflict and struggle that began in 1988. One development from that period was the decision to permit the NAC president to serve a longer term and to make the presidency a paid position, opening it up for consideration by women lacking secure careers or family support. Having a full-time president also made possible the pursuit of an increasingly busy political agenda both within NAC and by NAC in male-dominated political structures. NAC's development of a 'three nations' constitutional position, for example, required significant educational work among NAC's member groups. Moreover, NAC's eleventh president, Judy Rebick, because of her full-time status, was able to play an active role in the constitutional debates without putting other issues of pressing concern to women 'on hold' in order to do so.

NAC remains an institution of greater saliency for women in central Canada than for those in the East, North, and West. Efforts to regionalize NAC committee work have begun. Indeed, it was British Columbian women such as Megan Ellis who spearheaded the process of responding to the concerns identified by the organizational reviews. Currently, there is even debate concerning changes to NAC's umbrella structure: the possibility of creating chapters of individual NAC members – the current Friends of NAC – is under discussion.

NAC remains a favourite target of the anti-feminist Right. It has also become established as a permanent part of the broader political system in English Canada. Indeed, a recent study of its treatment in the *Globe and Mail* (Stone 1992) suggests that its development of a feminist approach to public policy has had a major effect in this country's political culture in terms of what gatekeepers of the public-policy agenda see as political. The debate between feminism and anti-feminism has carved out a new political spectrum in which sexuality and reproduction, and our representations of them, are considered to be as significant as work and the ownership of property. NAC has played a central role in achieving this result and will continue in the future to help Canadian women conceptualize and practise politics 'as if women mattered.'

Notes

1 We are grateful to Anne Molgat and Nancy Adamson for sharing their observations about this most recent period with us.

Appendix A
Ideological Forces among Anglophone NAC Delegates, 1984 AGM

During the winter of 1984, Chris Appelle, with the help of two other Carleton University graduate students, developed a questionnaire under the supervision of Jill Vickers. The questionnaire was designed to collect data for three distinct research topics. It was administered to the participants of the NAC Annual General Meeting, who met at the Chateau Laurier Hotel in Ottawa in March 1984. Questions relating to aspects of feminist opinion were adapted from a research questionnaire used by Alice Rossi at the First National Women's Conference in Houston, Texas, in 1977. This study focused on women active in the women's movement and asked specific questions about their family and socio-economic characteristics, feminist beliefs, organizational affiliations, and strategy preferences. No comparable Canadian study existed in 1984. Second, the spectrum of organizations at the Houston conference represented a broader ideological range than that represented in NAC's U.S. counterpart, the National Organization of Women (NOW). The diversity of groups at Houston made Rossi's sample similar to that of the more diverse NAC. The Houston conference included traditional women's groups such as the YWCA and the League of Women Voters; feminist organizations such as NOW and the Women's Action Alliance; and organizations focused primarily on ethnic, racial, or religious memberships, such as the National Council of Catholic Women and the National Urban League. Rossi analysed responses from 1,300 American delegates at Houston and reported her findings in *Feminists in Politics* (1982).

The NAC delegates surveyed were a self-selected group. The questionnaire was distributed to all participants at the conference, but, because of budgetary constraints, it was available only in English. (The withdrawal of the FFQ from NAC in 1981 had reduced the participation in the AGM of francophones to less than twenty in 1984.) Not all of those who filled out the questionnaire were official NAC delegates, but only questionnaires completed by the latter were used in the analysis. Participants at the conference included NAC executive members and official delegates as well as Friends of NAC and observers. Delegate status in NAC is conferred only on official representatives of member groups and involves the entitlement to vote. This group of official delegates was the focus of Appelle's study. Three hundred and twenty-five women attended the NAC AGM in 1984. Of these, 158 completed and returned the questionnaire; that is, 48.6 per cent. One hundred and twenty-five of the questionnaires (33.3 per cent of the 325 total), completed by official NAC delegates, were used in this analysis. It should be noted that the responses are the views of this self-selected group of delegates. They do not necessarily represent the views of other members of the groups that the delegates represented. Our generalizations cannot be projected beyond this narrow base and have no known applicability in Québec.

1. *Tactical Preferences*

This section deals with the tactics that the 1984 NAC delegates preferred for achieving greater equality for women. The findings clarify the degree of support that existed for both conventional and unconventional approaches to change. The statistics draw attention to these differences as a potential source of tension within NAC, but they also highlight the ability of NAC member groups to coexist despite these differences. Table A.1 shows a high level of agreement in support of the conventional tactics (pressuring government leaders to appoint more women to public office; forming coalitions to elect more women; and lobbying legislatures on women's issues). Public boycotts also received high endorsement, with 90 per cent favouring this strategy. The less conventional sit-ins and civil disobedience were viewed more warily: in the 'not sure' column, for example, we find sit-ins (33 per cent), public demonstrations (24 per cent), and civil disobedience (23 per cent).

2. *Opinion Forces within NAC, as Measured by Factor Analysis*

Factor analysis was used to construct a picture of the various forces represented in the responses of this group of anglophone NAC delegates. The factors that emerged stand for clusters of related beliefs (not groups of people). Put another way, individual NAC delegates *could* choose to support issues on more than one factor, but they were *more likely* to be consistent in devoting time and attention to the issues that load on one particular factor.

TABLE A.1
Summary of delegate support for various tactics to achieve greater equality for women*

	Very poor tactic	Not sure	Very good tactic
Pressuring provincial/territorial leaders to appoint more women	2.8%	11.2%	83.2%
Forming coalitions to elect more women to public office	2.4	4.8	92.0
Lobbying legislatures on women's issues	2.4	5.6	92.0
Boycotting firms that discriminate against women	3.2	6.4	89.6
Sit-ins to dramatize a bad situation affecting women	17.6	32.8	48.8
Public demonstrations/marches on women's issues	3.2	24.0	72.0
Civil disobedience when other tactics fail	25.6	23.2	49.6

*Columns may not total 100 per cent, because of rounding.

The fact that four factors emerged means that the priority assigned to each one was quite variable within the delegate body. Clearly, there are differences in the way people think and feel about issues that load on each factor. These four elements account for the 32.1 per cent variance of views within NAC.

Strong Feminist Force

Factor 1 (accounting for 10.2 per cent of the variance), the largest factor, represents a *strong feminist force* (see Table A.2). The origins of the commitments reflected here are radical feminist, although, as one past executive member of NAC stated, 'Today, in the mid-eighties, much of what was previously considered a "radical" platform is often supported by Business and Professional Women's clubs as well as radical-feminist groups within NAC' (R. Billings, personal interview with C. Appelle, 26 November 1985). All the items

TABLE A.2
Factor 1: Strong feminist force

	Factor 1	Factor 2	Factor 3	Factor 4
(strong) Position on sex equality	**.67736**	.06274	-.10525	-.02281
(approve) Civil disobedience	**.62970**	.03798	.27902	.02750
(disagree) Would not place child at child-care centre	**.62644**	.09694	-.09085	.03893
(disagree) Lesbian rights harms movement	**.55306**	.05247	.04381	-.13156
(approve) Sit-ins	**.55025**	-.01975	.19571	.12537
(disagree) Pre-school child likely to suffer if Mom works	**.51600**	-.08745	.01691	.09367
(agree) People cannot be feminist if they do not work for lesbian rights	**.51496**	.03319	.10954	-.24162
(high) Educational level	**.48845**	-.07722	.09032	.18389
(disagree) Prefer relative over child-care centre	**.47558**	.17004	-.00860	.03125
(agree) Demonstrations/marches	**.44034**	.00791	.08887	.11705
(disagree) More important to help husband than have a career	**.43900**	.06598	-.08382	-.11947
(agree) Pre-school child would benefit from child-care centre	**.43792**	-.04838	.07996	.17304
(agree) People cannot be feminist if oppose abortion	**.42734**	-.16474	-.08287	-.04111
(agree) People cannot be feminist if oppose Section 28	**.35443**	-.05957	-.09535	-.01857

that load on this factor represent role-transformation issues rather than role-equity or equal-opportunity issues. This primary concern for a change in role for both sexes is reflected in two strong challenges to the 'traditional' way of life: child care and 'careers for women ahead of support for husbands.' Associated with this factor is strong support for lesbian rights, the pro-choice stand on abortion, and the equality clause of the constitution. Consistent with a radical-feminist stance, little trust is placed in any political system to bring about change; therefore, a bias is displayed for the less conventional techniques, such as sit-ins, demonstrations, marches, and civil disobedience. Commitment to these issues and strategies is stronger than commitment to any one organization, since no single type of women's organization is included in this factor. These values likely express less support for narrowly defined groups, political or otherwise, and more for 'organic' organizations, such as collectives, self-help health groups, and support groups, which by

TABLE A.3
Factor 2: Traditional force

	Factor 1	Factor 2	Factor 3	Factor 4
Religious organizations	-.04213	**.88206**	.00237	.04616
Service organizations	-.12229	**.86034**	-.09876	-.01790
Educational organizations	-.00526	**.80097**	.01774	-.03662
Political organizations	.02148	**.78883**	-.09594	.20180
Job-related organizations	.12453	**.78214**	.09982	.22597
(lower) educational level of spouse	.19794	**-.31964**	-.16460	.15999

definition do not favour the internal structuring and hierarchical management that is typically associated with traditional organizations.

Traditional Force

Factor 2 (accounting for 9 per cent of the variance) profiles a commitment to traditional organizations (see Table A.3). In contrast to Factor 1, loyalties to particular organizations override a strong commitment to feminism or any single issue. It is important to note that a service commitment is underlined in this factor. This service component has been a consistent and stable part of NAC since its founding era. Religious and service organizations top the list, including groups such as the YWCA, the Anglican church, and the United church. Groups may also include newer services such as transition houses and rape-crisis centres. It is important to note, however, that the emphasis is on servicing a broad spectrum of the public. The quality of the service is seen as a priority above any single ideological concern. Commitment to educational, political, and job-related organizations ranks below commitment to religious and service organizations. That job-related organizations also loaded on the factor suggests a high level of participation in the paid workforce. This force is important because it represents women who are strongly committed to the issues but who do not necessarily identify with the feminist label.

Economic Force

Factor 3 (accounting for 7.2 per cent of the variance). Items on Factor 3 emphasize the economic aspects of women's oppression (see Table A.4). Economic concerns are linked with women's role in the family, and items in

TABLE A.4
Factor 3: Economic force

	Factor 1	Factor 2	Factor 3	Factor 4
(agree) Women should be considered for important jobs, even as PM	-.02726	-.00821	**.89689**	-.06634
(agree) Men should share housework	.07272	-.21948	**.78512**	-.08083
(agree) Women should have same job opportunities as men	-.01787	.01524	**.74881**	-.00956
(agree) Woman's job should be kept when she has a baby	.12242	.00339	**.70387**	-.01366
(agree) Working Mom can have just as secure a relationship with child as non-employed Mom	.14536	.06914	**.61965**	.06459
(agree) Men and women should be paid same wages for same work	-.02038	.01645	**.56066**	.04135

this factor relate to analysis of the sexual division of labour both at home and in the workplace. Although these concerns are in line with the Marxist view of liberation (a view that focuses on the relation of a class of people to the economic structure that defines them), concern is also expressed for equality of opportunity in the workplace and equal pay for work of equal value. Values around shared housework, issues of job security and maternity, and belief that 'a working Mom can have just as secure a relationship with a child as a non-employed Mom,' are items that load heavily on this factor. Similar to Factor 2, commitment to these issues is not linked to a strong feminist ideology.

Liberal/Reform Force

Factor 4 (accounting for 5.7 per cent of the variance) is labelled liberal/ reform (see Table A.5). Although similar to Factor 2, this force goes far beyond the expression of a service commitment. It reveals a commitment to influencing the current political system in definite ways, including lobbying legislatures, forming coalitions to elect more women to public office, and pressuring provincial and territorial leaders to appoint more women. These sentiments, which stress utilizing the political system to women's advantage, represent a reform or progressive force as opposed to a revolutionary one. The delegates who conform to this profile trust in the political system to bring about change and show a desire to partake in the existing power structure. Demographic variables of high family income and larger families,

TABLE A.5

Factor 4: Liberal/reform force

	Factor 1	Factor 2	Factor 3	Factor 4
(approve) Lobby legislature	-.03359	.00292	.04900	**.59361**
(approve) Form coalitions to elect more women to public office	-.16128	.00789	.17936	**.54756**
Older age group	.05981	.20885	-.18743	**.53432**
High family income	-.05594	.09977	-.10446	**.52153**
(approve) Pressure on provincial/territorial leaders to appoint more women	-.02073	.04803	.05370	**.51907**
Feminist organizations	.28648	-.10392	.02085	**.48450**
Social and cultural organizations	-.06123	-.03258	.00139	**.45838**
Civil-rights organizations	.33874	-.03758	-.10288	**.39495**
Civic organizations	.03480	.02856	.02334	**.34002**
(larger) Number of children	.08972	.20540	-.10673	**.31194**
(disagree) 'Men-only' club is discriminatory	.08826	.18327	-.09725	**-.30572**

as well as memberships in social/cultural organizations, reflect benefits already accrued from the system. Women who have already experienced a certain amount of status and power in society are likely to want more influence, and they are usually in a stronger position to vie for it. Women expressing these values are therefore more likely to favour political candidacies. Similarly, this force represents a strong commitment to feminist organizations, which are viewed as an effective means of promoting change. The profile is broadened further by active participation in civil-rights and civic organizations. These affiliations affirm the rights of the individual, a cornerstone of liberal-democratic theory. This commitment to individual liberty underlies support for men to retain 'men-only' clubs; it is also evident in the support for individual as opposed to collective rights. This factor is evident in the ongoing debate about pensions for housewives and who should fund them.

This factor analysis illustrates NAC's complex nature by showing that, in so far as this self-selected group of delegates can be considered representative, the organization embraced a full range of feminist ideologies in 1984. While the potential for disagreement is obvious, an important feature of the organization was the relatively balanced representation of each force (10.2%, 9%, 7.2%, and 5.7%, respectively). This balance also suggests that, in the context of this 1984 group of delegates, no single set of beliefs was sufficiently dominant to place at risk the internal balance of the organization. Rather, it tends to suggest a potential for each force to 'enrich' the whole, while at the same time underscoring the importance of *maintaining* the relative balance of the various ideological strains – a balancing act performed primarily by the executive. Significantly, no other women's movement outside Canada has achieved a comparable structure – one that effectively embraces such divergent interests and ideologies.

Appendix B
Groups Affiliated with NAC by Type, *circa* 1987–1988[1]

Action Committees

Alberta Status of Women Action Committee (ASWAC)*
Au Féminin: Sport and Fitness
Bay St George Status of Women Council
Calgary Status of Women Action Committee
Canadian Federation of University Women, Status of Women Committee
Central Newfoundland Status of Women Council
Corner Brook Status of Women Council
Gander Status of Women Council
Gateway Status of Women Council
Hamilton Status of Women Sub-Committee
Labrador West Status of Women Council*
Manitoba Action Committee on the Status of Women*
Mokami Status of Women Council
Mothers United for Metro Shelter (MUMS)
Northern Women's Action Group
Northwest (Saskatchewan) Status of Women
Northwestern Ontario Women's Decade Council
Notre Dame de Grace Women's Action
Ontario Committee on the Status of Women*
Outreach, A Women's Action Group
Perth County Status of Women Action Committee
Peterborough Women's Action Committee

* umbrella group
[1] *Source:* NAC membership brochures, 1972–88

Red Deer Status of Women
Riverdale Women's Action Committee
Saskatchewan Action Committee on the Status of Women*
St John's Status of Women Council
Sudbury Women's Action Group
Tamitik Status of Women
Vancouver Society on Immigrant Women
Vancouver Status of Women
Victoria Status of Women Action Group
Women's Action Coalition of Nova Scotia*
Women's Action Council of Peel
Women of Halton Action Movement
Yukon Status of Women's Council*

Advocacy Groups

Abortion by Choice (Alta)
Action Day Care (Ont.)
Action femmes handicappes (DAWN), Montreal
Alternatives for Single Parent Women
Association for Women's Equity in the Canadian Forces (AWECF)
Calgary Birth Control Association
Canadian Abortion Rights Action League (CARAL) – Fraser Valley Chapter
Canadian Association for the Advancement of Women in Sport
Canadian Association of Elizabeth Fry Societies
Canadian Day Care Advocacy Association
Canadian Organization for the Rights of Prostitutes
CARAL – Canadian Abortion Rights Action League
CARAL – Halifax
CARAL – London
CARAL – Ottawa
CARAL – PEI
Choice in Childcare Committee
Clef en Main
Committee against Pornography
Committee for '94
Concerned Citizens for Choice on Abortion (CCCA)
Concerned Women
Conseil d'intervention pour l'aces des femmes au travail
Co-operative Housing Federation of Toronto

DAWN, Toronto
DES Action Canada
Disabled Women's Network (DAWN) (BC)
Disabled Women's Network, Ontario
Disabled Women's Support Group
Equal Rights for Native Women
FAKE Women (Feminists for All Kinds of Equality)
Feminist Grandmothers of Canada (BC)
Femmes autochtones du Québec
Franco-Femmes
INFACT Canada (Infant Feeding Action Coalition)
La féderation des associations de familles monoparentales du Québec
Ligue des femmes du Québec
Ligue ouvrière révolutionnaire
Media Watch: National Watch Images of Women
Metro Action Committee on Public Violence against Women and Children
Midwifery Association of British Columbia
Midwifery Taskforce (Ont.)
National Household Careers
Ontario Coalition for Abortion Clinics
Organizational Society for Spouses of Military Members (OSSMM)
PEI Coalition against Pornography
Planned Parenthood, Alberta
Planned Parenthood Federation of Canada
Planned Parenthood, Ontario
Planned Parenthood (Nfld/Labrador)
Planned Parenthood, Ville Marie
Politics of Custody Coalition
POR No Women
Project Mom
Provincial Association on Family Violence
Québec Taskforce for Immigrant Women
Society against Family Abuse (NWT)
Supportive Action for Women
Toronto Women's Housing Cooperative
West End/Women Entering Marching
Women Initiating Responsible Change
Women of the North
Women Plan Toronto
Women Working With Immigrant Women

Business

Canadian Association of Women Executives and Entrepreneurs
Canadian Federation of Business and Professional Women's Clubs (CFBPWC)
BC Chapter CFBPWC
Ontario Chapter CFBPWC
  Local chapters:
  Hamilton
  Lakeshore, Ont.
  North Toronto
  Ontario
  Ottawa
  Sault Ste Marie
  Stratford, Ont.
  Toronto
  Toronto East
  Toronto West
  Yellowknife
  Montreal

Women's Networks

Association des femmes collaboratrices
Congress of Canadian Women – Grand Prairie, Alta.
Cornwall Women's Network
Councils of Women – South Peace Regional Council
Montreal Women's Network
Ottawa Women's Network
Prince Edward Island Women's Network Inc.
Renfrew County Women's Initiative Network
Windsor Women's Incentive Centre

Cultural

Canadian Women's Music and Cultural Festival
Fireweed
Hecate Players
Herizons
Hysteria

La vie en rose
Local Celebration of Women in the Arts
Newsmagazine for Alberta Women
Positive Images: Women by Women
Reel Women's Cable Collective
RFR (Resources for Feminist Research)
Women's Press
WOMONspace

Education

Action education des femmes
Affirmative Action Advisory Committee, George Brown College
Algonquin College – The Women's Program
Ban Righ Foundation for Continuing University Education,
    Queen's University
CCLOW (Canadian Congress for Learning Opportunities for Women) – NB
CCLOW – East Shore, NS
CCLOW – Québec
Canadian Association for Adult Education
Canadian Association of University Teachers (CAUT)
Canadian Congress for Learning Opportunities for Women
Canadian Federation of Students
Canadian Federation of Students (CFS) – Pacific Region
Canadian Psychological Association Section on Women and Psychology
Canadian Teachers' Federation
Canadian Women's Studies (York University)
Centre d'éducation et d'action des femmes de Montréal
Concordia Women's Collective
Interfaculty Committee on Women's Studies, Carleton University
Langara Student Society
Ontario Confederation of University Faculty Associations (OCUFA)
Ontario Federation of Students
Rexdale Community Microskills Development Centre
Ryerson Women's Centre Student Union
SAC Women's Commission, University of Toronto
Simone de Beauvoir Institute (Concordia)
UBC (University of British Columbia) Women's Committee
UNB (University of New Brunswick) Student Women's Committee

Western's Caucus on Women's Issues
Wilfrid Laurier Faculty of Social Work
Women Educators in Support of Public Education
Women's Centre, University of Toronto
Women's Counselling, Referral and Education Center
Women's Issues Commission, University of Western Ontario
Women's Program and Resource Center, Faculty of Extension
Women's Resource Centre for Continuing Education – British Columbia
Women's Resource Centre of Memorial University
Women's Studies Student Association, Simone de Beauvoir Institute
York University, Graduate Political Science Women's Caucus
York University, Women's Centre

Ethnic / Race

Arab Canadian Women's Network
Association of United Ukrainian Canadians
Chinese Canadian National Council, Women's Issues Committee
Comités des femmes Afro-Asiatiques du Québec
Congress of Black Women of Canada
Congress of Black Women – Montreal Committee
Costi Ilas Immigrant Services
FRAPPE – Moncton
Immigrant Women of Saskatchewan
India–Canada Association of Montreal
Labrador Native Women's Association
Multicultural Women's Association for Newfoundland and Labrador
NACOI (National Association of Canadians of Origins in India) – Montreal
NACOI (National Association of Canadians of Origins in India) – South
  Shore
National Federation of Pakistani Canadians
Pioneer Women Na'amat
Second Wreath
South Asia Community Centre
Women's Committee of NACOI

Foundations

Avoca Foundation

Health

Barbara Sclifer Commemorative Clinic
Birth Control and VD Information Centre – Ontario
Dalhousie Women Health and Medicine (WHAM)
International Institute for Public Health
Maternal Health Society – Ontario
Midwives' Collective of Toronto
South Riverdale Community Health Centre
Toronto Women's Chiropractic Council
Toronto Women's Health Network
Women Healthsharing
Women's Health Clinic (Man.)
Women's Health Education Information Network (WHEN) – Nova Scotia

Labour

FEDERATIONS
BC Federation of Labour
Confederation of Canadian Unions

CAUCUSES OF ORGANIZATIONS
Alberta Federation of Labour (Women's Section)
Canadian Auto Workers – Women's Department
Canadian Union of Educational Workers, Local 3, Women's Caucus
Labour Council of Metro Toronto, Women's Committee
Ontario Federation of Labour, Women's Committee

NATIONAL
Canadian Labour Congress (CLC) – Women's Bureau
Canadian Textile and Chemical Union
Canadian Union of Public Employees (CUPE)
Economists, Sociologists and Statisticians Association (ESSA)
National Union of Provincial Government Employees – Women's Committee

UNION LOCALS
Alberta Union of Public Employees
BC Government Employees' Unions
CUPW – Edmonton

Letter Carriers' Union of Canada (LCUC), Local 15 Women's Committee
Newfoundland Association of Public Employees
Ontario Public Service Employees' Union
OPSEU, Region 5, Women's Caucus
United Steelworkers of America, District 6
University and College Staff Union

QUÉBEC
Action travail des femmes du Québec Inc.
Comité et reseau de la condition des femmes (CEQ)
Comité National de la condition féminine de la CSN
Fédération Nationale des enseignants et enseignantes/Québec femmes CSN
Groupe d'aide et d'information harcelement sexuel au travail

INTER-UNION ASSOCIATIONS
Edmonton Working Women
Equal Pay Coalition
International Women's Day Committee – Durham
International Women's Day Committee – Toronto
Industrial Training Center for Women of Sudbury, Inc.
Vancouver Women in Trades Association
Victoria Women in Trades
Women Skills

Law

Association of Women and the Law, Ottawa Community Caucus
Calgary Association of Women and the Law
Civil Remedies and Rights Committee
Dalhousie Association of Women and the Law
Manitoba Association of Women and the Law
Nova Scotia Association of Women and the Law
National Association of Women and the Law, Osgoode Caucus
– Ottawa Caucus
– Queen's Caucus
– Toronto Area Caucus
– Windsor Caucus
– PEI Caucus
National Association of Women and the Law
Vancouver Association of Women and the Law
Women's Legal Education and Action Fund (LEAF)

Partisan / Political

Alberta NDP Women's Section
BC NDP Women's Right Committee
BC Women's Liberal Commission
Communist Party of Canada – Women's Commission
Feminist Party of Canada
Liberal Party of Canada – Women's Commission
NDP Nova Scotia Women's Rights Committee
NDP Ontario Women's Committee
NDP Participation of Women Committee
NDP Research
NDP Women's Committee, Algoma
NDP Women's Committee, Yukon
PC Association of Women of Ontario
PC Women's Caucus of Peel-Halton (Federal)
PC Women's Caucus of Metro Toronto
PC Women's Caucus of Ottawa
PC National Federation of Women
Women for Political Action

Peace

Nurses for Social Responsibility
Toronto Disarmament Network
Voice of Women
Voice of Women – Edmonton
Voice of Women – Québec
Women's International League for Peace and Freedom (WILPF)
World Federalists of Canada

Professional

ACTRA (Alliance of Cinema, Television and Radio Artists)
Association of Family Life Educators of Québec
BC Teachers' Federation
Canadian Association for Women in Science (CAWS)
Canadian Home Economics Association
Comité de condition féminine, Féd. Qué. des Infirmièr(e)s
Fed. SYN. Prof. D'Infirmières et D'Infirmiers du Qué. (FSPIIQ)
Federation of Women Teachers' Associations (FWTA) of Ontario

Federation of Medical Women of Calgary
Hamilton Women Teachers' Association (WTA)
L'Association des femmes de Radio-Canada-Moncton
Lincoln WTA
Newfoundland Teachers' Association, Women's Issues Council
Norfolk WTA
North York WTA
Northumberland and Newcastle WTA
Northwest Media Network Guild
Nova Scotia Association of Social Workers, Women's Issues Group
NS Confederation of University Faculty Associations, Status of Women
   Committee
Ontario Nurses' Association, Local 88
Organization for Women in Leadership, Board of Education – Ontario
Peel WTA
Professional Women's Association, University of Waterloo
Registered Nurses' Association of Ontario
Saskatchewan Teachers' Federation
Sudbury WTA
Toronto WTA
Toronto Women in Film and Video
University of Toronto Staff Association
Wentworth WTA
Women Active in Sport Administration – Ontario
Women in Planning
York Region WTA

Religion

Anglican Church of Canada
Toronto Hadassah – Wizo
Unitarian Universalist Women's Federation
United Church of Canada – Adult Ministry – Women
United Church of Canada – Women's Concerns Committee
United Jewish People's Order, Toronto Women's Committee
Women's Group, First Unitarian Congregation of Toronto

Research

Canadian Research Institute for the Advancement of Women (CRIAW)
Canadian Women's Movement Archives

CRIAW – NS
Housewives/Houseworkers in Training and Research
Institute for the Study of Women (Mount St Vincent University)
Pacific Women's Research Institute
WEB – Women's Information Exchange
Women's Research Centre
Women's Economic Agenda

Services

NATIONAL
Federation of Junior Leagues of Canada

NETWORKS OF SERVICES
Almonte Community Services Co-ordinators
BC/Yukon Association of Women's Centers
Cape Breton Transition House Association
CNP Women's Resource and Crisis Centre – Alberta
Halifax Transition House Association
L'R des centres des femmes du Québec
New Brunswick Women's Network
Newfoundland Organization of Women
Ontario Association of Interval and Transition Houses
Ontario Coalition of Rape Crisis Centres
Regroupment des gardières du Québec
Society of Transition Houses BC/Yukon

LOCAL
Battered Women's Support Services
Calgary Sexual Assault Center
Calgary Women's Emergency Shelter
Educate Wife Assault
Elizabeth Fry Society – Ottawa
Elizabeth Fry Society – Toronto
Emily Stowe Shelter for Women
Ernestine's Women's Shelter
Family Crisis Shelter
Fredericton Rape Crisis Centre
Gatineau Valley House/Maison de la Vallée de la Gatineau
Guelph Wellington Women in Crisis
Habitat Interlude

Haven House (Manitoulin Family Resource Centre)
Interval House
Interval House, Ottawa–Carleton
Kenora Family Resource Centre
Kirby House
La Maison Le Prelude Inc.
Lanark County Interval House
Leeds and Grenville Interval House
Libra House
London Battered Women's Advocacy Clinic, Inc.
Maison Halte Secours Inc.
Mouvement contre le Viol, Collectif, Femmes de Montréal
Nipissing Transition House
Northern Lights Resource Center Association
North Shore Crisis Services Society (Emily Murphy House)
Ottawa Rape Crisis Centre
Prince Edward Island Rape and Sexual Assault Crisis Center
Project Mayday
Rape Crisis Centre, Hamilton
Rape Relief and Women's Shelter
Sexual Assault Center – Edmonton
Sexual Assault Center – London
Sexual Assault Crisis Centre – Kingston
Sexual Assault Support Centre
Sistering: A Drop-In Centre for Homeless Women
Shuswap Area Family Emergency Society (SAFE)
South Okanagan Women in Need
Sudbury Sexual Assault Crisis Centre
Supportive Action for Women
Tearman Society for Battered Women
Times Change Women's Employment Service
Timmins Sexual Assault Centre
Thompson Crisis Centre
Thunder Bay Physical and Sexual Assault Crisis Centre
Toronto Birth Centre Inc.
Toronto Rape Crisis Centre
Town Daycare Centre
Transition House
WAVAW Rape Crisis Centre
WINS Transition House (Women in Need Society)

Women in Crisis Northumberlands County
Women's Career Counselling
Yellow Brick House Project H.O.S.T.E.L.

Umbrella Groups

Congress of Canadian Women, Grand Prairie, Alta.
Fédération des femmes du Québec

Women's Centres

Au bas de l'échelle – Rank and File
Beeches Women's Group
Bow River Women's Resource Center
Campbell River Area Women's Resource Society
Carrefour des femmes du Grand Lachute
Chatham Kent Women's Centre
Chetwynd Women's Resource Society
Contact Women's Group
Cranbrook Women's Resource Society
Fernie Women's Resource and Drop-in Center
Ft Nelson Women's Center
Ft St John Women's Resource Center
Golden Women's Resource Center
Halton Women's Place
Hay River Women's Centre
Howe Sound Women's Centre
Immigrant Women's Centre
Immigrant Women's Information Centre, Windsor
Kabayan Community Centre, Women's Collective
Kamloops Women's Resource Centre
Kelowna Women's Resource Centre
L'Escale, Centre des resources pour femmes
Langara Women's Centre
Lennoxville and District Women's Center
Lunenberg County Women's Group
New Experience for Refugee Women
North Bay Women's Centre
North Shore Women's Centre
Northern Options for Women Co-op Inc.

Northwestern Ontario Women's Centre
Penticton and Area Women's Centre Society
Pictou County Women's Centre
Port Alberni Women's Resources
Port Coquitlan Area Women's Centre
Prince George Women's Centre
Quesnel Women's Resource Centre
Richmond Women's Resource Centre
Rigolet Women's Group
Saskatchewan Women's Agricultural Network
Saskatchewan Women's Resources
Second Storey Women's Centre
South Surrey/White Rock Women's Place
St John's Women for Action Group
Terrance Women's Resource Centre Society
Tobique Women's Group
Victoria Faulker Women's Center
West Island Women's Center
Womanpower
Women for Women Sault Ste Marie
Women Like Me
Women Today
Women Zone
Women's Community House Semja Inc.
Women's Habitat
Women's Participation Group
Women's Place, Kenora
Women's Place/Place aux femmes
Women's Time Out
Working for Women (Sask.)

WOMEN'S ASSOCIATIONS
Antigonish Women's Association
Armstrong Women's Associations
Wellspring Women's Association of White Court
West Kootenay Women's Association

WOMEN'S COALITIONS
Okanagan Women's Coalition

WOMEN'S CLUBS
University Women's Club, North Vancouver
- Burlington
- Oakville
- Ottawa - Status of Women Committee
- North Toronto
- North York
- St Catharines
- Vancouver
Zonta Club, Halifax
- Burlington
- Hamilton II - Status of Women Committee
- Guelph Area
- Mississauga
- Montreal
West Bay Homemakers Club (Ankishnabequek)
Soroptimist Club of Regina
YWCA/YMCA
YWCA of Canada
YWCA Calgary
- Kitchener-Waterloo
- Metropolitan Toronto
- Montreal
- Peterborough
- Prince Albert
- Regina
- Saskatoon
- St Catharines
- St Thomas
- Sudbury
- Vancouver
- Yellowknife

Classification Unclear

Options for Women
Resau (Manitoba)
Vancouver Women in Focus Society
Women's Canadian ORT

Glossary

The purpose of this glossary is to define some of the basic terms and concepts relevant to this study of feminist politics in English Canada. It is important for the reader to recognize that the meanings given are specific to the context of the English-Canadian movement, and may not apply elsewhere.

Chapter-based organization
In densely populated countries, organizations often consist of multiple chapters, all sharing a similar purpose and structure, linked together in a hierarchical fashion to form larger state or provincial and national organizations. The result is a single organization with local chapters, all bearing the same name and affiliating individual chapter members to the organization directly. Most women's organizations in the United States are chapter based. Relatively few women's organizations in Canada employ this organizational form.

Christian socialism
In Canada, left-wing organizations have been influenced as often by forms of socialism inspired by Christianity as by Marxism. Among the founders and early leaders of the Co-operative Commonwealth Federation (CCF), the predecessor of the New Democratic party (NDP), were ministers and other men and women influenced by the radical social-gospel movement that had emerged out of Protestantism. This religious background lent a respectability to the leftist tradition in English-Canadian politics that was not granted the Left in the United States or Catholic Québec before the 1960s.

Collective rights
Although most feminist equality claims are based on the liberal concept of the rights of the individual, English-Canadian feminism has been challenged by women making equality claims based on concepts of collective rights.

Francophone feminists in Québec who support Québec nationalism and aboriginal women who advocate sovereignty for the First Nations argue that women's individual rights and their nations' collective rights cannot be separated. Some First Nations women have also argued that collective rights must supersede individual rights, although this is a matter of continuing debate among aboriginal women and between aboriginal women and men. Still other aboriginal women reject the concept of individual rights.

Conservative feminism
Although in other contexts this term might be considered an oxymoron, it identifies a distinct and coherent theoretical and political tradition in English Canada that finds its roots in the history of English-Canadian conservatism. The Progressive Conservative (PC) party, has historically been relatively supportive of state action, both to protect human and civil rights and to intervene in economic markets. The 'red Tory' strain within the party has included many self-proclaimed feminists, among both women and men. Former prime minister Joe Clark and former cabinet minister Flora MacDonald are two such examples. More recently, a new strain of feminism has emerged within the PC party. Its representatives, such as cabinet ministers Kim Campbell and Barbara McDougall, are less open to state intervention in the economy than were their 'red Tory' predecessors, but none the less support the use of state power to secure legal rights for women. Only recently has anti-statism been represented in a significant way within the federal PC party, although it has been evident for some time in certain of its provincial wings, especially in the Western provinces.

Cultural feminism
See Radical feminism

Élite accommodation
Canadian politics has been dominated by competition and cooperation among élites drawn disproportionately from higher socio-economic back-grounds. These élites share a similar socialization and therefore often hold common assumptions about how their interests can be best protected. Such élite accommodation characterizes not only politics, but also business and financial sectors. It frequently results in the movement of personalities back and forth between politics, the bureaucracy, and big business.

Equality-seeking movements
We have identified three distinct types of social movements in English Canada: equality-seeking movements, quality-of-life movements, and reactive

movements (the latter having developed in opposition to the first two). The women's movement is an equality-seeking movement that operates parallel to (and often overlaps with) other movements of equality seekers, including the gay- and lesbian-rights movement, the disability-rights movement, and anti-racism movements. It also operates parallel to, and may share personnel and resources with, the quality-of-life movements, which are dedicated to achieving such goals as peace, environmental protection, and secure communities. The reactive movements tend to be organized around the 'pro-life' movement, in opposition to abortion, although the 'pro-family' movement has brought together elements that oppose both the equality and the quality-of-life goals of the progressive movements.

Executive federalism
An approach to governing characterized by decision making that occurs outside the parliamentary system and instead relies on First Ministers' Conferences and consultations among high-level bureaucrats. This form of intergovernmental relations is undemocratic in that it bypasses legislatures and limits the number of participants involved in crucial decisions, in addition to curtailing debate. Women have been refused representation in such forums.

Free-enterprise feminism
See Conservative feminism

Gender-gap politics
Studies of women's political behaviour in terms of voting and support for specific policies reveal that women often vary significantly in their approach to politics. This phenomenon was first described in relation to the lesser support for Ronald Reagan by women than men. Evidence of a gender gap in political behaviour has been used to argue that women do have a distinct political culture.

Grass-roots feminism
In the context of this study, *grass-roots feminism* is defined in contrast to *institutionalized feminism*. The term has ideological resonance within the English-Canadian movement because it suggests the equivalent of radical feminism in the United States – that is, feminism untainted by involvement in male-dominated institutions. In this conception, 'grass-roots feminism is more community-based, emphasizing collective organizing, consciousness-raising, and reaching out to women on the street,' while 'institutionalized feminism operates within traditional institutions – inside political parties and

government ministries, for example' (Adamson et al. 1988:12). This dichotomy can be misleading, however, since many local, community-based forms of feminism work through institutions such as church groups, the YWCA, or the Women's Institutes. And, as this study makes clear, the women's movement has itself created many national institutions.

Identity feminisms
Identity feminisms emerged in the late 1970s and 1980s as part of the third wave of feminist activism, in opposition to the ideas of the majority of women in the movement during the late 1960s and early 1970s who defined themselves largely in opposition to male political ideas and practices.

The first 'identity' to emerge was lesbian feminism, which developed within radical feminism as women explored the nature of sexualities and the oppression, domination, and power built upon them. Today, not all lesbians would define themselves as feminists, and those who do may also hold other political identities within feminism, such as socialist-feminism. Other important feminist identities that have emerged are those of African-American and Latino women in the United States, black women and other women of colour in Canada, and women with disabilities. In each case, the identity is organized around minority women's differences from the women in the majority in the movement.

Integrative feminism
Angela Miles (1982) used this term to define a form of feminism that developed in the English-Canadian movement when women committed to different ideological positions within feminism developed a set of ideas based on their shared political practice of cooperation. Miles argues that their shared view of feminism as a 'potentially complete politics' 'unites them more closely with each other ... than with other feminists of like self-definition' (Miles 1982:12). The pursuit of a woman-centred politics creates an acceptance of ideological diversity and debate that is less common among feminists whose political practice is developed within the realm of male-centred politics.

Left feminism
We use this term to identify variants of feminism in the English-Canadian movement that share an emphasis on the material causes of women's oppression, including union feminism, working-class feminism, Marxist feminist, and socialist-feminism. Although these variants differ on certain points of theory and their adherents may be in conflict in some contexts,

they have tended to share a political analysis within feminism and similar choices in the strategies they adopt towards other movements and the state.

Liberal feminism

Liberal feminism is the ideological strain of feminism against which much contemporary feminism defines itself. Liberal feminism shares with liberalism the values of individualism, equality, freedom, autonomy, and self-fulfilment. A tension exists between liberalism's commitment to equality in law and opportunity and its commitment to freedom in defence of autonomy and in pursuit of individual self-fulfilment. Most liberal feminists argue that 'matter shouldn't matter'; that is, that societal rights, privileges, and opportunities ought to be equally available to men and women regardless of their material conditions.

In more concrete political terms, liberal feminism has taken a number of quite different forms in different political contexts. In the social-democratic countries of Scandinavia, liberal feminists have stressed the importance of the equality of outcomes, and have consequently accepted extensive state intervention in the 'private' realm. In the United States, liberal feminists have been committed to the absolute equality of opportunity represented by the Equal Rights Amendment. In Canada, liberal feminists have looked to state intervention for programs to assist women in achieving some measure of equality with men, especially in the public realm. There has been less emphasis in Canada on legal equality and more on the achievement of economic security than there has in the agenda of U.S. liberal feminism.

Marxist feminism

Marxist feminism conceptualizes 'the woman question' as a problem that is part of, but secondary to, the fundamental conflict between the classes – that is, between those who own property (the means of production) and those who do not. The oppression of women is understood as having arisen in the course of the development of property and the state. Marxist feminists argue that women were not oppressed in early classless, stateless societies, and that, once capitalism is overthrown, they will be liberated through their engagement in 'productive' (that is, non-domestic) work and through the socialization of child care and domestic work.

In political terms, strict Marxist feminism is quite uncommon in the politics of the English-Canadian women's movement, although the Communist party as been a member of NAC for several decades. Most left feminists hold views modified by the ideas of radical and liberal feminism.

Political culture

Political culture refers to the set of orientations, including attitudes, beliefs, and values, that people exhibit towards their political system. Political culture is influenced by socialization processes, as well as cultural, geographic, and class differences.

Political-opportunity structure

The political-opportunity structure refers to the ideological and organizational environment of the political system, which may enhance or deter women's participation in that system. Electoral systems, legislative systems, and political cultures can all affect the opportunity structure. In Canada, for example, the single-member constituency system, in which the member winning a plurality of votes wins the constituency ('first-past-the-post'), makes it harder for women to gain representation than would a multimember constituency system based on proportional representation. Similarly, the tight party discipline operating in the parliamentary legislative system protects members of Parliament from the extensive lobbying common in the U.S. congressional system, which is characterized by weak party discipline. The political-opportunity structure facing Canadian women comprises these and other structural elements of the political system along with aspects of the political culture. This concept is drawn from the work of Sidney Tarrow (1983) and Joyce Gelb (1989) on social movements.

Quality-of-life movements

See Equality-seeking movements

Radical feminism

As an ideology, radical feminism had its origins in the U.S. women's movement of the late 1960s. By arguing that patriarchy was a universal system of oppression of women by men based on sex, radical feminism opened up debate concerning sexual, reproductive, and domestic relationships that had previously been ignored by both liberal feminism and feminisms of the Left. Although radical feminism initially saw women's biology and psychology as 'enslaving,' it has more recently come to view them as the sources of women's power and special vision as nurturing beings.

In political terms, radical feminism began as a revolutionary reaction against the male-dominated civil-rights and anti-war movements in the United States. Radical feminists there were profoundly opposed to structure, hierarchy, and formal leadership. They were especially hostile to and suspicious of the state and other major social institutions. As we have argued in this book, these aspects of radical-feminist thought were influential within feminist organizations in the United States but had less impact on the English-Canadian women's movement, mostly because of its pro-statism.

Cultural feminism is an offshoot of radical feminism that involves a complete rejection of engagement with male-dominated institutions and politics, and therefore requires the creation of entirely woman-centred structures and a woman-centred culture. First-wave social feminism was similar in its valuing of a woman-centred culture, although social feminists were not fundamentally separatists (Black 1989).

Radical liberalism
This is a set of ideas about how to practise politics that was widely accepted by English-Canadian feminists in the period studied. (The particular ideas are developed in the text.) Radical liberalism has been partly at odds with the majoritarian political culture in English Canada, which has featured pro-statism (a belief in the value of state action), support for élite accommodation, and incremental policy making.

Reactive movements
See Equality-seeking movements

Red Tory
See Conservative feminism

Social feminism
See Radical feminism

Socialist feminism/socialist-feminism
Both of these terms refer to the product of encounters between left-feminist and radical-feminist ideas or practices. We have designated the hyphenated term (*socialist-feminism*) to represent what is largely a product of academic scholarship, involving attempts to revise Marxist feminism in order to respond to the major ideological points raised by radical feminism. We have used the unhyphenated term (*socialist feminism*) in reference to the experience of women working within the democratic-socialist movement in English-Canadian politics and dealing with the issues raised by radical feminism in practical political terms, within a socialist political practice.

State feminism
This term refers to the practice in the Nordic countries, especially Sweden, of

state institutions' implementing feminist policies beneficial to women, despite the limited presence of feminist organizing.

Working-class feminism
See Left feminism

Umbrella organizations
Umbrella organizations bring together in a more or less stable coalition groups of different sizes, ages, and structures for a political or other purpose. In the case of NAC, groups range in size from small collectives of ten to national organizations of many thousands. They range from those with local purposes, including self-help groups, to those with pan-Canadian goals. Some of the groups are long-standing institutions with complex histories; others have been created to achieve short-term goals. Unlike chapter-based organizations, umbrella organizations do not affiliate individual members directly; in other words, individual women consider themselves members of their own individual groups, and not of the umbrella organization. Umbrella organizations are limited in their ability to influence local activities without the cooperation of local leaders.

References

NAC Publications and Archival Materials

1972. Strategy for Change Report
1972–82. Index of Policy Recommendations
1972–88. Annual General Meeting reports
1972–88. Executive Minutes
1972–88. Membership brochures
1973–78. *Status of Women News*
1978–85. *Status*
1980–5. *NAC Memo*
1981. 'An Urgent Memo to Member Groups and Executive Members on Pensions and Procedures'
1981. 'A Past President's Report to NAC Member Groups and Executive Members'
1984–5, 1985–6. NAC Program Submission to the Secretary of State
1984–9. AGM briefing books, reports, and other literature
1984–9. Emergency resolutions
1985–8. *Feminist Action*
1988. Organizational Review Document [NAC ORD]
1988. 'A Summary of the Report of Nicole Lacelle'

Other Primary Sources

Canada. National Task Force on Child Care. 1987. *Report.* Ottawa: Supply and Services Canada
– Parliamentary Committee on Equality Rights. 1985. *Report.* Ottawa: Supply and Services Canada

- Royal Commission on the Economic Union and Development Prospects for Canada. 1985. *Report.* Ottawa: Supply and Services Canada
- Royal Commission on the Status of Women in Canada. 1970. *Report.* Ottawa: Queen's Printer
- Secretary of State. Women's Program. 1974. 'Pressure for Change: The Role of Canadian Women's Groups.' Ottawa: Supply and Services Canada
- Secretary of State. Women's Program. 1988. *Workshop on Federal Policy Development: The Consultative Process and Women's Issues.* Ottawa: Supply and Services Canada
- 1985. *Sessional Papers.* 'Discussion Paper on Equality Issues in Federal Law.' No. 331–416, tabled January 31

Ellis, Megan. 1985. 'Letter to the Executive of the NAC on the Status of Women.' August 30
- 1987. 'Women and Policing: Contact, Conflict and Considerations for Change.' Unpublished paper cited in Lisa Price, *In Women's Interests: Feminist Activism and Institutional Change.* Vancouver: Women's Research Centre

Emergency Consultation of Women's Groups Funded by the Women's Program, Secretary of State. 1986. *Final Report.* Ottawa: CRIAW

Public Archives of Canada (PAC). 1970a. Saskatchewan – Manitoba Waffle Resolutions. MG 28–IV–1, vol. 446
- 1970b. Waffle Conference Agenda/Study Papers. MG 28–IV–1, vol. 1
- 1970–2. Ontario Waffle. MG 28–IV–1, vol. 446

REAL Women. 1985–8. Brochures and pamphlets

Secondary Sources

Adamson, Nancy, Linda Briskin, and Margaret McPhail. 1988. *Feminist Organizing for Change: The Contemporary Women's Movement in Canada.* Toronto: Oxford University Press

Andrew, Caroline. 1984. 'Women and the Welfare State.' *Canadian Journal of Political Science* 27/4 (December): 667–83

Antonides, Harry. 1986. 'The Equality ... Campaign.' Circulated in brown envelopes in Ottawa, attributed to *The Guide*

Appelle, Christine. 1987. 'The New Parliament of Women.' MA thesis, Carleton University

Armour, Moira, and Pat Staton. 1990. *Canadian Women in History: A Chronology.* Toronto: Green Dragon Press

Aronowitz, Stanley. 1984. 'When the New Left Was New.' In Sohnya Sayres, Anders Stephanson, and Frederic Jameson, eds., *The 60's Without Apology.* Minneapolis: University of Minnesota Press

Aucoin, Peter. 1975. 'Pressure Groups and Recent Changes in Policy-Making Process.' In A. Paul Pross, ed., *Pressure-Group Behaviour in Canadian Politics.* Toronto: McGraw-Hill Ryerson

Aucoin, Peter, and Bruce Doern. 1979. *Public Policy in Canada.* Toronto: Macmillan

Bannon, Sharleen. 1975. 'The Women's Bureau Is 21.' *Labour Gazette,* Anniversary Issue, 629–31

Banting, Keith, and Richard Simeon. 1983. *And No One Cheered: Federalism, Democracy and the Constitutional Act.* Toronto: Methuen

Bashevkin, Sylvia. 1985. *Toeing the Lines: Women and Party Politics in English Canada.* Toronto: University of Toronto Press

Beaudry, Martha. 1990. 'The Politics of Child-Care: R.E.A.L. Women and the Patriarchal Family.' BA thesis, Carleton University

Bégin, Monique. 1988. 'Debates and Silences – Reflections of a Politician.' *Daedalus* 117/4 (Fall): 335–62

Bird, Florence. 1974. *Anne Francis: An Autobiography.* Toronto: Clark Irwin

Black, Naomi. 1988. 'The Canadian Women's Movement: The Second Wave.' In Sandra Burt, Lorraine Code, and Lindsay Dorney, eds., *Changing Patterns: Women in Canada.* Toronto: McClelland and Stewart

– 1989. *Social Feminism.* Ithaca, NY: Cornell University Press

Boles, J.K. 1979. *The Politics of the Equal Rights Amendment.* New York: Longmans

Bouchier, D. 1983. *The Feminist Challenge.* London: Macmillan

Briskin, Linda, and L. Yanz, eds. 1983. *Union Sisters: Women in the Labour Movement.* Toronto: Women's Press

Brodie, M. Janine. 1985a. 'From Waffles to Grits: A Decade in the Life of the New Democratic Party.' In Hugh C. Thorburn, ed., *Party Politics in Canada.* 5th ed. Scarborough: Prentice-Hall Canada

– 1985b. *Women and Politics in Canada.* Toronto: McGraw-Hill Ryerson

Brodie, M. Janine, and Jill McCalla Vickers. 1982. *Canadian Women in Politics: An Overview.* CRIAW paper no. 2. Ottawa: CRIAW

Burt, Sandra. 1986a. 'Different Democracies? A Preliminary Examination of the Political Worlds of Canadian Men and Women.' *Women and Politics* 6/4 (Winter): 57–79

– 1986b. 'Women's Issues and the Women's Movement in Canada since 1970.' In Alan Cairns and Cynthia Williams, eds., *The Politics of Gender, Ethnicity, and Language in Canada.* Toronto: University of Toronto Press

Burt, Sandra; Lorraine Code; and Lindsay Dorney, eds. 1988. *Changing Patterns: Women in Canada.* Toronto: McClelland and Stewart

Campbell, Judy, et al. 1988. 'Organizing at NAC.' *Broadside* 10/1 (October): 7

Canadian Educational Women's Press. 1972. *Women Unite!* Toronto: Canadian Educational Women's Press

Canadian Research Institute for the Advancement of Women. (CRIAW) 1987. *Women's Involvement in Political Life.* CRIAW papers no. 16–17. Prepared for UNESCO Division of Human Rights and Peace. Ottawa: CRIAW

Carden, M.L. 1974. *The New Feminist Movement.* New York: Russell Sage Foundation

Charter of Rights Coalition (BC). 1985. *Women's Equality and the Charter of Rights and Freedoms.* Vancouver: Legal Services Society of British Columbia

Christiansen-Ruffman, Linda. 1982. 'Women's Political Culture and Feminist Political Culture.' Paper presented at the Tenth World Congress of Sociology, Mexico City, August

Collins, Anne. 1985. *The Big Evasion.* Toronto: Lester & Orpen Dennys

Coote, Anna, and Beatrix Campbell. 1982. *Sweet Freedom.* London: Picador

Costa, Mariarosa D., and Selma James. 1972. *The Power of Women and the Subversion of the Community.* Bristol, England: Falling Wall Press

CRIAW. *See* Canadian Research Institute for the Advancement of Women

Crittenden, Danielle. 1988. 'REAL Women Don't Eat Crow.' *Saturday Night* 103/5 (May): 27–35

Dahlerup, Drude. 1986. *The New Women's Movement: Feminism and Political Power in Europe and the U.S.A.* Beverly Hills: Sage

Dawson, Helen. 1975. 'National Pressure Groups and the Federal Government.' In Paul Pross, ed., *Pressure Group Behaviour in Canadian Politics.* Toronto: McGraw-Hill Ryerson

Day, Shelagh. 1991. 'Constitutional Reform: Canada's Equality Crisis.' In David Schneiderman, ed., *Conversations among Friends/Entre Amis.* Edmonton: University of Alberta, Centre for Constitutional Studies

Deckard, Barbara Sinclair. 1983. *The Women's Movement.* New York: Harper and Row

Dixon, Marlene. 1971. 'Where Are We Going?' In Edith Altbach, ed., *From Feminism to Liberation.* London: Schenkman Publishing Company

– 1975. 'Women's Liberation: Opening Chapter Two.' *Canadian Dimension* 10/8 (June): 56–68

Doerr, Audrey, and Micheline Carrier, eds. 1981. *Women and the Constitution in Canada.* Ottawa: CACSW

Douglas, Mary. 1986. *How Institutions Think.* Syracuse, NY: Syracuse University Press

Dubinsky, Karen. 1985. *Lament for a 'Patriarchy Lost'? Anti-feminism, Anti-abortion, and REAL Women in Canada.* Ottawa: CRIAW

Duckworth, Muriel, and Peggy Hope-Simpson. 1981. 'Voice of Women Dialogue.' *Atlantis* 6/2 (Spring): 168–76

Dumont, Micheline. 1986. *The Women's Movement: Then and Now.* Feminist
Perspective no. 5b. Ottawa: CRIAW

Dumont, Micheline; Michèle Jean; Marie Lavigne; and Jennifer Stoddart.
1987. *Québec Women: A History.* Translated by Roger Gannon and Rosalind
Gill. Toronto: Women's Press

Eichler, Margrit. 1983. *Families in Canada Today.* Toronto: Gage

– 1986. 'The Pro-Family Movement: Are They For or Against Families?'
Ottawa: CRIAW

– 1988. *Non-sexist Research Methods: A Practical Guide.* Boston: Allen

Eisenstein, Zillah. 1981. *The Radical Future of Liberal Feminism.* Boston:
Northeastern University Press

Ferguson, Kathy. 1984. *The Feminist Case against Bureaucracy.* Philadelphia:
Temple University Press

Ferree, Myra Marx, and Beth Hess. 1985. *Controversy and Coalition: The New
Feminist Movement.* Boston: G.K. Hall and Company

Findlay, Sue. 1987. 'Facing the State: The Politics of the Women's Movement
Reconsidered.' In Heather Jon Maroney and Meg Luxton, eds., *Feminism
and Political Economy.* Toronto: Methuen

Finlayson, Judith. 1985. 'First among Equals.' *City Woman* 8/5 (November):
28–35

Firestone, Shulamith. 1970. *The Dialectic of Sex.* London: Paladin

Freeman, Jo. 1974. 'The Tyranny of Structurelessness.' In Jane Jacquette, ed.,
Women in Politics. New York: John Wiley

– 1979. *Women: A Feminist Perspective.* California: Mayfield

– 1983. *The Politics of Women's Liberation.* 2d ed. New York: Longman

Gelb, Joyce. 1989. *Feminism and Politics: A Comparative Perspective.* Berkeley:
University of California Press

Gertzog, Irwin N. 1984. *Congressional Women: Their Recruitment, Treatment, and
Behaviour.* New York: Praeger

Gidengil, Elisabeth. 1992. 'A Different Voice? Gender and Political Behaviour
in Canada.' Paper presented at the Annual Meeting of the Canadian
Political Science Association, Charlottetown, PEI, May/June

Gray, Elizabeth. 1981. 'Women's Fight to Get In from the Cold Political
Wind.' *Globe and Mail,* 30 January, 7

Greaves, Lorraine. 1988. 'NAC '88: Split Resolve.' *Broadside* 9/8 (June): 3

– 1991. 'Reorganizing the National Action Committee on the Status of
Women, 1986–1988.' In Jeri Dawn Wine and Janice Ristock, eds., *Women
and Social Change.* Toronto: James Lorimer and Company

Haavio–Mannila, Elina. 1985. *Unfinished Democracy: Women in Nordic Politics.*
London: Pergamon Press

Hamilton, Cheryl. 1972. 'Moderates, Radicals Clash at Women's Strategy Conference.' *London Free Press,* 10 April, 20

Hamilton, Roberta, and Michelle Barrett, eds. 1986. *The Politics of Diversity.* Montreal: Book Center

Hartsock, Nancy. 1983. *Money, Sex and Power.* New York: Longman

Hastings, Jane, and Judith Lawrence. 1981. 'Constitutional Conference: Valentine's Day Revenge.' *Broadside* 2 (March): 4

Hawthurst, Donna, and Sue Morrow. 1984. *Living Our Visions: Building Feminist Community.* Arizona: Temple University Press

Hošek, Chaviva. 1983. 'Women and Constitutional Change.' In R. Simeon and K. Banting, eds., *And No One Cheered.* Toronto: Methuen

Jackson, Edward, and Stan Persky, eds. 1982. *Flaunting It!* Vancouver: New Star Books

Janeway, Elizabeth. 1981. *Powers of the Weak.* New York: Morrow Quill

Jenson, Jane. 1982. 'The Modern Women's Movement in Italy, France, and Great Britain: Differences in Life Cycle.' In *Comparative Social Research* 5: 341–75

Jónasdóttir, Anna G. 1988. 'On the Concept of Interest, Women's Interests and the Limitations of Interest Theory.' In Kathleen B. Jones and Anna G. Jónasdóttir, eds., *The Political Interests of Gender.* London: Sage

Jones, Miriam, and Jennifer Stephens. 1988. 'Tempest in a Teapot: NAC Annual General Meeting.' *Rebel Girls Rag* 2/4 (July/August): 5

Kealey, Linda, and Joan Sangster, eds. 1989. *Beyond the Vote: Canadian Women and Politics.* Toronto: University of Toronto Press

Kee, Janet, and Nadine McDonnell. 1986. 'What Was Said: The Submissions of Women's Groups to the Parliamentary Committee on Equality Rights.' A project of the Charter of Rights Coalition, Vancouver

Kinsman, Gary. 1987. *The Regulation of Desire.* Montreal: Black Rose Books

Kirkpatrick, Jeane. 1974. *Political Woman.* New York: Basic Books

Kirkwood, Leone. 1972. 'Abortion a Non–Topic but Keeps Coming Up.' *Globe and Mail,* 10 April, 12

Koedt, Anne, Ellen Levine, and Anita Rapone, eds. 1973. *Radical Feminism.* New York: Quadrangle

Kome, Penney. 1983. *The Taking of Twenty-Eight: Women Challenge the Constitution.* Toronto: Women's Press

– 1985. *Women of Influence: Canadian Women and Politics.* Toronto: Doubleday Canada

Kornhauser, William. 1959. *The Politics of Mass Society.* Glencoe, IL: Free Press

Kostash, Myrna. 1980. *Long Way from Home.* Toronto: James Lorimer and Company

Kreps, Bonnie. 1972. 'Radical Feminism.' In *Women Unite!* Toronto: Canadian Educational Women's Press

– 1973. 'Toronto New Feminists.' In Anne Koedt, Ellen Levine, and Anita Rapone, eds., *Radical Feminism.* New York: Quadrangle

LaMarsh, Judy. 1969. *Memoirs of a Bird in a Gilded Cage.* Toronto: McClelland and Stewart

Lamoureux, Diane. 1987. 'Nationalism and Feminism in Québec: An Impossible Attraction.' In Heather Jon Maroney and Meg Luxton, eds., *Feminism and Political Economy.* Toronto: Methuen

Landholt, Gwen. 1972. 'Women's Conference Discriminatory.' *Toronto Star,* 7 April, 7

Landsberg, Michele. 1982. *Women and Children First.* Toronto: Macmillan

Laxer, James. 1960. 'The Americanization of the Canadian Student Movement.' In Ian Lumsden, ed., *Close the 49th Parallel.* Toronto: University of Toronto Press

Lemons, J. Stanley. 1973. *The Woman Citizen: Social Feminism in the 1920's.* Chicago: University of Illinois Press

Lerner, Gerda. 1986. *The Creation of Patriarchy.* New York: Oxford University Press

Levine, Helen, and Alma Estable. 1981. *The Power Politics of Motherhood: A Feminist Critique of Theory and Practice.* Ottawa: Carleton University Press

Lipset, Seymour Martin. 1990. *Continental Divide.* New York: Routledge

Loney, Martin. 1977. 'A Political Economy of Citizen Participation.' In Leo Panitch, ed., *The Canadian State: Political Economy and Political Power.* Toronto: University of Toronto Press

Lovenduski, Joni. 1986. *Women and European Politics: Contemporary Feminism and Public Policy.* Amherst, MA: University of Massachusetts Press

Lovenduski, Joni, and Jill Hills, eds. 1981. *The Politics of the Second Electorate: Women and Public Participation.* London: Routledge and Kegan Paul

Lynch, Charles. 1984. 'Women's Issues Debate Brings Campaigning Full Circle.' *Montreal Gazette,* 16 August, B1

McAdam, Doug. 1988. 'Gender Implications of the Traditional Academic Conception of the Political.' In Susan Hardy Aiken et al., eds., *Changing Our Minds: Feminist Transformations of Knowledge.* Albany: State University of New York Press

McConney, Denise. 1985. 'Untuned Ears: Political Violence in the Canadian Press.' MA thesis, Carleton University

McCormack, Thelma. 1975. 'Toward a Non–Sexist Perspective on Social and Political Change.' In M. Millman and R. Kanter, eds., *Another Voice.* New York: Doubleday

McDonald, Lynn. 1979. 'The Evolution of the Women's Movement in Canada.' Parts 1, 2. *Branching Out* 6/1: 32–5, 6/2: 39–43
– 1981. 'The Charter of Rights and the Subjection of Women.' *Canadian Forum* 61 (June/July): 17–18
MacKinnon, Catherine. 1989. *Toward a Feminist Theory of the State*. Cambridge: Harvard University Press
McLaughlin, Paula. 1980. 'Women's Leader Warns Militancy Will Combat Neglect.' *Ottawa Journal*, 18 March
Macpherson, C.B. 1966. *The Real World of Democracy*. The Massey Lectures. Toronto: Canadian Broadcasting Corporation
Macpherson, Kay. 1975. 'The Seeds of the Seventies.' *Canadian Dimension* 10/8 (June): 39–41
Macpherson, Kay, and Meg Sears. 1976. 'The Voice of Women: A History.' In Gwen Matheson, ed., *Women in the Canadian Mosaic*. Toronto: Peter Martin
Manley, John. 1980. 'Women and the Left in the 1930s: The Case of the Toronto CCF Women's Joint Committee.' *Atlantis* 5/2 (Spring): 100–119
Maroney, Heather Jon. 1987. 'Feminism at Work.' In Heather Jon Maroney and Meg Luxton, eds., *Feminism and Political Economy*. Toronto: Methuen
– 1988. 'Contemporary Québec Feminism: The Interrelation of Political and Ideological Development in Women's Organizations, Trade Unions, Political Parties and State Policy, 1960–1980.' PhD diss., McMaster University
Marsden, Lorna. 1980. 'The Role of the National Action Committee in Facilitating Equal Pay Policy in Canada.' In R. Ratner, ed., *Equal Employment Policy for Women*. Philadelphia: Temple University Press
– 1985. 'After 1984: Controlling the Agenda.' *Canadian Forum* 64 (January): 6–9
Meisel, John. 1985. 'The Decline of Party in Canada.' In Hugh C. Thorburn, ed., *Party Politics in Canada*. 5th ed. Scarborough: Prentice-Hall Canada
Michell, Gillian, and Lorraine Greaves. 1988. 'The Future of NAC: Some Questions of Feminist Process.' *Kinesis* (April): 15
Michels, Robert. [1915] 1962. *Political Parties: A Sociological Study of the Oligarchic Tendencies of Modern Democracy*. Reprint. New York: Free Press
Miles, Angela. 1982. 'Ideological Hegemony in Political Discourse: Women's Specificity and Equality.' In Angela Miles and Geraldine Finn, eds., *Feminism in Canada: From Pressure to Politics*. Montreal: Black Rose Books
– 1984. 'Integrative Feminism.' *Fireweed: A Feminist Quarterly* 19 (Summer/ Fall): 54–81
Miles, Angela, and Geraldine Finn, eds. 1982. *Feminism in Canada: From Pressure to Politics*. Montreal: Black Rose Books
Mitchell, Juliet. 1971. *Woman's Estate*. New York: Pantheon

Mitchinson, Wendy. 1981. 'The Woman's Christian Temperance Union: A Study in Organization.' In Sherri Clarkson, ed., *International Journal of Women's Studies* 4/2: 143–56

Molgat, Anne. 1992. '"An Action That Will Not Be Allowed to Subside": NAC's First Twenty Years.' Paper presented at the twentieth-anniversary NAC AGM, Ottawa, June

Morris, Cerise. 1980. 'Determination and Thoroughness: The Movement for a Royal Commission on the Status of Women in Canada.' *Atlantis* 5/2 (Spring): 1–21

– 1982. 'No More Than Simple Justice.' PhD diss., McGill University

– 1983. 'Pressuring the Canadian State for Women's Rights: The Role of the National Action Committee.' *Alternate Routes* 6: 87–108

Nelson, Barbara J. 1984. *Making an Issue of Child Abuse*. Chicago: University of Chicago Press

O'Brien, Mary. 1981. *The Politics of Reproduction*. Boston: Routledge and Kegan Paul

O'Neill, Brenda. 1992. 'Gender Gaps in Opinion: The Canadian Situation.' Paper presented at the Annual Meeting of the Canadian Political Science Association, Charlottetown, PEI, May/June

Phillips, Susan. 1990. 'Projects, Pressure and Perceptions of Effectiveness: An Organizational Analysis of National Women's Groups.' PhD diss., Carleton University

Pitkin, Hannah. 1967. *The Concept of Representation*. Berkeley: University of California Press

Piven, Frances Fox. 1984. 'Women and the State: Ideology, Power, and the Welfare State.' *Socialist Review* 74/4 (March/April): 11–19

Prentice, Alison; Paula Bourne; Gail Cuthbert Brandt; Beth Light; Wendy Mitchinson; and Naomi Black. 1988. *Canadian Women: A History*. Toronto: Harcourt Brace Jovanovich

Price, Lisa S. 1988. *In Women's Interests: Feminist Activism and Institutional Change*. Vancouver: Women's Research Centre

Pross, A. Paul. 1975. *Pressure Group Behaviour in Canadian Politics*. Toronto: McGraw-Hill Ryerson.

Randall, Vicky. 1987. *Women and Politics: An International Perspective*. 2d ed. Chicago: University of Chicago Press

Rankin, Pauline. 1989. 'The Politicization of Ontario Farm Women.' In Linda Kealey and Joan Sangster, eds., *Beyond the Vote: Canadian Women and Politics*. Toronto: University of Toronto Press

Rasmussen, Linda. 1975. *Harvest Yet to Reap: A History of Prairie Women*. Toronto: Women's Press

Richardson, Joan. 1983. 'The Structure of Organizational Instability: The Women's Movement in Montreal, 1974–1977.' PhD diss., New School for Social Research, New York

Ricks, Francie, George Matheson, and Sandra Pyke. 1972. 'Women's Liberation: A Case Study of Organizations for Social Change.' *Canadian Psychologist* 13/1 (January): 30–39

Roberts, Barbara. 1988. *Smooth Sailing or Storm Warning? Canadian and Quebec Women's Groups and the Meech Lake Accord.* Feminist Perspective no. 12a. Ottawa: CRIAW

Rooke, P.T., and R. L. Schnell. 1987. *No Bleeding Heart: Charlotte Whitton, A Feminist on the Right.* Vancouver: University of British Columbia Press

Rossi, Alice S. 1982. *Feminists in Politics: A Panel Analysis of the First National Women's Conference.* New York: Academic Press

Rothschild-Witt, Joyce. 1979. 'The Collectivist Organization: An Alternative to Rational-Bureaucratic Models.' *American Sociological Review* 44/4 (August): 509–27

Rowbotham, Sheila; Lynne Segal; and Hilary Wainwright. 1979. *Beyond the Fragments: Feminism and the Making of Socialism.* London: Merlin

Rucht, Dieter. 1991. *Research on Social Movements: The State of the Art in Western Europe and the U.S.A.* Frankfurt: Campus

Sangster, Joan. 1989. *Dreams of Equality: Women on the Canadian Left, 1920–1950.* Toronto: McClelland and Stewart

Sapiro, Virginia. 1983. *The Political Integration of Women: Roles, Socialization and Politics.* Chicago: University of Illinois Press

Sayres, Sohnya; Anders Stephanson; and Frederic Jameson, eds., 1984. *The 60's without Apology.* Minneapolis: University of Minnesota Press

Sheppard, Robert. 1980. 'Charter Would Enshrine Bias, NAC Says.' *Globe and Mail,* 21 November, 9

Smelser, Neil. 1962. *Theory of Collective Behavior.* New York: Free Press of Glencoe

Smith, Dorothy. 1979. 'Where There Is Oppression, There Is Resistance.' *Branching Out* 6/1: 10–15

Stone, Sharon. 1992. 'Feminists and the Toronto Press: A Study of Their Relations in 1988.' PhD diss., York University, Toronto

Strong-Boag, Veronica. 1986. 'Pulling in Double Harness or Hauling a Double Load: Women, Work and Feminism on the Canadian Prairie.' *Journal of Canadian Studies* 21/3 (November): 32–52

– 1988. *The New Day Recalled: Lives of Girls and Women in English Canada, 1919–1939.* Toronto: Copp Clark Pitman

Tarrow, Sidney. 1983. *Struggling to Reform: Social Movements and Policy Change during Cycles of Protest.* Western Societies Paper no. 15. Ithaca, NY: Cornell University

Vallance, Elizabeth. 1979. *Women in the House.* London: Athlone

Van Loon, Richard, and Michael Whittington. 1976. *The Canadian Political System: Environment, Structure and Process.* 2d ed. Toronto: McGraw-Hill Ryerson

Vickers, Jill McCalla. 1980. 'Coming Up for Air: Feminist Views of Power Re–Considered,' *Canadian Women's Studies* 2/4: 66–69

– 1983/4. 'Major Equality Issues of the Eighties.' *Human Rights Yearbook* 1 (Winter): 47–72

– 1986. 'Equality-Seeking in a Cold Climate.' In Lynn Smyth, ed., *Righting the Balance: Canada's New Equality Rights.* Saskatoon: Canadian Human Rights Reporter

– 1988a. *Getting Things Done: Women's Views of Their Involvement in Political Life.* Ottawa/Paris: CRIAW and UNESCO

– 1988b. 'Politics As If Women Mattered: The Institutionalization of the Canadian Women's Movement and Its Impact on Federal Politics, 1965–88.' Paper presented at ACSANZ '88, Canberra, June

– 1988c. *Politics Is a Man's Game, Isn't It?* A video in the Through Her Eyes series. Ottawa: Carleton University

– 1989. 'Feminist Approaches to Politics.' In Linda Kealey and Joan Sangster, eds., *Beyond the Vote: Canadian Women and Politics.* Toronto: University of Toronto Press

– 1990a. *The Politics of Getting Things Done.* A video in the Through Her Eyes series. Ottawa: Carleton University

– 1990b. *The Politics of the Women's Movement in Canada.* A video in the Through Her Eyes series. Ottawa: Carleton University

– 1991. 'Bending the Iron Law of Oligarchy: Debates on the Feminization of Political Process in the English Canadian Women's Movement, 1970–1988.' In Jeri Dawn Wine and Janice L. Ristock, eds., *Women and Social Change: Feminist Activism in Canada.* Toronto: James Lorimer and Company

– 1992. 'The Intellectual Origins of the Women's Movement in Canada.' In Constance Backhouse and David Flaherty, eds., *Challenging Times: The Women's Movement in Canada and the United States.* Montreal and Kingston: McGill–Queen's University Press

Vickers, Jill McCalla, and Janine Brodie. 1981. 'Canada.' In Joni Lovenduski and Jill Hills, eds., *The Politics of the Second Electorate.* London: Routledge and Kegan Paul

Walker, Gillian A. 1990. *Family Violence and the Women's Movement.* Toronto: University of Toronto Press

Whitaker, Reginald. 1977. *The Government Party: Organizing and Financing the Liberal Party of Canada, 1930–58*. Toronto: University of Toronto Press

White, Julie. 1990. *Mail and Female*. Toronto: Thompson Publishing

Willis, Ellen. 1984. 'Radical Feminism and Feminist Radicalism.' In Sohnya Sayres, Anders Stephanson, and Frederic Jameson, eds., *The 60's Without Apology*. Minneapolis: University of Minnesota Press

Wine, Jeri Dawn, and Janice L. Ristock, eds., 1991. *Women and Social Change: Feminist Activism in Canada*. Toronto: James Lorimer and Company

Women's Research Centre. 1987. *The Women's Research Centre and Our Assumptions about Action Research*. Rev. ed. Vancouver: Women's Research Centre

Yates, Gayle Graham. 1975. *What Women Want: The Ideas of the Women's Movement*. Cambridge: Harvard University Press

Young, Iris Marion. 1985. 'Humanism, Gynocentrism and Feminist Politics.' *Women's Studies International Forum* 8/3: 173–83

Index